When Research Matters

How Scholarship Influences Education Policy

When
Research Matters

How Scholarship Influences
Education Policy

Edited by

Frederick M. Hess

Foreword by

Lorraine M. McDonnell

HARVARD EDUCATION PRESS
CAMBRIDGE, MASSACHUSETTS

Library of Congress Control Number 2007941189

Paperback ISBN 978-1-891792-84-7
Library Edition ISBN 978-1-891792-85-4

Published by Harvard Education Press,
an imprint of the Harvard Education Publishing Group

Harvard Education Press
8 Story Street
Cambridge, MA 02138

Cover Design: Alyssa Morris

The typefaces used in this book are ITC Stone Serif for text and ITC Stone Sans for display.

Contents

Foreword

Although attention to the topic has waned in recent years, interest in the relation between social science research and public policy emerged almost as soon as policy analysis became a field of study in the 1970s.[1] Federal officials grew concerned that their increased investment in social science research and development (R&D) was not producing knowledge useful to them in their policymaking roles or, at least, not used often enough to justify the expense. Yet this insistence on greater relevance and accountability partially reflected the success of social scientists in penetrating government: policymakers now assumed that research could contribute to their decisionmaking.[2] Some disciplinary scholars viewed the federal government's growing interest in social science research as worrisome: They perceived it as diverting scholarly inquiry away from basic research to topics of interest to government, resulting in studies based on short-term political considerations rather than scientific principles.[3] However, for researchers in the emerging field of policy analysis, interest in the connections between research and policy mirrored that of government funders. These researchers recognized that usefulness to policymakers would be a major criterion by which the field would be judged, and that to make future work more valuable to policy audiences they needed to understand the process by which research was used (or not) in decision arenas.

Consequently, a variety of studies were conducted and committees formed to examine social R&D throughout the federal government—how it was funded, managed, and the results used. Some of these projects were supported by the National Science Foundation with synthetic and consensus studies organized under the auspices of the National Research Council. Research on knowledge utilization was also funded by other agencies such as the National Institute of Education (NIE) and its successor, the Office of Educational Research and Improvement (OERI). Most studies focused on research utilization in federal executive agencies, Congress, and the courts. However, as state officials became more central to education policy in the 1980s, a few studies focused on this level.[4] Analyses of research utilization were typically based on surveys or interviews with policymakers and their staffs, asking about information use generally (what types they used, whether any sources were especially influential and why), and sometimes asking respondents to judge the usefulness of specific studies or abstracts synthesizing multiple studies.

At first glance, changes in both the consumers and producers of policy research over the past 30 years suggest that earlier studies might have little applicability today. On the consumer end, analytical capacity within government has increased as staffs with advanced social science degrees have become an integral part of the executive and legislative branches at the federal and state levels. The result has been a greater valuing of research-based information, but also less dependence on those outside government to access and interpret it. On the producer side, there is now a broader array of information as the number and diversity of policy organizations and advocacy groups have expanded. Over time, policy-relevant databases have become more comprehensive and analytical techniques more sophisticated, resulting in more robust explanation and more reliable prediction.

Nevertheless, earlier studies of knowledge utilization still offer some guidance in assessing the connections between contemporary research and policy. First, they distinguish "ordinary knowledge" about the political consequences of policy actions that officials obtain from their personal experience and interaction with constituents, and the particularistic or distributional knowledge about the effects of policies on particular groups and communities that typically comes from interest groups, from the more systematic and balanced analytic knowledge provided through scientific inquiry.[5] Second, just as delineating among types of knowledge can help analysts focus research for more effective use, past studies also identify the different ways such research is applied. They conclude that policymakers primarily use research to support their existing political positions, but it also functions as warning—alerting policymakers to problems potentially requiring their attention—and as guidance in identifying policy strategies more likely to be effective than others. Perhaps the most enduring function research plays is what Carol Weiss calls enlightenment. It is not the findings of a single study or set of studies that directly affect policy, but rather it is concepts, new ways of thinking about an issue, and innovative frames for considering problems and remedies that influence policy.[6] Although education research has served all four functions, the enlightenment role has perhaps been the most visible and influential. Concepts such as fiscal neutrality, school choice, and standards-based reform are just a few examples of ideas that have shaped policy by combining normative theories with empirical evidence.

Finally, in addition to highlighting the need to understand the role of interests and ideas in shaping knowledge use, past studies point to the importance of institutional context. For example, Congressional committees use research differently than executive agencies; research is more likely to be influential at some points in the policy process than others; and the entrepreneurs who press particular options are often also critical brokers in introducing research findings into the policy process.[7]

With several decades' hindsight, some findings from earlier studies of research utilization seem outdated and even naive. Still, they highlight the centrality of institutional and political conditions in research utilization, and they underscore the importance of studying the impact of education policy research as systematically and with as much rigor as we study the effects of schooling. The chapters in this volume represent a valuable addition to that project.

—Lorraine M. McDonnell
President-Elect
American Educational Research Association

Acknowledgments

This volume was conceived at a May 2006 conference held at the Brookings Institution. Along with Tom Loveless, director of the Brown Center on Education Policy at Brookings, I was hosting a conference entitled Small Classes and Small Schools. Around the table sat a few dozen of the nation's most talented educational researchers and a handful of policy notables. Following a series of high-quality analyses regarding the effects of class size and school size, the discussion featured stellar researchers expressing frustration that nuanced evidence seemed to be ignored by federal and state policymakers, advocacy groups, and influential foundation officials. It was clear to several of us that the attention devoted to research design and analytic methods vastly exceeded that given to the manner in which research and policy interacted and that this reflected a familiar dynamic. In fact, while the sophistication of the research had improved dramatically since my first Washington, D.C., think-tank conference nearly a decade before, the discussion of how and why research influences policy seemed to have stagnated. That assessment—and the subsequent determination to explore whether it was accurate and, if so, why that might be—framed this volume.

I am indebted to all of the individuals who contributed to or assisted with the compilation of this volume. Primarily, I thank the contributing authors who wrote the conference papers that were presented at the American Enterprise Institute (AEI) in May 2007. I'd also like to thank the discussants who participated in that conference and provided invaluable feedback on those initial drafts, including Gina Burkhardt, CEO of Learning Point Associates; David Driscoll, former Massachusetts Commissioner of Education; Michael Feuer, executive director of the Division of Behavioral and Social Science and Education in the National Research Council; Pascal Forgione, superintendent of the Austin Independent School District; Ellen Condliffe Lagemann, Charles Warren Professor of the History of American Education at Harvard University; Reid Lyon, executive vice president for research and evaluation at Higher Ed Holdings and Whitney International University; Kathleen McCartney, dean of the Harvard Graduate School of Education; Lorraine M. McDonnell, president-elect of the American Educational Research Association; Michael McPherson, president of the Spencer Foundation; Roberto Rodriguez, senior education advisor to Senator Edward M. Kennedy (D-MA) on the Senate HELP Committee; Warren Simmons, executive director of the Annenberg Institute for School Reform; and Russ Whitehurst, director of the Institute of Education Sciences. At AEI, Juliet Squire did an admirable job of managing the conference and assembling and editing the papers for publication. Morgan Goatley, Rosemary Kendrick, and Thomas Gift also provided vital assistance.

As always, my thanks go to the American Enterprise Institute, and especially its president, Christopher DeMuth, for unwavering support and for providing an environment of collegiality and remarkable intellectual freedom. Funding for this project was generously provided by the Spencer Foundation, and for it, I offer my sincere gratitude. Finally, I'd like to thank Doug Clayton and production manager Dody Riggs for the wonderful work they did in translating the manuscript into the volume you hold before you.

—*Frederick M. Hess*

Introduction

Frederick M. Hess

In recent years, the rigor and quality of education research have drawn much attention. Heightening this interest have been the strides that states have made in collecting data on student achievement, the creation of the Institute of Education Sciences (IES), the explicit call for "scientifically based research" written into the No Child Left Behind Act (NCLB), professional interest in "data-driven decisionmaking," and the refinement of sophisticated analytic tools and methods. Proponents have hailed these developments as signaling the dawn of a new era in education research. Meanwhile, more jaded observers suggest that broader changes in the policy environment—including the dissemination strategies of advocacy groups, the role of the Internet, the impatience of public officials and private foundations eager to spur rapid and dramatic improvement in measured student performance, and increasingly polarized political debate—have made it *less* likely that even rigorous and reliable research will shape policy.

Increased attention to education research has primarily focused upon the relative merits of various research methodologies, how to identify "best practices" or "scientifically based" methods, and how to encourage classroom educators to utilize research findings. Far less notice has been devoted to the frustratingly vague but vital challenge of understanding how research does or does not shape policy. In this volume, respected scholars of politics and policy tackle that question, exploring when and why research influences policy; what role is played by intermediaries like scholarly journals, advocacy groups, and the press; and how this affects contemporary school reform. The travails of the billion-dollar Reading First program illustrate how inadequate attention to the challenges of employing research as a tool of policy, managing the relationships of researchers and public officials, or building new institutions make it likely that even well-intentioned efforts to promote the use of rigorous research will encounter stormy seas.

An emphasis on technical questions has obscured the reality that the impact of research on policy has as much to do with political behavior as with research design. In a democratic nation, where policy is the product of many competing interests, the influence of research and researchers will inevitably and appropriately be limited. Elected officials are rewarded for addressing the needs of their constituents. They may have good reason not to focus on the scientific merit of research—especially when "rigorous" research undermines a favored program or implies politically painful action. Appointees or career officials may be more insulated from popular sentiment, but are ultimately funded by and accountable to legislators.

Meanwhile, researchers are isolated from the pressures that confront public officials. The logic of the research world suggests that financial, reputational, and professional rewards are ultimately distributed according to the importance, rigor, and genius of the scholar's work rather than public popularity, though the reality is inevitably more complex. Researchers can stand to reap personal and professional rewards from "policy-relevant" scholarship and the dissemination of their findings, even when intermediaries misrepresent their work. The aim of this inquiry is not to determine how to free researchers from "politics" or to determine what research *should* influence policy, but to examine the research–policy nexus in the hope that fuller understanding might help researchers, public officials, and other interested parties play their roles more constructively.

More than twenty-five years ago, Aaron Wildavsky wrote the authoritative book, *Speaking Truth to Power*—an attempt to define the role and the responsibility of the policy analyst in bridging the gap between researchers and public officials. This volume seeks to build upon that inquiry in the context of twenty-first century education policy. How have changes in technology, communications, and academe determined the quantity and quality of research entering the public square? How has research factored into various policy debates? How have institutional and environmental forces like foundations, media outfits, and advocacy organizations affected the production and dissemination of research? And how do consumers of research—including elected officials, judges, educational leaders, and the public—understand and make use of findings?

IT'S NOT A QUESTION OF GETTING THE POLITICS "OUT"

One frequent but ultimately unfruitful line of thought begins with the presumption that the primary goal for those concerned about the research–policy nexus is to keep politics from coloring the interpretation or use of research. This notion has strong historic roots that trace back at least to the Progressive reformers of the early twentieth century. The Progressives were fond of arguing that there was no Republican or Democratic way to pave a road. Instead, they sought to base broad policy prescriptions on "expertise" and research. The reality, of course, is that expertise and research are contested terrains in a democratic nation. As Andrew Rudalevige quotes historian Carl Kaestle in chapter 2, "Politics can scale any walls in Washington, especially if the walls were built with federal dollars."[1]

In fact, when the Progressives first brought social science to bear on policy questions at the dawn of the twentieth century, they did so in unapologetically normative and political terms. The Progressive tradition presumed that upstanding policymakers could turn to researchers, who would use objective criteria to identify optimal policies. Given the nature of Progressivism, reforms typically involved regulation, new public spending, and the growth of government responsibilities in the process, aligning social science with what we today think of as "liberal" policy. This state of affairs dominated the research–policy nexus until the 1970s, when an aggressive challenge from free-market economists, ascendant conservative think tanks, and a number of political scientists and sociologists skeptical of what these efforts had wrought began to question the cozy relationship between research and expansive progressive policies. Today, both Right and Left tout research to support their social policy agendas and to argue the merits and designs of particular programs.

The meaning of "neutral" research itself has long been contested. As Alice O'Connor observed in *Social Science for What?*:

> Although it is often framed in terms of a stark and stylized opposition—as handed to us from Max Weber, "value-free" versus "normative" research—the concept of neutrality has been continually debated and redefined as a standard in social science, and as a strategy for establishing relevance and legitimacy.[2]

In short, as the chapters that follow make clear, it can be difficult for scholars tackling important educational questions to avoid engaging in contentious debates. Even to use test scores as a measure of learning is to take a firm stance about the appropriateness and utility of such measures, while researchers who evaluate teacher quality or reading progress inevitably make judgments about how to define a quality teacher or how to measure the success of a reading strategy.

Although such tensions are inescapable, Rudalevige observes in chapter 2 that "politics can help erect insulating walls as well as knock them over." It is possible for public officials to be buffered from day-to-day political pressures, leaving them more able to respond to the dictates of expertise and "science." Whether voters might wish for officials to operate in this fashion is, of course, an open question; but if they conclude that certain decisions ought to be based primarily upon technical or scientific considerations, institutions can be structured accordingly—as we have sought to do, with mixed success, in the case with the federal judiciary, the Federal Reserve, and the Food and Drug Administration (FDA).

EXPLORING THE RESEARCH–POLICY NEXUS

The modern era in education research can be traced to the 1960s, when President Lyndon Johnson launched the first concerted federal effort to promote education research and evaluation in his push for the Elementary and Secondary Education Act (ESEA) of 1965. ESEA called for substantial new federal spending on education and education research, while sparking debates over whether federal support for schools would be well spent and how to measure the benefits produced by the new spending.

In 1979, more than a decade after the enactment of ESEA and the same year that the Office of Educational Research and Innovation was created within the new Department of Education, Harvard University professor Carol Weiss asserted:

> Social scientists are concerned about making their research useful for public policymakers and policymakers are displaying . . . concern about the usefulness of the social science research that government funds support. There is mutual interest in whether social science research intended to influence policy is actually "used" but before that important issue can profitably be addressed it is essential to understand what "using research" actually means.[3]

Weiss was perhaps the leading scholar of a body of work on "knowledge utilization" that plumbed the research–policy nexus during the 1970s and 1980s. Academics like Weiss and University of Michigan professor Nathan Caplan found limited evidence that research had a significant impact on policymaking, tracing the failure to use social science to the lack of communication between research generators and users.

The critical point made by knowledge utilization scholars was that "using" research did not mean identifying simple answers that would translate directly into policy. They argued that policy-relevant research must extend beyond policy evaluation and help policymakers fully understand costs, benefits, possible unanticipated consequences, and implementation challenges. Weiss noted, "Governments don't often use research directly, but research helps people reconsider issues, it helps them think differently . . . it punctures old myths."[4] The value of research, then, was recognized not always for its ability to provide answers, but rather to change the way we understand the questions.

Weiss argued that understanding the use of research was not necessarily about the research itself but the incentives and demands acting upon researchers and policymakers. For instance, while time pressures and political imperatives in Congress worked against the use of research findings, the growth in staff professionalism and the creation of specialized congressional support agencies favored their use—though staff valued information more highly when they knew and trusted its source and understood its political motivations.[5] In a similar vein, University of Michigan political scientist John Kingdon authored the influential 1984 book *Agendas, Alternatives, and Public Policies*, in which he found that research played a modest but meaningful role when it came to legitimizing ideas and proposed policy solutions.[6]

Hampered by its ambiguous conclusions and limited ability to offer practical direction to policymakers, researchers, or reformers, knowledge utilization research was a vanishing presence by the early 1990s. Even as "evidence-based research" was becoming a mantra for education reformers, scholars of educational politics studied key questions in urban reform, mayoral control, school choice, and accountability—but no longer the questions of why, when, or how their results would enter the policy debate.

This is not to say that research has been ignored in the past fifteen years—far from it. In fact, much energy has been devoted to two distinct but related issues. First, organizations like the National Academy of Sciences and the National Academy of Education have assembled committees of leading scholars that have sought to provide guidance on the merits and limitations of various research methodologies. Second, much attention has been paid to the challenge of translating research into practice, so that findings are utilized by educators in classrooms and schools. This practical query has been a primary focus of professional associations and inspired the federally funded What Works Clearinghouse; it also holds out the promise of a relatively straightforward impact on student achievement. These two issues— the relative merits of various methodologies and the challenge of helping research to shape practice—while important in their own right, are not the focus of this volume.[7]

This volume focuses on a different issue—the link between research and policy. The importance of this link and the perils of failing to appreciate its dimensions can be illuminated by turning to a familiar and favored policy reform.

THE CASE OF CLASS SIZE

Why does it matter if we understand how research is explained, marketed, or utilized? The case of class size offers an instructive example. Efforts to reduce the number of students in a classroom are highly popular and have been a staple of school reform for decades. University of Wisconsin professor Doug Harris recently observed that 88 percent of parents support class size reduction and that teachers strongly endorse it.[8] Even the American Educational Research Association (AERA), the professional association of the nation's education researchers and presumably a fount of careful wisdom, issued an excited *Research Points* policy brief in 2003 that considered the extant research and then advised: "In the stockpile of educational policy initiatives that are worth finding resources for, small classes rank near the top of the list."[9]

Yet, the research is mixed on the actual merits of reducing class size. Far less prominent in the AERA policy brief were the warnings that "unintended consequences are possible," and that reducing class size "may not always be the best use of scarce resources."[10] In 1999, Stanford economist Eric Hanushek reported that 277 econometric studies of student performance conducted through 1994 had examined the impact of class size or student–teacher ratios on achievement.[11] Of those, 15 percent had found statistically significant positive effects and 13 percent statistically significant negative effects—offering little reason to believe that investments in reducing class size would offer a consistent pay-off. [12]

Why the vast popular and professional support for class size reduction if its merits are less than certain? Tellingly, the single most famous educational experiment conducted to date may well be the Student Teacher Achievement Ratio project—Project STAR—a class size experiment conducted in Tennessee in the late 1980s. STAR was described by distinguished Harvard University statistician Frederick Mosteller as "one of the great experiments in education in U.S. history."[13] Between 1985 and 1989, $12 million was spent on STAR to examine the impact of class size on student learning. The study entailed randomly assigning thousands of students at more than 70 schools around the state to either "regular" or "small" classes. Small classes consisted of 13 to 17 students and regular classes of 22 to 25 students. Researchers found significant achievement gains for those students in small classes in kindergarten relative to their peers in larger classes, and additional gains in first grade, especially for black students. While there was no evidence of continued gains in second or third grade, the benefits of being in small classes early on persisted through middle school—with a long-term effect on achievement that was equivalent to about 4.4 percentile points.[14] The STAR results suggested that a crowd-pleasing reform that eased teachers' working conditions could also boost student achievement. Not surprisingly, the research quickly found favor and was trumpeted by teachers unions and advocates for increased school spending.

While there was a desire to find straightforward policy lessons in the findings, would-be reformers seemed to conveniently forget that STAR was motivated by Gene Glass and Mary Lee Smith's theory that class size reduction would need to be administered in a heavy dose to be effective. They argued that the approach probably required reducing classes to fifteen students or less—otherwise the added expense might yield few benefits.[15] Yet the STAR findings were routinely trumpeted without regard to such subtleties.

The STAR findings were most famously and recklessly applied in California, with no attention to constraints or to the cautions implicit in the study. There, the results of STAR were touted as dramatic evidence for a statewide class size reduction program. California legislators adopted just such a program in 1996 that cost $771 million in its first year and $1.7 billion annually by 2005.[16] The program created an incentive for school districts to place first- and second-graders (and, soon after, kindergartners and third-graders) in classes of no more than twenty students. Of course, classes of twenty were substantially larger than those employed in Project STAR's small classes. The only major evaluation of California's program, conducted by the American Institutes of Research and the RAND Corporation, found no evidence that it had improved student achievement. Faced with the need to increase staffing dramatically, California's best school districts raided poorer neighbors for faculty, while schools statewide opened their doors to thousands of mediocre candidates.[17]

What happened? The success of class size reduction depends in large part on contextual considerations that were not self-evident in Project STAR, but have important consequences for public officials seeking to employ the experiment's findings. First is the obvious fact that resources devoted to smaller classes cannot be used elsewhere. Reducing class size requires devoting dollars to hiring more teachers rather than paying teachers more or investing in research, curricula, assessment, or other tools that might help teachers be more effective. In Project STAR, the program's limited size and the infusion of extra funding for participating schools meant this was not a consideration. Of course, the $12 million spent on STAR could have been used differently by Tennessee, but the participating schools were in a position where they would either receive the additional staff or they would not—they had no opportunity to redeploy the resources.

Second, while Project STAR showed that reducing class size may make sense in a given school or district, the benefits appear much harder to capture when the strategy is embraced by multiple schools forced to draw from a limited pool of teachers. The *widespread* adoption of class size reduction, as in California, creates a voracious appetite for new teachers and is likely to reduce teacher quality while siphoning teachers to more attractive schools and communities.[18]

Third, Project STAR only reported effects in kindergarten and first grade. Nonetheless, there is a tendency for constituents to demand, and for policymakers to provide, extra resources for a larger population. This may have diluted the impact of the intervention even as it aggravated problems related to cost and the need to locate more teachers.

Confronted with nuanced findings, parental pressure to place students in smaller classes, and unanticipated implementation challenges like a finite supply of quality teachers, it is not surprising that policymakers have touted rosy outcomes and overlooked the evidence suggesting that wholesale class size reduction may be a poor investment. Despite the cautionary experience of California, broadly drawn and expensive class size policies have been adopted in states including Utah, Nevada, and Florida. Policymakers have strong incentives to pursue prescriptive, popular policy solutions and, absent countervailing pressure, may well find ways to interpret mixed findings—even those reported by the most rigorous research—in order to support these aims.

THE UNEASY RELATIONSHIP BETWEEN RESEARCH AND POLICY

Scientific research is typically a painfully uncertain and frustrating endeavor. The most precise scientific techniques, such as randomized field trials, are expensive and slow. As Gerald Holton observed in the introduction to *ERRORS: Consequences of Big Mistakes in the Natural and Social Sciences*:

> Practitioners of science know well that the path is strewn with hurdles and pitfalls, [and] costly detours . . . The search may be so long and tedious, so demanding on one's energy and spirit that one of the persistent words in scientists' private correspondence is "despair."[19]

More pithily, renowned biologist Stephen Gould lamented, "Over 90 percent of the day's work generally turns out to be for naught, and then you still have to clean out the mouse cage."[20] The desire to speedily identify "effective" educational interventions that will make a difference in a three- or five-year time window yields a reluctance to accept the arduous realities of the scientific process. While researchers in both health care and education pursue advances with enormous personal stakes for individuals and for society, the health profession has won enough credibility that a substantial reservoir of support for basic research, which may not yield any visible benefits for decades, has developed. However, lacking a similar history of successes, education research has not earned similar trust or goodwill, and its advocates have been unsuccessful in making the case that research ought to be funded despite its painstaking pace and uncertain fruits.

In making the case for the creation of IES, Grover J. "Russ" Whitehurst, who would go on to serve as its first director, observed that the

> world of education, unlike defense, health care, or industrial production, does not rest on a strong research base. In no other field are personal experience and ideology so frequently relied on to make policy choices, and in no other field is the research base so inadequate and little used.[21]

As Arthur Levine, former president of Columbia University's Teachers College, dryly noted in his comprehensive study of education research in 2007, the "education school climate . . . does not make research a priority, does not put a premium on research productivity in faculty hiring, and does not provide the resources to support research."[22] This concern dates back to President Johnson's efforts in the mid-1960s when it gave rise to two sets of federally supported institutions intended to promote long-term, large-scale research and development. One was the Research and Development Centers and the other was the Regional Educational Laboratories. Plagued by the same concerns about funding levels, methodological limitations, inadequate data, and troubled governance, these efforts failed to deliver; instead, they produced mostly short-term and small-scale research that failed to provide anything resembling a breakthrough.[23]

This state of affairs has fostered a belief that education research may be inherently less likely to generate useful takeaways than research related to energy, defense, or medicine. Howard Gardner of the Harvard Graduate School of Education has argued:

> Education differs from medicine in crucial respects that need to be understood. Education is laden with human values. While almost no one disputes the medical goals of longer and healthier lives, citizens in a democracy differ deeply about the kind of education we value. How could we ever design an

educational system that would please Jesse Helms, Jesse Jackson, and Jesse Ventura? And we can't conduct meaningful scientific research on educational practices unless we articulate a value system with some specificity.[24]

In fact, some educational thinkers are so skeptical of the scientific research model when it comes to education that they encourage scholars to employ research approaches from other paradigms. For instance, William Ayers, a senior scholar at the University of Illinois at Chicago, has suggested that education researchers would benefit from "drawing upon the humanities—poetry, film, theater, and imaginative literature—in their search for knowledge and understanding."[25]

The creation of IES has the potential to change this landscape. The FDA, Federal Reserve, and National Institutes of Health (NIH) are powerful examples of public institutions that have changed public expectations and the way research informs public policy. Their insulation from daily political imperatives, their protocols and rules of evidence, and their expertise and prestige have made it more difficult and potentially embarrassing for advocates or public officials to disregard rigorous research or engage in the research-related machinations common in education. While these institutions are not immune to the challenges confronting IES, and while their autonomy, prestige, and technical rigor have certainly waxed and waned with time, their existence and design have profoundly shaped the relationship between research and relevant policy. NIH's funding decisions, FDA's required field protocols, and the Federal Reserve's processes for collecting and vetting data have altered the incentives for researchers while establishing clear norms for the research that public officials address in deliberations. Whether IES will play a similar role in education where its predecessors could not remains an open question.

THE "SOFT TISSUE" BETWEEN RESEARCH AND POLICY

In the pages ahead, authors explore the various dimensions of the research–policy nexus and the "soft tissue" that connects these two worlds. Their chapters illustrate the crucial role that informal incentives, practices, and private actors play in determining how research is translated and communicated. They illuminate at least four factors that help determine how, when, and why research is used to inform policy.

One key development is how technology and the proliferation of think tanks and advocacy groups have changed the manner in which research is disseminated. Because timeliness and accessibility have become increasingly important and new technology has allowed researchers to publish their work in new ways, researchers concerned about policy feel pressure to produce findings in a timely fashion—and funders push them to do so. This evolution has meant that many more technical critiques are now debated in the public square after work has been released, rather than simply in a review process within the confines of the academy. The consequences of this democratization are significant and raise new questions about how policymakers can make sense of these public conflicts, how researchers ought to negotiate them, and how observers gauge the reliability and validity of research.

A second consideration is the role played by intermediaries, including advocacy groups and journalists, who communicate research findings to the public and to policymakers. The authors particularly shine light upon how these groups can influence the visibility of research or the policy implications derived from it.

Third, how does the availability or absence of data dictate what researchers choose to examine, and how authoritatively can they contribute to the debate? The chapters highlight the role that the construction of major federal datasets can play, the impact of efforts to collect standardized student achievement scores, and the consequences of the tacit agreement that these are a valid proxy for learning and school performance.

Finally, the contributors shed light upon "feedback loops"—considering not only how the research community influences the policymaking community but also how policymaking and advocacy, in turn, affect the production of research.

OVERVIEW OF THE BOOK

The chapters that follow seek to break new ground on questions that have been rarely examined in recent years. While diverse in the topics covered and in the perspectives of the authors, they are linked by the conviction that researchers, public officials, educators, journalists, and advocates would all benefit from a clearer and deeper understanding of the complex relationship between research and policymaking. The book unfolds in four sections. The first two chapters consider the history of the federal role in education policy and the evolving nature of educational policy research. The following three chapters address the role of research in debates over reading, NCLB, and "out-of-field" teaching. The third section considers how research affects policy by shaping public opinion, influencing judicial decisions, and affecting the decisions of district and school leaders. Finally, the fourth section offers broader insights into the incentives that help explain the behavior of researchers and policymakers. I close the volume with some reflections on what the contributions imply for how we think about the link between research and policy.

In chapter 2, Andrew Rudalevige, an associate professor of political science at Dickinson College, explains that the organizational history of the research function in the Department of Education is one of institutional mutation. Each reinvention—from the National Institute of Education to the Office for Educational Research and Improvement to the present-day IES— has sought to make education research more "scientific" and thus more worthy of respect and Congressional funding. With the creation of IES in 2002, however, efforts to insulate education research from partisan interference seem to have advanced. That result has not occurred despite politics, but because of it: because the salience of educational accountability spilled over into the organizational arena. The question with which Rudalevige closes is whether those conditions will stay in place long enough to allow a new institutional culture to take root at IES—and in the U.S. Congress.

Jeffrey Henig, a professor of political science and education at Columbia University's Teachers College, opens chapter 3 with a paradox. Education policy research today is simultaneously charged with irrelevance and yet, at the same time, is often imagined as a powerful political weapon capable of swaying public opinion and legislative votes. High profile spats among prominent researchers have been presented to the public in a way that portrays research more as a swift sword for advocacy than a steady machine for generating knowledge. He notes that pursuing these scholarly debates in the public square has fostered an attendant focus on personalities and agendas rather than substantive questions. Henig examines the institutional transitions that may be simultaneously pushing research into the public eye and potentially eroding some of its traditional authority and independence, and considers what these developments mean for research and policy.

In chapter 4, Paul Manna, assistant professor in the Department of Government at the College of William and Mary, and Michael Petrilli, vice president for national programs and policy at the Thomas B. Fordham Foundation, examine the roots of NCLB's expansive call for "scientifically based research" and how such research influenced the law's development, in particular its "highly qualified teacher" provisions. While research had to compete with other considerations, including politics, ideology, logrolling, and the aspirations of public officials, they argue that it appears to have informed several of the substantive choices involved in producing NCLB. The authors discuss the crucial role that key "synthesizer groups" played in the highly qualified teacher debate, by helping to bridge the gap between researchers on the outside of government and policymakers on the inside, and what it can teach about the importance of relationships between scholars, advocates, and policymakers.

In chapter 5, James Kim, an assistant professor at the Harvard University Graduate School of Education, traces the history of the reading wars over the past four decades with an eye toward both the scientific community and the policy arena. His analysis suggests scientific research has played a major role in resolving controversies about reading by highlighting areas of substantial consensus and agreement. However, the very norms governing disciplined scientific inquiry—including the slow accumulation of findings in peer-reviewed journals and the reliance on expertise to adjudicate educational controversies—also explain why researchers may be frustrated by policy outcomes and explains the challenges in using research to shape policy. In his conclusion, Kim describes some recent trends in reading policy that may help address the limitations of research.

In chapter 6, University of Pennsylvania professor Richard Ingersoll offers a distinctive first-person take on the issue of teacher quality. In a chapter replete with insights drawn from personal experience, he explores how research has played out in one key strand of the teacher quality debate—the "out-of-field" teaching problem. Arguably the leading national authority on this issue as well as an influential voice in the teacher quality debates, Ingersoll briefly sketches his research on the problem of underqualified teachers, explains how his data has been used and misused by various groups to buttress their agendas, and offers some thoughts on how researchers might seek to ensure that their work is disseminated and utilized appropriately.

In chapter 7, William Howell, an associate professor at the University of Chicago's Harris School of Public Policy, examines the varying impacts of academic research on the views of average citizens. Drawing from a novel experiment embedded within a national public opinion survey, Howell finds that research can influence the preferences of a significant number of citizens, but only when its findings comport with deeply held views. He also finds that the willingness of individual citizens to believe academic research depends significantly upon their ideological commitments and biases. Even the most objective of academic studies, Howell reminds us, must ultimately persuade citizens who approach any research finding with their own beliefs and preconceptions.

As the courts' role in education policymaking has grown, so, too, has judges' apparent reliance on education research in crafting decisions. In chapter 8, University of Colorado–Colorado Springs assistant professor Joshua Dunn and Brown University assistant professor Martin West examine the judicial record on desegregation and school finance litigation. They report that research has been most influential in state courts, which are more closely tied to the political system than are federal courts, and in areas where constitutional texts and the judicial doctrine governing their interpretation are vague. Regardless of the venue, the absence of clear standards within the education research community about what constitutes compelling evidence has prevented judges from limiting the admissibility of dubious evidence and has allowed them to pick and choose evidence according to normative or legal arguments. Finally, they conclude, even the most rigorous of education research may be of limited use for courts because the scale of the remedies courts are asked to contemplate almost inevitably exceeds, by a vast distance, what can be reliably inferred from available studies.

In chapter 9, North Carolina State associate professor Lance Fusarelli argues that superintendents and principals face significant and unappreciated obstacles when it comes to using research to drive policy or decisions about school improvement. Even as school leaders embrace the tenets of data-driven decisionmaking and action research, they continue to ignore relevant scholarly research. Fusarelli traces this to the ambiguity of research findings, the questionable relevance of much education research, the nature of district and school decisionmaking, and a lack of expertise in making use of research findings. Fusarelli proposes several incentives or alterations that might lead district and school policymakers to make greater use of existing research, including restructuring the school day and calendar, more tightly linking evaluation of superintendents and principals to performance, addressing the reward structure for researchers, and creating more localized research consortiums.

In chapter 10, University of Washington professor Dan Goldhaber and University of Southern California professor Dominic Brewer argue that the proportion of the entire education research enterprise that would pass muster for scientific rigor in other fields is shockingly small. They propose a novel supply-and-demand model of education research to explore some of the reasons for this state of affairs, concentrating on the forces that drive the production of education research. They explore how factors like the availability of data and the structure of the tenure system help explain what questions researchers choose to address and the methodologies they utilize, and how funding and policy shifts affect the nature, quality, and policy relevance of the scholarship that is produced.

And, in chapter 11, Brown University professor Kenneth Wong focuses on the "political" side of the research–policymaker nexus. He considers the incentives that encourage or discourage public officials from using research and the conditions under which researchers can exercise greater influence in the policy process. Drawing on research from political science as well as his own extensive experience, Wong argues that electoral interests, distribution of power, and partisan-oriented agendas must be taken into consideration in understanding the use and influence of research in the policy process. He concludes by looking at several specific cases in which research has influenced policy and considering the implications of efforts to bridge the gap between research and policy.

Finally, in the concluding chapter, I try to distill some themes and insights from the foregoing and offer some thoughts about what these might mean for policymakers, researchers, advocates, and funders in the years ahead.

In part, the inattention devoted to these questions in the past decade has been a consequence of a reasonable desire to take advantage of newly available data on performance and increasingly sophisticated methodological tools, both of which have enabled researchers to focus more concretely on what does or does not appear to advance student learning. The result has been a wave of valuable new research on the impact of various educational reforms. The irony is that understanding how knowledge and research get produced, disseminated, and utilized has been largely ignored at precisely the time when a quantum leap in the availability of data, the enactment of NCLB and Reading First, the embrace of "scientifically based research," and the creation of IES have given these questions a new importance. My hope is not that the contributions in this volume will provide pat answers to thorny and complex challenges, but that they may help prompt a new wave of thought, scholarship, and sober reflection.

CHAPTER 1

Structure and Science in Federal Education Research

Andrew Rudalevige

The education research function has generally stood apart from the fierce controversies over the legitimate role of the federal government in education policy. Indeed, the creation of the earliest U.S. department of education, in 1867, centered on a national sanction for building and diffusing scientific knowledge in the field. Though such efforts have continued across a century and a half, longevity does not imply stability. The institutions housing the education research and development mission have changed frequently and rapidly. Since 1980 alone, when the modern Department of Education was created, the National Institute of Education (NIE) has yielded to the Office of Educational Research and Improvement (OERI), itself replaced in 2002 by the Institute of Education Sciences (IES).[1]

At the same time, the name of the legislation creating IES—the Education Sciences Reform Act (ESRA)—hints at one key consistency underlying these mutations. Proponents of each organizational reinvention sought to broaden the scope, utility, and use of education research and development, as well as the resources accorded to it. To reach those goals, they sought to make education more "scientific," on a par with research in the natural sciences or medicine. Only then, they reasoned, would education research receive the respect it required, to receive the support it required, to make a difference for students and society. Take, for instance, President Hoover's advisory committee on education. A section of its report, grandly entitled Truth vs. Partisanship, held that "governmental policy cannot hope to rise above partisanship . . . unless mere differences of opinion, tenaciously held, are dissolved by revelations of pertinent facts established by scientific method and presented in

understandable terms."[2] Seventy-five years later, IES touts a like determination to spark "the transformation of education into an evidence-based field
in which decisionmakers routinely seek out the best available research and
data before adopting programs or practices."[3]

If history is any guide, IES faces heavy odds against such a rationalizing
transformation. Christopher Cross, a former head of OERI, concludes that "of
all the potential federal functions, the research role remains the most unre-
alized in the course of the past half century."[4] Fault for this widely shared
view has been laid consistently at the feet of IES's predecessors. James March
lamented in 1978 that the NIE, "an organization dedicated to rational procedures, excellence, and the use of intelligence, came to be indecisive, incom-
petent, and disorganized."[5] The replacement of NIE by OERI changed little:
OERI director Diane Ravitch argued that her "agency itself bears a measure
of blame for the low status accorded federal educational research."[6] And by
the turn of the twenty-first century, congressional observers were describing
that agency in "language . . . [that] cannot be printed in a family-oriented
academic journal."[7]

Such assessments spring both from the nature of education research and
from the way the federal government has approached it. Education research,
as Carl Kaestle has noted, has an "awful reputation." It is accused of being
irrelevant, inconsistent, and fond of ratifying the obvious.[8] But just as importantly for the dictates of science, it is simply difficult to do well: education
is a field in which all else is too rarely equal to make ready claims of causality. Its subjects are moving targets motivated by multiple inputs for which
researchers cannot always account or control. Because students and teachers cannot be sent randomly to different schools or classrooms, or purposely
given less or worse educational "treatment," it is hard to know whether a
given variable or a myriad of other inputs caused the observed difference.[9]
Further, while facts might be determined by the scientific method, values
cannot be—and questions of education are naturally driven by value-laden,
aspirational lines of inquiry. Thus, while it is commonly observed that "education research has not yielded dramatic improvements in practice of the
kind one can point to in medicine,"[10] others object even to the metaphor.
Douglas Christensen, Nebraska's education commissioner, told Congress that
modeling education research on medicine was "abhorrent . . . Our children
are not sick or diseased. Education and instruction are not treatments."[11]
While in principle, then, the IES mission to conduct scientific research seems
uncontroversial—at least to outsiders—in practice, such aims have attracted
little consensus within the education community or its friends in government. In short, education is inextricably political.

As if this were not enough, education research has also been *politicized*. That is, it has been wrapped up in a "politics of bureaucratic structure"[12] that privileges influence over insulation and constituent service over science. Research has not been given adequate autonomy, separation from the projects and policies it is supposed to evaluate, or resources on a scale that might attract sufficient and sufficiently talented staff to convincingly conduct it. Instead, education research agencies have often been charged with serving partisan purposes by bolstering party-line arguments on everything from compensatory education to school choice to abstinence.[13] As a Senate task force noted in 1998, this engenders "little faith in our current education infrastructure to produce the needed research on policies and programs that work."[14]

Despite all this, there is general optimism—albeit cautiously expressed—that IES, the current organizational incarnation of that infrastructure, has a fighting chance to earn such faith. To understand why, we need to take the issues of science and structure raised already and show how the latter might help enable the former. This chapter lays out some basic issues of bureaucratic politics, then traces those insights across the political history of education research in the United States, especially with regard to the three major agencies (NIE, OERI, and IES) noted above. While the discussion focuses on the Department of Education, it is important to note at the outset that much federal sponsorship of education research occurs elsewhere. Indeed, as discussed below, agencies like the National Institutes of Health (NIH) and the National Science Foundation (NSF) have been longtime lodestars for education researchers seeking reform.

The final section of this chapter discusses the differences between IES and its predecessors, and evaluates its progress five years after its founding. Its experience begins, at least, to answer the question of what needs to happen—in terms of agenda setting, personnel policies, peer review procedures, insulation from party politics—for empirics to trump emotion in the field of federal education research.

BUREAUCRATIC STRUCTURE AND SCIENCE

This chapter is organized around the structural politics of education for a simple reason: structure matters to outcomes, and, thus, to political actors. The way a bureau is organized matters for its responsiveness to officials and interests of all stripes, as well as for the kinds of policy options that push to the top of its hierarchy. Structural choices, then, affect both the types of problems an agency perceives and the kinds of solutions it puzzles out—and their effectiveness. Structure shapes how well issues are coordinated and how resources can be distributed. Arguably, the struggle of organized inter-ests over agency structure means that practically no public bureau can live up to the purest tenets of public administration. Terry Moe posits that "any notion that political actors might confine their attention to policymaking and turn organizational design over to neutral criteria or efficiency experts denies the realities of politics."[15]

We should expect this observation to have particular bite in a values-driven policy realm such as education, as well as special ramifications for efforts to support "science" in government. If science requires neutral meth-odology, the ability to follow research where it leads and, not unimportantly, patience, then it should be particularly difficult to achieve through a political process driven by short-term electoral concerns in an era of partisan polariza-tion. A science agency needs, in some ways, to be left alone. Yet this is hard to pull off—especially since being left alone requires the appropriated cash to live independently. As March trenchantly observed of NIE, its creation "cel-ebrated the possibility of a new life; but it was conceived in the usual way, born innocent, and lost its virginity in a Senate subcommittee."[16]

Most important for our purposes, then, is the notion of autonomy (from that Senate subcommittee, say), and how to get it. Political scientist David E. Lewis lays out various measures of what he calls "insulation," battles over which are often played out through the politics that create a given agency. For instance, who chooses appointees, and which positions require Senate confirmation? Are there fixed terms? Are there limitations on appointments or removals? Most fundamentally, who governs the agency—a commission, a single administrator, a director with an advisory board? (A commission or empowered board makes it harder to politicize an agency because more actors must be influenced in order to change its direction.)[17]

In general, Lewis finds, agencies created by executive action (such as the 1985–1994 version of OERI) are less likely to be insulated than those created by statute (such as NIE or IES). The reason is that presidents tend to oppose insulation: they want control, a hierarchical bureaucracy responsive to execu-tive direction. Members of Congress would rather the president be constrained in his ability to manage a given agency, if only to keep their lines of influence open into the bureaucracy in ways that benefit their own favored interests. These preferences are hardened or mitigated by party control; divided gov-ernment generally enhances insulation, because a Congress (or even a cham-ber of Congress) controlled by an opposing party will be more cautious about allowing executive flexibility—as we will see with the long process that reau-thorized OERI in 1994, or the 2002 authorization of IES.[18]

To be sure, Kaestle is right to say that there is no structural "haven from politics. . . . Politics can scale any walls in Washington, especially if the walls were built with federal dollars."[19] Yet at the same time, the bureaucracy literature makes clear that politics can help erect insulating walls as well as knock them over. Politics, that is, is all about shifting incentives and imperatives, and the conditions under which they are altered. And in some cases, Congress has indeed been convinced to recuse itself from interference. The repeated rounds of military base closings, for example, attempt to rationalize the nation's overall security posture by imposing pain on numerous individual districts—achieved by delegating the task to an independent commission, whose work must be accepted or rejected as a whole. Likewise, legislators have periodically granted presidents "fast track" authority to reach agreements over tariffs and trade issues. Here, too, members of Congress agree to accept or reject the president's offering as a whole, without seeking to pick it apart to protect parochial interests.[20]

There are good examples, too, of bureaucratic autonomy. The Federal Reserve, for instance, is led by a board made up of appointees with long (fourteen-year), staggered terms. Better yet, the Fed is self-funding, and, thus, in a position both to avoid budget season pandering and to pay its analytic personnel well enough to compete for the best newly minted economics PhDs. NSF and NIH, as noted earlier, are also well-respected science bureaucracies. Their autonomies create what former education commissioner Harold Howe called, rather enviously, a "permanent cadre of really capable people" that give an agency "the kind of respect" that helps "fend off political invasions."[21] Such personnel also institutionalize a professional research ethos within an organization.

The key question, then, becomes whether there are conditions under which moving education research off the partisan target range can be made politically—that is, electorally—profitable. To be sure, the course of the educational infrastructure has rarely run this way. But as we will see, IES was a self-conscious effort to move in this direction, helped along, in part, by the high salience of the No Child Left Behind Act and the political cover it provided.

"SIMPLY TO COLLECT INFORMATION": EDUCATION RESEARCH, 1867–1954

As noted at the outset, the nineteenth-century department of education's statutory assignment was to gather and disseminate "statistics and facts" that would improve American education. Indeed, this was its *only* purpose.

"What is this bureau to do?" asked Representative Nathaniel Banks (R-MA) on the floor of the House. "Simply to collect information; nothing more than that."[22] Congress created a "department," in name. But this exalted status was not backed up in fact. The organization was to be headed not by a cabinet-level secretary but by a commissioner overseeing just four employees.

Still, that Banks' assurance was necessary illuminates the disputes over the new agency's structure and reach. Though some argued data gathering was sufficient reform—that information about good practices could be used as leverage to force (if only by embarrassment) educational improvement, an argument with obvious echoes today—many had wanted more, structurally and substantively.[23] Some urged a full department of public instruction or a national "agent for education," housed perhaps in the Smithsonian Institution. Horace Mann thought that secessionism could be forestalled by national education reforms, and after the Civil War, Congress debated a resolution to "enforce education, without regard to race or color, upon the population of all such States as shall fall below a standard to be established by Congress."[24]

National standards, even leaving race aside, represented a position that then, as now, scared off fans of state autonomy. In pushing, instead, for a circumscribed agency, critics joined constitutional concerns about the federal government's legitimate role in education with state education officers' reluctance to share authority. The first commissioner, Henry Barnard, had grand schemes "just shy of federal control" for leveraging centralized power over how states organized and implemented their educational systems.[25] Instead, in 1868, Congress quickly made the agency's nomenclature consistent with its limited powers, creating an "Office of Education" within the Department of the Interior and cutting the commissioner's salary by 25 percent.[26]

Under the long tenure of John Eaton, the bureau's second commissioner, the agency attained some organizational stability. Its functions remained limited, though, resolutely centered on information gathering and coordination. It watched rather than drove the field's research interests, and did not have the funding to adequately disseminate its findings.[27] Later commissioners such as William Torrey Harris (1889–1906) were well-regarded by educators but not by public administrators (who decried his "degree of indifference with regard to . . . detail") or members of Congress. These failings limited the agency's appropriations and undercut the efficacy of its services.[28] A small but telling detail is that the commissioner's salary remained at its 1868 level of $3,000 per annum until a decade into the twentieth century. At the same time, the bureau lost autonomy, attracting extraneous functions. Until 1907, for example, it ran a program in Alaska for purchasing and breeding reindeer and training Alaskans in their care.[29]

As Progressive ideals arose and spread, by 1914 the bureau was promoting its ability "to give"—though only "upon request"—"expert opinion to state, country, and city officials . . . for the promotion of education."[30] But it continued to oversee the territorial school system until 1931—a huge task that necessarily dwarfed other agency functions and obscured the research role. In 1929 the secretary of the interior recognized this problem, saying he would seek to reorganize the enterprise on the "principle" of "the establishment of the Office of Education as a research organization rather than an administrative agency."[31] In 1931, the national advisory committee cited earlier likewise denounced the half-hearted measures by which education policy, and in particular, research, had been advanced: the department, bureau, and office "have in this respect been minor agencies of the Government attempting to cope with a major interest."[32] To achieve the "truth" available through scientific management, more funding was necessary, but so was an organizational revamping. Research needed "adequate status," clout sufficient to make policymakers take it seriously and permit it "to present forcibly both to Congress and to the President" the scientific facts underlying educational needs.[33]

NATIONAL INSTITUTES

Such uses of force did not become immediately plausible. The number of professional positions in the Office of Education (OE) bumped up in 1931 but leveled off thereafter, and did not rise even during the New Deal's grand expansion of government.[34] The Office itself moved from the Department of the Interior to the new Federal Security Agency in 1939—thus, it no longer reported through a cabinet-level position.

However, the ethos behind the Advisory Committee Report, and the institutional structure it implied, remained ready to be reborn. This section traces that resurrection sequentially through the most recent agencies that have sought to give the education research function enhanced stature and independence: the NIE from 1972 to 1985, the OERI from 1985 to 2002, and the IES from 2002 to the present.

The Research Bandwagon

World War II and the science that sprang from it helped reinstate the early twentieth-century faith in rational administration; Richard Dershimer is one of many chroniclers of the era stressing "the exalted place that the concept of research had reached in the 1950s."[35] The natural sciences were the largest beneficiaries, with the creation of the Atomic Energy Commission (in 1946), the National Institute of Mental Health (1946), the NSF (1950), and the like, joining the older National Institutes of Health (1930, but made formally plural with a large expansion starting in 1946).

Education returned to the cabinet with the creation of the Department of Health, Education, and Welfare (HEW) in 1953. The next year, the Cooperative Research Act allowed HEW's Office of Education to fund "the conduct of research, surveys, and demonstrations."[36] While modestly funded—two-thirds of the first appropriation was earmarked for research on the education of the mentally retarded—the act was nonetheless OE's first officially sanctioned, substantive foray past the statistics-gathering function established in 1867. By 1960, some $3 million annually was being spent on education research and its dissemination; by 1965 the figure was $17 million.[37]

Yet even as technocracy ascended to new heights of prestige along the New Frontier, the research program seemed disjointed, small-scale, as "Miscellaneous," said the Chief State School Officers association, "as a list of dissertation titles."[38] A series of organizational efforts, combined with increased appropriations, were therefore undertaken to scale up both the scope and the science of education research. Indeed, they were modeled directly on how the federal government had managed research and development in the natural sciences.[39]

First, a series of research and development centers, intended to be large, national institutions affiliated with major universities, were created under the authority of the Cooperative Research Act in 1964. By 1967, 10 were in operation. Around the same time, President Johnson's education task force, led by John Gardner, proposed the creation of new educational laboratories to serve as educational equivalents of the "great national laboratories of the Atomic Energy Commission." These were authorized in Title IV of the Elementary and Secondary Education Act of 1965.[40] Further, using as a model the Clearinghouse for Federal Scientific and Technical Information, the Educational Resources Information Center (ERIC) was created as a means of disseminating exemplary research.

But by the late 1960s, key political actors were already dissatisfied with the science of education research and OE's ability to support or spur it. Despite the new centers and laboratories, the research agenda remained underwhelming, in part because the labs, when implemented, were not national, but regional and small-scale. This was based, in part, on two related political calculations by OE: to get many labs operating quickly, given legislative attention spans, and to place them strategically across the country to build local constituencies. "Title IV labs are going to be pork barrel," OE commissioner Francis Keppel told one interlocutor; "every Congressman is going to want one in his region."[41]

Further, while the centers and laboratories were created to match priority research needs with research projects, there was no definitive list of those priorities. Turnover and staffing were major problems, exacerbated by stifling micromanagement from the Johnson White House and frequent reorganizations in a quest for "central management and coordination of education research and development programs."[42] The result was, instead (at least after one 1965 reorganization), that "for days and weeks, people could not find each other's offices—sometimes not even their own."[43]

One dismayed observer was the Bureau of the Budget (BoB), the president's all-purpose supervisor and evaluator of executive branch action. The Bureau, which had high hopes and standards for rational research, supported White House efforts (pushed by Nixon advisor Daniel Patrick Moynihan and his aide Chester Finn) to start over by revamping the research function in a brand new organizational form. "Out of frustration with the failure of OE and belief in the power of scientific research, the NIE proposal was born."[44]

The National Institute of Education

The OE's Bureau of Research had been created in the 1965 reorganization. Though it united previously scattered programs within its purview, it remained buried bureaucratically. Its associate commissioner (one of 15) oversaw six divisions and reported to the OE commissioner, who reported to an assistant secretary for education, who reported to the secretary of HEW.[45]

Creation of a new, independent institute, as BoB and the White House saw it, would afford the research function a status equal to that of OE itself and, crucially, follow the successful models of NSF and, especially, NIH. Its autonomy would provide newfound prestige, which would attract better people both to its staff and to its advisory councils. These better people would spark, and produce, better (i.e., more scientific) research, which would attract other top researchers (and congressional support), thus forging a virtuous circle.

Accordingly, Nixon's message to Congress in March 1970 urged that policymakers "stop pretending that . . . we are significantly applying science and technology to the techniques of teaching."[46] The NIE he outlined would have the ability to hire a "permanent staff of outstanding scholars from such disciplines as psychology, biology and the social sciences, as well as education"; it would conduct its own research, as well as contract with other researchers; and serve as "a focus for educational research and experimentation in the United States." As such, Nixon anticipated a quarter-billion-dollar annual appropriation. The BoB's Emerson Elliott, who became the first acting director of NIE, has said it aimed even higher: "It was formulated by Moynihan as a billion-dollar agency."[47]

The result was significant structural change. After passage of the Education Amendments of 1972, NIE became, with OE, one of two co-equal parts of a new Education Division within HEW; its director had the same bureaucratic status as the commissioner of education. NIE was given a flexible personnel system that could evade civil service constraints and the authority to carry funds over from year to year, so as to underwrite long-term research programs. It could also spend 10 percent of its budget on its own internal research programs.[48]

These results are in line with Lewis's argument that divided government, especially when accompanied by marked distrust of the president by Congress, leads to additional insulation. Indeed, Democrats in Congress went so far as to endow the 15 members of the new agency's National Council on Educational Research (NCER) with fixed terms and a good deal of their own policymaking authority. NIE, legislators stressed, must be independent of OE—willing and able to "spit in [its] eye," as Rep. John Brademas (D-Ind.) put it.[49]

The Nixon administration (especially after Moynihan left the government) would prove apathetic toward the new institute, and Congress little more passionate.[50] Chester Finn calls Brademas "arguably the last member of Congress to give a damn" about education research or knowledge generation.[51] In the end, apathy turned to hostility, and structure could not overcome it. Michael Timpane, who directed NIE in the late 1970s, later noted that it "inherited at best a mixed bag of research projects, was slow to organize, inexpert at explaining itself, and soon fell from political grace."[52] As a clear indicator of the latter plunge, consider that Nixon's half-billion-dollar agency would wind up at $75 million by fiscal year 1974, $70 million the following year, and barely $50 million 10 years later. Even the $75 million was consumed by previously committed projects and did not allow for new work with an independent NIE imprint.[53]

One reason for NIE's failure, to be sure, was a dearth of political acuity. Certainly its first full-time director, Thomas Glennan, had few connections to the education research community, or to Congress.[54] Another reason was that OE continued to carry out activities that seemed to duplicate what NIE was funding. Yet even as NIE was criticized for, as Rep. Edith Green put it, "plowing the same ground over and over," when the agency sought to carry out new experimental work, members of Congress were slow to understand its import.[55] Sen. Warren Magnuson's (D-WA) 1974 exchange with NIE director Thomas Glennan sets the tone:

> *Magnuson:* You mean you cannot read about it?
> *Glennan:* No. It is set up as an experiment.
> *M:* They have got reports on it. I am sure they have.
> *G:* No, they do not. We are helping to produce them.
> *M:* They have their own reports.
> *G:* They have not introduced [these tests] as yet.
> *M:* You could get the reports.[56]

Thus, NIE's structural autonomy, so clear in statute, was never allowed to take tangible form. On Capitol Hill, Congress battered it with a lethal combination of cuts and earmarks. The education research community has rarely been a unified political interest, and NIE failed to attract support from local educators or (as its funding vanished) education researchers. NCER failed to help much in this regard; even when its members had individual clout, they rarely used it on behalf of NIE.[57] On the other hand, the R&D centers and, especially, the regional laboratories, had what OERI's Cross would call "a wonderful political network" centered on a Council for Educational Development and Research (CEDaR) that "protected them from everything" from budget cuts to NIE attempts to control their behavior.[58] As the centers and labs evolved, the former had become home to larger-scale research projects and the labs providers of technical assistance to states and school districts. The local focus of the latter had (as OE had, in fact, predicted) made them important to local constituencies and, thus, to members of Congress. Legislators therefore consistently mandated the preservation of their regional structure and their funding from NIE interference and/or competition, even during the huge cuts in NIE appropriations in the early 1980s. CEDaR was unsympathetic, arguing that NIE ("a disappointment from the outset") could have leveraged the labs' political connections instead of trying to hamstring them.[59]

At the other end of Pennsylvania Avenue, executive interference (in terms of both action and inaction) was also problematic. An early delay in appointing the members of NCER, given that board's many powers, proved problematic in developing agency priorities and requesting start-up funding—leading to a lawsuit when the agency sought to move ahead on these matters without the as-yet-nonexistent board's approval. As with OE, turnover was a constant problem in long-term planning; during NIE's 13-year tenure it had six directors plus five acting directors, and was subject to constant reorganizations—four between August 1972 and November 1974 alone. These did not succeed in repositioning the agency to gain congressional favor. A later reshuffle under director Patricia Graham simplified agency structure and better linked its organization to its research themes. While she felt this allowed her to regain some funding and improve staff recruitment, the energy spent in reorganization nonetheless proved hugely distracting to carrying out agency functions.[60]

In 1981, presidential attention increased, but in an unwelcome way. Upon taking office, President Reagan fired the entire NCER board, fixed terms or no, and appointed Edward Curran to direct NIE. Curran penetrated whatever agency insulation was left when he wrote to the president complaining of its (left-leaning) ideological rigidity and decrying NIE's basic "premise that education is a science, whose progress depends on systematic research and development. . . . I know that this premise is false."[61] Though Education Secretary Terrel Bell subsequently fired Curran, his successor shared much of his skepticism regarding the federal role in education.[62] Defenders fired back, catching NIE in a media crossfire that further undermined its mission.

One result was massive turnover of a professional staff that felt itself newly vulnerable to outside attack: only 7 percent of excepted service personnel and 25 percent of civil servants at NIE in spring of 1979 remained there in 1986.[63] Another result was the agency's demise. By now, as Finn notes, NIE was "unloved in Washington," whipped back and forth between the parties and "despised by both."[64]

The Office of Educational Research and Improvement

If "the NIE was a case study of how not to be effective in Washington," as Michael Kirst has noted, more successful by far was the National Education Association's (NEA) efforts to cash in on its support for Jimmy Carter's 1976 campaign with the creation of a new Department of Education.[65] Despite the increased salience the new department brought to education generally, NIE actually moved down one level in the federal hierarchy under a new umbrella Office for Educational Research and Improvement at the assistant secretary level. OERI also included the National Center for Education Statistics (NCES), which lost its independent status but did not gain control of relevant NSF programs, as Carter had hoped. A Federal Interagency Committee on Education (FICE) was created instead, with the idea of coordinating education programs across the bureaucracy. This proved "feeble."[66]

By 1985, after the sequence of events recounted above, Bell's successors as education secretary had begun to think about streamlining NIE. The Department of Education Organization Act provided authority to restructure the research function, and Secretary William Bennett did just that, merging NIE and NCES into OERI proper while wiping out NCER's policy authority. In the new OERI, an Office of Research joined a Center for Statistics and the Programs for Improvement of Practice under an assistant secretary for education research. This was Chester Finn who, after helping to create NIE, returned to government to help put it out of its misery.

While most in the educational community had not favored the reorganization, feeling that it downgraded the importance of the research function, they "recognized the importance of changing the entrenched public and congressional perception that federal education research and development was so politicized that it deserved little support."[67] This helped convince Congress to ratify Bennett's action in statute in 1986.[68] Still, OERI was structurally less independent from political line authority than it had been (at least in statute) as NIE. The replacement board for NCER, the National Advisory Council for Educational Research and Improvement, was "totally politicized" with little authority.[69] Further, Finn held the title "counselor to the secretary" as well as assistant secretary, making him part of the department's immediate political team. His efforts to compile and disseminate causal findings in comprehensible form, as in the 1986 volume *What Works*, attracted acclaim but also heated partisan charge and counter-charge. The head of the Office of Research at this time, Sally Kilgore, described the interaction between OERI and its critics as two sides that "would rather sink on a ship, if they could hold the flag they liked, than get the ship across to the shore."[70]

In any case, for Finn the research function did not hold much promise: it did not receive enough money and what was provided was already spoken for (Finn's fierce attacks along these lines on the laboratories, e.g., as "entrenched institutions whose primary goals seem to be self-perpetuation," tended merely to motivate their congressional defenders to provide additional protection for those institutions, as noted below).[71] On the other hand, NCES was revamped under old BoB hand Emerson Elliott and given additional structural protections. OERI's priorities became basic statistical and assessment data, and the notion that statistics could leverage reform received new life. As Finn told Congress, "the American people, equipped with reliable information, accurate data, and solid research findings, can be counted on to fix their own schools."[72]

Over time, the new OERI suffered from some of the same problems as the old NIE. It had frequent changes of leadership, each of which shifted the direction of the research agenda and, thus, undercut support for long-term projects.[73] Most new monies it received were encumbered by newly assigned duties, such as programs serving the gifted and talented, math and science students, or literacy. It was difficult to attract a first-rate staff, a problem assistant secretary Diane Ravitch attributed to the OERI's lack of autonomy and funding. She also noted that OERI provided an example of a "bizarre reversal of the classic 'iron triangle,'" whereby the interests supported by the agency and its legislative overseers did not protect it from interference, but rather sought actively to "keep it enfeebled" and permeable; "fearing that administrators would pursue political or ideological ends, lawmakers . . . had written into law every program that we manage, with strong safeguards that make each one almost impervious to legitimate review."[74] Among other statutory controls, legislators continued to keep the labs and centers independent forces. As a spoof performer at a 1996 retirement party at OERI crooned, "Centers and Labs, Centers and Labs / They play their game, while we pay the tab / They'll never lose their luster / And we can't have one."[75]

Reauthorizing OERI

OERI came due for reauthorization in 1991. Leading up to that date (and extending past it), a variety of new structural ideas were debated, with issues of politicization and, thus, insulation, front and center. Rep. Major Owens (D-NY) took the lead, arguing strongly that OERI needed to be "depoliticized, so that priorities can be properly identified and research activities can gain the kinds of credibility and support they merit." He favored the restoration of a powerful policy board composed largely of researchers and practitioners, supported by an independent staff from the department. The board would oversee OERI operations and spending; as with NCER in the days of NIE, this represented a structural means of keeping OERI out of "opposition" hands by limiting its flexibility and boosting field-initiated research proposals.[76] It was, as the AERA's Gerald Sroufe notes, a "distinctly researcher-friendly" draft, as abetted by the access his association had to the Democratic majority, and that majority's distrust of the administration.[77]

At the same time the NSF/NIH model came again to the fore. As Clinton OERI head Kent McGuire puts it, it was time "to take another shot at the same target."[78] Many in the education research community felt that OERI had been too amorphous to build coherent priorities that could gain legislative understanding and support. Thus, the idea was to organize the research field around distinct directorates or "institutes" within the agency. Each was to focus on addressing a different educational ill in the way that NIH's institutes address illnesses.[79] In the end, five national research institutes were created, centered on early childhood education, at-risk children, curriculum and assessment, postsecondary education and lifelong learning, and educational governance and management.[80]

While worried that there would be insufficient funds to support each, or any, of the institutes, the George H. W. Bush administration accepted this approach. However, OERI was not reauthorized until 1994's Goals 2000 Act: congressional Democrats decided to wait for the 1992 election, banking that happy days would come again. The delay highlights the politics of insulation: one result of President Clinton's victory was that the tight reins in the earlier legislative language were dramatically relaxed. In the end, the new National Educational Research Policy and Priorities Board did not keep control over the research agenda, but rather was tasked to "work collaboratively" and "in consultation" with the assistant secretary. Some funding streams were still constrained: for fiscal 1996, for example, a fifth of the budget given the institutes had to go to field-initiated research and another third to R&D centers.[81]

The institute idea, however, did not work as hoped. Christopher Cross would soon argue that the new structure "created a disaster. It has led to less communication and coordination, unhealthy competition for very scarce resources, excess overhead expenses, and Balkanization that would do Eastern Europe proud!"[82] Cross (and others) thought the institutes would need $50 million each and a staff of fifty or so. But funding in fiscal 1996 totaled just $43 million. Subsequent reviews of the research produced by the nine R&D centers now funded by the institutes were not encouraging; "with a few notable exceptions reviewers found little evidence of systematic development" but rather a focus on idiosyncratic settings with little hope of wide replicability.[83] Each institute director reported to OERI assistant secretary Sharon Robinson, who had other duties that made it hard for her to exercise direct supervision over their research. It did not help that this major reorientation of OERI was accompanied by an additional "reinvention" prompted by the Clinton administration's government-wide National Performance Review. Thus, even as the institutes divided the Office of Research into five, OERI reorganized its existing centers, for example, shifting the Programs for the Improvement of Practice office to an Office of Reform Assistance and Dissemination (ORAD).

Further, as new programs (such as one dealing with educational technology) were added to OERI by Congress, they were added not to the institutes but as discrete parts of the agency more generally, enhancing managerial difficulties and leading to the "balkanization" Cross decried. One result was that research was often bottom-up, dictated by field desires rather than what Kent McGuire termed a "robust research planning engine" guiding consistent priority planning. Subsequent reviews of the work produced by the nine R&D centers now funded by the institutes were not encouraging in terms of systematic development or wide replicability.[84]

During this period, staff turnover fed a "dilution of research orientation and research capacity" as fewer and fewer actual researchers remained part of the OERI hierarchy. Observers compared OERI unfavorably in this area even to NIE.[85] Further, after Robinson's relatively long tenure, a series of acting assistant secretaries were put in place; and these, some observers argued, were "those closely identified with the top political leadership of the Department." At the same time, the administration decided to use OERI staff and discretionary funds to develop and oversee a system of voluntary national tests for fourth and eighth graders, leading to further charges that the agency had been politicized for the president's policy purposes.[86] Congress reacted harshly to the testing proposal, finally forcing the issue out of OERI's purview.

Indeed, the legislative climate had cooled globally. With the elimination of the Select Committee on Education after the 1994 elections, research interests found themselves outside looking in. Rep. Michael Castle (R-DE), chair of the House Education Reform Subcommittee, had a long list of complaints about OERI, including "the creeping influence of short-lived partisan or political operatives, the funding and dissemination of questionable studies, programs, and practices, and an overly bureaucratic office with no real sense of mission, mired by duplicative programs and competing interests."[87] In this environment, not surprisingly, yet another new structure began to take form.

The Institute of Education Sciences

Reauthorization of OERI was due in 1999, but had to compete for attention with the higher-priority Elementary and Secondary Education Act (ESEA), also ready for reauthorization that year. The ESEA process was not completed until the very end of 2001 with the passage of the No Child Left Behind Act (NCLB); meantime, OERI legislation received subcommittee approval but moved no further. In early 2002, though, the bipartisan coalition that formulated NCLB proved important to passage of what would become the Education Sciences Reform Act (ESRA).

Rep. Castle, the legislative driver of the new reauthorization, introduced a draft as early as July 2000. Castle echoed some of Owens' rationale from the previous go-round: the purpose, he said at a later hearing, was to "insulate our federal research . . . from partisan or undue political influences." This would be achieved by producing research that "improv[ed] student achievement—not [by] protecting the current structure."[88] And indeed, the new legislation would dramatically reshape that structure.

Castle's original July 2000 draft set a basic template for the ultimate legislation. Blowing up OERI, it created a National Academy for Education Research, Statistics, Evaluation, and Information as an independent agency outside of the Department of Education. It was to be run by a director serving a fixed six-year term and working with a large (19-member) board of directors made up of educators, researchers, business leaders, parents, and various government officials. Instead of five institutes there would be three centers (for research, statistics, and evaluation), each headed by a presidential appointee serving a like six-year term with boards of their own and, in the research office, backed by a "senior scientist." Some regional technical assistance programs would continue to exist, but the extant lab/center structure was not mandated. The agency was to guarantee that its activities "conform to high standards of quality, integrity, and accuracy, and are free from ideological agendas and undue political influence." Indeed, strict prescriptive guidelines for what constituted valid research were to be set in statute. For quantitative studies, hypotheses would be

> evaluated using experimental designs in which individuals, entities, programs, or activities are assigned to different conditions with appropriate controls to evaluate the effects of the condition of interest through random assignment experiments, or other designs to the extent such designs contain within-condition or across-condition controls.[89]

Some changes were made over time as others—especially new Bush OERI staff, such as director Grover "Russ" Whitehurst—gave their input. The academy was moved back into the department, but retained its independent director, who gained appointment power over the centers' commissioners. The standards defining "scientific" research were shifted somewhat, in part to track those in NCLB. A regional role was retained and strengthened, with at least two entities in each of ten regions mandated; "the maintenance of this system," House Democrats noted when the committee reported the bill, "was a critical priority."[90] Contracts would be awarded by the education secretary but overseen by regional contract boards and advisory committees; extant labs were temporarily grandfathered.

The House majority was willing to give the president line control over the agency, for instance in the appointment of commissioners. But when Democrats regained control of the Senate in May 2001, Sen. Ted Kennedy (D-MA) took over the Senate HELP committee, and his staffers became "an irresistible legislative force" in ensuring that the Senate took action on the research agency bill.[91] New language restored the NCES commissioner as a direct presidential appointee (not subject to removal by the director of the new agency) and gave the post a six-year term that was calibrated to begin in June 2003—thus shielding the appointment process from the electoral cycle. The Senate draft also preserved the governing power of the National Assessment Governing Board over national achievement tests.[92]

Other insulating features of the bill remained intact, including the director's six-year term, and the first statutory definition of "scientifically based research standards" for education that, while not as proscriptive as in earlier drafts, still limited causal claims to research designs that could bear their weight—most notably, random assignment experiments. While IES was to be within the Education Department, its director ranked as a level II position on the executive schedule, just one rung beneath a department secretary and at the same rank as the director of the National Science Foundation. Assistant secretaries, by contrast, are normally at level IV. The director was to be aided by a deputy director for science, and commissioners in the three centers for education research, education statistics, and education evaluation and regional assistance.[93]

The new National Board for Education Sciences (NBES) was largely advisory, but did have formal approval powers over the institute's long-term research priorities and its revamped peer review process. For the first time, the board was to be composed of a majority of researchers, rather than practitioners or other consumers of research. Cementing the research focus of the institute, the bill removed technical assistance functions (as in the Office of Reform Assistance and Dissemination) from the new structure and instead gave it lead responsibility for evaluating programs implemented elsewhere in the department. Additional excepted service positions were authorized to aid in hiring skilled personnel on an expedited basis.

In urging passage of the bill in October 2002, both Castle and Kennedy hailed a new era of "scientific rigor" and (as ever) compared the new structure to NIH. As Kennedy said, "We want to be able to look to this Institute when we have education questions in the same way that we look to the NIH when we have medical questions. This bill provides a sound foundation to do so."[94]

A "TIPPING POINT"? FIVE YEARS LATER

Was Kennedy right? As we have seen, the magniloquent rhetoric pitting "truth vs. partisanship" has usually been met over time with meager resources, with small-bore structures that protect political constituencies and that don't aggregate research over time so much as they simply reshuffle it. As OERI's Cross laments, "when research contradicts personal experience or political ideology, research usually loses."[95]

Yet new IES director Russ Whitehurst, in 2002 testimony to Congress, argued that "we are close to a point where the right investment in the right structure could get us close to a tipping point, where education becomes an evidence-based field."[96] Has the field finally tipped past its envy of the "hard science" institutes? If so, what helped that to happen?

Certainly the language of "rigorous scientific standards" emanating from IES has been loud and consistent, extending the call for "scientifically based" education research across all program areas. But while such rhetoric is not unimportant—and in this case, of course, it has statutory backup—the narrative above shows that it is also not new. Along these lines, the American Association of School Administrators suggested that the IES legislation "is an extension of current law. Whatever the state of education research is now, it is going to be unchanged based on the work in that bill."[97] Has anything really changed?

The short answer is "yes," which might best be witnessed by the nervous complaints issued by those in the education community most skeptical about the applicability of "science" to education research. For them, the new focus on "transformation" via "evidence-based intervention" amounts (perversely enough) to a sort of faith-based recovery program—an unrealistically dogmatic view of what "counts" as research—namely, random-assignment controlled experimental methodologies. Not all good research is experimental or quantitative, after all. Should rigor, or relevance, be the goal? In mission and execution, IES clearly emphasizes the former, albeit as a tool to enhancing the latter, and the occasional heat of the debate suggests that some oxen have, indeed, been gored.[98]

Still, five years after its creation, IES receives what a 2006 *Education Week* survey termed "mixed, but mostly positive, grades."[99] Most observers, even those nervous about scientific single-mindedness, see the shift as "very positive in terms of structure" and personnel.[100] Its legislative authority is "much improved," noted former OERI head McGuire, in ways that are "not sexy but critical." "There is hardly anything in place now that is like it was in previous regimes," noted the AERA's Gerald Sroufe.[101]

For instance, peer review for grant applications has been revamped in a manner Whitehurst terms "explicitly modeled on NIH," emphasizing separation of the review and contracting processes. As noted, the peer review process was statutorily required to gain approval of NBES's cadre of researchers, who endorsed it in 2006 as "of the highest merit and comparable to" that at

NSF and NIH's National Institute of Child Health and Human Development (NICHD)—each of which has an ex officio member on the board.[102] Reports emanating from the agency are subject to a separate Standards and Review Office process modeled on that used by academic journals. The ERIC clearinghouse system is in the process of reinvention and an online What Works Clearinghouse (WWC) has been created to provide state and local practitioners with information on the impact of curriculum or programs, as vetted by strict methodological standards. (The standards were high enough that little was quickly approved; critics soon dubbed WWC the "nothing works" clearinghouse.)[103]

The shedding of the "whole Christmas tree" of programs extraneous to research and the addition of evaluation functions has helped "get the noise out of the agency" and attract new staff. Excepted service hiring approval, restored after being largely wiped out in the early 1990s, has been a valuable means of bolstering personnel. And new budget authority allows the agency to roll funds over multiple fiscal years if not enough worthy grant applications are received in a given cycle.[104]

The agency has so far displayed impressive independence vis-à-vis the Department of Education and the administration generally. For example, while the Reading First program has strongly pushed phonics-based reading curricula, the WWC gave high marks to the rival Reading Recovery program. Likewise, WWC found that widely (and expensively) touted math texts and test preparation software and technology had little effect on student outcomes.[105] Whitehurst himself was careful to cast caveats upon Secretary Margaret Spellings' claims that National Assessment of Educational Progress scores offered "proof" of NCLB's effectiveness. One insider noted a dramatic contrast between the "most *partisan* Department of Education I have seen since 1988, and the most *independent* research and stats agency."[106]

Such insulation is good for the perceived integrity of the institute, though it runs the risk of cooling departmental ardor for institute initiatives—or appropriations. And it can mean that the institute avoids (or is avoided in) shaping legislation with important ramifications for research—the administration draft of the NCLB reauthorization, for example. Whitehurst admits, "It can be somewhat difficult to be inside the tent while dropping stink bombs inside the tent." But, he argues, "better inside than out," in terms of influencing the decisions of the wider department, and says IES has received no "pushback" pressuring it to change its ways.[107]

Other observers also see "détente," so far, helped by the director's six-year term and status as a presidential appointee. They worry, however, that IES has dropped far down the list of secretarial priorities—as indicated, for example, by its relative lack of emphasis in a recent departmental strategic plan, compared to former Secretary Rod Paige's version in 2002.[108] It is worth noting, perhaps, that ESRA does not prevent the president from removing the director, even without formal cause. Further, in a statement issued upon signing the ESRA into law, President Bush claimed the ability to override provisions in the law imposing qualification standards upon appointees. And though one section of the law specifically authorized the IES director to "prepare and publish" research or reports "without the approval of the Secretary" of Education, Bush's signing statement ordered the IES "to implement" that section "subject to the supervision and direction of the Secretary of Education." Administrative action on these claims could perforate the agency's insulation.[109]

If IES seems to have successfully avoided centralized control by the president, it has also sought to impose its own. Chester Finn, for example, argues that NCES is "excessively subject to the IES hierarchy," which has centralized grant making authority and the review and reporting process.[110] Some would prefer an organizationally independent NCES; as it stands, the NCES commissioner is the only center head who also serves as a fixed-term, presidential appointee. That decision may be re-fought when IES is reauthorized.

The "knowledge utilization division"—grounded in the R&D centers and regional laboratories—has also felt the pinch of IES control. The centers have tightened their research foci, in part to reflect smaller funding allotments. At $2 million per year per center, down from $5.5 million or so, Jim Kohlmoos of the Knowledge Alliance, an advocacy group for education research, suggests there is enough to "fund a project, but not a program," and that the research infrastructure is being eroded. The labs, too, have been handed a new mandate to conduct experimental research in preference to their traditional role of local dissemination and "rapid response" technical assistance.[111]

For some observers, these developments showed IES was enhancing the labs' rigor at last. For others, especially in the regions themselves, they were less welcome. "It's kind of like we're left without something," complained Nebraska education official Polly Feis. And "when customers start complaining they're not being served," Kohlmoos notes, "they go to their member of Congress."[112] This raises the broader question of organized interests—the labs and centers, the large contractor sector supported by IES grants, and so on—and whether they might seek to threaten IES's hard-won autonomy through legislative appeals. Interestingly, IES seems to have taken some proactive steps itself to stock the interest pool. In 2006, for instance, the institute awarded a $760,000 start-up grant to the new Society for Research on Educational Effectiveness, which Whitehurst praised as a "professional association . . . organized around rigorous research designs."[113] The grant set off another round of argument over pluralism in education research—but the bitter edge of that conversation seems to have dulled over time (especially as IES does continue to fund descriptive research). That the conversation is happening at all is some tribute to the changes wrought by IES.

The Politics of Insulation

Any such success is contingent, of course, and so must be any early evaluation. Still, there are several reasons why the politics of bureaucratic structure at last favored insulation of and autonomy for the education research function—why the statute creating IES was different, in structure and emphasis, than past iterations with similar intent.

One, quite simply, was a sense of desperation born from deep dissatisfaction, a notion in Congress and the education community that this was a critical—even the last—chance to make significant change.[114] If OERI was strike two, the next swing might end the game.

At the same time, there was new reason to think that education research could pay dividends if properly nurtured. Ironically, this evidence came from outside the education department: Since the early 1980s, NICHD had funded a series of studies on reading and language development, arguing that illiteracy was its own health crisis. By the latter 1990s, this research generated evidence on the effectiveness of phonics curricula.[115] This appealed both to scientists and to conservative education activists, who often had additional reasons for promoting phonics over whole language approaches.

The election of George W. Bush provided a policy agenda around which such partisan synergy could rally. The president made education a centerpiece of his 2000 campaign and his 2001 legislative agenda, pushing especially hard on issues of measurement and assessment. Beyond rallying public and legislative support, Whitehurst suggests, such rhetorical leadership cut through bureaucratic inertia; it "provided context *within* the administration for thinking that education research was necessary."[116]

It was necessary, of course, because of the focus of the No Child Left Behind Act on "scientifically based research." NCLB was a critical Bush priority, its blueprint sent to Congress only days after the president's inauguration in January 2001. Though the definition of such research varies even within NCLB, its centrality clearly benefited ESRA. Indeed, in signing the latter bill into law, the president praised it as "an important complement" to NCLB that would "substantially strengthen the scientific basis" behind education research.

The Democratic members so crucial to the passage of No Child Left Behind similarly endorsed ESRA. As research became salient, so did producing "good" research: the link between the measurement required to enforce district progress under NCLB, and the broader rigor needed in measuring educational outcomes more generally, gave what would have been a bill of little interest to most members of Congress a needed push. And as the national debate over education became inseparable from a broad endorsement of "accountability," IES became an agency for which legislators of all stripes could claim credit as a contribution to that cause—at relatively low cost. Insulation became good politics.

Finally, as IES moved forward, its new mission was to be implemented by new personnel at top and bottom. Many of the new leaders of IES were scholars, but relative outsiders to the education research community. At lower rungs, the creation of the new institute led to a clean sweep of prior personnel either by transfer or (using a provision of the 2001 Patriot Act) via early retirement. NCES remained relatively stable, but the other centers (perceived as "tainted" by OERI's history) saw large-scale turnover. This meant the agency could be reshaped from the ground up—though it also meant the loss of extensive bureaucratic expertise, a trade that could have long-term costs.

Truth and Partisanship

No matter the organizational changes, education research will never work exactly like health-care research. Different market (and regulatory) forces apply to the two areas, and to the extent education is a values-driven enterprise, "the problems of educational research are not structural in nature."[117] But that does not mean that structure is irrelevant. If (as Rep. Castle suggested in 2002), agency independence depends on the quality of the research it underwrites, structure might matter to the extent it buys the credibility that gives processes that promote good research the chance to institutionalize. That has not occurred in the past, when incentives have, in fact, gone the other way—rewarding efforts to avoid cumulation, disparage one's predecessors, and leave a new, if transient, mark. Five years in, IES shows promise of revising this history.

Of course, OERI and NIE also had promise. Structure matters, but so do resources; and the "politics of knowledge" is no different from politics as a whole in being defined by who gets what, when, and how.[118] By this standard, IES remains undercapitalized. ESRA authorized some $400 million annually for IES research activities, a distinct increase, but less than half of that is currently available. Recall Pat Moynihan's 1970 vision of a billion-dollar NIE: that would be a $5.3 billion vision today.

One additional question remains, as the reauthorization of both NCLB and ESRA return to the floor of Congress: Will the politics of structure continue to reinforce insulation? That is, Can the tides of partisanship continue to run in favor of shielding education research from political manipulation? Ironically, we need that kind of partisanship—to get a chance for truth.

For their guidance in mapping my journey across this policy arena, I would like to thank—among others who have asked to remain unnamed—Gina Burkhardt, Christopher Cross, Emerson Elliott, Michael Feuer, Chester Finn, Carl Kaestle, Jim Kohlmoos, Ellen Condliffe Lagemann, Kent McGuire, Joe Schneider, Gerald Sroufe, Russ Whitehurst and, through his writings, Maris Vinovskis. Any errors in fact or interpretation are, of course my, own. Special thanks are due to Rick Hess and Juliet Squire. Finally, thanks to Ellen Simon for early research assistance.

CHAPTER 2

The Evolving Relationship between Researchers and Public Policy

Jeffrey R. Henig

If education research were a person, his ears would be burning. It is not that education research is hot on the gossip circle; most people do not talk about it much. But when it is talked about, the tone is critical, often harshly so. The reputation of education research among policymakers and many scholars is that it is amateurish, prosaic, politicized, unscientific, and generally beside the point. In a 1993 article, historian Carl Kaestle refers to the "awful reputation" of education research.[1] Maris Vinovskis notes that, compared to some of the other social and behavioral disciplines, "educational research appears to be relatively backward and underdeveloped . . . second-rate and rather unsophisticated methodologically."[2] And in perhaps the most biting analysis, Rick Hess provides a sarcastic review of the 2006 meetings of the American Educational Research Association, simultaneously lampooning its irrelevance and its leftist political slant by characterizing the "five major fields of educational inquiry: imperialism; ghetto culture; hegemonic oppression and right-thinking multiculturalism; cyber-jargon; and the utterly incomprehensible."[3]

At least at first glance, this appears to be a fall from grace. During the Progressive Era in the early twentieth century, urban reformers successfully pushed structural changes intended to put science and expertise in the forefront of policymaking and buffer these from political interference. Dewey, Thorndike, and others created something of a golden age in which education studies built a knowledge base, became institutionalized within universities, and earned the ear of policymakers.[4] In general, the stock of the social sciences was running high, with the perhaps outsized ambitions captured in one early New Deal observer's assertion that "mankind in a test-tube is the hope and aim of social science."[5] At the national level, attention to issues like the economy, poverty, and national security put education research somewhat in the shadows, but not entirely. Vinovskis notes that among the architects of the National Institute of Education in the early 1970s, including Daniel Patrick Moynihan, "frequent references were made to scientific and medical successes with the explicit suggestion that educational research now was poised to achieve the same breakthroughs."[6]

Paradoxically, though, education policy research today is simultaneously charged with irrelevance and with being a powerful political weapon capable of swaying public opinion and legislative votes.[7] Despite the criticisms leveled against it, education research is arguably of higher quality today than previously in its history, and it remains a prominent feature in many of the nation's most important policy debates, possibly even more visible than ever before. The No Child Left Behind legislation, with its frequent mention of evidence-based decisionmaking, has authoritatively underscored the important role that objective knowledge could and should play in democratic society. The Institute for Educational Sciences (IES) in its grant policies, promotion of randomized field trials, and its What Works Clearinghouse[8] has provided detailed roadmaps of what strong research design might mean (see Rudalevige, chapter 2 in this volume). Research findings and research debates get deep coverage in outlets like *Education Week* and instant coverage in the blogosphere. And advocacy groups—whether favoring or opposing such reform ideas as charter schools, small schools, small classrooms, alternative certification, merit pay, or mayoral control—appear anxious to enlist social science evidence and researchers-qua-spokespersons to add legitimacy to their cause.

In a forthcoming book, I examine in some detail the ways in which education research often becomes simplified and polarized as it moves into the public arena.[9] In this chapter, I distill some of the lessons from that analysis to highlight five broad structural changes that may help account for the paradoxical position of education policy research today. Especially for that highly visible subset of studies that address hot national issues on which partisan alignments are clearly drawn, the value of evidence that appears scientific is increasing as research and researchers are being drawn more quickly, and in less mediated forms, into an arena not conducive to moderate, probabilistic, and contingent claims. Sensitivity to the importance of strong research designs and good data is growing at the same time as some pressures are eroding institutions that historically played a role in enforcing quality control and guiding less expert consumers through the maze of conflicting evidentiary claims.

THE PARADOX ILLUSTRATED

The paradox of high visibility but problematic reputation is illustrated by the following minidramas. Each combines prominent attention to the importance of high-quality research with a flip-side portrayal of the research enterprise as personalized and partisan. What is significant here is not that researchers disagree about measurement, design, and interpretation. That is neither new nor a matter of concern. What is potentially important and problematic is that the way in which the debates end up being portrayed in the public arena may reinforce cynicism among the attentive public about the independence and potential contribution of good scientific techniques.

Minidrama 1.
Paul Peterson versus John Witte on Milwaukee Vouchers

Researchers frequently bemoan the fact that their work is ignored but, in October 1996, two political scientists had their research featured on the front page of the *Wall Street Journal*. The article focused on research into the effectiveness of the Milwaukee voucher program, the nation's first real experiment with school vouchers and one whose ins and outs, accordingly, have been the focus of much attention. It pitted John Witte, whose studies had found voucher parents highly satisfied but had concluded that voucher students' test scores were not better than those of comparable students in the Milwaukee public schools, against Paul Peterson, whose comparison between voucher lottery winners and losers suggested that there were substantial gains in both reading and math.[10] "Education scholars were hoping the Milwaukee experiment would finally settle the question," wrote Bob Davis, the article's author. "Fat chance." Instead of converging on a cooler and clearer understanding of how the abstract market-based theories behind vouchers translated into real world consequences, the research—at least as Davis chose to present it—appeared to have done little more than add a new kind of fuel to the fires of ideological debate. Although the article delved into some of the methodological issues that may have accounted for the differences in findings, readers could not be blamed for concluding that research was less a light of illumination than a snowball in a schoolboy spat. "The two men have come to despise each other, with Mr. Witte at the Milwaukee university calling his foe a 'snake' and Mr. Peterson shooting back that Mr. Witte's work is 'lousy.'"[11] In the years after the furor, long after the reporters had moved on and the public spotlight had shifted, Peterson and Witte resumed an amiable relationship, while agreeing that the reporters had taken incendiary quotes out of context and that the disputes were more professional and nuanced than the accounts had suggested. Of course, by then the public had already formed its impression of the debate.

Minidrama 2.
The AFT versus the Center for Education Reform on Charter Schools

On August 17, 2004, the front page of the *New York Times* prominently displayed a story about a new study of charter schools. "Charter Schools Trail in Results, U.S. Data Reveals," read the headline. The article, by *Times* reporter Diane Schemo, described a report by the American Federation of Teachers (AFT) comparing National Assessment on Educational Progress (NAEP) data on the performance of charter schools and traditional public schools. "The first national comparison of test scores among children in charter schools and regular public schools shows charter school students often doing worse than comparable students in regular public schools," Schemo wrote. In the second sentence, she described the findings as "buried in mountains of data the Education Department released without public announcement," suggesting that the Bush administration, a vocal and active proponent of charter schools, had tried to suppress the evidence.

Despite the summer doldrums, "All hell broke loose."[12] Within days, proponents of charters and other choice-based and market-oriented approaches to school reform had launched a counter-attack. Jeanne Allen of the Center for Education Reform, a Washington, D.C.-based organization supported by conservative foundations, tracked down prominent researchers, many on their summer vacations, to see whether they would be willing to have their names listed on a protest ad. The full-page ad, which cost over $115,000, ran just eight days after the article first appeared. At the same time, school choice proponents got busy placing editorials, providing supporters with talking points for discussion on television talk shows, issuing critiques on various electronic newsletters and blogs, and publicizing a report by Caroline Hoxby, a Harvard economist, which they claimed was much stronger methodologically, and which they said arrived at the opposite conclusion: that charter schools were working very well indeed. Hoxby, herself, in commenting on the AFT report, responded that "it was such a lousy study that it did not deserve a response. It did not deserve to be considered for even a few minutes."[13]

Minidrama 3.
Jesse Rothstein versus Caroline Hoxby on School Competition

Nine years after the Witte–Peterson altercation, readers of the *Wall Street Journal* were treated to another front-page story on school choice, one with almost eerie parallels. Like the earlier article, it gave an impressive prominence and space to arcane matters of measurement and research design. Like the earlier one, too, it featured drawings of the principal opponents (economists this time), lacing the description of social science methodology with comments about their personalities and backgrounds. And, once again, charges of bias and undertones of vitriol were prominent.[14]

Like Paul Peterson, Caroline Hoxby is a Harvard professor who has been highly vocal and highly cited in support of school choice, vouchers, and charter schools. The focus in the *Journal* article was a highly cited study she had done that indirectly assessed the impacts of markets by comparing what happens in metropolitan areas in which there is a lot of competition among school districts to those areas in which there is only a little. In metropolitan areas where there are many districts, she reasoned, families will have lots of options about where to live. School districts, in turn, would presumably have to compete in order to attract families. If competition provides the necessary spark for innovation and efficiency—as the market theories behind school choice proposals contend—those high-competition metropolitan areas should be the places where schools are doing the best job. Using an instrumental variable approach intended to account for the possibility that school performance might affect the number of districts, rather than the other way around, she found a clear relation between competition and school outcomes. Not only did increased choice among districts lead to substantially higher levels of student achievement, it did so while also leading to lower levels of per pupil costs.[15]

The *Journal* article zeroed in on the dispute that arose between Hoxby and Jesse Rothstein, a Princeton economist, who raised questions about the accuracy of her data and the substance of her claims.[16] Jon Hilsenrath, the *Journal* reporter, described the resulting attention as "a bitter dispute . . . that is riveting social scientists across the country." Rothstein released his analysis as a working paper on the National Bureau of Economic Research (NBER) website. The NBER is a private, nonprofit, nonpartisan research organization "committed to undertaking and disseminating unbiased economic research among public policymakers, business professionals, and the academic community,"[17] and its working paper series has become a favored vehicle for economics researchers to get their work out and widely read more quickly than could be

expected via the traditional journal route. After attempting to replicate Hoxby's analysis, Rothstein concluded that "Hoxby's positive estimated effect of
interdistrict competition on student achievement is not robust, and that a
fair reading of the evidence does not support claims of a large or significant
effect." Hoxby replied in kind. In a paper also posted on the NBER site, she
stated that she had reviewed every claim "of any importance" that Rothstein had made, and that "every claim is wrong." She charged Rothstein with
being confused, relying on innuendo, presenting her original work as his
own, making bad decisions "repeatedly" and worse. "It should surprise no
one," Hoxby wrote, "that if a person makes a determination to change data
and specifications until a result disappears, he will eventually succeed."[18]
Hilsenrath reported on the subsequent back-and-forth in which Rothstein
complained of Hoxby's "name-calling" and "ad hominem attacks" while she
accused Rothstein of "ideological bias." An economics blog, Hilsenrath concluded, "sums up the squabble as a 'nerdy Celebrity Death Match.'"[19]

Minidrama 4.
Reading Wars: Department of Education versus Itself
Not all of the public controversies over education policy research circle
around vouchers, charters, and choice. No Child Left Behind's heavy emphasis on the importance of scientific evidence as the basis for decisionmaking
arguably has increased the visibility—and controversy—surrounding research
debates in general. And the back-and-forth over the administration's Reading First initiative highlights another arena in which mixed messages accompany public visibility.

Some of the most assertive claims about scientifically based policy have
accompanied the administration's efforts to favor phonics-oriented instruction over curricula based on whole-language or balanced literacy. At the same
time that they were arguing that research should displace politics, federal
officials associated with Reading First used their interpretation of existing
evidence as a weapon with which to pressure state and local administrations
to reject curricula they disliked and to work with companies and products
they favored. And when the existing evidence was not sufficient, they sought
help from friendly researchers to marshal more. In initially resisting federal
pressure to adopt a more phonics-oriented program like Open Court, New
York City's Chancellor Joel Klein cited what his department considered to
be the mixed results of phonics curricula in other big cities. An influential
adviser to the federal Reading First initiative enlisted support from an education researcher with strong ties to Open Court, asking her to help provide
him with research he could use to make his case that New York should back

down: "I need good data fast," he wrote.[20] Ironically, in March 2007, one of the programs that the Bush administration had tried to shut out of the program received a strong endorsement from the What Works Clearinghouse, the Department of Education's unit established to critically assess the existing research literature and separate findings from strong studies from the weaker chaff.[21]

Looking beyond Personalities to Institutions

Even when it is done well—arguably *especially* when it is does well—research moves in a herky-jerky fashion marked by competing definitions, competing approaches, and seemingly contradictory findings. The notion that new policies might generate unambiguous and consensual empirical imprints is naïve, especially when the problems they address are thorny and multicausal, and when the political environment in which they are advanced is partisan and polarized. If there are insights to be drawn from these minidramas, then, they do not have to do with the specifics of the charges and countercharges, or fingering which of the participants are wearing white hats and which of them are wearing black. What is important is the way research enters into and is affected by the broader institutional context of democratic agenda setting, policymaking, and collective understanding. If the face of educational policy research is one of personalization, polarization, and partisanship, the loss of authority and fueling of skepticism toward social science research may be further fed and its potential contribution to democratic discourse diminished as a direct result. As one policy advocate I spoke to put it, summarizing what the public may conclude if researchers on opposing sides simply seem to cancel one another out, "Oh my God, these researchers, these social scientists, you know, piddling and piddling and one day it is this and one day it is that: a pox on all your houses." Certain tensions between the normal workings of research and the needs of the political process may be ingrained, but the way that tension plays out can be mediated by broader institutional factors and some, that I review below, may be changing in ways that exacerbate the problem.

NEW TECHNOLOGIES AND THE DISSEMINATION OF RESEARCH

New technologies have expanded the range of avenues through which research can reach the attentive public. Some researchers regularly use their own websites to post works in progress and solicit feedback. Think tanks and advocacy organizations regularly distribute electronic newsletters disseminating their own studies or summarizing the work of others. As one indicator of the scope of the emerging virtual world of education policy communication, Andy Rotherham's highly read blog, *Eduwonk*, includes 97 links to other education blogs, 12 links to sites providing education news and analysis, and 30 policy and political blogs that cover education along with other issues.[22]

In an earlier era, the normal cycle for policy research included submission to a peer-reviewed journal, double-blind review, often requirements for revision, nine months or more from acceptance to publication, and then—if the researcher, funder, or university public relations office was eager for impact—dissemination of a press release. Researchers who worked in similar areas might hear about forthcoming work at conferences—if they happened to attend the right ones and the right panels; but except in special cases, there was often a reluctance to publicly cite and respond to conference papers until they had been vetted through the slower and more meticulous processes of peer review.

Today's new technologies mean that studies—and even preliminary findings—often get tremendously broad dissemination within incredibly short periods. "I try very hard to favor breaking news in the *NewsBlast*," reports Howie Schaffer, who oversees the *PEN Weekly NewsBlast*:[23]

> The cycle of news is evolving. The weeklies like *TIME* don't try to break news anymore; they try to have relevant analysis. The daily papers try not to get burned breaking news that they know may evolve significantly throughout the day. The e-newsletters try to beat the bloggers to the story . . . so everyone is trying to keep their content fresh.

The speed with which research is disseminated means that some studies make an impact even before their final analysis is completed. In the case of the AFT charter report mentioned earlier, the Center for Education Reform (CER), which sponsored the advertisement criticizing the report and its coverage, felt it was important to act immediately, lest the impression the article left take root and linger. This concern was heightened by the belief that, in the era of the Internet, old studies and articles do not fade away; they remain on the Web poised to come up whenever a student, researcher, reporter, or government staffer conducts a Google search on the topic of charter schools.

Concerned about the attention being paid to the AFT study, "probably owing to the *New York Times'* irresponsible coverage," Caroline Hoxby told an audience at the Manhattan Institute, a conservative think tank, this "eventually convinced me that it would be a good idea for someone to produce evidence that addressed the AFT study's most egregious failings."[24] Within weeks of the *Times* article featuring the AFT report, Hoxby began disseminating a paper claiming to offer a methodologically superior and much more positive study of academic achievement in charter schools.[25] Rather than relying on statistical controls to account for the fact that charter school populations might systematically differ from those in traditionally public schools, Hoxby compared each charter school to a nearby school, which, she reasoned, would be likely to draw from a similar set of families. Based on this comparison, she concluded that charter schools were substantially outperforming the traditional districts. Charter school advocates were quick to promote Hoxby's study as a complete refutation of the AFT results. In mid-September, Chester Finn's electronic newsletter, *Education Gadfly*, announced that "Harvard economist Caroline M. Hoxby has just issued the most effective rejoinder to the misleading AFT 'study' of charter school achievement that's been much in the news of late: she's done a far better study, and it yields a far different result."[26] CER, on its website, judged that "Hoxby's study goes a long way in providing quantifiable proof of widespread charter success."[27]

Perhaps because it was rushed into the public arena, the September 2004 version of this paper included some serious errors. The most blatant of these involved Washington, D.C., where her report had claimed to find the sharpest advantages for charter schools. There are two public bodies with authority to charter schools in that city, but Hoxby included only schools chartered by the Public Charter School Board, an entity created by Congress and generally considered to be the more careful and professional of the two. As a result, her study failed to include almost half of the charter schools for which test score data existed at the time. In addition, and even more consequential, Hoxby made an error in the test scores she used to assess the performance of D.C. charter schools. For charter schools, she used figures used by the district to assess the No Child Left Behind Act (NCLB) proficiency standards (set at the 40th percentile on SAT-9 in 2003), while for her traditional public school comparison groups she used data that employed the much tougher definition of "proficiency" set by the company that designed the test. The AFT claimed that the huge charter schools advantage reported by Hoxby for Washington, D.C., actually turned into a small charter school deficit when these and other factors were taken into account.[28]

What is significant here is not that Caroline Hoxby made a mistake. Even the most careful researcher makes mistakes at least some of the time. This is one reason why researchers who want to be accurate and who care about their professional reputations usually prefer to let their work percolate a while—ask colleagues to look it over; present it at conferences; go through the slow and sometimes tedious scholarly journal process of peer review—before going fully public with a big bang.[29] What is significant, rather, is that the high speed, high stakes political debate over charter schools drew research into its vortex based more on whether the findings fit partisan arguments rather than on whether they were solid, reliable, and right.

When researchers buy too readily into the notion that speed is critical, normal processes for refining, checking, and simply deliberating about evidence can easily be short-circuited. This is especially the case in politically charged arenas in which other groups, with tactical interests in building or blocking momentum behind specific policy actions, can co-opt the dissemination and framing process. Researchers may acknowledge the limitations of their own data and design, the extent to which findings are contingent on time and setting, and the need for further study, but those caveats are often the first things to be stripped from a message as others take it up. In practice, research that aligns with major ideological cleavages is more likely to be pushed into the public realm, and the distinction between advocacy and rigorous analysis becomes more difficult to discern.

Foundations and advocacy organizations with the most intense interests in broad political battles are also those most likely to fund supportive research and actively support dissemination campaigns designed to get the results in the hands of journalists and policymakers. The result can be a selection bias in terms of what research gets attention, with studies that present mixed findings and make more moderate claims less likely to be carried into the stream of public discourse. The traditional media can play a role in muting this by taking on the responsibility to provide deeper and more discriminating coverage of research. But financial pressures, in large measure fueled by competition from the Web, mean that the traditional media are harder pressed than ever to provide the staffing and investment in longer-term reporting that this would require.

The blurring of the distinction between scholarship and advocacy, and the permeability of the lines distinguishing institutions devoted to the former from those devoted to the latter, make it more difficult for even discerning journalists, politicians, and citizens to sort through the competing claims and distinguish stronger findings from weaker ones. Such interested but nonexpert audiences often rely on academia (broadly defined) to enforce quality controls, sort out the wheat from the chaff, and put an authoritative stamp of legitimacy on findings that have stood up to rigorous scrutiny and have been replicated. Here, too, there are problems.

THE ACADEMY AS CONTEXT

Long-term trends in academia, including shifts in the relation between disciplinary and interdisciplinary programs, the declining status of education schools, and the fragmentation of journals and subfields, may affect the way researchers define themselves vis-à-vis different audiences and the extent to which outsiders perceive education research as having a coherent and authoritative voice. Academia, defined here as comprising universities, professional associations, and scholarly journals, is a powerful component of the institutional context within which policy researchers operate. Some of the factors discussed in this chapter suggest ways in which the independent influence of the academy may be waning,[30] but academia is still important as the institutional base for many scholars, the primary arbiter of research excellence and professional stature, and the training ground for successive generations of researchers. Behind the scenes, the basic structure of academia—the incentives it presents about what to study and where to publish and the ways in which it impedes or facilitates the flow and presentation of information—exerts a gravitational force that alters the way research enters the public domain.

A number of factors have contributed to an historic separation between education departments and schools and the more discipline-based arts and sciences faculty at the core of most universities. Faculty within education schools followed a path that led them progressively further from the mainstream of their universities—partly pushed by arts and sciences faculty who looked down on them from the first, but also pulled by their own and their students' more professional mission. Lagemann writes about historical tensions in education schools between a scholarly orientation favored by some faculty and the more applied concerns of education school students, who demanded training that helped them with the nitty-gritty day-to-day tasks they confronted on their jobs. "When educational scholarship was professionalized, it was viewed with contempt by noneducationists; when it was discipline-based, it was shunned by students, who had wanted 'recipes for practice.'"[31]

With the disciplines on the sidelines, policy research within education schools developed according to an array of signals that played out differently in different universities but had the overall effect of breeding an intellectually fragmented field and one that, in the eyes of many policymakers and discipline-based social scientists, was either overly abstract (e.g., neo-Marxist, post-structuralist, gender identity, or critical race studies) or overly applied (studies on the implementation of a particular program in a particular school or classroom). And whether abstract or applied, it was seen as insufficiently rigorous—leaning toward qualitative over quantitative research and less concerned with isolating causal mechanisms than telling convincing stories.[32]

Arguably, this has begun to change somewhat over the past decade, but the reconnection of the academic disciplines arguably creates a bit of a paradox. The paradoxical element lies in the trade-off between greater prestige, focus, and rigor, on the one hand, and less attention to and knowledge of the nitty-gritty of schooling on the other. Discipline-based researchers often speak from a higher perch of credibility; they are more likely to be associated with more prominent universities, for example, and less likely than those at education schools to be presumed to be apologists for the education policy status quo. To practicing educators, and to policymakers concerned with practical applications, however, the abstract framing and technological intricacies of disciplinary-based studies can make them seem both intimidating and arcane. Still unclear is whether the recent discipline-based visitors to education policy issues will be drawn into a deeper engagement with the field; and whether there will be a meaningful dialogue opened between them and their counterparts within the mainstream education research community, or each will operate independently, separated by unconnected networks and an atmosphere of mutual suspicion or indifference.

Re-engagement of the discipline-based scholars may, at least initially, be contributing to the already dysfunctional fragmentation of the landscape of academic and professional journals in the education research field. This fragmentation has consequences both for how research unfolds within the scholarly community and, more immediately to the point, its image and utility to journalists, policymakers, and citizens.

Within the sciences and medicine and within the social science disciplines there are typically one or two peak journals that hold a reputation both inside and outside the community as being a reliable arbiter of importance and quality. The *Journal of the American Medical Association* (*JAMA*) and *New England Journal of Medicine* play this role, for example. Within the field, such peak journals can provide a focal point, some common terms of discourse, and an arena for stimulating debate and exchange among scholars otherwise subdivided into multiple specialties. To outsiders, including journalists and policymakers, they provide an authoritative short-course in what constitutes the latest and best evidence. "You know, I pine for the sort of security that my colleagues who cover medicine have, where they can just say such-and-such is coming out in *JAMA* this week," one education reporter told me.

While there are several education research journals that are quite good, there is no comparable flagship publication. Good, important, and potentially policy-relevant research is just as likely to appear in any of dozens of narrow subfield publications as in those attracting a broader readership. Discipline-based researchers anchored in the academy already have strong incentives to seek to publish first in the major journals recognized by members of their departments, and the absence of a recognized peak journal in education exacerbates that tendency. Even as individual research studies become more sophisticated in design and richer in data, the lack of coherence in the field creates missed opportunities for positive spillover and feedback that could strengthen the collective learning enterprise.

PRIVATIZATION: THE GROWTH OF THE CORPORATE SECTOR IN K–12 EDUCATION

The growing corporate and educational management organization involvement in K–12 and supplementary educational services creates a new market for education research, with its own set of opportunities and constraints. For-profit companies in recent years have made substantial inroads into the K–12 education sphere. Nationwide there are more than fifty Educational Management Organizations (EMOs), for-profit companies managing charter schools or public schools under contract arrangements. The 51 EMOs identified by the Arizona State Education Policy Studies laboratory in school-year 2005–06 managed 521 schools in 28 states plus Washington, D.C.[33] Six of the largest EMOs are allied through the National Council of Education Providers; in 2003 they claimed to employ over 14,000 people, projecting employment growth of 24 percent the following year.[34] In addition, NCLB gave momentum to the for-profit sector providing Supplemental Education Services (SES), tutoring programs that provide services outside of the normal academic day.[35] A private-sector testing and publishing industry also was growing robustly before NCLB, but the federal law ensured that the state-initiated standards and accountability movement would continue to grow and to spread. Total spending for developing, publishing, and reporting required tests appears to be in the range of $500-750 million.[36] Large textbook publishing firms like Pearson, Houghton Mifflin, McGraw-Hill, and Harcourt Assessment are, as Tom Toch notes, "'full-service' companies that create tests; align them with state standards; ensure they are technically sound; publish, distribute, and score them; and analyze results."[37]

Still another form of privatization relevant to the research community comes from the growth of private research organizations that work under contract with private clients and all levels of government. For government, corporations, and some foundations, these private research firms can be an attractive alternative to university-based researchers when it comes to policy research. This may be especially the case in the education world, where the normal unwieldiness of academia, arguably, is exacerbated by the idiosyncrasies of education schools and what policymakers see as their almost obstinate indulgence of abstraction and narrative in preference to quantification, rigor, and contemporary standards for "scientifically based" research. When funders want answers quickly, and especially when they want to retain a measure of control over the design and dissemination of results, think tanks are emerging as a preferred partner. Among Institute of Education Sciences (IES) award recipients in FY2004–05, nonuniversity research organizations outnumbered universities and received awards that were, on average, 1.8 times larger.[38]

Growing privatization within the education sector increases the demand for research, but at the possible cost of introducing new constraints on researchers as far as what they can study, how they can access data, and how freely they can participate in public dialogue. In the era of NCLB, private providers of management, education, curriculum, professional development, and testing are under increased pressure to demonstrate that their products are research-based. The large firms require significant in-house research capacity, but for various reasons—including the occasional need for the greater credibility obtained with research by independent organizations—find it appropriate to contract with private research firms, universities, or university-based scholars acting independently from their home institutions. Edison Schools, for example, conducts its own analyses and uses these in its promotional material and to provide evidence of impact to their clients, but features more prominently on its website the result of a generally favorable but somewhat mixed study commissioned by the company but carried out by the RAND Corporation.[39] The highly touted Knowledge Is Power Program (KIPP) charter schools contracted with the Educational Policy Institute to evaluate the academic achievement of students at 24 of the 31 KIPP schools operating at the time. The report concluded that the program "has posted large and significant gains on a nationally norm-referenced standardized test. This performance is true across schools and throughout the nation" and is featured on the organization's website in a section labeled "independent reports."[40] In-house and contracted research for privately marketed products typically is regarded skeptically within the academic research community—but not always by clients or the media.[41]

While this makes the job market for education researchers rather promising, it can present challenges in data access and the free exchange of information within the scholarly community, not unlike those raised in medical science by the heavy role that drug companies play in footing the research bill.[42] Charter school researcher Gary Miron ran into this, for example, when he undertook research on Edison's charter schools. In return for providing data, Edison Schools maintained a right to prepublication review and an opportunity to comment. Six months after Miron submitted a draft for review, the company still had not replied. When he prepared to release the report, Edison threatened to sue him and his university.

SOURCES OF RESEARCH FUNDING

Funding is an important component of the researchers' environment.[43] Adequate funding is necessary to conduct research where original data collection is expensive and to make it possible to do the research better or faster. Even when researchers may not need funding to undertake a particular study, incentives within the research community can make external funding a priority: to help cover overhead and soft money needs of the organizations that employ them or for the status and legitimacy that winning competitive grants can confer.

Funding also can bring with it constraints of various kinds. Sources of funding have their own organizational priorities, and depending on formal and informal arrangements surrounding grants and contracts, researchers may need to trade off some independence to capitalize on funding opportunities. Some competitive grant opportunities come with elaborate formal protections that are designed to minimize political interference, require open dissemination of results, and ensure that criteria of excellence, as determined by the research community, play the dominant role in determining awards. But in other cases, funding sources can be quite precise about what they want researchers to find—either up front before committing support or after the research is conducted—by specifying how results are to be framed and whether and how they are disseminated. As a result, shifts in the funding environment can affect the kinds of research being done, the extent to which researchers or others are determining the research agenda and methodologies, and the ways in which research results are carried into the public arena.

Despite the fact that the federal government injects substantial amounts of funds into research and development, the amount available for education policy research is less than one might expect. Government support for research in the social sciences, generally, and funding for research on education policy, in particular, have been a much more minor affair than spending on such things as health, life sciences, military technologies, and the like. Most (about 60 percent) of the federal research and development budget goes to defense. For every $100 spent on research, less than $2.25 goes to the social sciences and less than 41 cents goes to research within the Department of Education.[44] Federal outlays for research and development in the Department of Education fell precipitously relative to those for the rest of the federal government during the early 1970s and again during the early

1980s, but they have been on the upswing since about 1997 (see Table 2.1). One reason for the historically low level of federal funding is the skepticism of some members of Congress toward what they see as the overly "soft" nature of social science research when compared to medicine and the physical sciences.

When Congress does choose to fund education, it is reluctant to support basic research, which is directed toward fuller understanding of the fundamental aspects of a phenomenon without specific uses in mind. Researchers tend to consider basic research to be the foundation on which knowledge is built, but Congress often finds it too far removed from the measurable pay-offs in constituents' lives that they need to point to in justifying public investment. Basic research in education competes rather unsuccessfully with "applied" research (intended to determine the means by which a recognized and specific need may be met) and spending for what might be referred to as the "four Ds:" development, dissemination, data, and direct services.

In 2005, considering all agencies combined, the federal government spent about $103 billion on research and development. About half of that was for development—the process of taking new ideas and converting them into "useful materials, devices, and systems or methods."[45] Figure 2.1 shows the breakdown of Department of Education funds for applied and basic research and for development.[46] Basic research makes up only 3.5 percent of the total departmental R&D budget.

Not only does the federal government spend relatively little on education research, but what it does spend tends in some ways to be more tightly defined and controlled. In addition to being more likely to emphasize applied research and development, federal education research funding is more likely to take the form of contracts than grants. Contracts accounted for just under one-third (32.4 percent) of the total number of awards IES made between FY2002 and FY2004, but contracts on average were more than three times as large and accounted in total for about 60 percent of the funds awarded.[47] Both the de-emphasis of basic research relative to applied research and development, and of grants relative to contracts, serve to narrow the degree of discretion left in the hands of researchers, reduce the role of peer review and other formal protections for scholarly autonomy, make the funding somewhat less attractive to university based researchers, give nonuniversity-based researchers some competitive advantages, and increase the ability of program administrators to shape the study and influence the dissemination of findings.

With federal funding less bountiful and more constrained than researchers might prefer, some education researchers have been increasingly turning to

TABLE 2.1   Federal Outlays for Research and Development, FY1967–2005
(Dollars in millions)

	1967	1977	1987	1997	2005 (preliminary)
All agencies	$16,066.34	$22,082.70	$51,611.70	$68,897.90	$103,086.90
Department of Education*	$69.97	$30.26	$122.60	$169.10	$327.90
Dept. of Ed. as % of all agencies	0.44%	0.14%	0.24%	0.25%	0.32%

*Office of Education through 1978.

Sources: National Science Foundation, Division of Science Resources Statistics, Federal Funds for Research and Development: Fiscal Years 2003–05, NSF 06-313, Project Officer, Ronald L. Meeks (Arlington, VA 2006).http://www.nsf.gov/statistics/nsf06313/tables.htm#group15; http://www.nsf.gov/statistics/nsf03325/tables/hist2.xls

private foundations as alternative sources of support. Foundation support for education research is not plentiful, and access to the available funds depends more on the fit between researcher interests and often-narrow foundation missions. But in a few areas of education reform where foundation interest is high, researchers can find ready support. This support typically comes with a different set of constraints than those accompanying federal funds.

Most foundations do not give money designated for K–12 education, and among those that do, research per se is not a particularly high priority. For the years 2000 through 2003, the Foundation Center's directory includes 331,186 grants, but only 25,384 (less than 8 percent) focused on K–12 education. There are indications that some of the largest foundations have soured on public education as an area for investment, concluding it is too big, too bureaucratic, and too resistant to needed reforms.[48] Of those focused on K–12 education, moreover, only 1,581 grants (about 6 percent of all the education-related grants) could be characterized as having a research component. Eliminating grants to non-U.S. recipients, and foundations that only gave a single education research grant, reduces the foundation activity to 1,280 grants awarded by 192 foundations to 563 organizations for a total amount of $401,984,124. Compared to federal grants, these are generally small in size. One out of three of the grants (32 percent) were for $50,000 or less and over half of the grants (55 percent) were $100,000 or less.[49]

Nonetheless, foundation funding can be quite influential in those niches in which it is concentrated. This appears especially to be the case in areas related to market-based reforms, including charter schools, school choice, and alternative routes to teaching.[50] In my interviews with researchers active

FIGURE 2.1   Preliminary Federal Obligations For Department of Education Research FY2005

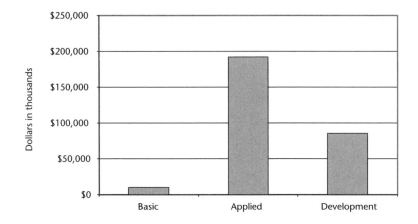

Source: National Science Foundation, Division of Science Resources Statistics, Federal Funds for Research and Development: Fiscal Years 2003–05, NSF 06-313, Project Officer, Ronald L. Meeks (Arlington, VA 2006).

in the area of vouchers, charters, and school choice, I found that foundations were about three times as important as federal funds as a source of support for their work.

The way in which foundations and researchers come together typically differs from the more formalized and regulated procedures of federal funding. Although this can vary, rather than formal requests for proposals and independent review, it is more common that researchers and foundations mutually seek and find one another based on style, trust, and compatibility with mission. Foundations in general are less concerned with peer review and sophisticated research designs, and more concerned with helping to shape and disseminate findings that accord with their organizational missions.

THE DYNAMICS OF FEDERALISM

While the federal courts have punted issues relating to equity down to the state level, elsewhere the center of gravity in education policymaking has been migrating up the ladder of federalism. Historically, K–12 education has been among the most localized of government functions. It is too soon to declare localism a thing of the past—its political roots are strong and resilient[51]—but it is equally clear that changes are underway. The states began asserting themselves both as sources of funding and promoters of academic standards during the 1980s. And NCLB marks a new era of regulatory aggressiveness from Washington, D.C., with public debates about school reform more and more likely to take place on the national stage.

The broad dimensions of this shift are familiar, and some of the causes have been discussed well by others.[52] But the implications for researchers and their role in the policy process have received much less attention. Localities, states, and the federal government differ from one another in ways that may bear upon the nature of the research they desire, their ability and willingness to generate and make available different types of data, and the political environment in which research is discussed.

Compared to state and national education departments, local school governance in the United States tends to be more bureaucratically insulated, possess more in-house analytic capacity, be more concrete and pragmatic in its data and analysis needs, and be less ideologically polarized in its political environment. The insulation derives from governance structures adopted during the Progressive Era in the early twentieth century. Designed to limit the influence of urban machines and narrow interest group politics, these structures—separate school boards often elected off-cycle from general elections, earmarked revenue streams, tenure and civil service protection for teachers and administrators—allowed local school bureaucracies to grow in size and autonomy, created career paths within the organizations that developed expertise combining general skills with locality-specific content, nurtured data systems tailored to meet administrative needs, and shielded much of the inner workings of the decisionmaking process from outside groups.

In lower-income rural districts, or those in which local culture does not support heavy investment in public education, localism can produce an extraordinarily thin research environment: nothing much gets done either inside or outside the district offices. In suburban districts that rely on strong schools to attract residents, and count on this to be capitalized into housing values, the in-house research capacity can be significant, but tends to be marked by bland competence. In large city school systems, the district research and data units are more likely to have developed a defensive posture, designed to generate data that is internally useful but limit access to that data out of concern that it will be used by organized interest groups to challenge the education bureaucracy's zone of autonomy.

For researchers who are unattached to local district offices, the end result in all of these settings means that data collected has tended not to be conducive to certain kinds of questions (for example, pinpointing inequitable distributions of resources across neighborhoods; disaggregating performance data by race, class, and special needs). Even when data are available and not directly tied to explosive issues, researchers at the local level have often found access difficult. Demand for high quality research from outside the district bureaucracy will tend to be narrow and episodic. Most practitioners do not have to ask the question of whether something would work somewhere else, and while replication and generalizability are important to researchers and national policy leaders, they are not as compelling within the window in which local practitioners are operating.

Uses of research at the local level occasionally can be quite politicized during the short and intense periods when education reform battles or union contract negotiations burst onto the local agenda, but this is a different kind of politicization than the ideological polarization that characterizes some national education wars. Local interests involved in the politics of big city education are arrayed less around ideology than material concerns—things like teacher salaries and competition among neighborhoods for capital investment or the best principals. While conflicts over material goodies can be intense, they are more subject to compromise—to a split-the-difference resolution—than battles over principles, ideologies, or claims to moral virtue.[53] The demand for research in such settings, accordingly, has been more narrowly focused and the uses of research less public and politically polarized than at the national level where partisan polarization generates a winner-take-all dynamic.

As involvement in education has migrated up the ladder of federalism, the environment has been altered in ways that appear relevant to the research community. The consequences of state involvement are less striking than those that follow when education gets drawn into national policy debates. Even as many states began to develop accountability regimes, most states lacked the person-power and in-house capacity to implement them. Some have addressed this capacity problem,[54] albeit to very different degrees. The most promising development for researchers has been the construction, in a handful of states, of administrative databases that make it possible to track individual students and their performance over time. This has had a major and salutary effect on research on some issues. Tennessee's Value Added Assessment System, for example, enabled influential research on teacher effectiveness.[55] State administrative databases in Florida, North Carolina, and Texas have featured prominently in some of the strongest research conducted on charter schools.[56]

Several factors are conducive to the formation of a strong partnership between education policy researchers and state government. Politics and governance within states, as at the local level, tend to be more pragmatic and less ideologically polarized than are the national battles. Most of the major media in the United States are structured to attend to either local or national audiences, and as a result, state-level decisionmaking is sometimes spared the hot glare of attention felt elsewhere. Because state departments of education have growing responsibilities but limited in-house research capacity, they may increasingly find themselves contracting with outside researchers; potentially, this can be done in a way that simultaneously promotes better governance and better access to data. That said, in the era of NCLB, it is at least as likely that state-level research will get drawn into the swirl of national politics, and that brings to bear a different set of pressures and incentives.

Broad structural changes have made the national political environment more polarized, with policy debates and partisan strategies shaped more by ideological purists than those seeking to find common ground based on pragmatism or the public's generally moderate center of gravity. The forces shaping this polarization at the national level do not appear to be ephemeral ones. They include state-level redistricting that creates increasing numbers of safe seats, changes in primaries that increase responsiveness to extreme elements within each party, changes in the structure and processes within Congress, and changes in the number and types of interest groups with influence in Washington, D.C.[57] The influence of membership organizations such as the national teachers unions and public interest groups representing local officials that are rooted in locally organizations, appears to be waning in national policy debates, while that of nonmembership policy organizations like Education Trust, that draw their support from the philanthropic community, is on the rise, making the wedge even greater between policy and practice.[58]

In this hothouse environment, education studies with policy implications—particularly research that maps directly onto core debates like that over the relative benefits of markets versus government—will be in high demand, although perhaps less based on the quality of their research design and analysis than on their particular rhetorical persuasiveness in ongoing battles to shape public opinion and mobilize electoral support.

CONCLUSION

So is it the best of times, or the worst of times? The current mixed picture, it seems to me, is partly a product of two good things. First, researchers have heard the message that they should descend from their ivory towers and engage the world. Second, the old model of "speaking truth to power" in which the scholar qua favored advisor whispers into the ear of elite leaders also is passé; in the age of mass media and the Internet, discourse about research has been democratized.

But it is a volatile time where promising opportunities are twinned with definite dangers. The very aspects of ivory tower research that can be so frustrating to many play double duty as important buffers against ideology and the politicization of the knowledge enterprise: abstract concern for theory, deliberately unhurried pace, fascination with technical aspects of research design, reliance on an internal network of peer review that can be stuffy and conservative, and journals where scholars talk to one another in terms no one else understands. These also play a role in maintaining a distinction between research and advocacy, between pursuit of knowledge and pursuit of advantage, between sounding good and being right; and it is an open question in my mind how far down the path of relevance researchers can travel without something of value being put at stake.

Double Standard? "Scientifically Based Research" and the No Child Left Behind Act

Paul Manna and Michael J. Petrilli

One of the most frequently reported facts about the No Child Left Behind Act (NCLB) is that the law features the phrase "scientifically based research" over one hundred times. That wording is supposed to provide a high standard by channeling federal dollars to activities with proven effectiveness based on rigorous standards.

Where did the phrase "scientifically based research" come from? What were NCLB's authors trying to achieve with this language? How closely has the actual construction of NCLB and its implementation lived up to this high standard? In other words, does the law itself rest on a foundation of scientifically based research? Or have Congress and the president enacted a higher standard for American schools than they themselves have been willing to uphold? We answer those questions by examining how research appeared to influence the development of NCLB, particularly its "highly qualified teachers" provisions. Our findings leave us cautiously optimistic that given the right conditions, research can help to guide political debate and the content of policy—to a point.

Our argument is based on several sources and methods of analysis. These include quantitative examination of NCLB's content and the hearings from which it grew. We also consider government documents, press coverage of NCLB, and other published secondary accounts. We also conducted personal open-ended telephone interviews (typically lasting less than 30 minutes) and exchanged email correspondence with a dozen members of the education policy community in Washington, D.C., during 2007. We chose this convenient sample of respondents by selecting people who have helped craft, implement, and oversee NCLB. Those individuals provided insights about how research has informed the law's development and its implementation, as does the personal experience of this chapter's second author, who was a Bush administration official in the U.S. Department of Education from 2001–2005.

INFORMATION AND INCENTIVES IN THE POLICY PROCESS

Considering how political leaders use research to inform education policy addresses a broader question of how information affects the policy process. Cynical observers argue that a politician will not care much about research unless it supports that politician's preferences and ultimate reelection. Given that members of Congress and American presidents typically possess no formal training in how to conduct or identify good empirical work, it also would be surprising if they chose policy based primarily on research. Granted, these officials have staff members who help them comb through the mountains of studies, reports, and articles released each year, but staff members themselves typically find their own workdays crowded with responsibilities and rapidly changing demands. Extinguishing the latest fire rather than reflecting on the latest research findings is usually how they allocate their time.

Limited opportunities for deep study mean that elected officials will rely much on gut instincts, ideology, riveting anecdotes, opinion polls, or the need to repay favors to colleagues—the proverbial logrolling of the legislative process—when formulating their positions. This cynicism is understandable, but it understates the potential of research to inform politicians' choices. Research can influence how policies develop, and its apparent absence from some debates may reflect the difficulties in wielding complicated findings, not mere laziness or politics. Three points elaborate this claim.

First, incentives exist for elected officials and their staff to consider research as they make policy. Even if reelection is a politician's primary objective, others exist, too. Selective use or nonuse of research may support the reelection objective, but goals such as having influence among colleagues and actually making good public policy also animate public officials' behavior. Not all information is of equal quality or merit, but clearly a search for what works means that solid research should have some chance to compete with other information sources. Further, even though most politicians never take their reelection for granted, those from relatively safe seats, including committee chairs, may have more time and motivation to study the latest findings in their preferred policy areas. A recent study of congressional decisionmaking illustrates that the reelection goal can even create political incentives for members to become steeped in research and to "favor the analytical aspects of policies that are of primary concern to organized groups."[1]

Second, elected and career officials allocate many resources to support research designed to inform policy. At the federal level, for example, agencies such as the Government Accountability Office, the Congressional Budget Office, the National Academy of Sciences, the National Institutes of Health, the National Center for Education Statistics, and several others inside and outside government annually spend millions of tax dollars studying salient policy issues. Professional researchers, many holding advanced research degrees from top universities, also populate government agencies.

The mere existence of these institutions and individuals does not guarantee that politicians will heed their advice or that partisanship will never trump objective analysis. As Rep. Michael Castle (R-DE) noted in a congressional hearing in 2000:

> The fact is that there has not been enough value placed on the need for education research as a means to drive good policy. The reasons are simple enough: sometimes good research tells us things we don't want to hear and good research is expensive and time-consuming—attributes which don't always conform to the reality of Washington budgetary priorities and political expediency.[2]

Still, if the information currency of politics consisted only of anecdotes, instincts, and political calculations, it would be hard to imagine government itself maintaining such an extensive research infrastructure. Even Castle's comment does not claim that officials never value research—rather, he says they do not value it enough.

Finally, the limited presence of research in policy debate may not reflect public officials' indifference. The limited cognitive ability of humans to manage information, what decision theorists call "bounded rationality," can also help explain why research does not always influence policymaking.[3] Public officials work in complex information environments that make it impossible for them to study a topic fully before proposing and enacting policy. Complicating matters further is that "research" comes in many forms, including randomized field trials, quasi-experimental designs, and more exploratory case-oriented work. Findings appear in peer-reviewed journals, government documents, think tank reports, and less-polished working papers, all operating with different quality standards.

Even public officials committed to serious study are stuck with the human brain's limited computing power as they confront this information flow. Studies have shown that the mind can stumble when processing tasks in parallel, weighing trade-offs among multidimensional issues, and weeding out irrelevant information from a complicated decision. In short, humans are not well equipped to perform the very tasks that the legislative process demands. These difficulties become compounded when research is not presented in terms that intelligent lay people can understand, a fair criticism that policymakers often express to academics. With many other sources available, public officials and their staffs will likely use cognitive shortcuts and reach for easily digestible information.

Overall, political pressures, issue complexity, and the limited cognitive capacities of humans can prevent dispassionate research from dominating political debate. However, research can and does influence policy content. The question is, when, where, and to what extent? With NCLB's grand ambitions and so many moving parts, it is worth asking: In which contexts and under what conditions has research-based decisionmaking influenced the law? And what has resulted from the law's impulse that federally funded interventions be "scientifically based"? We examine those questions in general terms, and in more detail for the law's highly qualified teacher provisions.

THE NCLB DEMAND FOR "SCIENTIFICALLY BASED RESEARCH"

Headlines following NCLB's passage focused on its high demands on states, school districts, and schools to increase student achievement. Supporting that ambition was, as one story called it, the "mantra-like" requirement that policies to improve education be based on scientifically based research.[4] That created a valuable opportunity, argued Grover J. "Russ" Whitehurst, assistant secretary for educational research and improvement: "There are a number of groups and individuals who have, for years, been interested in grounding education in a culture of evidence. That's always been their message. But there's an opening here."[5] In this section we examine how often and in what contexts the phrase "scientifically based research" appears in NCLB.

Our analysis began by identifying all uses of the word "research" that appear in the act. Overall, the word appears 266 times. Of those references, 50 are part of official titles (e.g., Office of Educational Research) or appear in the outline structure of the law itself (e.g., Subpart 2—Research, Evaluation, and Dissemination). Omitting those 50 cases reduces the total to 216 substantive references to the word "research."

Among those 216 references, in 54.6 percent of cases the modifier "scientifically based" appears. In other words, NCLB does not always consistently emphasize the "scientifically based" standard when it discusses or requires programs to be based on research. For example, in Title II of NCLB, which supports teacher and principal training and provides recruiting grants for states, the law requires that states provide:

> A description of how the activities to be carried out by the State educational agency under this subpart will be based on a review of *scientifically based research* and an explanation of why the activities are expected to improve student academic achievement.[6]

In contrast, later in Title II, local grants for applying instructional technology could support:

> Adapting or expanding existing and new applications of technology to enable teachers to increase student academic achievement, including technology literacy through the use of teaching practices that are based on a review of *relevant research* and are designed to prepare students to meet challenging State academic content and student academic achievement standards.[7]

This is just one example of how the "scientifically based" standard appears inconsistently in NCLB. Why these two passages should vary begs additional explanation.

Explicit ties to the "scientifically based" standard vary across NCLB titles, as Table 3.1 shows. Title I, which focuses on education of disadvantaged students and is the law's primary component, has the most overall references to research. The vast majority of those 84 references, 81.0 percent, are references to scientifically based research. A similarly large percentage, 71.4, appears for Title IV, 21st Century Schools (which funds afterschool programs), but the number of references in that title is much smaller. Other titles have fewer references to scientifically based research, including Title III on limited English proficient and immigrant students (46.7 percent of references to research are modified by the phrase "scientifically based"), Title II on high quality teachers and principals (35.7 percent), and Title V, which includes a grab-bag of individual programs (24.3 percent). Among titles with at least some reference to research, Title VII, Indian, Native Hawaiian, and Alaskan Native Education refers to research 17 times, but only 2 times (11.8 percent) does the reference include the "scientifically based" modifier.

Table 3.1 illustrates interesting variation, but it hides variability present within each title. For example, while 81.0 percent of Title I references to research are modified by the phrase "scientifically based," the percentage is even higher in Title I, Part B, which is dominated by the Reading First and Early Reading First programs.[8] That part contains 55 references to research and 50 of them (90.9 percent) link to the "scientifically based" standard.[9] In Title II, the Teacher and Principal Training and Recruiting Fund (Part A) and the Mathematics and Science Partnerships (Part B) combined have 13 references to research and 69.2 percent of those mention "scientifically based." In contrast, Title II, Part C, Innovation for Teacher Quality, and Part D, Enhancing Education Through Technology, contain 15 references to research and only 6.7 percent are paired with "scientifically based."

Title V, which promotes parental choice and several other small grant programs is also instructive. That title contains 37 references to research, but only 24.3 percent rise to the "scientifically based" standard. Within that title, Part B on Public Charter Schools—which supports charter school programs, credit for school facility acquisition, and other voluntary public school choice programs—contains no references to scientifically based research. Further, Title V, Part D, the generic Fund for the Improvement of Education, lists nearly two dozen specific programs, many of which are not tied explicitly to the "scientifically based" standard either, even though a blanket statement at the end of section 5411 (before the description of the specific programs) instructs the Secretary of Education to ensure the effectiveness of all programs based on "rigorous, scientifically based research and evaluations." Even that wording is curious because it states that program evaluations, not necessarily the evidence required to fund particular program activities in the first place, should be scientifically based. More generally, many programs in Title V, Part D, are less directly and less frequently admonished to uphold the "scientifically based" standard, unlike earlier sections of NCLB.

Comments from our interview respondents help clarify NCLB's inconsistent emphasis on scientifically based research. According to Republican and Democratic congressional staff members who helped develop the law, a push to ground NCLB programs in scientifically based research emerged from similar debates that transpired during the 1990s over federal reading policy. Work from the National Reading Panel, which Congress created in 1997, built momentum for grounding future federal education policy in what scientific research showed was effective.[10] Those debates produced the Reading Excellence Act of 1998, which itself includes 29 references to scientifically based reading research. These events from the 1990s suggest a desire to promote programs based on evidence, rather than only reading the polls or seeking partisan advantage. One Democratic staff member told us that as NCLB

TABLE 3.1   Where the Phrase "Scientifically Based Research" Appears in NCLB

	Number of references to "research"	Percent of "research" modified by "scientifically based"*
Title I. Improving Academic Achievement of the Disadvantaged	84	81.0
Title II. Preparing, Training, and Recruiting High Quality Teachers and Principals	28	35.7
Title III. Language Instruction for Limited English Proficient and Immigrant Students	30	46.7
Title IV. 21st Century Schools	14	71.4
Title V. Promoting Informed Parental Choice and Innovative Programs	37	24.3
Title VI. Flexibility and Accountability	2	50.0
Title VII. Indian, Native Hawaiian, and Alaskan Native Education	17	11.8
Title VIII. Impact Aid	0	—
Title IX. General provisions	4	100.0
TOTAL	216	54.6

Source: Based on authors' coding of NCLB.

* For example, of the 84 substantive references to the word "research" in Title I of NCLB, 81.0 percent use the phrase "scientifically based" to modify the word "research."

was taking shape during 2001, "it was already widely understood" that the law would incorporate the "scientifically based" standard.

Still, political considerations help explain why NCLB inconsistently applies this standard. Another Democratic staff member described a common back-and-forth dynamic that illuminates how negotiations unfolded:

- Democrats would push to include a new (or existing) program in the law.
- Republicans would counter by arguing that the scientifically based research language should be attached to ensure that federal funds support programs that work.
- Democrats would explain that scientifically based research did not necessarily exist in that particular area.

- Republicans would question why, then, federal funds should support the program at all.
- Democrats would accept the scientifically based research standard.

Hence, including the language throughout the law was, as another Democratic staff member said, an unavoidable "political reality."

Overall, a Republican staff member admitted it was "kind of silly" how many times the "scientifically based" language appeared in the law. But the emphasis was important, he said, because NCLB was "aspirational in so many ways," and therefore he and other Republicans "weren't worried about minimizing the concept. This was bleeding edge, meant to move the field forward." Similarly, the Democratic staff member who recounted the back-and-forth dynamic noted earlier conceded that "the intent was noble." The overall goal, after all, was not only to support practices based on scientific research, but to prompt additional scientific research in rarely studied areas. What is clear, though, according to this Democratic staff member, is that the law's inconsistent use of the scientifically based research language has watered down the practical meaning of the phrase. Without a strong scientific base in many education programs and practices that NCLB supports, both educators and regulators face no choice but to selectively ignore the provision.

The aspirational goals of policymakers did succeed in one respect. As measured by press coverage and shown in Table 3.2, an increase in popular attention to the links between research and education policy was almost immediate upon NCLB's passage. These topics received essentially no explicit attention from 1995–2001—the lifespan of NCLB's predecessor law, the Improving America's Schools Act (P.L. 103-382). The leading education news publication, *Education Week*, dramatically increased its coverage beginning in 2002, and published an average of almost 16 stories, op-eds, or letters per year that discussed the phrase "scientifically based research." Major newspapers broke their silence on the topic in 2001, albeit without producing a huge outpouring of stories. The relationship between scientifically based research and reading instruction is the dominant theme in these news stories and appears in nearly one-third of the *Education Week* articles. This connection also explains the surge during 2006 among the major U.S. newspapers.[11]

Additional stories illustrate the substantive reach of the "scientifically based" standard. Beyond reading, articles explored topics such as teacher training and recruitment; mathematics education; debates over teaching evolution versus intelligent design; anti-drug education; students with particular needs, such as bilingual or disabled learners; and the use of technology in the classroom. Local officials sometimes adopted this language, thus increas-

TABLE 3.2   Number of Articles Discussing "Scientifically Based Research" and Education, 1995–2006

Year	Articles in Education Week	Articles in major U.S. newspapers
1995	0	0
1996	0	0
1997	2	0
1998	0	0
1999	0	0
2000	1	0
2001	2	2
2002	16	6
2003	14	3
2004	16	2
2005	18	2
2006	15	9

Source: Based on authors' search of Education Week and Lexis-Nexis databases from January 1995 to December 2006. The full search algorithm is available from the authors.

ing its public profile. As an associate superintendent from Buffalo, New York, explained, fending off criticisms of a district plan for reading instruction, "We move on data. We're moving on scientifically based research. We're not going to rely on creativity to support these children. We're not looking for [teachers] to do their own thing."[12]

RESEARCHERS AND THE LEGISLATIVE PROCESS

Congressional hearings are one venue where researchers can speak truth to power.[13] Members of Congress use hearings for many purposes, including gathering information and building a record that informs policy debate. Hearings also enable members to have direct and extended access to researchers and their studies. Even though question and answer exchanges for any one witness and member can be relatively short, in preparing for hearings, staff members often review much published material, including empirical research. The congressional committee system and assistance from committee staff can attenuate the problems of information overflow and bounded rationality that we discussed earlier. Even if hearings themselves generally may be lackluster affairs, preparing for them gives committee staff and the members they serve opportunities to become informed on complicated topics.

In this part of our analysis, we considered all 155 hearings in what the Congressional Information Service (CIS) defines as NCLB's legislative history.[14] Those hearings occurred during 1995–2001 and featured 1,169 witness appearances (the same witness could appear multiple times), which we categorized by the primary witness affiliation in the CIS hearing abstract. The results from the coding are shown in Table 3.3.

The first three rows of Table 3.3 provide summary statistics on witnesses we categorized as members of the research profession. That group comprised 17.4 percent of all witnesses, which made these individuals more likely to appear than federal and state officials (12.4 and 11.8 percent, respectively), but less likely to appear than witnesses representing localities or groups and individuals (29.8 and 26.2 percent).

Two specific types of witnesses populate the research profession category. First are witnesses with university or college affiliations who work as professors, full-time academic researchers, or individuals running programs housed on a university or college campus. That group represented 9.1 percent of all witnesses. The second type, which comprised 8.3 percent, are those who work outside an academic environment at research-oriented think tanks (e.g., Heritage Foundation, 21st Century Schools Project) or at professional research firms (e.g., Mathematica, SRI International, RAND) and individuals who are applied program developers, whose work embraces several activities that include internal research on program design that is frequently broadcast to a wider audience (e.g., KIPP Foundation, Children's Scholarship Fund, Teach For America, Charles Stewart Mott Foundation).[15]

Even though witnesses from the research profession category represent less than one-fifth of all witnesses, the last column in Table 4.3 shows that when they testify, they typically appear in smaller hearings, as measured by the median number of witnesses per hearing. Members of the research profession, with a median hearing size value of 7, fare rather well when compared to other witness categories. Their median value means that half of all hearings featuring this witness category had 7 or fewer witnesses.

What are the characteristics of witnesses in the research profession category? Table 3.4 offers an initial answer by examining all witnesses who testified in more than one hearing. One obvious finding is that few witnesses received multiple invitations to testify. Given that fact, it is worth noting

TABLE 3.3   Affiliations of Witnesses from Hearings in NCLB's Legislative History, 1995–2001

Witness category and type	Percent by category	Percent by type	Median number of witnesses appearing
Research profession	17.4		7
University or college		9.1	9
Nonuniversity research or program development		8.3	6
Federal level	12.4		6
Federal agency		6.8	5
Federal House or Senate member		5.7	9
State level	11.8		9
State agency		7.2	8
Governor		1.4	7
State board of education		0.8	9
State legislator		0.8	12
Other state		1.7	14
Local level	29.8		9
School or district (but not types noted below)		8.2	10
Superintendent		7.2	8
Teacher		4.9	10
Principal		4.8	10.5
School board member		1.5	11.5
Other local		3.2	9
Groups and individuals	26.2		9
Association or advocacy group		13.9	7
Student		4.8	12
Parent		4.0	10
Business		3.5	6
Other affiliations or not ascertained	2.5	2.5	16

Note: N = 1,169. The unit of analysis is a witness appearance, which means that witnesses testifying more than once appeared in the dataset multiple times (see Table 3.4, for example). Results are based on the authors' coding. Coding rules are available from the authors.

that some of the most frequently appearing witnesses (Vinovskis, Finn, Hanushek, and Ravitch) have experience working in the federal government either in the executive or legislative branches. That familiarity with Washington, D.C., their relationships with members of Congress and staff, and an ability to communicate effectively with policymakers all might explain why they appear so often.

It is also notable from Table 3.4 that Ravitch is the only person affiliated with an education school, and only Feistritzer and Haycock have advanced degrees from such institutions. Others received their training and work in fields such as history, political science, economics, English, and sociology. Referring back to the full dataset, our witnesses in the university or college type came from several academic disciplines; those from education schools do appear, but they do not dominate the field.

Susan Fuhrman, Dean of the Graduate School of Education at the University of Pennsylvania, who testified in a House hearing in 2001, offered one reason why education school faculty appear less frequently than one might expect. In commenting on her profession, she said,

> [W]e have a premium in newness in education and, in education research, on fads, which are certainly closely related to one another. Part of that has to do with the incentive structure within the universities because tenure, promotion decisions and even dissertations are all prized for their unique contribution to the field, not for replicating existing studies.[16]

In contrast, policymakers might prefer discussing results from replications of the same study or program design across different sites to better understand how a program performs under varying conditions. That sort of replication often does not produce rewards within the academic community.[17]

Finally, Table 3.4 indicates that think tank researchers (Finn, Feistritzer, and Haycock) are popular hearing participants. In an interview, one Democratic staff member told us that people on Capitol Hill "don't connect" very well with academics, and instead they rely on policy think tanks to synthesize and translate important findings into lay terms. Given the complicated decisionmaking environment and competing incentives that we described in our opening section, it makes sense that popular witnesses would be able to identify general trends in the literature and communicate them in jargon-free language. Because many academics work in narrow niches and speak in limited scholarly circles, the synthesis and translation role that think tanks perform can ease the cognitive challenges that policymakers confront.

The hearings dataset further confirms this more general preference for synthesizers or hands-on researchers over academics. Table 3.3 shows that

TABLE 3.4   Most Frequently Appearing Witnesses from the Research Profession
Category

Name	Affiliation	Hearing appearances	
		No.	Years
Maris A. Vinovskis	Professor of History and Public Policy, University of Michigan	5	1997, 1999 (three times), 2000
Chester E. Finn, Jr.	President, Thomas B. Fordham Foundation	4	1997, 1999, 2000, 2001
C. Emily Feistritzer	President and Founder, National Center for Education Information	3	1998, 1999 (two times)
Eric A. Hanushek	Senior Fellow, Stanford University Hoover Institution, and former Professor of Economics, University of Rochester	3	1997, 1998, 1999
Diane S. Ravitch	Professor of Education, New York University, and Senior Fellow, Brookings Institution and the Stanford University Hoover Institution	3	1995, 1999 (two times)
Kati Haycock	Director, Education Trust	2	1998, 1999
E.D. Hirsch, Jr.	Professor of English, University of Virginia, and Founder, Core Knowledge Foundation	2	1998 (two times)
Lawrence W. Sherman	Professor of Criminology, University of Pennsylvania, and previously University of Maryland	2	1997, 1999

Note: See Table 3.3 for more information on the research profession category. Coding rules are available from the authors.

there are slightly more witnesses in the university or college type (9.1 percent) than the synthesizers in the non-university research or program development type (8.3 percent), but the latter tend to appear in smaller hearings (median hearing size of 9 versus 6 witnesses, respectively). Further, research or program development individuals were also more likely to testify in Washington, D.C., rather than in field hearings occurring away from the nation's capital. Within the university or college type, 58.5 percent of witnesses testified on Capitol Hill, while 71.9 percent of the non-university research or program development type witnesses did.[18] Those Washington appearances are important because they give witnesses greater access to congressional staff members who will be more readily available in Washington. That visibility also creates networking opportunities with government officials and others in the national policy community, including the press corps, who may attend those hearings.

The critical role of the synthesizer think tanks becomes even more apparent when we look in depth at the NCLB mandate that all teachers be "highly qualified." In the rest of our chapter we present a case study of that issue.

"HIGHLY QUALIFIED TEACHERS": A CASE STUDY

One of our key questions is, how did research influence the development and implementation of NCLB itself? The previous two sections looked broadly at this question. While it is difficult to offer a full response for the entire law (we could write a whole book about the topic), it is manageable to investigate one particular provision. In this section we present a case study to examine the act's mandate that all teachers be highly qualified. Through interviews with the key congressional staffers and Department of Education officials responsible for this policy area, as well as documentary evidence such as transcripts from related congressional hearings, we can piece together a picture of how research on teacher quality influenced this important part of the law. Readers might consider this case study a companion to this volume's chapter 6, by Richard Ingersoll, on how research has influenced the broader teacher quality debate.

Before examining that picture, it is worth considering what the "highly qualified teacher" mandate requires. Simply stated, NCLB demanded that states and districts adopt plans to ensure that all of their teachers were "highly qualified" by the end of the 2005–06 school year. The "highly qualified" definition has three parts. First, teachers must have at least a bachelor's degree. Second, they must have full state certification or licensure, which can include certification gained through alternate routes. (Charter school teachers need not be certified if their state charter laws do not require it.) Finally, all teachers must demonstrate their "subject-matter competency." For new elementary teachers, that means passing a broad-based test. For new middle or high school teachers, it means passing a test or having an academic major or advanced certification in their subject area. Veteran teachers can meet the requirement by passing tests, having relevant majors, or through a portfolio process called HOUSSE, which stands for High Objective Uniform State Standard of Evaluation. In most states, this allows veteran teachers to earn the "highly qualified" designation based on years of successful teaching experience, service on curriculum committees, professional development credits, and so forth.

So how did the "highly qualified teacher" provision come to be? Our interviews with former congressional staff members highlighted the influence of three "synthesizers"—organizations that had packaged their own take on the teacher quality research into appealing, accessible, actionable, and ideologically persuasive documents with recommendations that policy-makers could understand, embrace, and then enact. These organizations—The National Commission on Teaching and America's Future (NCTAF), The Education Trust, and the Thomas B. Fordham Foundation—played a key gate-keeper role; the research studies they highlighted became extremely influential, in part because the groups' missions appealed to important policymakers in Congress and the Bush administration.

A former aide to Sen. Edward Kennedy (D-MA, and the ranking Democrat on the Health, Education, Labor, and Pensions Committee who became chair when Republicans lost the Senate in June 2001) identified NCTAF as critical to the teacher quality discussions. This staffer explained, "This one was big for Kennedy. They didn't just provide the research, they also had ideas about what you should do." Meanwhile, a former aide to Rep. George Miller (D-CA, and the ranking Democrat on the House Education and the Workforce Committee), credited Education Trust. "What drove the highly qualified teachers conversation was all of the subject-matter stuff—the data coming out showing that teachers of disadvantaged kids didn't know their subjects as well... the Ed Trust report was the big push." Indeed, a recent study by *Education Week* found that the teacher quality publications by these two organizations were among the ten most influential studies in all of education policy over the past decade or so.[19]

Meanwhile, for Republicans, work by Fordham played an important role. One former House GOP staff member remembers frequent conversations with Fordham's president about the teacher quality issue. As we explore below, researchers highlighted by Fordham reports appeared at congressional hearings and were cited in prominent administration documents. Thus, the story of the "highly qualified teacher" mandate, and the role that research played in its development and implementation, begins with the work of these three organizations in the mid- to late-1990s.

The Key Synthesizers

National Commission on Teaching and America's Future

In 1996, NCTAF published *What Matters Most: Teaching for America's Future.*[20] The commission was chaired by North Carolina's Democratic governor Jim Hunt, and led by executive director Linda Darling-Hammond, who at the time was a professor at Columbia University's Teachers College. The commission included two dozen respected educators, business executives, and civil rights leaders. It set a goal that by the year 2006, "we will provide every student in America with what should be his or her educational birthright: access to competent, caring, qualified teaching in schools organized for success."[21] This ambitious vision foreshadowed NCLB's call for all teachers to be "highly qualified" by the end of the 2005–06 school year. The commission made twenty recommendations; these included requiring accreditation for all schools of education; licensing teachers based on demonstrated performance, including tests of subject-matter knowledge, teaching knowledge, and teaching skill; and insisting that districts hire only qualified teachers.

In a section titled Fatal Distractions, the commission also criticized other perspectives. Most notably, it attacked alternate routes to the teaching profession (such as Teach For America) for "offering a few weeks of summer training before new hires are thrown into the classroom."[22] It defended the importance of formal teacher preparation, writing that "literally hundreds of studies confirm that the best teachers know their subjects deeply, understand how people learn, and have mastered a range of teaching methods."[23] And it rebutted critics of teachers unions, arguing that "teacher groups have often been at the forefront of the movement to improve schools and enact greater quality assurances in teaching."[24] It is understandable, then, that Senator Kennedy—with his close ties to the National Education Association (NEA) and himself an education leader in the Senate—could comfortably embrace this report.

So which research did NCTAF highlight? First and foremost, the commission report emphasized the work of Darling-Hammond herself; approximately 25 percent of the citations referenced pieces she authored, co-authored, or edited. Other research studies featured prominently included those by Ingersoll (who used the federal Schools and Staffing Survey to examine teacher qualifications); Ronald Ferguson (who examined the benefits of investing in higher-quality teachers); and Emily Feistritzer (who collected data on the teacher labor market).

Education Trust

Education Trust is a liberal research and advocacy organization whose president, Kati Haycock, spent her formative years in the affirmative action movement in California and came to believe in the urgent need to close America's achievement gaps in education.[25] With funding from several prominent national foundations, her organization conducts and publishes original research, provides assistance to educators, and meets with policymakers to discuss education reform.

In the summer of 1998, Haycock penned "Good Teaching Matters: How Well-Qualified Teachers Can Close the Gap."[26] This breezy 14-page policy brief presents several well-designed charts and graphs that emphasize four compelling overall points: (1) Teachers have a big impact on student achievement. (2) Teacher effectiveness is most clearly linked to strong verbal and math skills and deep content knowledge. (3) Findings are inconclusive on the importance of teaching skill, as developed by traditional teacher preparation programs. (4) Effective teachers are inequitably distributed. The report recommended making teacher licensure exams tougher; holding colleges and universities accountable for the quality of teachers they produce; improving professional development; ensuring that poor and minority students get teachers at least as qualified as their peers get; informing parents about the qualifications of their children's teachers; providing financial incentives for candidates to teach in high need schools; and widening the pathway to rigorous alternate route programs like Teach for America.

So which research did Education Trust highlight? Perhaps most importantly, this policy brief introduced Tennessee's William Sanders to the Washington policy world. Sanders had completed research using the Volunteer State's "value added" data system, which he developed, to show the enormous cumulative difference having three effective teachers in a row could make for low-performing students. A brilliantly designed chart depicting these findings is displayed prominently at the front of the Education Trust brief.

Perhaps due in part to promotion by the Education Trust, Sanders's work has been found to be among the most influential education studies of the past ten years.[27] Sanders's most frequently cited paper appearing in Google Scholar, a piece he co-authored with June Rivers on the effects of teachers on student achievement, was cited an average of 7 times per year from 1997–2001. That average increased to 35 cites per year from 2002–06.[28] *Good Teaching Matters* may have also provided Sanders with added popular exposure, at least in the short run. A search of major newspapers in Lexis-Nexis for "William Sanders" and "school" produced only 8 articles total for the 1995–98 period, but 11 articles in 1999 and 25 in 2000, before the totals decline back to single digits for the ensuing years.

The Education Trust paper highlighted other researchers, too. Eric Hanushek is quoted as saying "The difference between a good and a bad teacher can be a full level of achievement in a single school year."[29] Also highlighted were Ferguson's findings about the importance of teachers' verbal abilities in raising student achievement; work by Dan Goldhaber and Dominic Brewer looking at the relationship between teachers' subject-matter degrees and student performance; and separate studies by Richard Ingersoll, John Kain, and Ferguson showing that minority children are much more likely to have out-of-field instructors.

Thomas B. Fordham Foundation

The Fordham Foundation is a private foundation that supports research, publications, and action projects in elementary and secondary education reform at the national level and in the Dayton, Ohio, area. Its president, Chester E. Finn, Jr., was assistant U.S. secretary of education in the Reagan administration; as a result, Fordham is typically viewed as a conservative voice on education policy.

In April 1999, Fordham published a 16-page manifesto, "The Teachers We Need and How to Get More of Them," ghost-written by Finn and his research director, Marci Kanstoroom.[30] More than fifty policymakers, educators, and reform advocates signed on immediately, including Pennsylvania secretary of education Gene Hickok, who would later become responsible for the implementation of NCLB as deputy U.S. secretary of education (and who wrote the preface to a 1999 Fordham book, *Better Teachers, Better Schools*, which also reprinted the Fordham manifesto).[31]

"The Teachers We Need" directly attacked some of NCTAF's major recommendations. It characterized that group's approach as "more of the same… tightening the regulatory vise, making it harder to enter teaching by piling on new requirement for certification."[32] Instead, the Fordham report advocated pluralism: "In a deregulated environment, good teacher education programs will thrive and prosper….Principals should be able to decide for themselves whether to hire teachers who have been trained in certain pedagogical methods and theories."[33] The report further recommended holding schools (and their leaders) accountable for results while granting principals greater authority to hire the best person for the job, requiring teachers to either possess a major in their field or pass a rigorous subject-matter test, and opening the door to the profession to talented individuals regardless of their training or background.

And what research did Fordham highlight? Some familiar names return: Sanders, Hanushek, and Ferguson all receive top billing, again for demonstrating the link between effective teachers and improved student achievement. Feistritzer appears, though this time for her data on alternative certification. But there are some new names, too. Labor economists Michael Podgursky and Dale Ballou are cited for their studies about the (negative) impact of teacher certification; and Robert Strauss's examination of Pennsylvania's teacher quality reforms also receives prominent attention.

Explaining the Behavior of the Synthesizers

For all three synthesizers, it appears that organizational mission drove decisions about which research to highlight. Take NCTAF's optimistic assessment of the evidence base for teacher certification, for example, which paralleled Darling-Hammond's views as an education school professor that these teacher preparation programs were essential to improving teacher quality. This also aligned with NCTAF's mission, as stated in *What Matters Most*, which includes "connecting the quest for higher student achievement with the need for teachers who are knowledgeable, skillful, and committed to meeting the needs of all students" and "helping develop policies and practices aimed at ensuring powerful teaching and learning in all communities."[34]

Or consider Education Trust's use of the Sanders studies. While Kati Haycock had expressed public concerns about some of Sanders' views (he was skeptical about schools' ability to close the achievement gap),[35] she simultaneously promoted his work demonstrating a vast unevenness in the distribution of quality teachers. This, after all, squared with Education Trust's focus on inequity as the primary problem facing American schooling. Its mission, as printed in *Good Teachers Matter*, is to "promote high academic achievement for all students at all levels—kindergarten through college," with a focus "on the schools and colleges most often left behind in efforts to improve education: those institutions serving Latino, African American, Native American and low-income students."[36]

Or look at the Fordham Foundation's use of studies by Podgursky and Ballou that raised concerns about the impact of rigid certification rules. The obvious conclusion—free principals' hands to hire the best person for the job—fit perfectly with Fordham's preference for deregulated solutions. It also fit with Fordham's mission, which is to support "the educational needs of children, not the interests of institutions or adults."[37]

The link between the synthesizers' perspectives and the research they highlighted is not surprising, or even pernicious. Education researchers themselves, inside the academy or outside it, also frequently disagree about appropriate policy solutions to educational problems. In effect, the synthesizers' different perspectives help to expose members of Congress and the executive branch to these wider debates in the research community. We see that as a good thing.

Finally, what sets these three synthesizers apart from the alphabet soup of Washington, D.C.-based associations and advocacy groups (who testified in large numbers before Congress, as shown in Table 3.3) is that their positions are formed by organizational missions rather than self-interest. That is a key reason that policymakers consider their advice credible; plus, it appears that many politicians (who are partisans by definition, after all) enjoy a dose of ideology with their research. Perhaps the growing polarization of the U.S. Congress[38] also serves to drive congressional representatives and their staffs toward organizations with clear ideological positions that are in sync with the Republican or Democratic base, rather than broad-based, consensus-oriented membership organizations such as the Education Commission of the States (ECS), National Governors Association, or the Council of Chief State School Officers. Recent political history could thus help explain the rise of mission-oriented organizations such as NCTAF, Education Trust, and Fordham, whose ideas now compete with and in some cases assert more influence than work from these other groups.

Legislation and Implementation

Into the Mixing Bowl

This quick review of these three policy statements on teacher quality shows that, the many differences aside, areas of agreement did exist. First and foremost, the synthesizers all argued that teacher quality mattered—and mattered a lot. This prompted calls to do something on the issue. Consensus also existed on the importance of teachers' subject-matter knowledge, indicated either by a subject-specific major or passage of a subject-matter exam. There was also concern about poor and minority students having an unfair share of ineffective, unqualified teachers. And while strong disagreements persisted over specific programs such as Teach For America, all three groups at least nominally supported "rigorous" alternate routes to certification.

This lowest common denominator agreement set the stage for what would become NCLB's highly qualified teacher provision. In fact, by October 1999, the House of Representatives had passed H.R. 2 (The Student Results Act), which included a provision mandating that each state submit a plan for ensuring that all its teachers be "fully qualified" by December 31, 2003.[39] Interviews with congressional staff members indicate that Education Trust, working closely with ranking Democrat George Miller, was primarily responsible for creating this requirement and ensuring its inclusion in the bill. One former staffer described a "real push" from Education Trust, putting pressure on Miller, who offered enthusiastic support.

But the fingerprints of all three "synthesizers" are apparent. Consider a House hearing held in February 1998. The focus was on teacher preparation (Congress was still working on finishing the Higher Education Act reauthorization) but it helped frame the subsequent larger teacher quality debates. The witness list included several familiar names: several people from Table 3.4 (Feistritzer, Hanushek, Hirsch, and Haycock), Ballou, Hickock, and Ingersoll, as well as Barnett Berry, associate director of NCTAF, and Paul Steidler, director of the Alexis de Toqueville Institution. Recall that Hanushek, Ingersoll, Feistritzer, and Ballou were featured prominently in at least one of the three synthesizer reports. Through Haycock and Berry, Education Trust and NCTAF had direct representation. And three of the witnesses—Hickok, Hirsch, and Hanushek—were original signers of the soon-to-be-published Fordham manifesto.

Not surprisingly, then, ideas from the key synthesizer groups helped shape the "fully qualified" definition in the House bill. The requirement for subject-matter knowledge was front and center; all three promoted the evidence for its importance. Haycock's testimony from the February 1998 hearing noted that many teachers "have only a very, very thin grasp of the subject matter they are teaching and get almost no support to deepen that knowledge after they get into the classroom."[40] The requirement that teachers be "fully certified" implied a victory for NCTAF. Berry's testimony argued that "teacher ed matters for both teacher performance and student learning...the best teacher ed programs in this country have certain characteristics. First and foremost, they require a minimum of 40 weeks of extensive clinical experience."[41] And allowing alternative certification affirmed Fordham's viewpoint. Hickok stated in his testimony that "it is very important...that it is possible for people to enter the teaching profession who do not go through the traditional teacher preparation programs. We propose alternative certification to attract the best and the brightest from other areas and other fields to become teachers because we think they have something to offer."[42]

Politics Take Over

The House of Representatives passed the Student Results Act in late 1999, but, running out of time before the 2000 presidential campaign, the bill died in the Senate. All Elementary and Secondary Education Act reauthorization efforts ground to a halt. But when they resumed in 2001, after President George W. Bush offered his 25-page proposal, "No Child Left Behind" (which, notably, did not say anything about requiring "fully qualified teachers"), Congress rekindled its teacher quality debates. According to several congressional aides, John Boehner (R-OH), then chairman of the House Education and the Workforce Committee, gave Miller authority to flesh out NCLB's teacher quality provisions. Miller more or less maintained the language from 1999 in the version of NCLB that the House passed in the summer of 2001, though now the goal was for all teachers to be "highly qualified" by the end of the 2005–06 school year. All teachers, both rookies and veterans, would need to attain full certification and demonstrate their subject-matter knowledge through a major or a test in their field.

Understandably, the specter of veteran teachers needing to pass a subject-matter test (and the possibility that thousands could fail) roiled the teachers unions, especially the NEA. So, according to several congressional aides, NEA put heavy pressure on Senator Kennedy to offer an alternative: the HOUSSE provision. (As explained above, this loophole allowed experienced teachers to show their knowledge through a portfolio system; it soon came to be ridiculed for its lack of rigor.) It was tucked into the Senate version of NCLB, and, after many negotiations with Miller, also included in the final version.

Simply for political reasons, then, the law's subject-matter requirements were effectively neutered, at least for veteran teachers. In the end, interest-group politics proved more influential than education research—even in this one area, the importance of teachers' subject-matter knowledge, where broad consensus existed from left to right.

Implementation Time

No Child Left Behind's highly qualified teacher mandate put the Bush administration in an awkward position. The president had not proposed this provision, nor did senior Department of Education officials favor it. We have already seen that Hickok was skeptical about traditional teacher certification requirements. So, too, was Susan Sclafani, who also played a key role in NCLB implementation as counselor to Secretary of Education Rod Paige during the first several years of President Bush's first term. Her views on teacher quality emerged from her own personal experience working in the Houston Independent Public Schools, and specifically from leading the district's "urban systemic initiative" grant from the National Science Foundation. As she said in an interview,

> I saw how our alternative certification candidates did in terms of their scores on required exams, and they were much better prepared than new people coming through traditional routes…At the same time, I looked at what the research was showing on math—that teachers who had majored in math had students with much higher levels of performance.

These formative experiences taught her that alternate route teachers could be quite effective—and that subject knowledge mattered most. Yet the actual provision required full certification for all teachers, and a watered-down mandate on subject-matter knowledge.

Perhaps not surprisingly, then, the Bush administration focused its early efforts on protecting alternative certification by using the bully pulpit, most notably in the June 2002 publication *Meeting the Highly Qualified Teachers Challenge: The Secretary's Annual Report on Teacher Quality*.[43] The Higher Education Act required the Secretary to report annually on the nation's education schools and their candidates' success rates on teacher certification exams. The administration used the report as a clarion call for states to open their schoolhouse doors to qualified teaching candidates from non-traditional backgrounds.

In Secretary Paige's voice, the report argued:

> at the same time that states should be seeking teaching candidates with solid content knowledge and high verbal ability, our system of teacher certification is thwarting the aspirations of our most talented individuals—while at the same time maintaining low academic standards and failing to prepare teachers for the reality of the classroom. There must be a better way.[44]

It continued by asserting, "a model for tomorrow would be based on the best alternate route programs of today."[45]

This line of thinking was straight from the Fordham Foundation playbook. That is not a coincidence—a former Fordham staffer (and the second author of this chapter) led the development and ghost-writing of the report. As with the original Fordham manifesto, it prominently featured research by Goldhaber and Brewer (on the importance of teachers' subject-matter knowledge), Feistritzer (on the growth of alternative certification programs), and Podgursky and Ballou. It also cited much of Fordham's work, as well as Education Trust's. And it incorporated new voices and research: Kate Walsh's review of the literature on teacher certification; Frederick M. Hess's manifesto, *Tear Down This Wall*; and a new study of Teach For America's impact on student achievement in Houston by Margaret Raymond and Stephen Fletcher.[46]

These arguments—and the research backing them—informed countless speeches of Secretary Paige and other senior officials during NCLB's early implementation. In those remarks, they argued for states to raise their subject-matter standards for teachers while lowering all other barriers to certification. Though the law allowed states to follow this path, it did not require it. Eventually, evidence emerged that many states were using the HOUSSE provisions to water down their already-meager subject-matter standards, while maintaining their rigid certification requirements. It was a quagmire, and the administration soon abandoned the battle, unable to undo the damage the law itself had wrought.

CONCLUSIONS AND RECOMMENDATIONS

Our analysis of how research influenced NCLB's development and the implementation of its highly qualified teacher provisions leads us to several observations, including some recommendations for producers and consumers of education research.

Contrary to the cynics' views that political gamesmanship always drives the behavior of public officials, it appears that research can add substantive value to policymaking. Our evidence showed that researchers and their ideas did influence the legislative debates that helped develop NCLB. Plus, Republicans and Democrats in Congress did intend to move educational practice in a more research-based direction through their use of NCLB's scientifically based research provisions. And further, specific findings from researchers across several social science fields did appear to animate discussions about the law's teacher quality provisions.

Still, and perhaps not surprisingly, members of Congress and their staff used research selectively. They tended to gravitate toward findings that supported their own ideological views, behavior that the synthesizer groups facilitated and mediated. Regarding the highly qualified teacher provision, NCTAF, Education Trust, and the Fordham Foundation promoted research studies that backed their preferred narratives. Thus, these synthesizers were less philosopher kings than kingmakers. They used research to drive their agendas, rather than allowing research alone to drive policy. And when the synthesizers found consensus—such as around the import of teachers' subject-matter knowledge—they helped foster bipartisan action.

It is not hard to understand what motivates these and other synthesizer groups. Not tethered by the views of a membership, inspired largely by their own mission and creed, dependent on financial support from foundations with generally identifiable ideological perspectives, they are incentivized to pursue their own deeply held convictions about what makes for good education policy. Research becomes just another arrow in their quiver. It is futile to call on them to become more research-based and less mission-based because their missions give them purpose and credibility in the first place. And one must not forget that these groups, which are typically strapped for staff and other resources (at least compared to congressional committees or government agencies), must also confront the cognitive challenges of mastering large bodies of literature. Their organizational missions help to clarify and simplify that complicated landscape by providing guidance about which studies to consider and how to evaluate their quality.

So if the synthesizers are unlikely to change their behavior, what about other producers and the consumers of research? Among the producers, academic researchers who want to influence the policymaking process have a choice, it seems to us. One option is to bring their research findings to the attention of one or more of the synthesizer groups—the ones whose missions line up nicely with the policy conclusions of their studies. A second option is to circumvent the synthesizers entirely by making their research accessible directly to policymakers. They could execute both of these options relatively easily by converting their academic publications (e.g., journal articles and university press books) into more accessible and shorter op-eds or user-friendly policy briefs. Academics with more flexibility, especially those who have made tenure, might invest more time conversing or visiting with staff in Washington, D.C., or their state capitals. To make these activities more workable at scale, researchers might band together to develop their own synthesizer groups—ones that develop user-friendly products but without the ideological edge, as some research centers on university campuses already do. Of course, without such an edge, their work might be less appealing to policymakers. Academic researchers who build these connections may pay a cost in the short term (e.g., they burn time that they could be using to publish in peer-reviewed journals), but they may benefit eventually if these links produce funding opportunities, via foundation or government grants, for example, that will earn them credit on the academic tenure track. And as we see from the William Sanders example, greater exposure in Washington does seem correlated with greater attention in academia and in the popular press.

And what about the ultimate consumers of policy research, the policymakers? How might they better use research in their deliberations? First and foremost, they should be aware of the perspectives that synthesizer groups—and academic researchers, for that matter—bring to their work. Of course, they likely share these same perspectives, which is why they rely on these groups. Second, they might make the extra effort to identify researchers that the synthesizers have not highlighted. Some of the best at this in the policy world are staff members on Capitol Hill who work for congressional committees. Creating incentives for these seasoned staff members to continue their public service, rather than leaving the government or jumping to new issue areas on different committees, would be one way to help expose elected officials to crucial perspectives. That's not to say that politicians will necessarily change their views (you can lead a horse to water . . .), but having talented staff on both sides of the aisle working in these policy trenches would certainly improve the chances for research to make a difference.

Finally, perhaps the easiest way for elected officials to promote even-handedness without acting against their own personal interests would be for them to always ask researchers to come clean about the limits of their scholarship. After all, social science fields that study human behavior often contain much legitimate disagreement about what policy levers society might pull to improve results. Within any study—even those meeting the highest design standards and that pass peer-review—researchers make judgment calls that some other credible researcher would see as flawed. Thus, any time public officials claim to be hearing a researcher describe "the truth" in congressional testimony, some other committee member should ask the witness a simple follow-up question: What are the best arguments that other researchers would offer against your conclusions? Academic researchers, especially, will be familiar with that question because they hear variants of it all the time in interviews on the job market, at academic conferences, and in written exchanges with article reviewers.

In the end, though, it is probably a mistake to assume that any of these actors—researchers, synthesizers, or policymakers—will change their behavior in fundamental ways. They are simply responding to the incentives that will help them advance their careers, ideas, and preferred solutions. The best researchers, especially those on academic tenure tracks, produce studies that their peers find compelling contributions to knowledge, often of a theoretical but not necessarily practical nature. (Researchers outside academia at professional firms such as Mathematica, and others, are certainly exceptions to that rule.) Synthesizers develop and use research to promote their organizational missions. Policymakers frequently use research to bolster their preexisting points of view. And when No Child Left Behind is reauthorized, we can expect many of the same dynamics to unfold once again. It's not pretty, and it's certainly not "scientifically based policymaking," but its democracy.

We thank our interview respondents for being generous with their time and sharing their experiences. Frederick M. Hess offered super feedback on earlier drafts, and Chad Aldeman provided great research assistance.

CHAPTER 4

Research and the Reading Wars

James S. Kim

Controversy over the role of phonics in reading instruction has persisted for over 100 years, making the reading wars seem like an inevitable fact of American history. In the mid-nineteenth century, Horace Mann, the secretary of the Massachusetts Board of Education, railed against the teaching of the alphabetic code—the idea that letters represented sounds—as an impediment to reading for meaning. Mann excoriated the letters of the alphabet as "bloodless, ghostly apparitions," and argued that children should first learn to read whole words.[1] The 1886 publication of James Cattell's pioneering eye movement study showed that adults perceived words more rapidly than letters, providing an ostensibly scientific basis for Mann's assertions.[2] In the twentieth century, state education officials like Mann have continued to voice strong opinions about reading policy and practice, aiding the rapid implementation of whole language–inspired curriculum frameworks and texts during the late 1980s. And scientists like Cattell have shed light on the processes underlying skillful reading, contributing to a growing scientific consensus that culminated in the 2000 National Reading Panel report.[3]

This chapter traces the history of the reading wars in both the political arena and the scientific community. The narrative is organized into three sections. The first offers the history of reading research in the 1950s, when the "conventional wisdom" in reading was established by acclaimed leaders in the field like William Gray, who encouraged teachers to instruct children how to read whole words while avoiding isolated phonics drills. In the 1960s and 1970s, Jeanne Chall's research on first-grade reading instruction indicated that phonics instruction was effective in helping children become skilled readers. Whole-language theorists, however, conducted research to challenge Chall's findings, arguing that context clues helped children read more effectively than teacher-directed phonics instruction.

The next section shows how both the federal government and state education agencies mediated the reading wars. In the 1980s and 1990s, the federal government turned to experts to undertake syntheses of research and to highlight areas of scientific consensus, which could form a solid foundation for improving instruction. At the same time, advocates of whole-language pedagogy persuaded numerous states to adopt new curriculum frameworks and instructional materials that pushed phonics instruction to the periphery of the classroom. Eventually, the decline in fourth-grade readings scores on the National Assessment of Educational Progress (NAEP) prompted many state legislatures to pass mandatory phonics bills.

The third section discusses how findings from the National Reading Panel (NRP) synthesized three decades of scientific research in reading and formed the basis for the Reading First legislation. Since 2000, the NRP's findings have continued to fuel the ongoing debate about evidence-based practice in reading among state and federal policymakers, professional organizations, and teachers. In sum, this chapter seeks to describe *how* research has helped resolve controversies in the reading wars; and to explain *why* good research alone cannot ensure sound instructional policy and practice.

1967–1979: THE GREAT DEBATE IN EARLY READING INSTRUCTION

Phonics versus Look-Say: And the Winner Is?

In the mid-twentieth century, the conventional wisdom about effective reading instruction in the early grades was heavily influenced by William S. Gray, a leading reading scholar. In his 1948 book, *On Their Own Reading*, Gray objected to the dominant method of teaching children the letters of the alphabet, the sounds represented by letters, and the blending of groups of letters to sound out words. Echoing Mann's earlier criticism of phonics instruction, Gray objected to "the old mechanical phonic drills . . . that inevitably result in dull, word-by-word reading."[4] Instead, he endorsed a meaning-first and word-analysis-later approach that became a hallmark characteristic of the classroom texts used to instruct children in reading. Gray and his supporters theorized that reading skill would develop more rapidly if children learned to look at and quickly recognize whole words much like adults. This method of instruction was called "look-say" because it taught children to recognize and say whole words by sight rather than using knowledge of letter–sound relationships to read words.

In *Why Johnny Can't Read*, Rudolph Flesch attacked the basic premise of a meaning-focused instructional approach proposed by Gray. Flesch exhorted teachers and parents to instruct children how letters represented sounds and how to blend those sounds to identify unknown words. According to Flesch, phonics was the best way to teach reading, and the only hope for curing our nation's reading woes. Furthermore, Flesch directed his message to parents, teachers, and the general public, seeking to win the debate about how best to teach children to read.[5] In the context of the cold war, Flesch's back-to-basics, phonics-first, message was embraced by many politicians and citizens who feared that the American educational system was losing ground to the Russians.[6]

With the support of a Carnegie Corporation grant, Jeanne Chall, a professor at Harvard University's Graduate School of Education, undertook a research synthesis to assess the competing ideas about early reading instruction. The title of Chall's 1967 book, *Learning to Read: The Great Debate*, captured the essence of the reading wars that erupted in the middle of the twentieth century. Chall noted that the many issues and controversies about reading instruction in first grade boiled down to one question: "Do children learn better with a beginning method that stresses meaning or with one that stresses learning the code?"[7] To address this question, Chall interviewed teachers, inspected basal texts, and reviewed earlier research on elementary school reading. However, the heart of Chall's analysis was an assessment of the efficacy of three instructional approaches, based on a methodological strategy for aggregating findings from experimental studies. The *look-say* method emphasizes the visual recognition of whole words, the reading of whole sentences, and the acquisition of meaning; it involves little or no phonics instruction. The *systematic phonics* program teaches phonics early and instructs children how to separate letter–sound relationships and to blend these sounds. The *intrinsic phonics* program stresses sight-word reading, teaches children how to learn the sounds of letters by analyzing sight words, and encourages children to use context clues and pictures to identify words. Chall's classification system placed programs on a continuum from instruction emphasizing the code (systematic phonics) to programs emphasizing meaning (look-say) and the programs in-between (intrinsic phonics). Finally, Chall tallied the number of experimental studies favoring each of the three approaches to beginning reading.

Consulting research from 1900 to 1965, Chall reviewed 30 experimental studies that compared at least two different approaches to beginning reading instruction. As shown in Table 4.1, 27 studies showed superior outcomes in phonics programs (18 favored systematic phonics and 9 favored intrinsic phonics) and 3 favored look-say methods. Contrary to the conventional wisdom, Chall found that an early code emphasis produced better word recognition outcomes in the early grades and helped children read with better comprehension up to fourth grade, relative to the dominant look-say method of reading instruction, in which little phonics was taught and emphasis was placed on reading whole words and whole sentences. A code-emphasis also produced larger benefits for less-skilled readers and children from low-income families. However, Chall emphasized that the dichotomy between code- and meaning-emphasis was a simplistic dualism and a matter of emphasis—all programs had some dose of instruction about letter–sound relationships and whole-word reading. Because the findings were based on few quality experiments, Chall viewed her findings as "hypotheses to be tested further."[8]

A Psycholinguistic Theory of Reading: Theoretical Roots of Whole-language Pedagogy

Chall's findings were immediately challenged by two scholars—Kenneth S. Goodman and Frank Smith. In a 1967 journal article, Goodman challenged the idea that reading involved the "exact, detailed, sequential perception and identification of letters, words, spelling patterns and large language units."[9] To Goodman, reading was a "psycholinguistic guessing game," in which good readers used context and background information rather than precise identification of letter–sound relationships to predict, confirm, and guess at the identification of an unfamiliar word.[10] In a 1969 article in *Reading Research Quarterly*, Goodman went on to criticize "recent attempts by Chall and others to justify the separation of code-breaking from reading for meaning."[11] According to Goodman, syntax (grammatical structure of language) and semantics (relevant background knowledge) were as important as grapho-phonetic cues (letter–sound correspondences) in aiding word recognition processes. In the conclusion, Goodman hoped that his research would "generate hypotheses about the reading process which can be empirically tested and lead to new insights into methods and materials for reading instruction."[12]

As he hoped, Goodman's theory fueled research on the processes underlying word recognition ability among linguists, cognitive psychologists, and educational researchers. In the 1970s, Goodman's ideas were echoed most prominently in the writings of Frank Smith, who began to publish research originating from the Harvard University Center for Cognitive Studies under the direction of the eminent psychologist George Miller. In *Understanding*

TABLE 4.1   A Comparison of Three Approaches to Reading Instruction, 1900–1965

Period	Prevailing method	Total studies	Found systematic phonics superior	Found intrinsic phonics superior	Found look-say superior
1900–1920	Systematic phonics	3	1	0	2
1920–1935	Look-say	6	4	2	0
1935–1955	Intrinsic phonics	8	4	3	1
1955–1965	The debate: intrinsic phonics still the prevailing method with a push toward earlier and heavier emphasis on phonics	13	9	4	0
TOTAL		30	18	9	3

Source: Jeanne Chall, Learning to Reading: The Great Debate (New York: McGraw-Hill, 1967), 132.

Reading, Smith hypothesized that reading was natural, like speaking, and that children knew a good deal about language.[13] Consequently, skilled readers used their knowledge of a meaningful context, like a story or paragraph, to recognize individual words in a sentence. Furthermore, Smith argued that phonics rules were too complex, had too many exceptions, and were unnecessary for helping the beginning reader become a proficient reader. "Learning to read," Smith argued, "is akin to any other skill; there are perhaps some specialized exercises that one can undertake to iron out particular difficulties, but there is no substitute for the activity itself."[14] In other words, one of the best ways to become a skilled reader was simply to read.

In trying to bridge the divide between theory and practice, Smith directed his message to practitioners. The final section of Understanding Reading was titled The Teacher's Role, and Smith acknowledged that his model of reading was unconventional. He explained,

[Readers] are not usually regarded as "predicting" their way through a passage of text, eliminating some alternatives in advance on the basis of their knowledge of the redundancy of language, and acquiring just enough visual information to eliminate the alternatives remaining . . . But nothing that I have said should start a classroom revolution. There is no suggestion that teachers of reading should throw away their instructional procedures, or their years or experience, and start all over again.[15]

The direct appeal to teachers and the deference to practitioner judgment became a theme in Smith's writing throughout the 1970s, and both Goodman and Smith started to make explicit instructional recommendations based on their theories about reading.

Smith published two books in the 1970s that were squarely focused on persuading teachers to change instruction in their classrooms. In *Psycholinguistics and Reading,* Smith reiterated his basic hypothesis that the primary goal of reading was to acquire meaning from print and dismissed the importance of teaching the systematic relationship between letters and sounds. Pre-packaged phonics programs, Smith claimed, undermined teacher autonomy. Indeed, Smith argued that teachers "do not act as brainless purveyors of predigested instruction (that is why there is the frightening trend these days to produce 'teacher-proof' materials)."[16] In *Reading Without Nonsense*, Smith argued that phonics instruction was unnecessary for efficient decoding of words and actually interfered with the process of learning to read. When confronted with a struggling reader, Smith advised teachers: "The first alternative and preference is—to skip over the puzzling word. The second alternative is to guess what the unknown word might be. And the final and least preferred alternative is to sound the word out. Phonics, in other words, comes last."[17]

By the end of the 1970s, Smith's writings reflected the actions of a policy entrepreneur seeking to persuade teachers to reject phonics instruction and to encourage children to use context clues to identify words. Moreover, his recommendations evoked earlier arguments put forth by William Gray, who suggested that teaching children to read whole words was superior to phonics instruction.

Testing the Psycholinguistic Theory of Reading in Laboratory Experiments

Starting in the early 1970s, cognitive psychologist Keith Stanovich notes that Smith's top-down model of reading piqued the curiosity of scholars, who began to undertake experiments to examine whether good readers, in fact, relied more on context to recognize words than poor readers.[18] The more immediate goal of these studies was to understand the basic processes underlying reading rather than the application of these findings to schools and classrooms. Much to the surprise of Stanovich and his colleagues, experimental data indicated that it was poor readers, not good readers, who relied more heavily on context to facilitate word recognition.[19] Working independently on related questions, other scholars replicated the finding that context effects were largest for poor readers.[20] Studies based on eye-movement technology also indicated that good readers did not engage in whole-scale skipping of letters and words but processed all the visual information in text.[21] Mounting evidence also indicated that children needed to develop phonemic awareness—the knowledge that words are composed of units of sounds (phonemes) represented by letters (graphemes)—and master the alphabetic principle in order to become independent readers.[22] Contrary to Goodman and Smith's top-down model of reading, research findings also showed that good readers had fast and accurate word recognition ability that freed attention to focus on meaning, whereas poor readers had to rely more heavily on context to decode words.[23]

Although basic research produced knowledge about the acquisition of reading skills among young children, these findings were disseminated primarily in peer-reviewed journals and academic conferences and did not have an immediate and direct impact on education policy and practice. In assessing the state of reading research in 1977, Richard Venezsky argued, that "[if] reading research is to influence instruction, then more experimental psychologists will have to be persuaded to interact professionally with educational planners and developers and to concern themselves with the practical side of reading."[24] Venezsky's recommendations for using research to shape practice took two forms in the 1980s. The federal government convened expert panels to synthesize basic research and its implications for teachers, while whole-language advocates worked with state education agencies to disseminate their ideas about reading instruction to teachers.

1983–1997: HOW CONSENSUS PANELS OF EXPERTS AND STATE EDUCATION AGENCIES MEDIATED THE READING WARS

Consensus Panels and the Call for Balanced Literacy Instruction

In 1983, the National Institute of Education (NIE) authorized the National Academy of Education's Commission on Education and Public Policy to gather a panel of experts "to survey, interpret and synthesize research findings" on beginning reading and the comprehension of language.[25] Under the direction of professor Richard C. Anderson, the Commission on Reading convened eight leading professors, one first-grade teacher, and one member from the Department of Education to conduct the review. Housed at the Center for the Study of Reading at the University of Illinois, the panel synthesized recent findings from linguistics, cognitive psychology, and child development in a 1985 publication, *Becoming a Nation of Readers*. The report affirmed the value of (1) early language experiences in kindergarten and at home, (2) phonics instruction (in helping children master the alphabetic principle), and (3) opportunities to read connected text orally and silently. The recommendations emphasized the developmental needs of children as they moved from a basic understanding of the form and function of print to an understanding of letter–sound correspondences and on to independent, fluent reading of books.

In addition to offering recommendations for practitioners, the 1985 NIE report helped reframe the debates about reading instruction in two ways. First, it rejected the dualism between activities designed to foster knowledge of the alphabetic code and opportunities for children to read good literature. New findings from related academic disciplines were shedding light on "the intricacies of the reading process" and "lay at rest once and for all some of the old debates about the role of phonics and comprehension."[26] Second, it raised new questions and encouraged researchers to broaden their study of the reading process and the instructional strategies that facilitated the development of reading comprehension. According to one federal policymaker, the reading research begun by NIE and the publication of the 1985 report "shifted the entire agenda for research and development in that area."[27] It did so by moving the field away from a dominant concern with decoding and early reading instruction to a broader focus on comprehension and language development.

In a second research synthesis, authorized by the federal government and sponsored by the Center for the Study of Reading, Marilyn J. Adams completed a synthesis of the theory and practice of beginning reading. In the 1990 publication *Beginning to Read: Thinking and Learning About Print*,[28] Adams echoed many of Chall's findings and the 1985 NIE report by explaining why phonics instruction facilitated word recognition skills. She also reviewed the growing research literature that undercut the validity of the psycholinguistic theory of reading advanced by Goodman and Smith. Skilled readers used knowledge of letter–sound relationships to process all the graphic information contained in identifying a word. Once lower-level word recognition processes were automated, children could read connected text with speed and focus on comprehending what they read. Thus, the strategy of using context to aid word recognition and the rejection of phonics instruction, as advocated by whole-language theorists, had little support in empirical research by the late 1980s.[29]

Additional evidence challenging the effectiveness of whole-language practices emerged in a 1989 study published in the peer-reviewed journal *Review of Educational Research*. In this meta-analysis, Steven Stahl and Patricia Miller reviewed the efficacy of whole-language approaches to reading instruction. In addition to informing the scientific literature, the authors hoped to shed light on the heated debate between proponents of whole-language theories and phonics instruction.[30] Stahl and Miller defined whole-language/language–experience methods as having four characteristics: (1) an emphasis on using children's language as a medium for instruction, (2) child-centered lessons, (3) trade books rather than basal texts, and (4) lessons in decoding and phonics only as they arose in the context of reading stories and text.

Their quantitative synthesis revealed that whole-language approaches had some benefits as an instructional approach in kindergarten, but produced inferior results relative to systematic code-emphasis approaches in first grade. To explain this finding, Stahl and Miller suggested that whole language might help children in kindergarten when reading instruction is more romantic and focused on learning the form and function of print. They noted that whole language might be less useful in first grade when children must master the alphabetic code to decode new words. Perhaps most importantly, the findings indicated that whole-language/language–experience methods had the greatest benefit for middle- and upper-class students. Why? According to Stahl and Miller, students from advantaged backgrounds were more likely than low-income students to have learned about the code through exposure to storybooks and language experience at home. Echoing the findings from Chall's earlier research, Stahl and Miller hypothesized that low-income children and poor readers needed explicit instruction in sound–symbol relationships in first grade to become skilled readers.

The Rise and Fall of Whole Language in California

During the late 1980s, research indicating that phonics facilitated efficient decoding skills and that whole language practices lacked evidence of efficacy had little direct influence on state policy and classroom practice. On the contrary, whole-language pedagogy formed the latest conventional wisdom in reading. In a 1990 special issue of *Elementary School Journal* on whole language, P. David Pearson observed that whole language had become a grassroots movement of educators supported by state education officials and professional organizations. Pearson noted that in his 25–year career as an educator,

> Never have I witnessed anything like the rapid spread of the whole-language movement. Pick your metaphor—an epidemic, wildfire, manna from heaven—whole language has spread so rapidly throughout North America that it is a fact of life in literacy curriculum and research.[31]

In the same special issue of *Elementary School Journal*, Jerome Harste and Kenneth Goodman argued that one goal of whole-language philosophy and practice was to empower practitioners. The school curriculum, Harste argued, should not be "left in the hands of those who only rarely come in contact with students."[32] Echoing Harste's ideas about teacher empowerment, Kenneth Goodman asserted that "teachers are not relying on gurus and experts to tell them what to do."[33] The whole-language movement, according to Goodman, was generating a knowledge base "passed from teacher to teacher in person contacts, in teacher support groups, and in local conferences."[34] Rather than following the findings of experimental research published in academic journals, Goodman urged scholars to do research that was useful for teachers, and predicted that "practitioners will move ahead, with or without this support."[35]

By the late 1980s, whole-language theorists had communicated their ideas to decisionmakers in state government in order to change curriculum and instruction. One direct path to changing classroom instruction was to work through state legislatures that had centralized control over textbook adoption policies and the authority to shape the content of the basal texts used in all public school classrooms. According to reading scholar Timothy Shanahan, whole-language advocates were able to persuade the commissioner of education in California, Bill Honig, to adopt new textbooks that de-emphasized skill instruction and phonics skills. According to Shanahan, "[w]hole language-influenced policies translated into a ban on the use of state money to purchase spelling books (whole language proponents opposed spellers)."[36] This change in reading curriculum and text represented a radical shift away from traditional basal texts and a move toward child-centered pedagogy. For example, the 1987 California language arts framework supported an integrated language arts curriculum critical of phonics instruction, and advanced the idea that children should construct knowledge on their own, based on their interests.[37] It specifically noted that learning English "cannot be limited to a daily list of ten or 15 skill objectives or to the completion of meaningless worksheets."[38] Given these recommendations, there was little emphasis on teaching all children to master the 26 letters of the alphabet or the 44 speech sounds that make up the English language. Although some educators embraced the literature-based curriculum and new textbooks, many parents and teachers were alarmed to find that the new materials were too difficult for many children.

The major challenge to whole-language pedagogy eventually came from fourth–grade reading scores on the National Assessment of Educational Progress (NAEP). With the first wave of 1992 data from the newly authorized NAEP administrations at the state level, the federal government supplied the public and policymakers with comparative information on state performance. Thus, Californians were alarmed to find that 52 percent of fourth graders read below the basic level on the 1992 administration of NAEP. More bad news followed when the 1994 NAEP scores were released in spring of 1995. Policymakers, parents, and educators learned that the average performance of California's fourth-graders put the state near the bottom relative to other states, and that the decline in scores from 1992 to 1994 was evident among all ethnic and socioeconomic groups. On the 1994 NAEP, 56 percent of fourth graders read below basic, including 46 percent of children from families with college-educated parents.[39]

The perceived reading crisis was eventually linked to whole-language practice. Survey data indicated that a larger percentage of California teachers employed whole-language practices than their peers in other states. For example, surveys of classroom instruction from the 1992 NAEP indicated that 69 percent of California teachers put a "heavy" emphasis (versus "moderate" or "little or no") on whole language compared to a mean response of 40 percent across other states. Moreover, 87 percent of California teachers indicated heavy reliance on literature-based reading and 52 percent reported little or no reliance on phonics, compared to a mean of 50 percent and 33 percent in other states.[40] Despite the difficulty of drawing firm causal links between instruction and achievement, many policymakers implicated the California language arts framework and poor teaching as the primary cause behind the decline in state reading scores.[41]

Since whole language had become the conventional wisdom in reading instruction, any decline (perceived or real) in reading achievement was easily linked to the dominant method of reading instruction. Legislators in California and elsewhere reacted to the educational crisis of low literacy attainment by enacting a flood of phonics bills during the mid-1990s. From 1994 to 1997, 18 states had one or more phonics bills introduced in legislative sessions and California had the largest number of bills introduced during this time period. By 1997, a total of 33 state legislators had passed bills that stressed instruction to improve phonemic awareness or explicit phonics.[42] Moreover, the growing number of phonics bills appeared to reflect the public's dissatisfaction with an educational establishment that seemed unwilling to adopt evidence-based practices in the classroom.[43] The reading wars were now being fought in the political arena, as legislators sought to stem the reading crisis by passing laws to govern classroom instruction.

In explaining the political reaction of state legislatures to the reading crisis, Keith Stanovich argued that whole-language theorists had failed to respond to evidence and enact norms of practice rooted in scientific research. In short, whole-language theorists and advocates left the teaching profession vulnerable to intrusive legislative mandates by failing to police itself. According to Stanovich,

> In holding to an irrationally extreme view on the role of phonics in reading education—for failing to acknowledge that some children do not discover the alphabetic principle on their own and need systematic direct instruction in the alphabetic principle, phonological analysis, and alphabetic coding—whole language proponents threaten all of their legitimate accomplishments. Eventually—perhaps not for a great while, but eventually—the weight of empirical evidence will fall on their heads. That direct instruction in alphabetic coding facilitates early reading acquisition is one of the most well established conclusions in all of behavioral science.[44]

In many ways, Stanovich's criticism of whole language was echoed by California's former commissioner of education. In retrospect, Bill Honig admitted that the 1987 language arts framework and whole-language practices were not based on proven strategies. "It is the curse of all progressives," said Honig, "that we are anti-research and anti-science, and we never seem to grasp how irrational that attitude is. This is probably our deepest failure."[45]

1993–2000: THE FEDERAL GOVERNMENT TURNS TO EXPERTS TO END THE READING WARS

Political scientist John Kingdon points out that public policy issues and agendas are most likely to capture the attention of legislators when three streams coalesce.[46] In the 1990s, the merging of the problem, political, and policy streams made federal lawmakers eager to convene a panel of experts to prevent reading failure in the early elementary grades.[47] First, the problem stream flowed from state-level NAEP data in California, which revealed that a majority of fourth-graders could not read at a basic level of performance. Second, the political stream originated from state policymakers' reaction to efforts to win the reading wars by mandating phonics instruction in classrooms where whole-language texts and instruction prevailed. Third, the policy stream emerged from the National Institute of Child Health and Human Development (NICHD), which began to ask and answer timely questions for policymakers and practitioners. In 1993, NICHD encouraged the research community to submit applications for research that addressed the practical question, "Which single treatment/intervention or combination of interventions, provided in which setting or combination of settings, has (have) the most effective impact on well-defined domains of children functioning, for how long, and for what reasons?"[48] Under the leadership of G.

Reid Lyon, NICHD advanced its research agenda by funding a programmatic series of experimental and longitudinal studies that showed how appropriate interventions targeted from kindergarten to third grade could reduce failure levels in reading.[49] Converging lines of evidence from basic and applied research began to show that early intervention and direct instruction in phonics could reduce reading failure before third grade.

Given the substantial body of research on the basic processes underlying reading development and the efficacy of different instructional strategies, the National Research Council (NRC) convened leading scholars to synthesize findings from the scientific literature. Published in 1998, *Preventing Reading Difficulties in Young Children* sought to provide lay audiences and decisionmakers with an integrated picture of how reading skills develop and how to prevent reading failure. According to Catherine Snow, the chair of the NRC report, the consensus about early reading, how it developed, and how instruction facilitated reading ability was "not difficult to reach."[50] The NRC's "core message" to practitioners was that instruction should "integrate attention to the alphabetic principle with attention to the construction of meaning and opportunities to develop fluency."[51] In making its final recommendations, the NRC report exhorted scholars and federal lawmakers: "Research toward increasing the efficacy of classroom reading instruction in kindergarten and the primary grades should be the number one funding priority."[52] It concluded with 18 additional questions to guide a research agenda on effective primary-grade interventions. Similar to earlier expert panel reports from the 1970s and 1980s, the 1998 NRC report rejected the simplistic dualism between phonics and whole language and raised new questions for fruitful inquiry and research. However, since the panel did not focus its review on questions about the efficacy of different instructional methods, Congress authorized a second panel of experts to conduct an objective review of studies that could provide clear instructional guidance to classroom teachers.

On July 24, 1997, the Senate Committee on Appropriations authorized the director of NICHD to assemble a national panel to synthesize the best research on the effectiveness of different approaches to teaching reading. Senator Arlen Specter stated that the committee was

> impressed with the important accomplishments reported from the NICHD research program on reading development and disability, and is eager to have this information brought to the attention of educators, policymakers, and parents.[53]

The goal of including panelists with diverse professional backgrounds was reinforced in the authorizing statute, which called for a National Reading

Panel of "leading scientists in reading research, representatives of colleges of education, reading teachers, educational administrators, and parents."[54]

On balance, the 15 panelists were primarily tenured professors in psychology and education and many were leaders in the field of literacy research.[55] Given the unique expertise of each panel member, the NRP eventually formed subgroups that each focused on one of six areas of research: alphabetics (phonemic awareness and phonics instruction), fluency (oral guided reading and independent silent reading), comprehension (vocabulary and text comprehension instruction), teacher education, computer technology, and methodology. By reviewing multiple instructional strategies, the NRP's review implicitly rejected the idea that either phonics or whole-language instruction could produce superior reading achievement. In the words of one of the panelists on the NRP, Congress wanted to settle the "Reading Wars," and put an "end to the inflated rhetoric, partisan lobbying, and uninformed decisionmaking that have been so widespread and so detrimental to the progress of reading instruction in America's schools."[56]

To make credible causal inferences about the effects of instructional approaches on student outcomes, panelists reviewed only published studies using experimental and quasi-experimental designs.[57] Given the inclusion criteria, panel member Timothy Shanahan asserted that the report "will be, perhaps, the most thorough and explicit review of these topics ever conducted in reading."[58] And by describing in detail the steps that went into the meta-analytic review, the NRP hoped to encourage public scrutiny and review of its procedures and findings.

THE IMPACT OF THE NRP ON RESEARCHERS, POLICYMAKERS, AND PROFESSIONAL ORGANIZATIONS

In 2000, two NRP reports went to press—a 464-page full report with technical details, filled with tables of coding schemes, effect sizes, and p values, and a 33-page summary of the full report. The meta-analysis showed that instruction in phonemic awareness, phonics, and guided oral reading fluency improved children's ability to read words, to read connected text with speed and accuracy, and to comprehend text. Moreover, the report underscored the importance of embedding specific instructional strategies in a comprehensive reading program. For example, although phonics improved word recognition ability, the NRP emphasized that "systematic phonics instruction should be integrated with other reading instruction to create a balanced reading program. Phonics instruction is never a total reading program."[59] In addition, the NRP found that providing support and guidance during oral reading of text helped children improve their ability to read connected text with greater speed, accuracy, and comprehension. However, the NRP cautioned that guided oral reading should be used as part of "an overall reading program, not as stand alone-interventions."[60]

More broadly, the empirical findings affirmed the vital role that teachers played in improving children's reading skill. The NRP concluded that explicit instruction involving phonemic awareness, phonics, oral guided reading, and comprehension strategies was more effective in improving children's reading skills than student-centered approaches like sustained silent reading, in which children received little or no guidance from teachers in selecting and reading text.[61] Thus, the NRP concluded that teacher-directed instruction was essential to improving children's reading, a robust finding that has been documented in over 100 years of education research.[62]

Since 2000, the NRP's findings have garnered the attention of researchers, policymakers, and practitioners. The findings of the NRP have been widely cited by researchers and subjected to creative re-analyses that have shed light on new questions and influenced federal policy.[63] In particular, the NRP's findings on (1) phonemic awareness training, (2) phonics instruction, (3) fluency, (4) comprehension strategies, and (5) vocabulary instruction eventually shaped the Reading First legislation. States and districts must show how federal dollars will support each of the five pillars of scientifically based reading instruction in Reading First schools.[64]

Professional organizations also helped translate the NRP's findings for its members. The International Reading Association, an organization for reading researchers and practitioners, published a 2002 book titled *Evidence-Based Reading Instruction: Putting the National Reading Panel Report into Practice*. This edited volume included recent publications from *Reading Teacher* (an International Reading Association publication with wide circulation to teachers), to guide research-based practice based in each of the five components of instruction reviewed by the NRP, and, according to the editors, "will be a useful tool for educators as they implement practices consistent with scientifically based reading research and the provisions of Reading First."[65] For the members of the of the American Federation of Teachers (AFT), the NRP reiterated findings from Louisa C. Moats's 1999 publication, *Teaching Reading Is Rocket Science*, a lay-friendly publication that summarized research on phonemic awareness, phonics, fluency, vocabulary, and comprehension instruction. Echoing Chall and Adams's earlier works on the value of literature-rich and skill-based instruction, Moats asserted that "teachers need to connect the teaching of skills with the joy of reading, and writing, using read-alouds and the motivating activities popularized by the whole-language movement."[66]

Because Moats's book had already been disseminated to a large number of teachers, many practitioners were also familiar with the five pillars of scientifically based reading instruction articulated by the NRP report.

Furthermore, the full-length NRP report was condensed into a simpler 33-page summary report for teachers and lay audiences. Critics charged, however, that the summary report misrepresented the findings on the efficacy of phonics instruction. Although the full NRP report provided insufficient data to draw conclusions about the effects of phonics instruction above first grade, the summary indicated that systematic phonics benefited children from kindergarten to sixth grade.[67] Agreeing that the translation of findings was less than perfect, panel member Timothy Shanahan concurred that the summary was an incomplete and inaccurate summary of the full report. More specifically, he noted that the summary "conveys the idea that good, older readers should be taught phonics, something neither stated nor implied in the report."[68] Shanahan added that one remedy to this problem was to make sure that more teachers read the entire full report and enacted evidence-based practices in their classrooms.

Some scholars, however, have challenged the notion that the NRP has promoted good instruction and supported professional autonomy. Richard Allington, a reading professor at the University of Tennessee, charges that the National Reading Panel's findings have been used by proponents of direct instruction and intensive phonics to impose external mandates on teachers. According to Allington, legislative mandates and expert panel reports strip teachers of the autonomy to make curricular and instructional decisions. And if lawmakers and professors have the power to govern curriculum and instruction, Allington wonders whether teachers will continue to feel like autonomous professionals who hold themselves accountable for helping children become independent and skilled readers.[69]

DISCUSSION

"The history of medicine has been written as an epic of progress, but it is also the tale of . . . conflict over the emergence of new hierarchies of power and authority," writes sociologist Paul Starr in his Pulitzer Prize–winning book, *The Social Transformation of American Medicine, The Rise of a Sovereign Profession and the Making of a Vast Industry.*[70] In many ways, the history of the reading wars might aptly be characterized as an "epic of progress" and a "tale of conflict." The story of progress shows how research findings converged over four decades to form the basis for national policy, most notably in the 2001 Reading First legislation. The story of conflict suggests that research was also a weak countervailing force in the pendulum swings between whole-language and phonics instruction that took place in state legislatures during the 1980s and 1990s. In the following discussion, my goal is describe *how* controversies about instruction in beginning reading have been resolved through normal scientific inquiry and *why* good research alone cannot shape sound instructional policies and practices in reading.

Jeanne Chall's 1967 book *Learning to Read: The Great Debate*, the National Institute of Education's 1985 report *Becoming a Nation of Readers*, the 1998 National Reading Council book *Preventing Reading Difficulties in Young Children*, and the 2000 National Reading Panel report share several qualities of "normal science." According to historian of science Thomas Kuhn, "normal science" builds on "past scientific achievements" and "is sufficiently open-ended to leave all sorts of problems for the redefined group of practitioners to resolve."[71] Major research syntheses of reading traveled down the path of normal science by recognizing the convergent, cumulative, and replicated findings in the scientific research literature. These reports, however, did not immediately or directly impact reading policy and practice. After all, it took the accumulation of three decades of research before a substantive meta-analysis of instruction in phonemic awareness, phonics, fluency, vocabulary, and comprehension could be undertaken in the late 1990s. Nonetheless, the reports showed how substantial agreement in the scientific community was needed before firm recommendations could be made for policymakers and practitioners.

In the conclusion of *Learning to Read: The Great Debate*, Jeanne Chall asserted that scholarship in reading "should follow the norms of science" by building on the past and raising new questions and hypotheses; a scholar "must try to learn from the work of those who preceded him . . . knowing that neither he nor anyone following him will have the final word."[72] Chall's observations about the conduct of normal science were realized in the ensuing debates about the merits of phonics instruction. Although Chall found experimental evidence supporting phonics instruction over whole-word reading methods in first grade, Kenneth Goodman challenged these conclusions by speculating that context cues were equally, if not more, important than knowledge of spelling–sound relationships in helping children read new words. Like debates in any scientific field, the novel "psycholinguistic theory of reading" proposed by Goodman sparked the interest of other scholars. According to psychologist Keith Stanovich, "Ken Goodman conducted the well-known 1965 study that focused so many of us in the early 1970s on the study of the effects of context on reading."[73] Eventually, Stanovich and others found that reliance on context slowed down word recognition abilities and was a strategy used by poor readers. Skilled readers, on the other hand, were able to apply knowledge of the alphabetic principle to quickly and automatically read new words. The dispute about the role of context in word reading underscores a truth about scientific progress: No single scholar or individual study dictated the scientific consensus about the processes underlying skillful reading. As Thomas Kuhn points out, the progressive accumulation of research findings produces a discernible "shift in the distribution of professional allegiances" of members in the scientific community.[74]

That shift in professional allegiances among scholars was captured in consensus panel reports from the 1970s and 1990s, which sought to reject simplistic approaches to reading instruction. In *Toward a Literacy Society*, a 1975 publication sponsored by the National Institute of Education, Chall argued that neither phonics nor sight-word approaches were sufficient to help children become skilled readers. Instead, she reminded educators and the general public that inflexible approaches "may fail with a child if in the long run it plays down either of these aspects of learning to read. What is important is a proper balance between them."[75] A second NIE publication in 1985, *Becoming a Nation of Readers*, extended Chall's work and synthesized new findings from cognitive psychology and related disciplines. It argued for the need to go beyond word reading and decoding strategies and emphasized the importance of oral language and text comprehension. By broadening its survey of the scientific literature, the report encouraged the scientific community to undertake multi-disciplinary studies of reading and to examine the efficacy of diverse approaches to instruction. In 1998, the National Reading Council publication, *Preventing Reading Difficulties in Young Children*, recognized convergent findings from diverse scientific disciplines and deepened the foundation on which to base evidence-based reading instruction.

The culmination of nearly three decades of research resulted in the 2000 National Reading Panel report. By raising questions about the efficacy of different instructional approaches and by restricting its review to findings from experiments and quasi-experiments published in peer-reviewed journals, the NRP influenced federal policy and classroom practice. Scientifically based reading instruction needed to focus on word-, sentence-, and text-level outcomes, and claims about the efficacy of different instructional strategies needed the backing of experimental data. Pushing the public and decision-makers to think beyond the phonics–whole-language dichotomy, the NRP helped reframe definitions about scientifically based research and practice in reading. Moreover, the findings from the National Reading Panel eventually shaped the Reading First legislation in the No Child Left Behind Act, which required eligible Title I schools to adopt scientifically based research practices in five areas of reading instruction: phonemic awareness, phonics, fluency, vocabulary, and comprehension instruction. The five pillars of good reading instruction articulated a new grammar of schooling in education by encouraging practitioners to focus on a broad set of instructional strategies and reading outcomes.

Tracing the evolution of scientific consensus in reading may paint an overly simplistic and teleological version of history—a kind of inevitable and progressive accumulation of research toward the ultimate goal of improving instruction and achievement. However, the reading wars are also a tale of conflict and of pendulum swings between externally mandated whole-language practices and phonics legislation during the 1980s and 1990s. The story of conflict offers some reasons why research alone cannot protect educators from unproven theories and policies, whether originating in the minds of an academic researcher or the actions of a state education official. In particular, I elaborate on three characteristics of scholarly research and the scientific community that help explain why research does not immediately influence and shape education policies.

First, the results of normal scientific inquiry are usually reported in peer-reviewed journal articles, slowing down the dissemination of scientific research findings to decisionmakers and lay audiences. From the 1960s to 1980s, scientists began to undertake basic research on the processes underlying skillful reading in laboratories, and applied research on the efficacy of different instructional approaches in classroom settings. However, it took several decades for researchers to highlight convergent findings and make recommendations for teachers.[76] Louisa C. Moats has observed, "there is always a long delay between developments in academic research disciplines and their incorporation into teaching practice."[77] Research often takes several decades to bear fruit, but decisionmakers cannot wait for decades to help struggling readers. Consequently, the demands facing a state education official, superintendent, or teacher create pressures for immediate action and quick solutions. Research that is unavailable for decades cannot inform decisionmaking today.

Speeding up the process by which scientific controversies are resolved may equip practitioners with more relevant and timely information. Adversarial collaboration represents a recent effort among scientists to accelerate the process for resolving controversies. Expounded in the journal *Psychological Science*, the editors expressed hope that adversarial collaboration would become a more widely used protocol for adjudicating disputes between scholars and disseminating findings quickly to avoid ongoing controversy.[78] The procedure requires adversaries in a scholarly debate to agree on basic design issues and research questions *before* they conduct the study. In addition, it requires antagonists to collaborate on a prospective study and agree on an arbiter who imposes the rules of engagement over the entire process. The arbiter helps adversaries decide on the design of the experiment, controls the data, determines the final venue for publication, and can even declare in the final publication if an uncooperative participant failed to comply with the agreed-upon protocol. In other words, adversarial collaboration represents a potentially valuable and under-utilized tool for mediating conflict in scientific debates. In the future, it might help to adjudicate debates in reading and the many education policy controversies outlined in this volume.[79] Ideally, encouraging adversaries to collaborate on prospective studies would accelerate the resolution of conflict in the research community and provide the kind of scientific consensus that informs good practice in schools.

Second, normal science depends on the validation of research findings by a community of experts who are expected to remain objective participants in democratic debates. Scientists are asked to educate, not advocate. "One of the strongest, if still unwritten, rules of scientific life is the prohibition of appeals to heads of state or to the populace at large in matters scientific," observes Thomas Kuhn.[80] These strong professional norms create disincentives for scholars to jump into the policy area and advocate for specific policies or educational curricula. Therefore, the mere existence of good research is no guarantee that such knowledge will be communicated to policymakers. Nonetheless, the critical perspective of scientists performs a valuable function in a democracy where public policies are crafted by politicians in local school boards, state legislatures, and Congress. Scientists do not have power or authority to mandate phonics instruction, to adopt literature-based basal texts, or to define scientifically based reading instruction in federal statutes. They can, however, encourage legislators to evaluate untested policies before they are brought to scale.

For example, the critical perspective of a social scientist played a vital role in causing Tennessee legislators to require an evaluation of class size reduction in the mid-1980s. Although state lawmakers wanted to enact class size reductions to improve student achievement in the early grades, Steven Cobb, a sociologist by training, encouraged a randomized experiment to evaluate the efficacy of small class sizes on student learning.[81] Tennessee lawmakers eventually passed legislation to undertake a statewide experiment called Project STAR (Student Teacher Achievement Ratio), which has been hailed by scholars as one of the most influential studies in education.[82] "The role of social science research," writes Daniel Patrick Moynihan, "lies not in the formulation social policy, but in the measurement of its results."[83] When sociologists like Steven Cobb and Daniel Moynihan enter the political arena, they often contribute to democratic debate by encouraging critical evaluation of unproven and costly policies. Had social scientists shared findings from Stahl and Miller's meta-analysis of whole language with state legislators, perhaps California's state officials would have called for a smaller pilot study or an evaluation of whole-language practices before it was implemented in all districts and schools.

Third, the federal government has frequently turned to scientists, not teachers, to determine evidence-based practice. The assumption, of course, is that scientists have the tools and knowledge to understand research and can therefore establish norms of practice that buffer the teaching profession from fads, ideology, and political intrusion. To practitioners, however, experts can be viewed as novices who know little about teaching in the public schools, and effect sizes from a meta-analysis can be viewed as irrelevant tools for addressing the range of skills and performance in a classroom of 30 first-graders. Indeed, Joanne Yatvin, the lone practitioner on the National Reading Panel, wondered how professional standards could be determined primarily by scholars who do not teach children how to read. In filing a Minority View in the appendix of the NRP, Yatvin argued that panelists failed to subject their results to the scrutiny of teachers. "Outside teacher reviewers," Yatvin argued, "should have been brought in to critique the panel's conclusion, just as outside scientists were to critique its processes."[84]

Without being represented on these expert panels, teachers and their allies have frequently asserted that external mandates by federal and state lawmakers and consensus reports by university researchers undercut the professional autonomy of K–12 teachers. Professionally eclectic expert panels in reading—perhaps even an equal number of teachers and professors—might address these criticisms by giving voice to teachers. For example, by including an equal number of teachers and nonteachers on the United Kingdom's National Literacy Task Force, political leaders encouraged recommendations for improving reading instruction that integrated the practical knowledge of teachers and findings from researchers.[85] Recent efforts to bridge the gap between researchers and practitioners provide hopeful signs that collaborative efforts may deepen the legitimacy of scientific evidence among teachers and encourage researchers to pursue answers to relevant, practical questions. For example, the International Reading Association (IRA) and the National Institute of Child Health and Human Development (NICHD) jointly sponsored a research seminar on teaching English-language learners. According to Peggy McCardle, the chief of the Child Development and Behavior Branch for NICHD, the long-term goal of these collaborative meetings is to "get researchers talking both to each other and to practitioners."[86] In addition to fostering dialogue, inviting teachers and researchers to make policy may empower teachers to shape the norms governing their profession.

CONCLUSION

By design, normal science proceeds slowly and convergent findings take decades to evolve. By tradition, scientists must embrace neutrality in public policy debates and avoid partisanship in controversies about reading instruction. And by necessity, government has usually turned to university professors to translate scientific research and technical findings in academic journals for classroom teachers and lay audiences. The defining characteristics of normal science are in many respects virtues of the scientific enterprise. Waiting 30 years for scientists to conduct enough studies to be included in the National Reading Panel's meta-analyses seems worthwhile if these research findings are helping to improve the quality of teaching and learning in classrooms. Recent efforts to speed up the resolution of scientific controversy, to encourage communication between social scientists and policymakers, and to forge collaborations between research and practitioner communities may help resolve conflict in reading and other areas of education policy and practice. In the long-run, it is unclear whether any of these initiatives will create an enduring peace in the reading wars.

Perhaps the surest path to protecting reading policy and practice from radical pendulum swings, fads, and ideology is to create a sovereign profession. Ultimately, teachers must be involved in establishing and regulating professional norms. Sociologist Paul Starr asserts that the legitimacy of professional authority and competence rests on "three distinctive claims: first, that knowledge and competence of the professional have been validated by a community of his or her peers; second, that this consensually validated knowledge and competence rest on rational, scientific grounds; and third, that the professional's judgment and advice are oriented toward a set of substantive values, such as health."[87]

Few would dispute that the teaching profession is oriented toward a substantive and valuable goal—the education and cognitive development of young children. Today, it would also be noncontroversial to suggest that substantial progress in reading research has built a strong empirical foundation for improving reading instruction. Yet the first claim of professional authority—the validation of professional competence by a community of peers—remains an elusive goal in American education. Among the professions, teachers remain in the unenviable position of lacking the power and authority to insulate good practice from the misguided theories of academic researchers or the faddish policies of political leaders.

In the future, will a community of practitioners validate the knowledge and ability of their colleagues' to instruct children how to read? Will teachers belong to a sovereign profession that compels its members to meet norms of excellence agreed upon by a community of peers, applies scientific research in shaping professional standards, and serves its clients well? Or will teaching remain a partial profession where professors and lawmakers possess the primary authority to mandate policy and shape practice? Empowering teachers to establish professional norms rooted in scientific research may help create a sovereign profession. Ultimately, teachers must have access to truth and power if they are to establish professional norms that support their efforts to help children become skilled readers and active participants in our democracy.

CHAPTER 5

Researcher Meets the Policy Realm: A Personal Account

Richard M. Ingersoll

Few educational problems have received more attention in recent times than the failure to ensure that our nation's elementary and secondary classrooms are all staffed with qualified teachers. Over the past couple of decades, dozens of studies, commissions, and national reports have bemoaned the quality of our teachers. As a result, there have been numerous policies and initiatives enacted at the federal, state, and local levels. The most significant of these efforts has been the No Child Left Behind Act (NCLB), enacted in 2002, which set an unprecedented goal to ensure that students are all taught by "highly qualified" teachers. These policies and initiatives have for the most part focused on either upgrading the education and preparation requirements for teachers, or on increasing recruitment and the incoming supply of teachers.[1]

Such concern with the quality and qualifications of teachers is neither unique nor surprising. Elementary and secondary schooling are mandatory and it is into the care of teachers that children are legally placed for a significant portion of their lives. The quality of teachers and teaching are undoubtedly among the most important factors shaping the learning and growth of students. Moreover, the largest single component of the cost of education in any country is teacher compensation.

However, though staffing all of the nation's classrooms with qualified teachers is a perennially important issue in our schools, it is also among the least understood. Like many similarly worthwhile reforms, I have come to conclude that the array of recent efforts, alone, will not solve the problem of underqualified teachers and low-quality teaching in this country, because they do not address some of the key causes.

One of the least recognized of these causes is the phenomenon known as out-of-field teaching—teachers assigned to teach subjects for which they have little preparation, education, or background. This is a crucial factor because highly qualified teachers may actually become highly unqualified if, once on the job, they are assigned to teach subjects for which they have little background or preparation. Educators, and those closely familiar with the way schools operate, have long known of the existence of out-of-field teaching. James Conant called attention to the widespread "misuse of teachers" through out-of-field assignments in his landmark 1963 study *The Education of American Teachers*.[2] Albert Shanker condemned out-of-field teaching as education's 'dirty little secret' in a 1985 opinion piece in the *New York Times*.[3] But this seemingly odd and irrational practice has been largely unknown to the public and to policymakers. Until recently, almost no empirical research had been done on out-of-field teaching. Indeed, very few writings on schools have even acknowledged the existence of this practice.

One of the reasons for the lack of recognition of this problem was an absence of accurate data. This situation was remedied beginning in 1990, with the first release of the Schools and Staffing Survey (SASS), a major new survey of the nation's elementary and secondary teachers conducted every few years by the National Center for Education Statistics (NCES), the statistical arm of the Department of Education. Working with this dataset in the early 1990s, several of us discovered that we could, for the first time, accurately calculate how much out-of-field teaching goes on in this country.

My interest in these issues originally stemmed from previous experiences as a secondary school teacher, first in western Canada and then later in New York, Pennsylvania, and finally in Delaware, near where I had grown up. The job of teaching, I found to my surprise, was very different in Canada than in the United States. One of the major differences was out-of-field teaching. In the Canadian schools in which I taught, misassignment was a frowned-upon and rare occurrence. In contrast, out-of-field teaching was neither frowned upon, nor rare, in the secondary schools, both public and private, in which I taught in the United States. Indeed, it seemed commonplace. My field of training was social studies, but hardly a semester went by in which I was not also assigned a couple of classes in other fields, such as math or special education. In my experience, being a successful teacher required knowing both the subject matter and how to get that across to the students. I found teaching subjects for which I had little background very challenging. Two such experiences in particular stood out to me.

At one point in my career, I accepted a job at an expensive private boarding school in New England as a history and social studies teacher. Upon arriving at the school, I was surprised to find that my job had been changed by the headmaster; for half of my course load I was re-assigned to one-on-one teaching of remedial language skills to dyslexic students. I approached the headmaster to ask if this change might be re-considered, as I had no knowledge of, nor experience with, dyslexia and its remediation. He was unhappily surprised at my response and it became clear that misassignment was a normal and unquestioned administrative prerogative in his school. The headmaster concluded that I was not sufficiently "committed," was not a "team player," and demanded that I quit, or be fired. I quit and was quickly and easily replaced with a new teacher, less resistant to misassignment. Although out-of-field teaching was a normal practice at this setting, knowledge of it was carefully kept from parents and of little interest to the relevant authorities. Indeed, when I reported this incident to the regional school accreditation agency, charged with overseeing school quality standards, they responded that such "internal management" affairs were not their concern.

The second experience took place in a public high school in Delaware. In late August one year, just prior to the start of the semester, I received a memo from the principal indicating that my course assignments for the year had been changed. In place of teaching my most prized course—a senior elective in social problems—I had been assigned to teach two classes in 9th- and 10th-grade algebra. I went to the principal to ask why he had made this change and to stress that I had little background in math and could hardly recall what algebra was. His response was to wish me good luck. In the ensuing weeks, I rushed to search out the math teachers in the school, from which to beg and borrow texts, worksheets, and tests. I learned that it is not easy to teach algebraic equations to teenagers. A great deal of trial and error ensued, and the year was spent staying up late at night trying to stay one chapter ahead of my students.

My experiences left me with a number of questions: Were the schools in which I taught unusual in this regard? Or, was out-of-field teaching a common practice in other schools across the country? And, if so, why? Later, after leaving secondary teaching and completing a doctorate in sociology, I got the opportunity to investigate these questions in a large-scale research project using the Schools and Staffing Survey.

Even I was surprised by what I found—that out-of-field teaching is a widespread and chronic practice in a large number of American schools. The data indicated, for instance, that about one-third of secondary-level math teachers have little formal preparation in math. Notably, my results were replicated by several NCES analysts.[4] I began publishing the results in the mid-1990s, first in two reports contracted by NCES.[5] Over the next decade, I published dozens of pieces on the issue of underqualified teachers, ranging from brief op-ed essays, to short summaries of the data, to lengthy scholarly articles laden with statistical analyses.[6]

The results also surprised others and captured widespread interest. Out-of-field teaching and the data from my research, and that of others, began to be widely reported in the media, beginning with an article in 1996 in the *Atlanta Journal Constitution*. Numerous newspaper editorials and syndicated columnists also took up the topic and put their spin on the data, representing a variety of political orientations.

Simultaneously, numerous education advocacy groups began to pick up on the problem of out-of-field teaching and featured my and others' research in reports and documents. Among the first of these was the National Commission on Teaching and America's Future (NCTAF), an organization advocating for upgrading and professionalizing teacher education and certification, led at the time by Linda Darling-Hammond. NCTAF issued two widely distributed reports—*What Matters Most* in 1996 and *Doing Want Matters Most* in 1997—both of which featured the new data on out-of-field teaching.[7] This group's early interest and wide influence turned out to be significant for how the data were to be subsequently framed and interpreted. The Education Trust, an advocacy group focused on educational equity, was another prominent organization that featured my data early on, first in a 1996 report titled *Education Watch*, and subsequently in their ongoing newsletter, *Thinking K–16*, as well as in a number of later reports.[8]

Over the next few years, interest multiplied. I received many dozens of invitations to speak on my research from a wide range of groups. My data were included or featured in numerous other documents and reports by groups such as the National Governor's Association, the Gannett News Service, the National Center for Public Policy and Higher Education, and in *Education Week*'s annual supplement, "Quality Counts," in 1998 and 2003.[9] In some cases, these groups simply used already published data, in other cases they contracted with me to do data "runs," that is, to generate specific indicators and statistics using the SASS raw data files, and in even other cases they commissioned me to write papers and reports presenting the data, which they would then publish.

As a result of all of the attention generated by the data, by the late 1990s the problem of out-of-field teaching became a concern in the realm of education policy. Findings from my and others' research were frequently used by federal and state lawmakers. President Clinton cited my data and even used my own words in some of his speeches in 1997 promoting his various teacher training and recruitment initiatives. I found myself invited to address numerous legislative groups and forums at local, state, and federal levels, beginning with the House congressional hearings on education in 1998.[10] The research and data had a direct influence on NCLB, which explicitly requires secondary-level teachers to establish competency in each of the academic fields they are assigned to teach.[11]

At first glance, this story seems to be an example of success from the perspective of advocates of data-based decisionmaking and of greater use of "scientifically based" data and research to inform policy in education. The release of new data provided a first-time opportunity for researchers, the public, and policymakers to learn about a little-known but widespread phenomenon. And indeed, a national problem was seemingly "discovered." The data were widely disseminated and had—and still have—an influence on policy. Moreover, the data provide a rare "teaching moment." Examining the practice of out-of-field teaching opens an unusual window into the internal workings of schools. It has the potential to allow the public to glimpse how schools really utilize and manage—or mis-utilize and mismanage—their key human resource: teachers.

But, in some ways this story is not an example of success from the perspective of data-based decisionmaking and the use of data and research in education policy. Indeed, in some ways this has been an example of where having a little bit of information may prove to be worse than having no information at all. Despite a growing awareness of this problem and its importance, out-of-field teaching remains, unfortunately, widely misunderstood—and in ways that have strong implications for fixing the problem. Rather than using the data to understand the character and sources of out-of-field teaching, the data have at times been used to draw attention to other problems and have been misunderstood and misrepresented to advance normative agendas. Sometimes, such misinterpretation seemed to be a result of honest misunderstanding; other times, it appeared willful. Indeed, rather than data-based decisionmaking, at times my experience seemed to resemble James March's famous garbage can model of decisionmaking, where data, goals, interests, and actors are incoherently coupled, mixed, and matched.[12]

For me, this professional experience has been both personally gratifying and personally frustrating. One the one hand, it can be very gratifying and flattering to see interest taken in, and use made of, one's work and research. After all, this is not common in academia and most of the research we academics do lies unread in dusty journals. On the other hand, it can be very frustrating to see one's work and research widely misrepresented and used to promote policies and remedies that are not supported by that same research—policies and remedies that may do more harm than good. My response to this turn of events has been to spend much time over the past decade writing and speaking, trying to counter these misrepresentations and to develop, test, and disseminate an alternative interpretation of the data. This response, in turn, posed career challenges for me because applied and policy-oriented research is frowned upon in some parts of academia, especially departments in the arts and sciences. It can be difficult to publish such research in mainstream academic journals. And such research may count little toward promotion and tenure. Like other academics who undertake policy research and who engage in public debates, at times I felt I had to carry on something of a double life and hide my nonacademic research interests from my colleagues.

In this chapter I will try to tell this story. I begin by briefly summarizing what my research revealed about out-of-field teaching. Following that, I turn to the larger policy context and several influential, but incorrect, interpretations of the data that have gained widespread currency. Subsequently, I summarize my own interpretation of the data, and conclude by laying out the implications for research and for policy.

THE RESEARCH

When I began analyzing the SASS data in the early 1990s, I quickly discovered that undertaking empirical assessments of the extent of underqualified and out-of-field teaching presents serious methodological problems. Research on out-of-field teaching has not occurred in a vacuum. The environment surrounding issues of teacher quality and qualifications has been highly charged and highly politicized (a subject I will turn to in more detail in the next section). Although there is almost universal agreement that teachers do matter, and that student learning is affected by the quality of teaching, there is a great deal of disagreement, often heated, concerning how many and which kinds of preparation and credentials teachers ought to have to be considered "adequately qualified." This debate and lack of consensus over how to define a qualified teacher has serious implications for anyone attempting to do research on underqualified teachers.

Those of us who do this research have developed a couple of dozen different measures of out-of-field teaching, which vary depending upon whether the measures focus on the numbers of teachers doing it or the numbers of students exposed to it, according to which fields and subjects they examine, according to which school grade levels are included, and, most importantly, according to how they define a qualified teacher. Because there have not been national databases available with accurate information on teachers' college course transcripts or test scores, in addition to their course assignments, those of us who do this research typically turn to whether teachers have one or more credentials, such as a college degree or teaching certificate, in the fields they teach. Each of our different measures has its own advantages and disadvantages, and whatever definition and measure one chooses will have its critics.[13]

Early on I decided to try to skirt the endless debate over how to best define an adequately qualified teacher by adopting a minimal definition and by focusing on the most compelling case. My primary focus became discovering how many of those teaching core academic subjects at the secondary level do not have at least a college minor in their teaching fields. Having a college minor, of course, does not guarantee quality teaching, or even a qualified teacher. I viewed a college minor in the subject as a minimal prerequisite. In short, I assumed that few parents would want or expect their teenagers to be taught, for example, 11th-grade trigonometry by a teacher who did not have a minor in math—or something related like math education or physics—no matter how bright the teacher.

From my personal perspective as a former high school teacher, and as a parent myself, I had assumed such an assumption was unexceptional and a matter of common sense. However, I quickly discovered that I was naïve. Some skeptics doubted the necessity of teacher background preparation in a subject, argued that out-of-field teaching is not really "much of a problem," and devalued the necessity or relevance of research or policy on it. I quickly found such skeptics could be quite strident and aggressive.[14] Rather than debate endlessly whether the existing research does or does not support such an assumption, I found that the best response was to bring the debate down to a concrete and personal level by asking the skeptic if, other things equal, they would be comfortable if their child's science teacher did not have at least a college minor or major in one of the sciences. This may have not been a scientifically based method, but it seemed to work to quiet most such critics.

The SASS data show, indeed, that millions of teenagers were and are in this situation. As illustrated in Figure 5.1, over a third of all secondary school teachers who teach math do not have either an undergraduate or graduate major or minor in math, math education, or related disciplines like engineering or physics. About one-third of all secondary school English teachers have neither a major or minor in English or related subjects such as literature, communications, speech, journalism, English education, or reading education. In science, just over one-quarter of all secondary school teachers do not have at least a minor in one of the sciences or in science education. Finally, about a quarter of social studies teachers are without at least a minor in any of the social sciences, in social studies education, or in history.[15]

Moreover, teachers in broad multidiscipline fields, such as science and social studies, are routinely required to teach any of a wide array of disciplines within the larger field, but may be qualified to teach only some of them. For example, a teacher with a degree in biology and a teaching certificate in science may not be qualified to teach physics. So, when I raised the standard for a qualified teacher within science and social studies to a major or minor in the subfield taught, I found high levels of within-department but out-of-field teaching. For example, over half of those teaching physical science classes (chemistry, physics, earth or space science) are without a major or minor in any of these physical sciences. Likewise, over half of all those teaching history are without a major or minor in history itself.

Out-of-field teaching is chronic—levels have changed little from 1987 up to the present. In each of the fields of English and math and history, every year well over four million secondary-level students are taught by teachers with neither a major nor a minor in the field. However, there are striking differences in the amount of out-of-field teaching across different types of schools. In particular, teachers in high poverty schools are more likely to be out-of-field than are teachers in more affluent schools.

Of course, some of these out-of-field teachers may actually be qualified, despite not having a minor or major or a certificate in the subject. However, the starting premise in my research was that even a moderate number of teachers lacking the minimal prerequisite of a college minor signals the existence of a serious problem. To advocates of raising standards of teacher quality, whether they were teachers, policymakers, or parents of school-age children, the data raised a red flag. They also raised numerous questions.

For instance, given the ongoing national concern over the relatively low achievement test scores of U.S. students in comparison to students in numerous other nations, many viewed the data on levels of out-of-field teaching as particularly relevant. Is it any surprise, they asked, that science achievement is so low given, that even at the 12th-grade level, 41 percent of public school students in chemistry, physics, or other physical science classes in the United States are taught by someone with neither a major nor a minor in either chemistry, physics, or another physical science? In a recent cross-national study, I found nations with high-scoring students, such as Korea and Japan and Singapore, tend to have very little out-of-field teaching.[16]

FIGURE 5.1 Percentage of Public Secondary School (Grades 7–12) Teachers in the Core Academic Fields Without a Major or Minor in That Field (1999-2000).

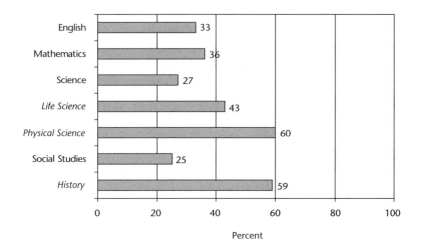

Source: Ingersoll, R. (2003) Out-of-Field Teaching and the Limits of Teacher Policies. Consortium for Policy Research in Education, University of Pennsylvania

Some of the most important consequences of out-of-field teaching are, however, probably those not easily quantified. The effects of being taught by a teacher without a strong background in a field may be just the kind of outcome not captured in student scores on short-answer standardized examinations. Teachers assigned to teach a subject for which they have little background are probably more likely to overly rely on textbooks (as was my own case), and the kinds of learning obtained from textbooks is probably what standardized examinations best capture. One can easily imagine the limitations imposed by a lack of subject background on a teacher's ability to teach for critical thinking and to engage the students' interest in the subject—the kinds of learning probably not well captured by standardized examinations.

Moreover, teachers who do a lot of out-of-field teaching most likely do not have the opportunity to acquire what has been called pedagogical content knowledge—knowing which approach to use with particular subjects in particular kinds of settings. Much of what constitutes effective teaching may not necessarily be generic, but may be highly nuanced, depending on the specific situation, subject matter, grade level, and type of student.

High levels of out-of-field assignments could also negatively affect the learning environment for all students in schools, not just for those students unlucky enough to be taught by out-of-field teachers. The assignment of teachers to teach fields in which they have no background could change the allocation of their preparation time across their courses—decreasing the amount of time they spend preparing for their other courses in order to prepare for the one(s) for which they have no background.

There are, moreover, consequences for teachers to be considered. Having to cope with out-of-field assignments comes on top of an already burdensome teaching load for most public secondary teachers, who are assigned an average of 128 students and five classes per day. What is the impact on teachers' sense of efficacy of having to teach courses for which they have little formal preparation? Are out-of-field assignments associated with decreases in teachers' morale and commitment and increases in turnover? Moreover, one might also ask, does out-of-field teaching have any effect on the legitimacy and authority of teachers and, hence, classroom discipline?

THE TEACHER QUALITY DEBATE

Research on out-of-field teaching has not occurred in a vacuum, and it is useful to discuss its context because this shaped how the data have been greeted, interpreted and used. While recently undertaking a cross-national study of teachers, I learned that the subject of teacher quality is a source of much debate and disagreement in many nations.[17] But, I also learned that nowhere has this debate been more pronounced and more divisive than in the United States. Indeed, parallel to the much-discussed "reading wars," it is probably not an exaggeration to refer to analogous "teacher quality wars." Over the past two decades, the quality of teacher education and the quality of teachers have been widely criticized in the United States, by those inside and outside the educational sector.[18] However, while there is widespread consensus that a problem exists, there is little consensus in regard to the sources and reasons behind the problem and, hence, the best strategies to improve things.

One of the most prominent viewpoints in this debate traces the problem of teacher quality to teacher preparation. In this view, college and university teacher education programs, and state certification standards, all too often lack adequate rigor, breadth, and depth. Accordingly, the solution, from this viewpoint, lies in making the entry and training requirements for teaching more restrictive, deeper, and more rigorous, as in the traditional higher prestige professions such as medicine, academia, and law. To this group, the surest way to upgrade the quality of teaching is to upgrade the qualifications standards required of new teachers. NCTAF has been among the prominent advocates of this view.[19]

An opposing viewpoint argues for deregulating entry into teaching. This viewpoint also holds that the quality of teacher education and certification is poor. But, rather than increasing requirements, this view holds that entry into the teaching occupation already is plagued by unusually restrictive and rigid bureaucratic barriers. These critics argue that there is little or no solid empirical research documenting the value of such entry requirements, and that such barriers discourage large numbers of high-quality candidates from getting into the occupation. By doing away with these regulatory impediments, this argument concludes, schools could finally recruit the kinds and numbers of candidates they deem best and this would solve the quality problems that plague teaching. The Fordham Foundation and a leading educational economist, Eric Hanushek, have been among the prominent advocates of this view.[20]

One of the more popular variants of this deregulation perspective favors a preparation model analogous to that utilized for entrance to post-secondary academic careers. The pre-employment preparation of professors in the United States usually includes little formal training in pedagogical and instructional methods. The assumption here appears to be that what holds in higher education also should hold in lower education, especially at the secondary level. Content or subject knowledge—knowing *what* to teach—is considered of primary importance for a qualified teacher. Formal professional training in pedagogical and methodological knowledge and skills—knowing *how* to teach—is considered less necessary, or even irrelevant.

Proponents of de-regulation have pushed a range of initiatives, most of which involve a loosening of the traditional occupational entry gates. Among the most widespread of these reforms are alternative certification programs, whereby college graduates can postpone formal education training, obtain an emergency teaching certificate, and begin teaching immediately.

It is important to note that proponents of each viewpoint—professionalization and deregulation—claim the same rationale: the enhanced recruitment of high-quality candidates into teaching. But often left unsaid are each view's differing implications for a crucial issue—costs. Professionalization and increased training would most likely necessitate increases in teacher compensation and, hence, increased labor costs. Deregulation and decreased entry requirements could lead to increases in teacher supply and, hence, decreases in teacher compensation and decreased labor costs.

Given such implications, the teacher quality debate has often been highly ideological and charged, making it difficult for neutral observers and policymakers to separate rhetoric from reality. Debate over teacher quality may be neither unique nor surprising, but it is illuminating to place this in context. Reflecting my own bias and training, one useful context is a cross-occupational comparison. How does teaching, its entry requirements, and research on their value compare with other lines of work?

In the United States, teaching as an occupation has an oddly ironic character. Compared with other occupations and professions, teaching has relatively low pre-employment entry requirements but, nevertheless, relatively high empirical scrutiny and skepticism of these low requirements.

Compared to other occupations and, especially to the traditional professions, such as law, medicine, engineering, dentistry, and academia, teaching has a relatively low entry bar, and a relatively wide entry gate.[21] Placed in this context, entry to teaching is among the least restrictive and least burdensome. However, though teaching's entry training and licensing requirements are lower than those for many other lines of work in the United States, they are subject to far more skepticism and empirical evaluation than for other lines of work. For most occupations and professions there has been little, if any, empirical research done assessing the value-added of practitioners having a particular credential, license, or certification.[22] Nevertheless, such barriers, whether enforced by precedent or by law, are common. Indeed, it is illegal to do many lines of work, from plumbing and hairstyling to law and medicine, without a license. In short, scientific-based decisionmaking is rare in regard to occupational and professional entry requirements.

In contrast, empirical assessment of teacher's qualifications is a well-worn path. There are literally hundreds of empirical studies, going back decades, devoted to evaluating the effects of elementary and secondary teacher qualifications on teacher performance.[23] Typically, such studies try to assess the relation between various measures of teacher preparation and various measures of student performance. And, contrary to skeptics, a number of rigorous studies have indeed found teacher education and preparation, of one sort or another, to be significantly related to increases in student achievement.[24] These are telling findings given the widespread criticism from both insiders and outsiders that teacher education is of low quality in the United States.

However, accurately isolating and capturing the effects of teacher's qualifications on their students' achievement is difficult, and not surprisingly, the results of such research are, at times, mixed and contradictory. Moreover, there also are large gaps in this research.[25] All of which provides further fuel for the ongoing debate and further fosters interest in, and funding for, ever-more-exacting and sophisticated scientific studies in this line of research. But, placed in a cross-occupational context, the mixed and limited quality of research documenting the value of the qualifications required of elementary and secondary teaching is not unusual; what is unusual is the existence of any such empirical research at all.

Comparing lower education with higher education is illuminating. Almost all universities and colleges in the United States require a doctorate degree for full-time professorial positions. Doctorates are a relatively high bar and require a relatively long time commitment. Some studies have put the average duration to obtain a PhD at over seven years. However, there are almost no examples of a "professor effects" literature examining the value-added of doctorate degrees and whether professors' qualifications have any effect on outcomes such as student achievement.[26] Moreover, there has been little research attempting to compare the quality of teaching in lower and higher education. I have uncovered one such study; it concluded that the caliber of instruction is far higher in lower education than in higher education, but it was not a systematic or rigorous study and examined only one university.[27] At least for the issue of instructional quality, the widespread desire and pressure for data-based decisionmaking and for greater use of data and research to inform policy in lower education does not appear to hold in higher education. Indeed, recent attempts by the Department of Education to introduce relatively minor forms of evaluation of the quality of instruction and learning in higher education have been met with great resistance and even scorn by some higher-education leaders and some higher-education professional organizations. I find myself wondering what would be the reaction of the professoriate if the kind of high stakes, value-added teacher accountability now being proposed for teachers in lower education were to be proposed for those of us teaching at the higher-education level.

Hence, from a cross-occupational perspective, the interesting empirical question is not solely, Do teacher qualifications matter? Of equal empirical interest are additional questions: Why is this an important question? Why is there not as much concern with data-based decisionmaking in other occupations and in the traditional professions, such as law, medicine, engineering, and academia? Is elementary and secondary teaching held to a different standard in regard to empirical documentation and justification of its training and licensing requirements and, if so, why? In short, why pick on elementary and secondary teaching?

MISUNDERSTANDING THE PROBLEM

Reviewing the context of this debate is useful because it has shaped how the data on out-of-field teaching have been greeted, interpreted, and used. The release of the data brought out-of-field teaching to the attention of the public. However, it did not necessarily bring understanding of the problem. Indeed, the problem of out-of-field teaching remains, unfortunately, widely misunderstood. The major area of disagreement and misunderstanding concerns what is perhaps the most crucial question: Why are so many teachers teaching subjects for which they have little background? Correctly identifying the reasons for, and sources behind, the problem is crucial because incorrect diagnosis can result in flawed remedies.

Typically, policymakers, commentators, and researchers have offered three explanations (and sources of fault) for the high rates of out-of-field teaching: inadequate preparation or education of teachers, inflexible teacher unions, and shortages of teachers. A close examination of the data reveals that each of these views seriously misunderstands the source of the problem—with strong implications for prescription.

A Teacher Education Deficit

Most observers, researchers, and policymakers have assumed that out-of-field teaching is synonymous with a deficit in teachers' education or preparation. Teachers too often lack appropriate coursework or certification, it is widely believed, resulting in the alarming statistics on out-of-field teaching. The root of this problem is assumed to largely lie with either teacher education institutions or with state certification standards. Accordingly, the remedy for out-of-field teaching is to change and upgrade the preparation requirements for prospective teachers.

Blaming out-of-field teaching on a deficit in teachers' preparation certainly seems plausible. This interpretation was adopted by Linda Darling-Hammond in two widely disseminated reports released by NCTAF,[28] and has come to be the conventional wisdom among a wide range of observers and groups, including politicians such as President Clinton and education professional organizations such as the National Association for State Boards of Education. This view is also embedded in NCLB.

However, parallel to the opposing positions in the teacher quality debate discussed earlier, more than one variant of this view of out-of-field teaching has appeared. One version tends to emphasize certification and tends to assume out-of-field teaching results from hiring uncertified and under-credentialed candidates. This variant assumes that the problem can be largely solved by upgrading licensing and entry standards. A second highly popular variant emphasizes subject-matter preparation, in particular, and holds that the source of the problem lies in a lack of preparation and coursework in a particular academic discipline on the part of teachers. This latter version assumes the problem can be remedied by requiring prospective teachers to complete a "real" undergraduate or graduate major in an academic discipline or specialization. I have found this variant to be especially popular in the media and among news columnists, across a variety of political orientations, from David Broder to Maggie Gallagher to Thomas Sowell. It has also been popular among business advocacy groups, such as the Committee on Economic Development.[29]

Those who subscribe to one or another variant of the teacher-education-deficit view also vary widely in how sympathetically they view teachers and teacher education. Some, such as NCTAF, used the data to advocate for upgrading teacher preparation institutions; other consumers used the data to denigrate "the education establishment." An extreme example of this latter line of thinking appeared in a late-1990s syndicated column titled "The Same Old Story" by Thomas Sowell, a senior fellow at the Hoover Institution. He traced the problem to an "education school monopoly" that purveys "gobbledygook that passes for education" and ignores the academic preparation of teachers.[30]

As a former teacher, I found myself personally sympathetic to the idea that teaching is complex and difficult work, and in agreement with advocates calling for professionalizing teacher preparation requirements, both subject-matter and pedagogical. However, regardless of the variant, the teacher-education-deficit view of out-of-field teaching is incorrect. My own case provides an illustration of just how misleading it is. I graduated magna cum laude from the University of California with a bachelor's degree in sociology, and with an additional concentration in history. Several years later, I returned to academia to take part in an intensive fifth-year teacher certification program in social studies. None of this background, however, precluded me from later, as a high school teacher, being assigned to teach subjects out of my field of social studies on a regular basis.

The data show that only 1 percent of all teachers in the United States have not completed a college education, that is, do not have bachelor's degrees; indeed, almost half of all public school teachers have graduate degrees. Moreover, over 90 percent of public school teachers and, surprisingly, well over half of private school teachers hold regular teaching certificates. In short, those teaching a subject out of field, such as math, do not lack degrees or preparation, they lack a degree in math, or in something related, such as physics, engineering, or math education.

Of course, at least since the *Nation at Risk* report in 1983,[31] critics of teacher education have pointed out that subject-area education degrees, such as math education, have tended to be overloaded with required courses in pedagogy and education to the neglect of coursework in the subject itself. Indeed, it is precisely because of such problems that many states have, over the past couple of decades, upgraded teacher education by, among other things, requiring education majors to complete substantial coursework in an academic discipline.[32]

The teacher-education-deficit view of out-of-field teaching confounds and confuses two different sources of the problem of underqualified teaching. One source lies in the adequacy of the qualifications teachers bring to the job. A second source lies in how teachers are utilized and assigned once on the job. Out-of-field teaching is not due to a lack of education on the part of teachers, but to the lack of fit between teachers' fields of preparation and their teaching assignments. The data show that out-of-field teachers are typically experienced and qualified individuals who have been assigned to teach part of their day in fields that do not match their preparation or education. Hence, mandating more rigorous academic or certification requirements for prospective teachers may be a good thing to do, but will help little if large numbers of such teachers continue to be assigned to teach subjects other than those for which they were prepared.

This distinction between pre-service education and teacher in-service assignment may seem a simple one. But I have found it has proved to be anything but simple to communicate to others. I have puzzled over why so many observers, researchers, and policymakers have so readily assumed the former is the case, when the data so clearly point to the latter. My sense is that timing was a factor. There is no question that there are widespread problems with teacher education and teacher quality, and, as a result, both have been a major focal point of educational reform and policy for the past two decades. The data on out-of-field teaching arrived at an opportune time, with the teacher quality debate at an especially hot point. The data were new, compelling, readily available, and not already explained—in a sense, the data were up for grabs. As a result they could readily be made to fit and serve pre-existing viewpoints. Data have different uses and, in this case, the objective did not seem to be hypothesis testing, but hypothesis confirming—in the service of a cause.

Teacher Union Work Rules

A second, less-widely held explanation for out-of-field teaching assumes the fault lies with teacher unions. An example of this anti-union line of thinking appeared in a late-1990s cover story in *U.S. News and World Report*, "Why

Teachers Don't Teach: How Teacher Unions are Wrecking our Schools."[33] The author, Thomas Toch, used data from my research to provide support for his critique of teacher unions and, in particular, their seniority rules. In his view, work rules promulgated by teacher unions are a main reason that classrooms are often staffed with out-of-field teachers. The use and abuse of such rules, according to this view, is especially prevalent in times of teacher oversupply, when school officials face the need to cut or shift staff as a result of fiscal cutbacks or declining enrollments. In such situations, "last-hired, first-fired" seniority rules require that more experienced teachers be given priority, regardless of their competence. As a result, this argument continues, veteran teachers are often given out-of-field assignments, while junior staff are transferred or laid off. Students suffer accordingly.

Nothing in my research or data has ever provided support for this explanation of out-of-field teaching. Public and private schools with unions usually have less, not more, out-of-field teaching. Moreover, teacher oversupply and layoffs are not common—only a small percentage of public school districts report that they lay off teachers because of budget limitations, declining enrollments, or elimination of courses, and these layoffs account for a very small percentage of the teaching force. Union work rules certainly have an impact on the management and administration of schools and, depending upon one's viewpoint, this impact may be positive or negative, but eliminating teacher unions will not eliminate out-of-field teaching.

As with the teacher-education-deficit explanation, I wondered about the origins of this unions-at-fault explanation of out-of-field teaching. Again, timing seemed a factor. Debate over the virtues and vices of teacher unions has been ongoing and antagonistic. My sense is that the data on out-of-field teaching provided some new compelling ammunition to advance a small part of this larger pre-existing attack on unions.

Teacher Shortages

If out-of-field teaching is due to neither a lack of preparation, nor union work rules, what is its source? To outsiders, assigning teachers to teach subjects they may not know may seem like an odd, inefficient, and irrational use of an important human resource. Why are so many teachers assigned to teach subjects for which they have little background? This brings us to the most popular explanation of the problem of out-of-field teaching—teacher shortages. This conventional wisdom holds that shortfalls in the number of available qualified teachers, primarily due to increasing student enrollments and an aging teaching workforce, have forced many school systems to resort to lowering standards to fill teaching openings, the net effect of which is high levels of out-of-field teaching.[34] From this view, the solution is to recruit more quality candidates into teaching through a wide variety of initiatives.

Shortages seem to provide a sensible and plausible explanation for out-of-field teaching. But the data show this view is only partly correct. It is true that demand for teachers has increased in recent years. Since the mid-1980s, student enrollments have increased, the majority of schools have had job openings for teachers, and the size of the teacher workforce has increased. Most important, substantial numbers of schools do, indeed, report difficulties finding qualified candidates to fill their teaching openings.[35] These staffing difficulties are clearly a factor that contributes to out-of-field teaching.

But, there are several problems with teacher shortages as an explanation for out-of-field teaching. First, shortages cannot explain the high levels of out-of-field teaching that exist in English and social studies, fields that have long been known to have teacher surpluses (see Figure 5.1). Second, not all schools experience recruitment and staffing problems, and the data indicate that about half of all misassigned teachers in any given year are employed in schools that reported no difficulties whatever finding qualified candidates for their job openings that year. Indeed, in any given year much out-of-field teaching takes place in schools that did not have any vacancies or openings for teachers in that year. In short, recruiting thousands of new qualified candidates will not solve the problem if large numbers of such teachers continue to be assigned to teach subjects other than those for which they were prepared.

AN ALTERNATIVE HYPOTHESIS

In contrast to the above three explanations of out-of-field teaching, over the past decade I have tried to develop, test, and disseminate an alternative explanation for out-of-field teaching. This alternative view is drawn from the field of organizational theory, and from my own experiences as a high school teacher. Rather than a problem of teacher education or teacher supply, I've concluded that the data point in another direction—the occupational and organizational conditions of teaching.

Unlike traditional professions, teachers have only limited authority over key workplace decisions. Teachers, for instance, have little say over which courses they are assigned to teach. The data tell us that decisions concerning the allocation of teachers to course and program assignments are primarily made by school principals.[36] These administrators are charged with the often-difficult task of providing an increasingly broad array of programs and courses with limited resources, limited time, a limited budget, and a limited teaching staff.[37]

School principals not only have the responsibility to decide who teaches which courses and programs, they also have an unusual degree of discretion in these decisions. While teaching candidates are subject to an elaborate array of state certification requirements designed to ensure their basic preparation and competence, there has been little regulation of how teachers are employed and utilized once on the job.[38] In this context, assigning teachers to teach out of their fields has been a useful and acceptable managerial practice.

For example, rather than trying to find and hire a new science teacher to teach a newly state-mandated, but underfunded, science curriculum, a school principal may find it more convenient and cost-effective to assign a couple of English and social studies teachers to teach a class or two in science. Similarly, when faced with the choice between hiring a fully qualified candidate for an English position and hiring a less-qualified candidate who is also willing to coach a major varsity sport, a principal may find it more expedient to do the latter. If a full-time music teacher is under contract, but student enrollment is sufficient to fill only three music classes, the principal may find it both necessary and cost effective in a given semester to assign the music teacher to teach two classes in English, in addition to the three classes in music, in order to employ the teacher for a regular full-time complement of five classes per semester.

All of these managerial choices to misassign teachers may save time and money for the school, and ultimately for the taxpayer, but they are not cost-free. Moreover, they have become illegal with the advent of NCLB and its mandate to have academic classes taught by teachers qualified in the subject.

My view is that the prevalence of these management practices can, in turn, be explained by the occupational status of teaching. Unlike many European and Asian nations, in the United States, elementary- and secondary-school teaching is deemed as relatively lower-status work, and teachers as semi-skilled workers. The comparison with traditional male-dominated higher status professions is stark. Few would require cardiologists to deliver babies, real estate lawyers to defend criminal cases, chemical engineers to design bridges, or sociology professors to teach English. The commonly held assumption is that such traditional professions require a great deal of skill and training, that is, expertise, and, hence, specialization is assumed necessary.[39] The prevalence of out-of-field teaching suggests this assumption does not hold for elementary- and secondary school teaching.

An occupational-status perspective also provides an explanation for the irony, mentioned earlier, surrounding the relatively high empirical scrutiny of teachings' relatively low entry requirements. Why is there such ongoing interest, compared to other occupations, in challenging whether teacher qualifications matter? From my perspective, underlying the skepticism and double standard is the assumption—as yet scientifically untested—that teaching is not especially difficult work to do well and requires less ability and expertise than, for example, working with buildings (engineers), teeth (dentists), financial accounts (accountants) or doing academic research (professors). Hence, treating teachers as low-skill interchangeable employees is viewed as a matter of efficiency.

IMPLICATIONS FOR RESEARCH AND POLICY

Understanding or misunderstanding the reasons behind out-of-field teaching assignments is important because of their implications for both research and for policy. Differing interpretations of the data have differing implications. For instance, underlying the earlier teacher education and teacher shortage interpretations is the common assumption that the primary source of underqualified teachers in schools lies in deficits in teachers themselves—their numbers, preparation, knowledge, ability, and licensing, etc. The impetus is for ever-more-research on understanding, addressing, and erasing these teacher deficits. In short, the assumption is that to understand what is wrong with schools we need to understand what is wrong with the quality and quantity of teachers. Which kinds of preparation and certification are best? Does certification matter? Are those with higher test scores better teachers? How can we recruit more candidates into teaching? What are the effects on student achievement of whether teachers do or do not have particular degrees?

Accordingly, in recent years we have seen a mushrooming in the development and use of ever-more-sophisticated value-added and econometric statistical techniques using ever-more-detailed and expensive data bases to try to more accurately define, isolate, and measure teaching effectiveness. Such efforts are useful and have provided illumination, however, there are probably inherent methodological limits to this quest. Social science evaluation research is not new and has always faced steep hurdles in discerning the impact of human-based interventions, programs, and "treatments." Indeed, in my field we often cite fellow sociologist Peter Rossi's law: "The expected value for any measured effect of a social program is zero," when analyses fail to turn up significant effects.[40] When reading highly complex statistical analyses, striving to quantify the results of these essentially human interactions between teacher and student, I am reminded of Raymond Callahan's classic,

Education and the Cult of Efficiency, published almost a half-century ago, that tellingly critiques the 1920s and 1930s movement to rationalize teachers' work through the use of "scientific methods" borrowed from industry.[41]

The application of scientifically based research to education issues is also selective. In contrast to the abovementioned mushrooming lines of inquiry, there is very little research on many of the kinds of questions raised by the data on out-of-field teaching. There are very few studies looking at the effects of in-field or out-of-field teachers on other outcomes such as student engagement, critical thinking, teachers' expertise, over-reliance, rote textbook teaching, the classroom environment, student discipline, or teacher turnover.

Moreover, there has been little cross-occupational comparative research and little effort to contextualize teacher research itself. How do teaching's entry requirements and routes compare to those of other occupations? How does the complexity and character of the work itself compare to that in other occupations? What are the differences in teaching quality at lower and higher education levels?

In addition, the ongoing emphasis (and blame) placed on teacher education and teacher supply diverts attention from other sources of the out-of-field teaching problem—especially the way schools and teachers are managed and mismanaged—and other kinds of research questions. The data tell us there are large cross-school differences in out-of-field teaching, but we know little of why this is so. In a series of exploratory multivariate analyses, I have found that, after controlling for school recruitment and hiring difficulties and after controlling for school demographic characteristics, factors such as the quality of principal leadership, average class sizes, the character of the oversight of school hiring practices provided by the larger district, and the strategies districts and schools use for teacher recruitment and hiring are all significantly related to the amount of out-of-field teaching in schools.[42] Such findings are suggestive of lines of further inquiry. What are the processes behind school staffing and teacher assignment? What are the decisionmaking processes surrounding the hiring, assignment, and utilization of teachers in particular kinds of schools? What are the hidden incentive systems within which administrators make staffing decisions? How do particular teachers come to be teaching particular classes? What are the reasons behind the misassignment of teachers? In short, there is almost no research on the role of schools, and their management, in the problem of underqualified teachers. In my view, this is unfortunate. Rather than confirm old lines of argument, the new data on out-of-field teaching provide a "teaching moment"—an opportunity to broaden our understanding of how schools work and don't work.

Answering these questions and deepening our understanding of the reasons behind out-of-field teaching assignments is not only useful from a scientific perspective, but is also important because of the implications for policy. Parallel to the research realm, most recent federal, state, and local teacher policies and initiatives, including those in NCLB, have also focused on the same two general approaches to trying to ensure that all classrooms are staffed with qualified teachers: upgrading the qualifications of teachers and increasing the quantity of teachers. And, again, underlying these kinds of methods is a teacher deficit perspective—the source of the problem lies in deficits in the numbers, preparation, knowledge, ability, and licensing of teachers. Hence, the assumption is that the way to fix schools is to fix these deficits in teachers.

Of course, upgrading teacher recruitment, preparation, and certification practices and requirements can be useful first steps. But, the above methods do not address the ways schools themselves contribute to the problem of underqualified teachers. The data tell us that solutions to the problem of out-of-field teaching must also look to how schools are managed and how teachers are utilized *once on the job*. In short, recruiting thousands of new candidates and providing them with rigorous preservice preparation or inservice professional development will not solve the problem if large numbers of such teachers continue to be assigned to teach subjects other than those for which they were prepared.[43]

Our analyses of the most recent SASS data provide an independent assessment of how things have progressed in terms of the highly qualified teacher requirements of NCLB. The data indicate that out-of-field teaching declined very little between the 1999–2000 school year (two years before NCLB) and 2003-04 (two years into NCLB). This is a discouraging finding, but perhaps also to be expected. If assigning teachers to teach out of their fields has been a prevalent school administrative practice for decades because it is more efficient and less expensive than the alternatives, then its elimination will not be easily accomplished simply by legislative fiat. To meet the goal of ensuring all students are provided with qualified teachers, states will need to rethink how districts and schools go about managing their human resources—a tall order. There is a clear role here for scientific data and research, but this is a cautionary tale and one that is also not yet finished.

CHAPTER 6

Education Policy, Academic Research, and Public Opinion

William G. Howell

Perch yourself atop a stack of every education study published in the last couple of decades, and you will be looking down a good number of world-class skyscrapers. Universities, colleges, think tanks, testing organizations, and the public school system itself now employ an army of academics who study the single most prevalent public institution the world has ever known—schools. And each foot-soldier is eager to make a mark, to demonstrate that his or her research illuminates something crucial about how we educate our children, and about how we might do a better job of it. It is difficult to identify a single issue in education, no matter how arcane, that has not been the subject of sustained academic inquiry appearing online or in academic journals, industry trade publications, books, and edited volumes.

Given its sheer volume, education scholarship ought to hold a prominent place in public conversations about how best to characterize the state of education domestically, about which reforms hold the greatest promise in redressing persistent inequalities, and about how the nation ought to allocate billions of dollars each year to schools. It does not. For the most part, the U.S. citizens who vote for school board members and education bond initiatives, debate the merits of different education reforms, and ultimately decide the fate of proposed education policies, know very little about this research. These citizens do not subscribe to academic journals. They do not attend academic conferences. They do not follow the latest academic debates. Their awareness of education research is dismayingly thin. And their interest in the kinds of methodological issues that consume education researchers is thinner still. Put a table of regression results in front of them and behold the many faces of bewilderment.

Do not confuse disinterest in education research, however, with disinterest in education. Citizens care greatly about America's schools and the children who attend them. Polls that ask citizens about the single most important issue facing the nation generally, and their local communities in particular, often rank education at or near the top. Citizens, moreover, are not wanting for opinions about education. They have plenty to say about what is wrong with the nation's schools and what needs to be done to fix them. When they attempt to close down a school, introduce a new family planning curriculum, implement an inter-district school choice program, or cut funding for the high school football team, districts reliably confront varying levels of outrage expressed by parents, public school employees, booster clubs, parent–teacher associations, and interested citizens.

And occasionally, education research does manage to percolate into the public conscience. General interest newspapers, specialty journals, and even television media outlets devote modest levels of coverage to education issues, at least some of which is dedicated to scholarly research. Increasingly, think tanks and universities are employing teams of well-connected consultants whose sole purpose is to publicize the latest education studies of their scholars and faculty. Their labors often pay considerable dividends. In the last several years, stories about new research on the effectiveness of charter schools, public schools, social promotion and discipline policies, and the federally mandated No Child Left Behind Act (NCLB) have been splashed across the nation's newspapers. Moreover, these news stories are often accompanied by editorials and op-eds that distill key findings and proffer a bevy of policy recommendations.

This chapter examines the possibility that citizens' mediated and sporadic exposure to education research influences their attitudes toward education policies. It reflects upon how citizens—who are not direct consumers of education research and who lack basic training in the modes of social scientific inquiry—use the paucity of information made available to them in news stories to formulate opinions about public education. After briefly surveying the relevant literatures on political behavior and survey design, the chapter introduces a simple experiment designed to further elucidate the varying impacts of academic research on public opinion about education policy.

A FEW REFLECTIONS ON PUBLIC OPINION

From the outset, we must dash hopeful notions that citizens interpret the world around them as do social scientists. The public engages education research—to the extent that it is even aware of education research—in fundamentally different ways than those who produce it. The basic principles of social scientific inquiry do not preoccupy your average citizen, who has never fixated on the tradeoffs between type one and type two errors, the appropriateness of a particular instrument designed to solve some selection problem, or the generalizability of findings from one study to a larger population of students, teachers, or parents. Citizens do not know the difference between an estimator's bias and efficiency—they do not have a clue what an estimator even is.

What citizens know about an education study, instead, is limited to what journalists tell them. Upon learning about a study that purports to show that charter schools outperform public schools (or any other policy issue), few if any citizens run down to their local library, download the original report, and formulate an independent and reasoned opinion about its strengths and weaknesses. Instead, citizens rely upon the media to tell them about the existence and relevant implications of important academic research. Citizens evaluate academic research on the basis of information found within the news story itself—typically, the identity of the individual or institution that produced the report, a core finding or two, and a handful of quotes from experts providing commentary. Rarely more, and often less.

Massive literatures detail the ways in which citizens' political views are poorly informed, unorganized, and unstable—leading Phillip Converse some 40 years ago to declare that citizens are best understood as having "nonattitudes."[1] People know very little about factual matters involving politics generally, and specific public policies in particular.[2] Their stated opinions on one issue (say, the privatization of education) often have little relationship to those expressed on another related issue (say, federal grants to Catholic schools). There is little evidence that average citizens organize their views into anything resembling a coherent ideology. And the views that citizens express on any particular issue often change dramatically over time.

In many ways, the field of political behavior since Converse's seminal article can be understood as an ongoing effort to understand how, and whether, poorly informed and inattentive people navigate a complicated and evolving political universe, using as guides their partisan affiliation,[3] retrospective voting,[4] stereotypes,[5] or other shortcuts.[6] To be sure, disagreements linger about whether people succeed or fail in this endeavor, and what implications this has for the health of our democracy. And much about the cognitive processes that people use to understand politics remain poorly understood. Still, the facts that motivate these higher-order debates, for the most part, remain uncontested—namely, average citizens know very little about politics, and they know even less about specific policies that do not have a direct bearing on their own lives or on those around them.

Given the state of public opinion, the persuasive appeal of academic research could turn out to be either weak or strong. On the one hand, public inattention would appear to mute possibilities for academic research to inform and persuade a broader citizenry. Most citizens, after all, rarely participate in the kinds of discussions about education policies that feature academic research. The problem is not merely that citizens do not subscribe to academic journals or attend professional education conferences. Rather, the problem is that citizens receive very little information about academic research in any form. And with the decline of newspaper readerships, the displacement of television news with soft news, and the massive proliferation of cable entertainment, streams of information appear to be running dry.[7] Even those citizens who regularly sit with a newspaper in the morning and turn on the television at the end of a workday worry more about the cleanliness of their kitchens than they do about the state of American education (or the depletion of the ozone layer, the decline of American cities, trade imbalances with China, or the rising violence in the Middle East). Many citizens devote about the same amount of time and reflection to academic research on education as they do to imagining what it would be like to play a round of golf on the moon.

On the other hand, because citizens know so little about public policy, even small doses of research may induce large changes in public attitudes. A number of scholars have shown that citizens who know less about a chosen policy are especially susceptible to persuasion.[8] If the views of citizens with low levels of information are generally pliable, they may be especially receptive to new research findings, which carry airs of objectivity and authority. Precisely because citizens lack substantial information about a range of education policies, they may willingly adopt conclusions from research studies that contradict their current views, such as they are. Told that a major study demonstrates that a popular program does not help children, or that an unpopular program does, citizens may concede the point and adjust their views accordingly.

WHETHER TO BELIEVE RESEARCH

Scholars of public opinion have made much of the fact that a poorly informed citizenry is especially vulnerable to demagoguery. Simple changes in the ways in which policies are discussed, the order of policy options put before an electorate, and subtle cues about the efficacy of a proposed reform can have a substantial influence on the expressed views of an inattentive public. Often, scholars have found, surveys can elicit policy choices that do not in any meaningful sense reflect the true views or deeper interests of a citizenry. And by tapping latent stereotypes or priming certain emotions or misrepresenting a body of evidence, elites also can direct public discussions in ways that serve their private interests, to the detriment of the larger public good.

The potential value of research, then, would appear profound. Through fair-minded presentations on the state of public education in America and the merits of a variety of education policies, scholars and the journalists who speak on their behalf can both inform average citizens (allowing citizens to discern their own, independent views) and inoculate them against the appeals made by interest groups on both the left and right (allowing them to more meaningfully participate in public debates about education). Indeed, academic research ought to serve the greatest need, and have the most influence, when citizens are asked to evaluate the merits of public policies about which they know very little.

It is important, though, not to be too Pollyannaish about the promise of academic research. Before heralding education scholars and the journalists who spread their good word as saviors of an ill-informed and easily manipulated public, we ought to face up to some less comforting truths. Too often, researchers unjustifiably advance conclusions that are not supported by their evidence. Interest groups and teachers unions fund their own research departments that churn out findings that, amazingly, again and again confirm their institution's favored positions. And from a purely methodological standpoint, much of what passes for education research—even that which is peer reviewed—is just plain poor.

Journalistic reports on academic research, meanwhile, are not without their own biases and shortcomings, as the various chapters in this volume make plain. Rather than carefully assessing the strengths and weaknesses of a particular study, journalists all too often conjure up controversy where it does not exist, focus on the personalities of the parties involved, look to vested interest groups for commentary, and give equal time and attention to two sides of an issue even when the preponderance of evidence suggests that only one is right.

How do citizens, then, go about distinguishing bald rhetorical appeals (warranting disregard) from genuine scholarly advancements (demanding serious consideration)? Because they lack the time, inclination and training, citizens are obviously ill equipped to formulate independent judgments about the quality of the research itself. When deciding whether to update one's views in light of new research, therefore, citizens may look to the organization that produced it or the media outlet that reported on it. And depending upon a host of factors, some citizens may update their views, and others may not.

To understand the variable impacts that research can have on different citizens, it is worth recalling a well-established truth within the social sciences: Like-minded individuals have an easier time communicating with one another than do individuals with divergent worldviews;[9] hence, average citizens tend to view fellow partisans as more reliable sources of political information than partisan opponents. Why? Citizens believe like-minded elites not because they have independent information to corroborate their views, but because citizens know that, on average, these elites will likely draw the same conclusions about the merits of a specific policy that the citizens would were they privy to the elites' private information. It is quite possible, then, that research will persuade only those citizens who trust the source that produced it. Conservative citizens may believe conservative research organizations, and liberal citizens may believe liberal research organizations, while across ideological divides, considerable discounting may occur.

Evidence of academic research's influence may further depend upon the current state of public opinion and the nature of the scholarly findings themselves. If it merely confirms citizens' prior views about the merits of a proposed education policy, then academic research may not disrupt the current constellation of public attitudes, at least not in the short term. Though citizens have a stronger basis upon which to justify their opinions, they may disregard any compunction to reconsider their prior views in light of new research. It is only when research conflicts with citizens' existing views that changes of opinion are likely to be detected. The influence of research on public opinion is most consequential when new findings offer citizens a substantive reason to abandon their current beliefs and adopt altogether new ones.

Academic research also may have an especially large impact on people's views when it allows them to realign their specific policy preferences with their more general ideological orientation. By way of example, consider two citizens, one conservative and the other liberal, who both believe that most poor people do not work hard. Imagine, then, a research study that refutes this view, showing rather that the poor actually work longer hours than the rich. How are the two citizens likely to respond? The conservative, being conservative, has strong reasons to resist the finding. After all, this research would appear to challenge the various policy preferences—for instance, opposition to redistributive programs—that define conservatism. In contrast, this research is likely to have a relatively large impact on the liberal citizen. For him, after all, this research facilitates a realignment of his views about how the world works with the relevant beliefs that define his liberal orientation—in this instance, support for redistributive programs. If true, then the power of academic research would appear to depend upon the relationship between a study's precise findings and a citizen's ideological orientation.

Similarly, academic research may prove especially persuasive when it affirms an individual's private choices. To see this, consider the varying impacts of a hypothetical *Consumer Report* study on the relative quality of a $40K BMW and a $20K Honda. Most citizens naturally would believe that the BMW outperforms the less expensive Honda. Imagine, though, that the research found the Honda to be just as reliable as the BMW. People who drive BMWs, one can well imagine, will discount the study, clinging to whatever information they have that justifies their decision to spend twice the amount of the Honda. People who drive Hondas, however, are likely to find the study eminently persuasive. For these individuals, after all, the study vindicates their choice, demonstrating their acuity of judgment for having made the better automobile purchase. In this sense, the influence of academic research would appear to depend upon the interaction between a study's substantive findings and the people's prior choices in the relevant issue domain.

Even under ideal conditions, however, academic research simply may not resonate with the larger public. Just because it reaches citizens, comes from a trusted source, challenges conventional wisdom, or affirms either ideological inclinations or past choices, academic research may not influence the content of public opinion. On some issues, at least, some citizens simply may not care about the current state of scholarship. A study finding that the death penalty effectively deters criminal activity may not influence by one iota the views of citizens who believe that all life is precious and that the government, as a matter of principle, should not be granted the power to kill any of its citizens. Similarly, findings that school vouchers improve the test scores of African American children may appear irrelevant to those citizens who retain an abiding belief in the value of public education, and whose preferences are informed more by ideology than a dispassionate reading of existing scholarship. If the foundation of public discourse on matters involving education rests entirely upon normative claims about right and wrong, vested interests, and ideological commitments, academic research may not serve any role whatsoever.

Ultimately, it is an empirical question whether academic research can shape the thinking of citizens who oversee the education of their own children and who hold accountable those elected officials charged with overseeing the education of all children. In the next section, I examine survey data that speak to this issue, identifying the differential impacts that research can have on the education views of diverse segments of the American public.

SOME EMPIRICAL FINDINGS ABOUT, WELL, THE IMPACT OF EMPIRICAL FINDINGS

To gauge the willingness of different segments of the American public to update their views about education in light of new research findings, I conducted a simple experiment. With a stratified, nationally representative survey of 2,000 adults, I randomly assigned individuals to one of five (one baseline, four treatment) conditions that presented short vignettes about research conducted on the test scores of students in public and private schools.[10] I then asked respondents their own views about the performance of students in the two sectors. Because respondents were randomly assigned to each of the five conditions, differences observed in their answers can reliably be attributed to differences in the vignettes themselves, and not the background characteristics of the respondents.

Table 6.1 summarizes the conditions of the experiment. In the baseline condition, respondents were told: "A prominent research organization in Washington, D.C., recently released a study comparing the test scores of similar students in private and public schools." Neither the findings from the study nor the ideological orientation of the research organization were presented. The respondent was only told that research had been conducted, and then was asked, "What about you? Do you think similar students who attend private or public schools score higher on standardized tests?" Respondents then could choose from three response categories: private school students score higher; public school students score higher; there is no difference. The structure of the treatment conditions looks much like that of the baseline condition. The differences are that the vignette informs the respondent that either a prominent liberal or a prominent conservative research organization released the study finding; and that private school students either do or do

TABLE 6.1   Study Design

Baseline condition	"A prominent research organization in Washington, D.C., recently released a study comparing the test scores of similar students in private and public schools."
Treatment condition 1	"According to a prominent conservative research organization in Washington, D.C., students in private schools score higher on tests than comparable students in public schools."
Treatment condition 2	"According to a prominent liberal research organization in Washington, D.C., students in private schools score higher on tests than comparable students in public schools."
Treatment condition 3	"According to a prominent conservative research organization in Washington, D.C., students in private schools do not score higher on tests than comparable students in public schools."
Treatment condition 4	"According to a prominent liberal research organization in Washington, D.C., students in private schools do not score higher on tests than comparable students in public schools."
Question	"What about you? Do you think similar students who attend private or public schools score higher on standardized tests?"
Response choices	a. Private school students score higher b. Public school students score higher c. There is no difference

Note: Subjects were randomly assigned to one of the five conditions. All subjects were asked the same question and offered the same response categories.

not score higher than comparable public school students. The two types of research organizations and two sets of findings generate the four treatment conditions ($2 \times 2 = 4$) that complete the experiment.

To determine whether respondents update their views in light of new research conducted by different types of organizations, answers observed in each of the treatment conditions are compared to those in the baseline condition. Again, because we have randomly assigned subjects to each of the survey conditions, to discern the influence of different research findings on public attitudes about education we do not need to include controls for socio-economic characteristics, their television viewing habits, or anything else. Instead, unbiased estimates can be recovered from direct comparisons of people's responses in the baseline and four treatment conditions. We therefore focus on the average proportion of people who claim that private school students outperform their public school peers.

From the outset, though, we should recognize that this constitutes a hard test of the proposition that research can meaningfully inform the views of average citizens. Indeed, one might expect that research will prove incapable of dislodging the essentially normative underpinnings of the public's views about public and private schools. Indeed, if we find that at least some elements of the American public respond to research about the performance of students in public and private schools, we can reasonably expect many others to find research persuasive on education issues that are not so politically charged.

Findings for the Overall Population

Table 6.2 presents the main findings. Overall, roughly three in four adults nationwide believe that private school students outperform their public school peers. We do not know why respondents express this belief. Perceptions about the relative quality of school teachers or facilities, the strength of peer groups, the selection processes that place students into schools, differences in schooling climates, or the simple fact that private schools charge tuition and public schools are (nominally) free may guide their responses. Whatever the source, though, in the eyes of the general public, private school students stand a notch above their public school peers.

Interestingly, being told that academic research confirms this view does not have any systematic effects on the public's overall responses. Whether it is a liberal or a conservative organization that purports to find that private school students outperform their public school peers, registered responses vary by just a percentage point or two from the baseline condition—differences that do not even approach standard thresholds of statistical significance. When told about research that public school students score just as high as private school students, however, public responses change dramatically. Again, on average it does not matter whether the research organization is liberal or conservative. The mere acknowledgment of a research study finding that public school students score just as high as private school students is enough to convince almost 30 percent of surveyed adults to express a different perspective about the issue.

On the basis of these findings alone, advocates of private schools would appear to be engaged in a losing battle. Academic research that confirms their preferred view—namely, that private school students score higher on standardized tests than public school students—does not influence the views of the broader public. A single study that finds no difference between the test scores of students in the two sectors, meanwhile, can have devastating consequences. Without any discussion of the study's characteristics (the population of students, schools, and cities sampled, for instance) or quality (the comparability of public and private school students, the number of subjects tested, the availability of baseline data, etc.), the mere mention of a negative

TABLE 6.2   Beliefs of Overall Population

	Average %[†]	n
Baseline condition	74.5	403
Differences between treatment conditions 1–4 and baseline condition		
Private higher, report by conservative think tank	2.6	389
Private higher, report by liberal think tank	–1.0	403
Private not higher, report by conservative think tank	–27.1*	395
Private not higher, report by liberal think tank	–25.5*	394

Note: The baseline condition reports the average percentage of people who believe, after only being told that a prominent think tank recently issued a report on the topic, that students in private schools perform higher on standardized tests than similar students in public schools. In the treatment conditions, respondents are told the ideological orientation of the think tank (liberal or conservative) and the finding of the report (private school students did or did not score higher than comparable public school students). Reported figures for treatment conditions indicate the percentage-point differences relative to the baseline condition. Positive values indicate a higher percentage of people who believe that private school students score higher than public school students; negative values indicate a lower percentage.

* Significant at $p < 0.10$, two-tailed test. Post-stratification weights employed.

† Percentage of people who believe that students in private schools score higher than similar students in public schools.

finding reduced by roughly 26 percentage points the number of people willing to adopt the common view that private school students outperform their public school peers on all matters academic.

Findings for Liberals and Conservatives

Table 6.3 disaggregates the findings for self-described liberals, moderates, and conservatives. In the baseline conditions, the three groups of respondents look almost identical to one another. Across the ideological spectrum, roughly three in four adults profess that private school students outperform public school students. The groups respond quite differently, though, across the various treatment conditions. Neither liberals nor moderates appear at all affected by research from either liberal or conservative research organizations finding that private school students score higher than public school students. Indeed, only the responses of conservatives appear affected by research that confirms the view endorsed by most people in the baseline condition. And the only instance when the effect is statistically significant is when conservative respondents learn about research from conservative research organizations. Told that a conservative research organization recently released a study

TABLE 6.3　Beliefs among Liberals, Moderates, and Conservatives

	Liberals		Moderates		Conservatives	
	Average %†	n	Average %†	n	Average %†	n
Baseline condition	74.5	84	73.9	154	75.4	155
Differences between treatment conditions 1–4 and baseline condition						
Private higher, report by conservative think tank	4.1	114	−4.5	148	7.9*	138
Private higher, report by liberal think tank	−7.8	94	−1.6	143	4.7	152
Private not higher, report by conservative think tank	−30.6*	115	−34.7*	125	−17.2*	161
Private not higher, report by liberal think tank	−36.9*	99	−25.5*	153	−16.8*	142

Note: See note to Table 6.2.

* Significant at $p < 0.10$, two-tailed test. Post-stratification weights employed.

† Percentage of people who believe that students in private schools score higher than similar students in public schools.

finding that private school students outperform public school students, conservatives appear roughly 8 percentage points more likely to endorse the view than in the baseline condition.

Differences across the three ideological groups are also observed in the other treatment conditions. When told that either a liberal or conservative research organization released a study finding that public school students scored just as high as private school students, liberals abandon in droves the common view represented in the baseline condition. Indeed, belief in the superiority of private school students is cut in half among liberals in the third and fourth treatment conditions. Conservatives, in contrast, do not appear as affected by the research findings described in the last two treatment conditions. Though the observed differences are in the same direction and statistically significant, the magnitudes of the effects are roughly half as large. Told that a liberal research organization issued a report finding that public school students score just as high as private school students, fully 59 percent of conservatives continue to believe that private school students score higher than public school students, as compared to just 38 percent of liberals.

TABLE 6.4   Beliefs among School Voucher Supporters and Opponents

	Support Vouchers		Oppose Vouchers	
	Average %†	n	Average %†	n
Baseline condition	78.7	178	76.7	156
Differences between treatment conditions 1–4 and baseline condition				
Private higher, report by conservative think tank	3.6	179	−7.1	165
Private higher, report by liberal think tank	0.5	162	−5.0	150
Private not higher, report by conservative think tank	−20.8*	161	−33.1*	169
Private not higher, report by liberal think tank	−17.3*	171	−39.0*	140

Note: See note to Table 6.2. Voucher supporters and opponents were identified on a prior survey question.

* Significant at $p < 0.10$, two-tailed test. Post-stratification weights employed.

† Percentage of people who believe that students in private schools score higher than similar students in public schools.

These findings are not altogether surprising. Though liberals and conservatives share a common view about public and private school students generally, their willingness to update these views in light of new research critically depends upon the extent to which this research comports with their ideological priors. As previously discussed, citizens resist findings that challenge their ideological priors, and endorse those that confirm them. We know that liberals are much more likely to support increased spending for public schools and higher salaries for public school teachers than are conservatives; and that conservatives are more likely to support choice-based initiatives like charter schools and vouchers. Armed with research that would appear to bolster their positions—as conservatives are in treatment conditions 1 and 2, and liberals are in treatment conditions 3 and 4—evidence of updating is observed. But where academic research challenges the wisdom of one's policy preferences—as treatment conditions 3 and 4 do for conservatives, and treatment conditions 1 and 2 do for liberals—the estimated effects either disappear or attenuate substantially. Plainly, the assessed value of academic research depends upon its congruence with previously held policy preferences.

Table 6.4 drives this point home. Rather than distinguishing liberals from conservatives, here adults who support school vouchers are differentiated from those who oppose them—a distinction made possible by a prior question in the survey.[11] Again, in the baseline condition, both groups look almost identical; the views of neither group appear to change much when told that academic research confirms the view held by most people in the baseline condition. The estimated differences from the baseline condition in the final two treatment groups, however, vary markedly for supporters and opponents of vouchers. When told that a liberal research organization just released a report finding that public school students score just as high as private school students, the expressed views of voucher opponents dropped by a whopping 39 percentage points relative to the baseline condition. For voucher supporters, however, the change was a more modest 17 percentage points. Additionally, there is some evidence that voucher proponents are more sensitive to conservative research organizations, while voucher opponents are more prone to update their views in response to liberal research organizations. Within-group differences across treatment conditions 1 and 2 and conditions 3 and 4, however, are not statistically significant.

Findings for Public and Private School Parents

Table 6.5 shifts tack slightly. Rather than disaggregate respondents according to their ideological predispositions or policy preferences, this comparison looks at public school parents, private school parents, and nonparents. Here, for the first time, there are differences within the baseline conditions across the three groups. Private school parents are 14 percentage points more likely than public school parents to claim that private school students score higher than their public school peers. Given that the former group has opted to pay the extra costs of sending their child to a private school, this finding can hardly come as a surprise. Comparable findings can be expected when comparing the assessments of comparable consumers in virtually any other domain of life (including those who purchase Hondas and BMWs).

As one would expect, public school parents appear especially sensitive to treatment conditions 3 and 4, and completely unaffected by conditions 1 and 2. When told about research that public school students score just as high as private school students, less than 50 percent of public school parents claim that private school students outperform their public school peers. Private school parents, meanwhile, appear unaffected by any research findings from liberal organizations, though they update their views by comparable magnitudes and in the expected directions when told about research from conservative organizations. Though the effects are never statistically significant—largely because of the small number of available observations—support for the conventional wisdom increases by 11 percentage points in the

TABLE 6.5   Beliefs among Public School Parents, Private School Parents, and Nonparents

	Public School Parents		Private School Parents		Nonparents	
	Average %†	n	Average %†	n	Average %†	n
Baseline condition	70.4	136	83.5	35	75.3	244
Differences between treatment conditions 1–4 and baseline condition						
Private higher, report by conservative think tank	6.7	170	11.2	43	−0.4	226
Private higher, report by liberal think tank	−0.6	159	1.5	35	−3.7	222
Private not higher, report by conservative think tank	−24.8*	155	−13.4	27	−28.9*	248
Private not higher, report by liberal think tank	−29.2*	147	−4.7	31	−26.3*	239

Note: See note to Table 6.2. Public school parents, private school parents, and nonparents were identified on a prior survey question.

* Significant at $p < 0.10$, two-tailed test. Post-stratification weights employed.

† Percentage of people who believe that students in private schools score higher than similar students in public schools.

first treatment condition and declines by 13 percentage points in the third. In fact, private school parents support the conventional wisdom at roughly the same rate in the third treatment condition as public school parents do in the baseline condition.[12]

In this instance, the willingness of adults to update their views in light of new research depends less upon their ideological priors, and more upon the individual choices that they have made on behalf of their children. Public school parents appear unaffected by research that challenges their decision to send their children to public schools; they are quick, though, to update their beliefs in light of research that confirms their decision to send their children to public schools. Having decided to pay the extra costs of a private education, private school parents appear less susceptible to persuasion of any kind; when they are, their belief in the superiority of private school students increases in light of confirming research by roughly the same magnitude as it drops in light of evidence to the contrary; and never does less than 70 percent of the population profess that private school students outperform public school students.

TABLE 6.6   Beliefs among Individuals from Households with Different Levels of Education

	Up to Some College		Associate Degree or Above	
	Average %†	n	Average %†	n
Baseline condition	75.1	212	73.7	182
Differences between treatment conditions 1–4 and baseline condition				
Private higher, report by conservative think tank	−1.6	226	11.7*	177
Private higher, report by liberal think tank	−3.3	220	4.1	169
Private not higher, report by conservative think tank	−33.3*	207	−18.5*	196
Private not higher, report by liberal think tank	−24.0*	242	−30.5*	153

Note: See note to Table 6.2. Education of head of household was identified on a prior survey question.

* Significant at $p < 0.10$, two-tailed test. Post-stratification weights employed.

† Percentage of people who believe that students in private schools score higher than similar students in public schools.

The precise cognitive processes that generate these findings remain unclear. It is possible that public and private school parents are merely searching for ex post justifications for their decisions to send their children to different types of schools. Alternatively, at least some public school parents may have investigated private schooling options and decided that they are no better than public schools. It is also possible that at least some private school parents remain convinced that public school students simply do not measure up to their private school peers. If true, then the research findings presented in the various treatment conditions have to be weighed against the different types and amounts of information that public and private school parents already retain about the quality of students in the two education sectors. Whichever the explanation, though, the persuasive appeal of new academic research appears conditional upon the personal educational choices that different parents have made on behalf of their children.

Findings for Selected Other Subgroups

Next, we compare more and less educated respondents, the results for whom are presented in Table 6.6. For reasons previously outlined, one might expect the responses of less-educated individuals to be more pliable, and those of

TABLE 6.7   Beliefs of Individuals with Different Evaluations of Public Schools

	Give Schools Grade of A or B		Give Schools Grade of C, D, or F	
	Average %†	n	Average %†	n
Baseline condition	66.4	186	79.5	197
Differences between treatment conditions 1–4 and baseline condition				
Private higher, report by conservative think tank	5.0	188	–3.6	194
Private higher, report by liberal think tank	0.3	194	1.2	198
Private not higher, report by conservative think tank	–27.3*	209	–24.6*	184
Private not higher, report by liberal think tank	–24.4*	185	–25.2*	212

Note: See note to Table 6.2. Grades that parents gave public schools in their communities were identified on a prior survey question.

* Significant at $p < 0.10$, two-tailed test. Post-stratification weights employed.

† Percentage of people who believe that students in private schools score higher than similar students in public schools.

more-educated parents to be more resistant to new information. In this experiment, however, no such evidence emerges. The baseline answers of people with "some college" or less and those with at least an associate's degree are virtually identical. Both groups, meanwhile, reveal considerable evidence of updating when told about research findings showing that public school students perform just as well as private school students on standardized tests. Interestingly, though, well-educated individuals also appear receptive to new research findings that private school students outperform public school students—at least when such research comes from a conservative research organization. Indeed, the recorded responses of higher-educated people in the first treatment conditions are fully 12 percentage points higher than those in the baseline condition.

As a final cut at the data, Table 6.7 disaggregates the data according to respondents' own assessments about the quality of public schools in their districts. As one would expect, large differences across the baseline conditions are observed. Almost 80 percent of respondents who gave the public schools in their community a grade of C or below claimed that private school students outperform public school students, as compared to just 66 percent of respondents who gave the public schools in their community a grade of A or B. Interestingly, though, the impacts of the treatment conditions appear virtually identical for the two groups. Research findings that private school students score higher on standardized tests did not influence the thinking of either group. By contrast, research findings that public school students score just as high as private school students lead approximately 25 percent of both groups to adopt a different position than what was observed in the baseline condition. Whether research confirms or challenges people's general views about an issue, as long as these views are not tied to distinct ideological commitments or personal choices, proves immaterial. The direction and magnitude of opinion changes appear relatively constant.

SOME CONCLUDING THOUGHTS

The findings presented in this chapter appear consistent with most, though not all, of our expectations about the variable impacts of academic research on public opinion. Most dramatically, the influence of academic research on school sector effects appears asymmetric. Findings that confirm the widely held view that private school students outperform public school students do not appear to influence the thinking of an especially large portion of the American public; findings that challenge this view, in contrast, persuade a significant portion of the public to adopt an altogether different view. Indeed, the mere mention of a single academic report finding that public school students score just as high as private school students is enough to convince over one-quarter of the American public to express a different view on the matter.

The magnitudes of the treatment effects, meanwhile, varied dramatically for different populations. Consistent with our expectations about the alignment of a study's findings and citizens' ideological orientations and private choices, the effects of our treatment interventions appeared especially large for liberals, voucher opponents, and public school parents. Evidence of trusted signals, meanwhile, appears more sporadic. Though in some comparisons the magnitudes of the treatment effects appear slightly larger when the ideological orientation of the respondent and research organization align, the differences are not especially large. For the most part, in fact, whether the research organization was liberal or conservative did not matter nearly as much as the particular findings of the study.

The results from this simple experiment have clear implications for those scholars who conduct academic research on school sector effects. If your sole objective is to make the biggest possible splash, you should issue an academic report finding that public school students score just as high as private school students, and then you should distribute the findings to liberals, voucher opponents, and public school parents. By contrast, a surefire way to underwhelm the public is to issue a study—as I myself have done—that finds that private school students outperform public school students, and then to distribute the findings to almost any segment of the American public, with the possible exception of conservatives, private school parents, and the more-educated.

Obviously, one simple experiment cannot possibly identify all of the various ways in which academic research impacts public opinion on education. One wonders, for instance, whether the findings would substantially differ had the subject involved the performance of children in smaller and larger classes, rather than the more politically charged issue of private and public education. It also is quite possible that the particular venue in which citizens learn about academic research—whether on CNN or Fox News, for instance—may either enhance or mute the influence of the particular findings. It further remains unclear how consecutive studies that either complement one another or that challenge one another may influence the content of public opinion. Finally, nothing in the experiment considered here identifies the strength of people's convictions, measured either by the intensity of their views at any given point in time or the stability of their views over time. Plainly, this issue is ripe for continued study.

One thing, though, now is clear. For at least some segments of the public, some studies can shape popular views about the state of public education in America. Indeed, the relatively mild treatment effects examined here probably underestimate the potential influence of academic research. It is certainly true that citizens generally pay little attention to prominent academic debates, they lack the basic skills required to evaluate the quality of any particular study, and their views about education can be laced with ideological and personal biases. Nonetheless, scholarship can penetrate the public conscience—and for at least some citizens, the consequences can be dramatic.

For helpful feedback, I thank Chris Berry, Rick Hess, Sunshine Hillygus, Paul Peterson, and Martin West. For financial support, I thank the Program on Education Policy and Governance at Harvard University and IES grant R305A040043, National Research and Development Center on School Choice, Competition, and Student Achievement. Standard disclaimers apply.

CHAPTER 7

Calculated Justice: Education Research and the Courts

Joshua Dunn and Martin West

The role of the courts in education policymaking has, by any account, expanded in recent decades. In 1949, constitutional scholar Edward Corwin complained that the Supreme Court had established itself as a "super board of education for every school district in the nation" by striking down a Champaign, Illinois, program that allowed students to attend religious classes in school buildings during the regular school day.[1] This, however, was only the tip of the iceberg. Federal courts soon took the lead in banning de jure segregation and forcing districts to integrate their schools. Curricular decisions, disciplinary policies, the free speech rights of students, and state testing systems have all been the subject of numerous decisions since the 1970s.[2] Perhaps most remarkably, many state courts have claimed jurisdiction over the level of funding provided for public education, a question previously left to state legislatures and local taxpayers.[3]

As the scope of the courts' influence on education policy has grown, so, too, has judges' apparent reliance on social science evidence when crafting their decisions. Footnote 11 of the Supreme Court's landmark *Brown v. Board of Education* decision, which cited studies purportedly documenting the psychological harm of segregated schooling for black children, received widespread attention at the time—in part because the notion that social science was relevant to constitutional questions was largely unprecedented.[4] Yet contemporary decisions in education cases are invariably replete with references to studies commissioned for the case at hand, the testimony of scholars serving as expert witnesses, and the voluminous literature to which they have contributed.

This chapter does not assess whether courts *should* be making education policy; in fact, they do. It instead seeks to inform debates over the role of the courts by examining how education research has influenced judicial decisions in desegregation and school finance cases. Together, these two sets of cases represent the most sustained attempts to enlist the courts in the struggle for equal opportunity in American education.[5] Moreover, similarities and differences in the role education research has played in shaping jurisprudence in these areas shed light on the conditions under which social science evidence is likely to be pivotal.

In discussing the influence of education research on court decisions, we focus on studies that seek to establish a causal relationship between alternative schooling policies and outcomes for the students exposed to them. We therefore do not include descriptive data gathered to characterize facts relevant to a case, even though this type of evidence is frequently introduced in court, may be highly technical, and is often gathered by social scientists. For desegregation and school finance cases, the most relevant bodies of evidence examine the effects of integration, of overall school spending, and of investments in specific policies or programs on student outcomes.

Although the now-ubiquitous citation of this type of evidence in court decisions appears to make it difficult to draw distinctions between different areas of education litigation, our survey of the post-*Brown* era suggests that the role played by research varies based on the venue and nature of legal dispute under consideration. Specifically, recent history suggests that social science evidence has become less influential in federal courts but more influential in state courts. State courts, as we discuss below, are more political than federal courts, making them more likely to base decisions on the kinds of evidence traditionally relied upon by legislatures and executive agencies. This dynamic has been most evident in the area of school finance litigation, which, since the Supreme Court's 1973 decision in *San Antonio v. Rodriquez*, has been confined to state courts.[6]

Perhaps more important than the venue in determining the influence of education research, however, is the nature of the legal dispute. If the constitutional text is sufficient to decide a controversy, social science testimony is far less important. Deciding whether vouchers for religious private schools or affirmative action admissions policies are constitutional, for example, does not obviously require social science evidence. Relying on purely legal analysis, judges can and do arrive at decisions on either side of the issue. Social science is frequently used to clarify or sharpen the issues—or cited to enhance the authority of an opinion—but it is not essential.

Some disputes, on the other hand, by their very nature *require* that social science evidence play a determinative role. Most notably, the latest and ongoing wave of school finance litigation, the adequacy movement, could not have gained traction if courts were unwilling to base rulings squarely on purported research findings. The notion that spending is too low to provide a constitutionally acceptable standard of education rests on a finding of a direct causal relation between spending and student outcomes at current resource levels. Moreover, calculating a precise dollar figure at the remedial phase of litigation requires deference to expert consultants who have developed methods of doing so. Adequacy judgments therefore turn on social science evidence at both the liability and remedy phases.

In the end, we conclude that the courtroom has not proven to be an effective venue for aligning education policy with the findings of high-quality research. Yet the blame does not fall exclusively on judges and the constraints of judicial procedures for handling research-based evidence. A fundamental obstacle facing the courts has been the absence of clear standards within the education research community regarding what constitutes compelling evidence. Only in recent years have researchers begun to subject educational interventions to rigorous experimental and quasi-experimental evaluations of the type that are widely accepted in other policy domains.[7] Even today, the merits of this approach to the development of policy-relevant evidence remains contested.[8]

Strangely, the mixed quality of education research *increases* its significance in the courts by making it almost impossible to challenge the admissibility of particular experts or studies. Existing judicial standards for assessing the reliability of scientific evidence rely heavily on indicators of acceptance within the relevant scholarly community, such as publication in peer-reviewed journals. The lack of methodological consensus among education researchers ensures that such tests are of limited use, forcing judges to admit as evidence anything that has surface credibility and trust the adversarial process to reveal its flaws.

While education research has, under certain conditions, clearly influenced judicial decisions, the courts have also influenced the production of education research. When rigorous evidence is altogether lacking on issues central to legal disputes, litigants work assiduously to fill in the gaps. This dynamic is again most evident in the area of school finance, where the courts have emerged as important drivers of the production of new research evidence. "Costing-out" studies intended to specify precisely the amount of money required to raise student achievement to constitutionally acceptable levels are rapidly proliferating and now find audiences not only in the courtroom but in legislatures and within the scholarly community. The fact that all of the existing methods for addressing this question are fundamentally flawed has not yet limited their use.

BACKGROUND

Judicial reliance on social science evidence is hardly unique to the field of education. In fact, it was an inevitable byproduct of the vast expansion of judicial activity in the latter half of the twentieth century, which saw courts take an active role in matters as diverse as prison and mental hospital administration, welfare and employment policies, car safety standards, and environmental and land use regulation. Judicial decisions in each of these areas are marked by more affirmative and detailed remedies than had historically characterized American jurisprudence, often including specific appropriations decrees.[9] As courts accepted the invitation to engage in wholesale problem-solving rather than addressing particular grievances, they grew increasingly reliant on research evidence in order to justify their decisions and to anticipate their likely consequences.

Judicial Activism and Social Science Evidence

Judges' use of social science has not gone unnoticed by scholarly observers—nor by the courts. Indeed, it has played a central role in normative debates over the new model of public law litigation and the appropriate degree of judicial activism.[10] In his trail-blazing 1977 analysis of federal court involvement in social policy, Donald Horowitz asserted that the judicial system is ill-equipped to handle the inherently probabilistic evidence offered up by social scientists. He noted that federal judges are generalists, selected for their broad legal expertise and lacking in the specialized knowledge necessary to reach nuanced judgments about the quality of evidence on specific policy questions. Moreover, while the traditional adversarial fact-finding process is effective for ascertaining the historical facts of a particular case, Horowitz argued that it is poorly suited to discern the social facts about recurrent patterns of behavior on which policy decisions must be based.[11] According to the rules of procedure, trial court determinations of fact are upheld unless they are "clearly erroneous." A judge, therefore, may draw on social science evidence to establish as fact what studies are unable to show with certainty, and there are no available means to challenge such a determination.

A perhaps more fundamental problem underscored by Horowitz's analysis is the poor fit between available social science evidence and specific legal questions facing the courts: There are often no studies germane to the question at hand. Research can always be commissioned for the purposes of a particular lawsuit, but it is likely to be of lower quality due to constraints on time, resources, and data—and may even be biased. "The problems of social science do not disappear in litigation," Horowitz concluded, "but are instead compounded by the litigation setting, the different ways in which lawyers and social scientists ask questions, and the time constraint."[12]

The courts themselves have acknowledged a need to improve judicial procedures for dealing with scientific evidence. Specifically, the Supreme Court recently tightened the requirements for the admission of expert testimony in both the natural and social sciences in a trilogy of cases starting with *Daubert v. Merrell Dow Pharmaceuticals*.[13] These new standards were intended to limit the influence of "junk science" by requiring trial court judges to determine the reliability of expert testimony before admitting it as evidence. The Court said that judges should ask if the research was produced using the scientific method and offered a four-pronged test—now known as the *Daubert* standard—for determining this:

1. Could the evidence be empirically tested?
2. Has the method used been subjected to peer review?
3. Does the method used have a known error rate?
4. Is the method generally accepted within the relevant scientific community?

Evidence currently does not have to meet all of these criteria in order to be admissible, but they are to serve as a rough guide.[14]

The *Daubert* standard has had mixed success in keeping unreliable evidence from the natural and medical sciences out of the courtroom, and many states have since adopted it in their own court systems.[15] It remains unclear, however, whether the test could have any use in the social sciences, particularly in education research, because of the lack of consensus about methodological standards.

Political Venues: Federal and State Courts

Of course, there would be no debate about judicial capacity to interpret and apply social science evidence if judges refused to do so. Yet the distinctly political nature of American courts, both federal and state, makes them willing to entertain social science evidence when making constitutional decisions. Compared to other constitutional democracies, our method of selecting federal and state judges is shockingly political, regardless of whether they are elected or appointed. Aspiring federal judges, both district and appellate, are well-advised to be active in partisan politics. Senatorial courtesy, which effectively gives Senators in the president's party control over district court judgeships from their state, makes those positions a source of political patronage. As a result, more than 50 percent of federal judges have an established record of "party activism" before their appointment.[16] And, as high-profile fights over judicial nominations show, political considerations routinely intrude into the confirmation process.

State court judges by background and method of selection are even more political than federal judges, making them, in our view, even more likely to base their rulings on social science testimony. State judges are often elected in the first instance and are almost universally subject to retention elections.[17] Both types of elections, which used to be fairly sedate affairs, have become increasingly politicized since the 1980s. While trial court elections generally remain uncompetitive, elections at the intermediate appellate level and even more so at the high court level, are now highly competitive.[18] The increasingly contentious nature of judicial elections is best illustrated by exponential growth in campaign spending. For example, prior to 1984, candidates for the Texas Supreme Court spent, on average, less than $200,000.[19] By 2004, this number had risen to more than $2,000,000.[20] One reason for the growing intensity of state judicial elections has in fact been school finance litigation. Since 2000, for example, antitax and business groups in Ohio have spent substantial sums trying to unseat members of the state supreme court who ruled in favor of the plaintiffs in the state's adequacy litigation.[21]

The political vulnerability of state court judges would seem to give them reason to avoid relying on dubious social science research when wading into obviously political disputes over education funding. However, the logic could just as easily work the other way. Because state judges are subject to political retaliation, accepting the claims of experts who call for increased educational spending has appeal—voters tend to support the adequacy movement's abstract goal of improving education. Not only do decisions ordering additional spending find support from teachers unions, which are often part of the plaintiff group, but also judges can expect many parents to favor them as well. In short, political considerations not only make judges likely to consider social science evidence, but could also influence their interpretation of it.

DESEGREGATON

The Supreme Court's use of social science is notorious for its inconsistency. The Court, and even individual justices, often cite research-based evidence when it supports their position, and disparage or ignore it when it does not.

In *Craig v. Boren*, for example, Justice William Brennan dismissed the social science evidence underpinning Oklahoma's different legal drinking ages for men and women. The state defended its policy by producing statistical studies showing that young men were responsible for a disproportionate number of arrests for driving while intoxicated. After criticizing the studies, Brennan confessed that he actually did not understand them, saying,

> It is unrealistic to expect either members of the judiciary or state officials to be well versed in the rigors of experimental or statistical technique. But this merely illustrates that proving broad sociological propositions is a dubious business, and one that inevitably is in tension with the normative philosophy that underlies the equal protection clause. [22]

Brennan had an entirely different disposition to social science evidence presented in *McCleskey v. Kemp*. The famous "Baldus" study had shown that the race of a defendant in Georgia's capital cases was highly correlated with receiving the death penalty. The majority rejected the claim that this evidence was constitutionally significant. In his dissent, however, Brennan expressed complete confidence in both the study and his ability to understand it, saying that in reaching its conclusions, the study "relentlessly documents," "reveals," "shows," and "has particular force."[23]

More recently, the Court's decisions on all-male education at the Virginia Military Institute (VMI) in *United States v. Virginia*[24] and affirmative action in *Grutter v. Bollinger*[25] show the Court adopting completely different positions on social science. As David Faigman noted:

> In *Virginia*, the Court rejected VMI's contention that admitting women into its adversative training method would destroy that model, despite the considerable social science evidence that supported this judgment; in *Grutter*, the Court was deferential to the law school's contention that racial diversity would bolster its training methods, and used social science as window dressing to buttress this conclusion while ignoring any research that questioned it.[26]

The preferences and values of justices, it appears, not social science evidence, generally control the outcomes of cases in the nation's highest court.

Footnote 11

Of course, in education, desegregation is one area in which social science testimony has appeared to play a key role both in Supreme Court and lower federal court decisions. *Brown's* famous—or infamous—Footnote 11 was the first drop in a flood of research-based testimony that would find its way into judicial decisions in the following decades. However, while the volume of social science testimony only increased after *Brown*, its importance in shaping judicial decisions has fluctuated. In the first two decades of desegregation cases, including *Brown*, social science evidence played a supporting but hardly essential role. In the cases following *Milliken v. Bradley I*, however, social science evidence was integral in the remedial phase of litigation.

In *Brown*, the unanimous Court ruled that segregated education was "inherently unequal" and therefore in violation of the 14th Amendment's guarantee of equal protection.[27] Yet the Court did not ground its decision solely on the "inherent" inequality of segregated schooling. Instead, it sought to buttress its argument by noting the psychological damage segregation inflicted on minority children. "To separate them," the Court wrote, "from others of similar age and qualifications solely because of their race generates a feeling of inferiority as to their status in the community that may affect their hearts and minds in a way unlikely ever to be undone."[28] As evidence for this claim, the Court cited in Footnote 11 several studies that maintained that forced segregation caused permanent psychological harm to black children.

The significance of the psychological harm thesis to the Court's opinion is still a contentious matter. Even at the time, Legal Defense Fund attorneys were divided over whether to draw upon social science evidence. Jack B. Weinstein, for instance, recalled referring to the available studies as "crap" and not wanting to "build our case on a gimmick."[29] Still in dispute is whether the evidence was central to the Court's ruling in *Brown*. Some legal scholars have argued that it was insignificant and unnecessary for the decision.[30] Others have defended it on both legal and scientific grounds.[31] At the very least, evidence of psychological harm helped to distinguish segregated schooling from the segregated transportation facilities the court had upheld 60 years earlier in *Plessy v. Ferguson*, and it may, therefore, have been essential for Chief Justice Earl Warren to win the votes of his more conservative colleagues.[32]

Regardless of this continuing debate, the dangers of basing constitutional rulings on social science evidence were quickly evident in the wake of the Court's ruling in *Brown*. Most distressing was the fact that Kenneth Clark's famous "doll study" highlighted by the Court could plausibly lend support to segregationists.[33] Clark showed black children from segregated southern schools and integrated northern schools brown and pink dolls and then asked them a battery of questions to determine their feelings about each doll, assuming that the children's attitudes toward the brown doll indicated perceptions of themselves. The children generally preferred the pink doll, considering it "nice" and the brown doll "bad." But black children in segregated schools exhibited less negative reactions to the brown doll and showed less desire to play with the pink doll. This disconcerting fact allowed southern critics simultaneously to defend segregation as efficacious and to mock the Court for relying on specious evidence. This, Morroe Berger noted three years after the decision, "is the garden path down which the argument about damage to personality leads."[34]

Perhaps because of the less than reliable nature of existing social science evidence, the Court abandoned the psychological harm thesis in striking down other forms of segregation. In the decade following *Brown*, the Court overturned state laws mandating segregated golf courses, public transportation, and public beaches, all without resorting to the psychological harm thesis. Such laws were inherently unequal. In later generations of school desegregation cases, however, *Brown*'s psychological harm thesis would greatly influence the scope and structure of lower court remedies. In fact, district courts would routinely cite it to justify desegregation remedies.

Shifting Judicial Doctrine

Changes to judicial doctrine, though, soon altered the role of social science in desegregation cases more significantly. A series of decisions from 1968 through 1974 changed the standards for proving segregation, and forced judges to order remedies designed to improve education in addition to fostering racial integration. These new remedies effectively required the introduction of social science expertise in the remedial phase of desegregation cases in order to devise an appropriate strategy for school improvement. The first case, *Green v. New Kent County*,[35] held that segregated school districts had an "affirmative duty" to desegregate. In practical terms, this meant that school districts had to show that their policies led to meaningful integration. Superficially neutral policies were insufficient because they allowed segregationists to maintain racially isolated schools, often through blatant intimidation. This decision was followed by *Swann v. Charlotte Mecklenburg*,[36] which approved busing as a remedy for segregation and held that racially imbalanced southern school districts were presumptively segregated. The Court then took desegregation north in *Keyes v. Denver School District*,[37] and held that an entire school district could be considered segregated if segregation could be proved for even a small portion of the district. In the aftermath of *Keyes*, Gary Orfield said, "Courts almost always found school districts guilty of unconstitutional segregation whenever litigation was seriously pursued."[38]

While social scientists were routinely called upon during the trial phase of desegregation cases to prove or disprove claims of segregation, most of the time their testimony did not play a decisive role. Courts would cite it in their decisions, but the standards set by the Supreme Court made basic descriptive facts sufficient to reach a verdict. Compiling the racial composition of individual schools and comparing their deviation from the district's overall composition was often enough to demonstrate unconstitutional segregation.

The court's 1974 and 1977 decisions in *Milliken v. Bradley*, however, dramatically increased the role of educational experts in desegregation cases. In *Milliken I*, the Court forbade metropolitan-wide busing remedies unless suburban districts had participated in creating the constitutional violation.[39] Thus, while *Green*, *Swann*, and *Keyes* required judges to combat segregation, *Milliken I* deprived them of their primary tool. Busing would not work within urban school districts, which were already overwhelmingly racially isolated. The only alternative, sanctioned by the Court in *Milliken II*, was to order compensatory educational remedies.[40] This required educational experts to design magnet school programs to accomplish the dual purpose of improving the quality of education in racially isolated districts and drawing white students from the suburbs.

Importantly, by the time the Court decided *Milliken I*, a dramatic change had occurred in the social science literature on desegregation. In the 1960s, a naïve optimism pervaded the literature on desegregation, assuming that racial mixing alone would naturally lead to dramatic improvements in the educational lot of minority children. By 1974, that optimism had vanished.[41] The surprising victory of George Wallace in Michigan's 1972 Democratic presidential primary also revealed the anger that busing generated.[42] In short, both social-scientific and political considerations had made compensatory remedies increasingly attractive.[43]

Early compensatory remedies, though, tended to create "two-tiered" schools systems. Magnet schools at times provided a good education for the small percentage of students attending them. But most students remained in racially isolated and poorly performing schools, creating pressure to expand the scope of compensatory programs.

This dynamic led ultimately to *Missouri v. Jenkins*, the federal judiciary's most ambitious attempt to reform an urban educational system.[44] In this case, Judge Russell Clark was all but compelled to accept the proposals of educational experts who testified that the Kansas City, Missouri, School District (KCMSD) should undergo a massive program of "magnetization." This meant converting all of the district's high schools and middle schools and half of its elementary schools into magnets. The new school designs included such special facilities as a robotics lab, a petting zoo, a planetarium, a model United Nations with simultaneous translation capability, a natatorium with underwater viewing room, and a greenhouse. Additionally, the expert witnesses called for reduced class sizes, early language development programs, more school counselors, and more teacher training. All of this, according to the experts, would draw tens of thousands of suburban white students into the KCMSD.

Shockingly, one of the expert witnesses for the plaintiffs, Daniel Levine, testified that "in four or five years' time average achievement [in the school district] will be raised to the national average."[45] Levine was steeped in the "effective schools" approach to education research, which had emerged in the 1970s as perhaps the dominant paradigm among scholars studying school improvement. The effective schools literature claimed that it had identified "correlates" of school success, such as strong instructional leadership, a clear sense of mission, demonstrated effective instructional behaviors, high expectations for all students, frequent monitoring of student achievement, and a safe and orderly environment.[46] Aside from being vaguely tautological—effective schools tend unsurprisingly to have effective habits—the great mistake of the effective schools movement was the idea that mimicking attributes of effective schools would by itself turn around failing schools.

The predictions of the plaintiffs' experts were transparently unbelievable and, needless to say, unsupported by the evidence. The plaintiffs' own polls showed that the magnet schools were almost universally unattractive to suburban parents. Even the local branch of the NAACP (National Association for the Advancement of Colored People) urged presiding judge Russell Clark not to order the programs, saying that they would not improve the quality of education in the KCMSD. Defense witnesses such as Herbert Wahlberg explained in detail the obstacles the plan would face, and how it would only exacerbate the district's existing problems by adding another layer to its bloated administration and distracting attention from basic educational skills. Most importantly, the research presented in support of "effective schools" relied solely on small-scale studies. In short, the judge had more than sufficient information to expect that the programs he was ordering were unlikely to work, but ordered them anyway. The reason for such apparent irrationality was that Supreme Court doctrine required it. Based on Court precedents, the KCMSD was unconstitutionally segregated, the suburban school districts could not be included in the remedial plan, and small-scale programs were known to be ineffectual.

The result of having the interpretation of social science driven by judicial doctrine was an indisputable waste of resources. The court spent more than $2 billion dollars over fifteen years and every indicator of both segregation and student achievement in Kansas City got worse. Ironically, of the few schools that improved during the course of the case, most were "traditional" schools that remained largely untouched by the recommendations of the expert witnesses. In 2001, after the plan's failure, the plaintiffs' attorney confessed that the problem was that no one "understood the problems of scaling something up to a district-wide remedy."[47]

Judicial Pullback

As a result of cases such as *Missouri v. Jenkins*, the local hostility desegregation remedies often provoked,[48] and the seemingly unending demands the cases placed on federal judges, the Supreme Court pulled back from its involvement in desegregation in a series of three cases decided from 1991–95: *Board of Education of Oklahoma City v. Dowell, Freeman v. Pitts,* and *Missouri v. Jenkins III.*[49] In *Dowell,* the Supreme Court lowered the standard for removing judicial supervision of a school district; in *Freeman,* it allowed for partial removal of supervision if a school district could show that it was "unitary" in some areas of district operations; and in *Jenkins III,* it held that remedial plans such as the one ordered by Judge Clark conflicted with *Milliken I* since they constituted an "interdistrict" remedy for an "intradistrict" violation. As a result of these decisions, the federal judiciary's involvement in desegregation remedies receded, decreasing the influence of educational experts as well.

Today there are two remaining types of federal desegregation cases. The first are attempts to end judicial supervision by claiming unitary status. The second are challenges to voluntary integration plans like the ones recently considered by the Supreme Court in *Parents Involved in Community Schools v. Seattle School District No. 1* and *Crystal Meredith v. Jefferson County Board of Education.*[50] In both types, social science plays a limited role. Unitary status decisions require judges, as James Ryan has noted, to make "value judgments" about "federalism and the proper role of the courts" when deciding to end supervision—not to engage in an elaborate statistical analyses about the nature of current segregation and its effects on students.[51] This, in fact, is also how the Court decided the voluntary integration cases. Justice Roberts, writing for the majority and striking down the Seattle and Jefferson County programs, dismissed the competing social science evidence on the educational value of integration and diversity. While noting that "the parties and their amici dispute whether racial diversity in schools in fact has a marked impact on test scores and other objective yardsticks or achieves intangible socialization benefits," Roberts asserted that "the debate is not one we need to resolve."[52] Justice Kennedy, in his concurring and likely controlling opinion, paid no attention to social science evidence. Kennedy, as the swing vote in the 5–4 decision, refused to join the rest of the majority in condemning voluntary integration plans altogether. Instead, in his typical Delphic style,

Kennedy said that efforts to alleviate racial isolation could survive strict scrutiny if they did not treat "each student in a different fashion solely on the basis of a systematic, individual typing by race."[53]   The lack of clear principles in Kennedy's ruling makes it unlikely that lower courts will be able to find a discernible standard, which social science could help to resolve in future disputes.

SCHOOL FINANCE

Of the many areas in which courts have engaged in education policymaking, the extent of their involvement has been perhaps greatest when it comes to school finance. In contrast with desegregation litigation, which proceeded mainly within the federal court system, the locus of activity in school finance has been the states. At first, plaintiffs claimed that disparities in spending between districts ran afoul of the equal protection clauses of state constitutions. By the 1990s, however, equity claims had given way to lawsuits claiming that the level of funding provided school districts was too low to provide a constitutionally acceptable level of education. The shift from equity to adequacy as a litigation strategy brought school finance plaintiffs considerable success in the courtroom. It also heightened the courts' reliance on research investigating the relation between spending and student outcomes.

That relation has been controversial, at least since the 1966 publication of *Equality of Educational Opportunity* by sociologist James Coleman and colleagues.[54] Mandated by the U.S. Congress in the Civil Rights Act, the "Coleman Report" presented data from the first large-scale, nationwide survey of student performance in public schools. The report's startling conclusion that academic achievement was more strongly related to students' family backgrounds than to school resources triggered a scholarly debate over whether and how "money matters" for student outcomes—a debate that continues to this day. Economist Eric Hanushek, among others, has argued forcefully that there is no systematic link between levels of spending on public education and student outcomes.[55] Some scholars, however, dissent from this interpretation, arguing that the highest quality studies paint a more optimistic picture of the effects of spending on achievement.[56] While the contours of this debate have remained roughly fixed for four decades, the way in which the courts have responded to this controversy has evolved.

Equity Litigation

The guiding principle of equity litigation was the notion that the quality of a child's education should not be related to individual or community wealth, but only to the wealth of the state as a whole.[57] This approach departed from the earliest school finance cases, in which plaintiffs asserted that children were entitled to an education that met their needs. Federal courts had consistently denied these claims on the grounds that there was insufficient evidence on which to base a ruling. For example, in a 1968 case filed in Illinois, *McInnis v. Shapiro*, plaintiffs asked the court to redistribute tax revenues in "keeping with the needs of children."[58] The district court declined to intervene, explaining that there were no judicially manageable means for assessing those needs and determining whether they were being met. Similarly, in *Burrus v. Wilkerson* a district court in Virginia concluded in 1969 that "courts have neither the knowledge, nor the means, nor the power to tailor the public moneys to fit the varying needs of these students throughout the State."[59]

The equity principle seemed more amenable to judicial consideration, yet it required the development of an objective measure of school quality. The leading proponents of equity-based school finance litigation took a clear position as to how this should be done, arguing that, "Quality is the sum of district expenditures per pupil; quality is money."[60] In building the case for a judicial intervention, their decision to focus narrowly on inputs rather than on indicators of student outcomes may have reflected the lack of consensus among education researchers about the strength of the connection between the two.[61] Given the state of the research evidence in the wake of the Coleman Report, only an argument based on spending disparities pointed to a remedy that was conceivably within the capacity of the courts to achieve.

The equity argument was first embraced in the celebrated California decision of *Serrano v. Priest*, handed down by the state's high court in 1971.[62] Within eighteen months of that verdict, plaintiffs filed 53 separate lawsuits challenging the school finance systems in 38 states.[63] A federal district court in Texas in 1971 adopted the *Serrano* standard of fiscal neutrality and ordered the state to bring its finance system into compliance, opening the possibility of a single federal ruling applicable to all states.[64] The state of Texas, however, appealed the decision to the U.S. Supreme Court.

The Supreme Court's 1973 decision in *San Antonio Independent School District v. Rodriguez* effectively ended school finance litigation in the federal courts.[65] A 5–4 majority ruled that Texas' system of financing public schools, which allowed substantial disparities in local spending between property-rich and property-poor districts, did not violate the equal protection clause of the 14th Amendment of the U.S. Constitution. The Court's opinion centered not on the empirical question of whether spending determined school quality, but on the appropriate legal standard to apply. It reasoned that differences in wealth did not create a suspect class afforded special protection under the federal constitution, and that public education, despite its importance, is not a fundamental right which can only be abridged for a compelling governmental interest. The Court therefore concluded that the district court had erred in applying a "strict scrutiny" standard, and that the state's articulated interest in maintaining a locally controlled and financed school system provided a rational basis for the spending disparities that were its result. Judicial precedent guiding the interpretation of the equal protection clause made recourse to social science evidence unnecessary.

While education research did not figure prominently in the majority's legal reasoning, the *Rodriguez* Court did comment in passing on the state of the field. "On even the most basic questions in this area," it noted, "the scholars and educational experts are divided. Indeed, one of the most basic questions concerns the extent to which there is a demonstrable correlation between educational expenditures and the quality of education—an assumed correlation underlying virtually every legal conclusion drawn by the District Court in this case."[66] Embracing a position advanced in oral arguments by state's attorney Charles Alan Wright, the majority offered the lack of consensus among educational experts as an additional rationale for its decision. Specifically, they worried that inflexible spending constraints "could circumscribe or handicap the continued research and experimentation so vital to finding even partial solutions to educational problems and to keeping abreast of ever changing conditions."[67]

In the wake of the *Rodriguez* decision, litigants returned their attention to the states. If educational equity were not a fundamental federal right, they claimed, it was certainly guaranteed by state constitutions that explicitly ordered the legislature to provide for the education of its citizenry. The California Supreme Court, which had previously relied in part on the federal constitution to strike down intra-district spending disparities within that state, issued a new decision in 1976 based solely on its state constitution. Ruling that education did constitute a fundamental right under the California Constitution, the only remaining question was whether wealth-related disparities in spending affected the quality of education. Crucially, the court also rejected an outcome-based measure of educational quality, which would have forced an inquiry into the research controversy over the correlation between spending and school quality discussed in *Rodriguez*. Rather, it explicitly restricted its analysis to educational inputs, which were transparently related to spending. The court ultimately ruled that the state had to reduce disparities in spending across districts to less than $100 per pupil and substantially equalize tax rates within six years.[68]

Although equity plaintiffs in several states won cases in the 1970s, many judges refused to follow the California court's logic. Some were reluctant to interpret their own states' equal protection clauses in a way that differed from the Supreme Court's reading of the federal Constitution, while others worried about the implications for other policy domains in which spending also varied within the state.[69] It is also likely that some judges took notice of the political fallout in states that implemented strict equity verdicts. By reallocating funds from districts with higher property values and forcing wealthy districts to cut back their own spending, the implementation of the *Serrano* decision provoked a backlash among California voters and appeared to contribute to the passage of Proposition 13, which limited increases in residential property taxes.[70] By the late 1980s, equity claims had been successful in less than half of the states in which they were litigated.[71]

Notably, even those courts that have accepted equity claims have generally avoided taking a strong position on the relation between spending and school quality. One of the only equity-based cases to be decided in favor of the plaintiffs in the past decade, *Brigham v. State of Vermont*, provides a telling example.[72] The justices on the Vermont Supreme Court ruled unanimously that the state's system of funding public education, which depended heavily on local property taxes and created wide disparities in district revenues, deprived children of equal educational opportunity. In reaching this conclusion, the court emphasized the clear evidence on the "essential point" that "wide disparities in student expenditures exist among Vermont school districts and that these disparities correlate generally with taxable property wealth." It conceded that the record was "relatively less developed" on the plaintiffs' additional claim that funding disparities lead directly to unequal educational opportunities—despite the extensive expert testimony that had been offered.[73] Yet, in the court's view, the state's constitution did not require a firm conclusion on this point. So long as property-poor districts did not have substantially equal capacity to make educational investments, educational opportunities were inherently unequal and in need of remedy.

Adequacy Litigation

By the time the Vermont court issued its ruling in *Brigham*, however, the adequacy lawsuit had long since emerged as the dominant approach to school finance litigation. In 1989, the Kentucky Supreme Court declared the state's entire public education system unconstitutional and ordered the legislature to increase funding statewide so as to provide "funding sufficient to provide every child in Kentucky with an adequate education."[74] Since that time, courts in more than 35 states have heard claims that state finance systems fail to provide sufficient funding for many students to receive a constitutionally adequate education. Plaintiffs have won victories in roughly three-quarters of these cases, establishing state courts as de facto arbiters of the amount of funding school districts receive.[75]

The descriptive evidence presented to the courts in adequacy cases differs from equity cases in the emphasis placed on student outcomes. As Richard Briffault has pointed out, however, "A judicial determination of educational inadequacy in a particular school district is often predicated on some finding of inequity."[76] This determination could be based on evidence of raw disparities across districts in indicators such as graduation rates or the percentage of students performing at proficient levels on state exams. Alternatively, as was the case in the landmark Kentucky decision, evidence on the academic performance of students compared with students in other states may play a pivotal role. Either way, the vagueness of the state constitutional language on which these cases are based means that relative rather than absolute comparisons are usually essential to reach a judgment that a school system is inadequate.

While descriptive evidence of inequity plays a key role in both equity and adequacy cases, adequacy decisions turn on the additional inference that a lack of resources is to blame for shortcomings within a particular school system. The evidence on the relationship between overall spending and student outcomes, however, remains, at best, ambiguous. There is a growing body of rigorous evidence demonstrating the effectiveness of particular educational interventions, some of which would clearly require additional funds. This evidence is typically highlighted by adequacy plaintiffs in the courts and cited by judges who prove sympathetic to their claims. Yet the self-evident claim that more money, if spent well, would lead to improved student outcomes has no bearing on whether current spending levels are sufficient to provide students with an education of a particular quality. Inevitably, then, judicial decisions about the adequacy of school spending go well beyond what has been established conclusively by research.

Moreover, once a judge rules that funding in a particular state is inadequate, settling on a remedy requires evidence on the additional question of just how much money is needed to lift student outcomes to constitutionally acceptable levels. This is a question that education researchers had not, in the absence of judicial inquiries, felt compelled to ask. In light of the unclear relationship between current spending levels and student outcomes, researchers had sensibly focused on evaluating the efficacy of specific interventions, hoping to improve the cost-effectiveness of educational operations. Yet evidence on "what works" in education, while clearly useful for informing policy decisions, is tangential to the question of how much money is required to raise student outcomes to desired levels.

As discussed above, however, the absence of evidence on empirical questions made relevant by novel legal doctrine does not necessarily constitute a barrier to judicial action. New studies can be conducted and new methods devised to fill the void. In the case of adequacy litigation, the professional and financial rewards to researchers of providing information to the courts have been enough to drive the proliferation of "costing-out" studies intended to determine objectively the amount of funding necessary to provide students with an adequate education. Since 1990, formal costing-out studies have been conducted in more than 37 states, often as a result of a court mandate, with 17 studies in 15 states conducted since 2005.[77] The leading professional association for scholars studying school finance, the American Education Finance Association, offered a workshop on costing-out at its 2005 annual meeting featuring proponents of the most widely used approaches.[78]

Importantly, the two most common approaches to costing-out have their origins in particular adequacy cases. Researchers developed the "professional judgment" method, which relies on panels of educators to determine the resources needed to ensure adequate levels of achievement, to comply with a 1995 decision of the Wyoming Supreme Court. In *Campbell County School District v. State*, the court found the state's school finance system to be unconstitutional on both equity and adequacy grounds and ordered the legislature to calculate the costs of the "basket of goods and services" needed to establish a "visionary" school system equal in quality to the very best in the world.[79] Because Wyoming did not have a statewide achievement test at the time, James Guthrie and his colleagues at Management Analysis and Planning modeled their casting-out analysis on practices at federal agencies with limited access to performance measures such as the Food and Drug Administration, Air Traffic Control Administration, and the Veterans Administration, which had all relied on expert panels to estimate the costs of operations.[80]

Although professional judgment studies initially appeared to offer a relatively analytic and objective means of calculating educational costs, the method's weaknesses when conducted in the context of politicized debates over school finance are increasingly clear. The panels convened to identify the resources necessary to meet judicially mandated quality standards often include educators from the districts which stand to receive increased funding as a result of their study, creating a clear conflict of interest. Tellingly, the costs estimated by professional judgment panels in different states vary enormously in ways more easily attributed to the political context than to real differences in resource costs, student needs, or court-established standards for adequacy. As Guthrie himself has noted, "An increasing number of professional judgment studies are devoid of methodological rigor and have been infected with self-serving biases hardly worthy of legislative, executive, and judicial consideration."[81] Nonetheless, professional judgment studies have been used to inform judicial and legislative deliberations in at least 18 other states to date.[82]

The most widely used alternative to professional judgment, the "successful schools" or "empirical" methodology, was first employed by John Augenblick and colleagues in 1995 as the Ohio Supreme Court considered an adequacy claim in *DeRolph v. State*. Researchers using this approach first identify a group of school districts where student outcomes exceed whatever benchmarks have been established by the court as indicators of adequacy. After removing unusually high- and low-spending districts, average spending levels within this group are used to estimate the cost of an adequate education elsewhere in the state (sometimes after making adjustments for differences in student characteristics assumed to influence costs). The glaring internal contradiction that results—that half of the "successful" districts inevitably spend less than the amount determined to be adequate—highlights the fundamental problem with this approach: it ignores the fact that districts operate at different levels of efficiency.[83] Despite this shortcoming, however, successful school studies have been conducted in at least ten states to date.[84]

More recently, developed costing-out methods include the "state-of the-art" model, which is based on analysts' reading of the research literature on the effects of various educational interventions, and "cost-function" techniques, which base cost estimates on the overall correlation between expenditures and student achievement within the state. All, however, are fundamentally flawed. As a disclaimer included in one recent costing-out study puts it, "The effort to develop these approaches stems from the fact that no existing research demonstrates a straightforward relationship between how much is spent to provide education services and performance, whether of student, school, or school district."[85] That being the case, it is impossible to use data on existing school operations to identify the amount of money needed to produce an adequate education.

Of course, some courts finding for the plaintiffs in adequacy cases choose not to specify a precise dollar amount by which spending must be increased, leaving that matter instead to be determined by the legislature. While this approach may initially appear to diminish the influence of the problematic costing-out studies presented in the courts, in fact it merely transfers the problem into the legislature, where the social science the court's ruling relied on inevitably holds the trump card. A reluctant legislature may choose to ignore a study's findings, yet this guarantees future litigation.

Still another strategy courts have taken is to mandate a detailed set of policy changes to accompany spending increases, as they did in New Jersey's *Abbott* decisions and the *Leandro* decisions in North Carolina. Courts adopting this approach do tend to base their orders on rigorous and methodologically transparent research evidence, such as randomized controlled trials, but they tend to ignore questions of scale and judicial capacity. Most of the evidence demonstrating the effectiveness of early childhood education, for example, comes from small, intensive interventions for extremely disadvantaged students, and may not generalize to other types of programs and populations. In much the same way, experimental evidence shows that class size reduction in the early grades can raise achievement, but it is not at all clear that wholesale class size reductions represent the most effective use of funds. Moreover, while experience suggests that courts can drive the implementation of popular reforms, there is no guarantee that popular reforms will be effective on their own. Indeed, case study evidence on the implementation of adequacy judgments suggests that they have not been accompanied by meaningful attempts to increase accountability for results within public education—even when such measures have been mandated by the courts.[86]

Recent decisions in several states suggest that courts may be growing more reluctant to engage in long, drawn-out deliberations over school finance. The Ohio Supreme Court, in 2005, after several failed attempts to win compliance with an earlier adequacy judgment, opted to leave the matter to the legislature to resolve. In 2007, the state supreme courts in Nebraska and Oklahoma dismissed adequacy claims altogether on the grounds that the adequacy of educational spending was a nonjusticiable issue. Previously, Rhode Island (1995), Pennsylvania (1998) and Illinois (1999) had been the only states to reject adequacy claims on those grounds. Also in 2007, the Arizona Supreme Court reversed a trial court ruling that an adequacy claim filed in the state was nonjusticiable, yet granted the state's motion for a summary judgment to dismiss the case.

CONCLUDING THOUGHTS

While the recent trend in adequacy litigation indicates that courts are weary of school finance litigation, any belief that judicial involvement will end abruptly would be premature. In fact, if suggested revisions to the No Child Left Behind Act (NCLB) are adopted, a new wave of litigation could begin. Both the Aspen Institute and Education Trust have suggested adding a private right of action allowing parents to bring suit if they believe that their state has failed to implement NCLB appropriately. While the proposals differ in their particulars, either would be a boon to the adequacy movement. Leaders of the movement, such as Michael Rebell, have always been optimistic about the potential of NCLB to support their litigation. The data on student achievement that states must now collect, he thinks, provide ready-made evidence of inadequacy.[87] A private right of action under NCLB would open a new avenue for judicial involvement in education and undoubtedly increase the volume of education research evidence entering the courtroom. The issues raised by our analysis, then, are likely to remain central to how education policy is made and implemented.

Two of these issues appear to be especially troubling. The first is that even if courts rely on rigorous research when ordering reforms, that research is unlikely to be applicable to the fundamental question of how to generate improved student outcomes at scale. Examples from both desegregation and adequacy litigation illustrate this problem. Proponents of the effective schools literature relied on in *Missouri v. Jenkins* could point to isolated success stories when individual schools followed the example of successful schools. But, as the plaintiffs' attorney later acknowledged, the experts' assurances that this model of improvement could be applied to an entire district were wholly unfounded. Similarly, randomized controlled trials indicate that the Success For All (SFA) reading program ordered by the New Jersey courts in the *Abbott* adequacy litigation can enhance students' reading ability. Teachers in plaintiff districts, however, resented having the program thrust on them, which naturally undermined its effectiveness.[88]

In short, even the most rigorous experimental evaluation is unlikely to approximate the conditions facing administrators who implement a program across a district—much less an entire state. Unfortunately, as Nathan Glazer has pointed out, increased judicial oversight of administrative organizations serves only to "exaggerate theoretical considerations and reduce practical considerations." For example, he notes, "In a school desegregation case, it is not a teacher or principal who will testify, but experts and administrators from distant universities on both sides of the argument."[89] Plaintiff attorneys can call on expert witnesses who will testify that rigorous research supports their demands even if there are serious obstacles to effective implementation. Measures aimed at limiting the admissibility of expert testimony, such as the *Daubert* standards, are thus unlikely to enhance judicial capacity to drive large-scale educational improvement.

The second, and perhaps most troubling, issue is that education research can mask the inherently political judgments courts inevitably make when ordering educational reforms. Having a cadre of experts pointing to ostensibly scientific evidence makes adopting the textually slender claims of adequacy litigation seem far more defensible because judges can say that it is science, not politics, that underpins their judgment. This dynamic is hardly unique to education litigation. Shep Melnick, for instance, has documented the same phenomenon in litigation over issues ranging from air quality to disability insurance.[90] In all of these areas, judges have justified their actions with an appeal to expert judgment, which is allegedly free of political bias. Adequacy litigation presents a particularly compelling example, though, because it is the absence of clear constitutional or statutory standards that makes expert testimony essential in the first place.

But the consequences of judicial reliance on educational research extend beyond dubious constitutional or statutory decisions. Instead of having education policy made in an open, deliberative process through representative institutions such as legislatures and school boards, it is made through a closed, adversarial legal process which encourages extremism in the claims made by the parties and thus extremism in the testimony of expert witnesses. The increased judicialization of educational policy, which expert witnesses encourage, directly affects the kinds of research scholars produce. The incentives are powerful, as James Guthrie has noted with respect to costing-out studies, to shape your conclusions to fit the claims of those who have hired you.[91] Moreover, while representative institutions must consider the evidence from a variety of perspectives, the policy horizons of courts are far narrower. Researchers who think that neither side is correct will not have an audience before the court because no one will call on their services. Of course, school boards and legislatures routinely make policy mistakes and often ignore research evidence altogether. But given the complexity of the American education system—it is a vast domain connected to other equally vast domains—arbitrarily narrowing the range of policy choices is unlikely to yield successful reforms.

We are grateful to Martha Derthick, John Dinan, James Guthrie, Al Lindseth, Shep Melnick, Paul Peterson, Michael Podgursky, James Smith, and Matthew Springer for helpful discussions of this subject. Chris Bennett and Arthur Kim at Brown University provided valuable research assistance.

CHAPTER 8

Flying (Partially) Blind: School Leaders' Use of Research in Decisionmaking

Lance D. Fusarelli

Critics bemoan the seeming lack of impact that education research has on the practice and improvement of schooling.[1] Researchers commonly lament that educators do not read or use all of the valuable research produced in universities, think tanks, and regional development labs. If only school leaders would pay more attention to research, the argument goes, "they would make better decisions about improvement strategies and resource allocation, and we would see better results."[2]

Drawing from a limited body of research on knowledge utilization in education and on research utilization in other areas, such as business, the military, and public sector organizations, coupled with an extensive review of professional association journals and personal correspondence with eighteen superintendents, district officials, principals, and evaluators from four states, this chapter examines how research is used (and why it isn't used more often) in decisions about school improvement.[3] If research is not used systematically in decisionmaking, what barriers exist and what can be done to create incentives to ensure greater research utilization in education? The chapter concludes with recommendations about how policymakers can facilitate greater utilization of research by school leaders for school improvement.

RESEARCH UTILIZATION WITHIN AND ACROSS ORGANIZATIONAL SECTORS

Research has had a greater impact on some sectors of society than others, particularly in the private sector. Organizations that utilize research and actively incorporate it into decisionmaking are more effective than other organizations. To compete and survive in a hostile and increasingly competitive environment, businesses both large and small have been forced to adopt research-based best practices to improve organizational performance, although some would suggest that the startlingly high number of annual business failures in the United States, particularly among start-ups, suggests that research utilization in the private sector is uneven.

In the public sector, increased competition and increased public dissatisfaction with poor organizational performance has forced organizations to adapt research-based best practices to ensure organizational survival, although the degree of research utilization within the public sector is uneven as well. The scope, variety, and organizational complexity of public sector organizations rivals, if not surpasses, that found in the private sector. Despite their differences, all are faced with the challenges of eliminating poor quality, empowering employees, eliminating waste, improving customer service, and increasing productivity with limited resources. Some public sector organizations have been able to adapt and learn effectively, while others have struggled. For example, in Vietnam, the military was criticized for its inability to adapt to the changing reality of warfare; its leaders were thought to be fighting the last war rather than preparing for the next one. Yet, post Vietnam, military leaders are generally credited with putting strategic plans and processes in place that have improved organizational performance. As another example, in response to withering criticism of its unresponsiveness to citizen complaints, the Internal Revenue Service implemented Total Quality Management (TQM) throughout the organization. The IRS sharply reduced the average account problem-resolution time from 45 days to 2–3 days, reduced the turnaround time for inquiries from weeks to four days, reduced interest charges to the federal government four-fold, increased internal and external customer satisfaction, improved morale, and in the process saved taxpayers nearly three million dollars.[4]

Other public organizations, however, have been slower to adopt research-based best practices to improve organizational performance. Let us take, for example, schools. Organizations that utilize research-based best practices for continuous improvement are what Peter Senge refers to as learning organizations. So, are schools learning organizations? At first blush, the answer is obvious—of course they are; that's what they are supposed to do. Well, yes, that is at least partially true; students learn, albeit unevenly, but it is much less clear whether adults in schools, particularly teachers and school leaders, also learn (and whether what they learn is research-based best practices or survival skills). It is assumed that education leaders use research in making decisions about school improvement, that they draw lessons from the research and from successful practices of others, and that they don't reinvent the wheel every time they make a curriculum or programmatic decision. Denis Doyle, co-founder of SchoolNet, asserts that the idea is "so obvious and commonsensical it is hard to imagine why it is not the norm. Is there any other way to make decisions? Unhappily, the answer is yes."[5]

For example, a scathing report on problems in the Los Angeles Unified School District (LAUSD), the nation's second largest, sharply criticized school officials for their failure to implement the recommendations of program and system performance evaluations, and for their failure to replicate successful programs throughout the district. Unfortunately, Los Angeles may not be atypical. If public organizations can and do learn, then possibly education reform could produce its intended objective—the improvement of practice—if internal organizational learning processes are incorporated into the institutional design framework. We turn now to an exploration of the ways in which research has been used by school leaders to improve practice.

THE USE OF RESEARCH IN EDUCATION

In her extensive review of the role of research in policymaking, Carol Weiss found that policy actors claim to be influenced by social science research but, "when pressed to give examples, often cite broad generalizations . . . or social science concepts. . . . Not single findings, one by one, but *ideas* from social science research appear to affect the development of the policy agenda," a finding which has been confirmed by a study of principals' use of research in decisionmaking in Missouri.[6] Mary Kennedy refers to such research as conceptual research—research that impacts the climate of opinion as opposed to instrumental research (highly prescriptive—method A is superior to method B), which she asserts is not really possible in an education context due to the difficulty of conducting randomized, controlled trials.[7]

Surprisingly little research exists as to the extent to which educators use research in decisionmaking. Undoubtedly, some school leaders use research and many incorporate it into their professional practice.[8] A survey of principals in the United States and Australia found that most principals hold positive opinions about research and use it to inform decisionmaking.[9] In interviews with superintendents, Gary Huang and colleagues found that nearly all of them reported that they "read reports of research studies and program evaluations at least occasionally." Two-thirds reported that research helped them to "sort out the effective methods we ought to copy."[10] However, school leaders are more likely to cite general research traditions or concepts such as brain research or emotional intelligence rather than specific studies.

Unfortunately, these examples notwithstanding, instances of how research has informed decisionmaking or improved schooling are relatively rare. Victoria Bernhardt, the author of several books on data-based decisionmaking in education, observed the irony that the penal system in the United States uses education data (the number of elementary students not reading on grade level) to predict "the number of prison cells to build ten years hence," yet educators themselves rarely use data in their strategic school improvement plans.[11] Psychological research on children's self-image and legal research on school finance have been cited by the courts in decisions ending de jure segregation and inequities in school finance, which have significantly influenced education practice. Research on elements of effective schools and whole-school reform models has helped some schools and school districts to significantly improve education outcomes, as has research on some early reading programs, class-size reduction, and value-added accountability systems.[12] However, other programs, even those that have been extensively studied, such as Head Start, charter schools, and vouchers, have failed to provide school leaders with clear, consistent, and definitive evidence of effectiveness. Moreover, even if research was to conclusively demonstrate the effectiveness of certain reforms, the personal ideologies and beliefs of school leaders would likely override or supersede research findings.

Although use of academic research to inform policy is uneven, particularly in "soft" social science areas such as education, research is sometimes used as a guide in crafting better education policies. For example, Tennessee lawmakers used the value-added assessment system developed by William Sanders as the centerpiece of the state's school improvement efforts. Several states, most notably Florida, Kentucky, South Carolina, and Texas, have undertaken comprehensive systemic reform initiatives and improved their education systems over time, based in part on policy feedback from school leaders. Incoming reports on these initiatives suggest some degree of organizational learning is occurring.[13] Unfortunately, these examples represent only a tiny fraction of the vast amount of education research produced every year. This begs the question: Why hasn't research been used more often by school leaders to improve education practice?

BARRIERS TO RESEARCH UTILIZATION IN EDUCATION

Why don't educators use research more often as they make decisions about how best to improve schools? Several barriers exist—some institutional and structural, others personal—that impede the use of research in education decisionmaking.

The Ambiguity of Social Science and Education Research

Through organizational learning processes, school leaders may use research to discover what policies and programs work best and why. The problem is that it can be challenging to find many examples of the direct impact of social science or education research on practice. Petrilli notes that "it is notoriously difficult to determine the impact of research and scholarship on public policy."[14] Daniel Callahan and Bruce Jennings found that "occasionally the findings of social scientific studies are explicitly drawn upon by policymakers in the formation, implementation, or evaluation of particular policies. More often, the categories and theoretical models of social science provide a general background orientation within which policymakers conceptualize problems and frame policy options."[15]

Often in the social sciences, research produces new arguments and further complicates reality, which can be confusing to school leaders seeking clear direction and prescriptive solutions to complex education problems. As research proliferates, it often crosses disciplinary boundaries—produces greater methodological complexity, generates competing paradigms, and becomes less accessible to practitioners—leading to confusion and frustration.[16] This clearly is the case with much education research, which all-too-often becomes embroiled in paradigm wars, competing ideologies, or becomes so specialized that school leaders have difficulty making sense out of the noise.

Furthermore, the "it depends" response of researchers to many issues tends to freeze out researchers from having a significant impact on decisionmaking.[17] Social science research is complex, contextual, and seldom provides clear direction for school leaders. In her review of the history of education research, Ellen Condliffe Lagemann observes that the research community rarely reaches consensus about what education policies work best and rarely conducts research on the practical problems faced by school leaders.[18] School leaders are faced with a confounding mass of often-conflicting research. A veteran superintendent remarked, "I've been in education for 35 years. Honestly, nobody really knows what's going on in the area. . . . Today, you read reports about this and this, next day you read reports about just the opposite. There is no consistency. That's frustrating. Education research is not a science, not scientific. It is not objective."[19] Christopher Cross, former assistant secretary for the Office of Educational Research and Improvement, calls this the "Cross' corollary, that is, for every study in education research, there are an equal or greater number of opposing studies."[20] The four research minidramas highlighted by Henig (chapter 3 in this volume) exemplify this phenomenon.

From the perspective of many school leaders, the inconclusive nature of some education research, particularly the existence of conflicting studies, suggests significant disagreement about what works best, where, and under what conditions. This makes it problematic for superintendents and principals to learn and leads to confusion and mistrust among educators.[21] While the view that educational research too-often produces inconclusion or, worse yet, conflicting results, is not shared by all researchers, it is an article of faith among school leaders. Learning is difficult, if not impossible, when the lessons themselves are conflicting and unclear. Thus, unlike research on nuclear energy, transportation safety, defense, or medicine, the very nature of research in education makes it comparatively less useful as a clear guide for decisionmaking, which is what school leaders most want and need from the research community.[22]

This is not to say that all education research is irrelevant or useless. For example, many useful insights have been gleaned from studies of teacher turnover, school choice, the value of phonics mastery in the early grades, and special education. Further, many districts, particularly larger districts, regularly bring in education researchers to work with school leaders and staff on research-based school improvement processes and strategic planning initiatives. Thus, it is clear that school leaders are not unaware of research-based best practices, nor do they always ignore research in decisionmaking. However, the extent to which events such as attending a one- or two-day professional development seminar get translated into research-based decisionmaking at the district or school level varies widely from district to district, from school to school.

Education Research as Advocacy

Many school leaders view education research with skepticism. As state and federal officials have become more deeply involved in education reform, research is often used by politicians "in an advocacy fashion, i.e., to buttress one's position or to attack an opponent's."[23] In such cases, research "becomes ammunition for the side that finds its conclusions most congenial and supportive. Partisans brandish the evidence in an attempt to neutralize opponents, convince waverers, and bolster supporters."[24] Research supplies school leaders with knowledge to be used for influence and persuasion—policy analysis is reduced to policy argument.[25]

This skepticism is widely shared among school leaders who are constantly bombarded by companies promising the latest "magic bullet" to eliminate the achievement gap. Reid Lyon, former chief of the Child Development and Behavior Branch at the National Institute of Child Health and Human Development, notes that many companies that market instructional software manipulate research—in fact, many produce their own supportive research—in order to convince school superintendents to purchase their products. Few of these studies meet the gold standard of scientifically based research. According to Lyon, claims are often "based on any kind of document—whether it's an unpublished technical manual, an opinion piece, or an editorial."[26] Superintendents and principals are busy enough without having to shift through research spin and marketing hype. One veteran superintendent commented that her principals regularly return from mega-conferences where they hear a presentation or two about "something touted as a fix for what ails the schools and they come home primed to purchase it." A principal in North Carolina concurred: "Generally, I think we just jump on the bandwagon of the latest, flashiest consultants . . . and they may or may not have research on their side." This leads some school leaders to mistrust statistics, research, and slick marketing gimmicks, viewing them "as blatant attempts to distort or manipulate an audience."[27]

Others distrust research because it is frequently used to promote political agendas.[28] The active involvement of state legislators, governors, big business, and interest groups in education reform in the past two decades contributes significantly to the skeptical view that education (including education research) has become increasingly politicized. Everyone wants to be the "education governor" or the "education president" and has his or her preferred reforms to fix what is broken. A superintendent in Texas questioned the meaning of research-based programs. He observed that the state requires that school programs be research-based in order to qualify for state funds. However, "When the list of 'research-based' programs came out, companies owned by two former Commissioners of Education for the State of Texas were on the list." The superintendent asked if this was "politics or research-based?"[29]

School leaders' skepticism of research has been heightened by the influx of policy research produced by think tanks and policy centers, which, according to a professional evaluator, do "a much better job of putting their research in the hands of decision makers in user-friendly formats" than do academic researchers.[30] The media further contributes to this malaise, reporting the latest he said/she said findings from high-profile researchers and think tanks. The tendency of some academic researchers and policy wonks to bypass peer review in an effort to quickly disseminate their findings to the widest possible audience contributes to this "research noise" and confusion by disseminating sometimes poor-quality, nonvetted or nonblind reviewed research directly into the hands of policymakers.

Incomplete Information in a Loosely Coupled System

In addition to concerns about the ambiguity and bias of research, school leaders tend not to incorporate research into their daily practice because they rarely have the luxury of complete information. Critics argue that models premised on organizational learning rely too heavily on an idealized or rationalized policy paradigm that fails to adequately capture the uncertainty and interpretive nature of policymaking, exemplified by garbage can models of the policymaking process.[31] Decisionmaking in education often takes place under conditions of uncertainty and with incomplete information.[32]

Decisionmaking in organizations, especially public organizations such as schools, "takes place in a context where 'rational information' is but one among many contending forces."[33] These forces include conflict over the values, goals, and objectives of the organization.[34] This is particularly true in schools, which are hotbeds of conflicting values regularly played out in school board elections and in leadership turnover. Resolving questions over conflicting values "involves a contest of personal preferences in which reason plays little role, [and] political criteria rather than scientific principles govern the determination of value disputes."[35] A veteran superintendent in Texas agrees: "Policy is based on politics," which reflect "closely held beliefs, not research-based beliefs. There is a saying . . . 'It's their kids, their schools, and their money.' If the public wants something, then it is their children, their schools, and their money." She asked, "Why does Texas spend so much on high school football? We spend it because that is what the public wants us to spend education dollars on. If research proved that football reduced student IQ's by 20 basis points, we would still offer and support football as long as the people who are paying the bills put a premium on offering it. Public schools are political units, and the public, by damn, pay the bills and determine the standards of quality."[36] Many school leaders who emphasized the politics involved in education decisionmaking in school systems at both the district and local school level share this superintendent's sentiments.

Organizational learning and research utilization is much more common in highly technical areas such as airline deregulation, communications, and energy policy—where science more clearly identifies best practices—than in areas such as education, where disagreement exists about many issues—from pedagogy and curriculum to school finance and governance.[37] Unlike virtually all other major institutions in society, schools remain loosely coupled organizations consisting of multiple, often conflicting, and indeterminate goals. For example, scholars who have studied the reading and math wars note that political forces have privileged particular approaches to teaching and researching those subjects, which has produced swings in both dominant pedagogies and competing research paradigms.[38] Furthermore, the participation and involvement of organizational members is fluid (the number of participants is exceeded only by the various degrees of involvement of stakeholders). Schools are notorious for their lack of horizontal and vertical alignment of core instructional processes.[39] The political nature of the education process leads to situations where data is easily distorted and where power is often more important than data in decisionmaking.[40] Organizational learning under these conditions is exceedingly difficult.

Decisionmaking and program adoption in education is shaped by and often determined by ease of use, good marketing, lack of threat to current practice, "philosophical commitments, political necessities, and the attractiveness or popularity of ideas" rather than research-based evidence of program effectiveness.[41] One veteran principal who has led schools in New York and Connecticut stated that many superintendents and school boards he has worked for "pick research [adopt reforms] that meets their budget needs" rather than that which has the most credible scientific support.[42]

Ideology and Professional Culture

The professional culture of many schools "in which the 'good' and the 'popular' [are] valued more than the effective" further mitigates against the use of research in decisionmaking.[43] School leaders play a key role in this process. Sometimes, differences exist between the anecdotal professional experiences of principals and superintendents and what the research says is most effective—a difference which may be attributed to conflicting professional cultures. For example, in Los Angeles, the district's chief instructional official admitted that she did not examine the research on the Waterford Early Reading program before recommending that the district invest nearly $50 million to purchase the program. When asked why she ignored the research, she responded, "Every classroom situation is different. And nothing compares to L.A. I'd rather listen to my own teachers."[44]

The ideological and professional beliefs of school leaders—beliefs about what is right or about what works based on individual experience—feel more relevant than abstract statistics and often trumps findings from meta-analyses of research. A veteran district leader in North Carolina expressed her belief that, "Many educators have always made decisions from their 'gut,'" so using research and data to make decisions "is new to them," especially "for older educators who were not raised in their careers in the era of accountability." As an award-winning principal in North Carolina stated, "anyone can find research to support what they are doing." A veteran New York principal concurred, asserting that, "Principals try to find [*Phi Delta*] *Kappan* articles that support their views."[45] This clash between the professional culture of researchers and those of school leaders explains in large part why research is so often ignored in school decisionmaking.

School leaders are also heavily influenced in their adoption of programs and reforms by what their peers are doing (the regional research diffusion model). Sometimes, school leaders learn and apply good lessons or best practices from neighboring districts, while at other times they apply poor lessons or find that what worked in one district is not working in their own.

Uneven Quality of Research

Complicating the uneven use of research in decisionmaking is the fact that although much education research is produced, we have comparatively little high-quality research; what we have is of such uneven quality that it is of limited utility as a guide to school leaders to improve practice.[46] This situation is the result of several factors. Unlike medicine, where a handful of top journals such as the *New England Journal of Medicine* (*NEJM*) and the *Journal of the American Medical Association* (*JAMA*) and specialized journals reporting advances in medical specialties, serve as the gold standard for advancing knowledge in the field, no comparative education equivalents exist, in part because of serious and fundamental disagreement about what constitutes valid, reliable research. Although many scholars would argue that the *American Educational Research Journal* and other journals published under the auspices of the American Educational Research Association (AERA), or journals such as *Educational Administration Quarterly*, published by the University Council for Educational Administration, are the educational equivalent of *NEJM* or *JAMA*, the varying quality and conflicting findings of education research published in even these top-tier journals contributes to the research noise and policy confusion that school leaders sometimes hear when they seek to utilize research in decisionmaking.[47]

This situation is compounded by the fact that so many education research journals exist. *Cabell's Directory*, which contains a description of journals devoted to education research, contains 1,025 entries (comprising six volumes).[48] More than 20,000 articles are published in education journals each year.[49] It is virtually impossible for even fulltime education researchers to keep abreast of the latest research in the field, let alone school leaders busy managing the increasingly complex daily operations of schools.

Personal and Professional Barriers to Research Utilization

Even if the research community could somehow come to agreement on what works best, some personal barriers exist which limit school leaders' use of research in decisionmaking. The most common reasons why school leaders do not use research in decisionmaking are: questionable relevancy to users' needs, lack of expertise, lack of time, cultural conflict, and poor communication between researchers and practitioners.[50] Some educators have plenty of data but poor data analysis skills and lack a firm grasp of statistics.[51] Few school leaders are adequately trained in data collection and analysis, with many either uncomfortable with using it or viewing it as just another mandate that takes time away from the real work of educating students.[52]

The sheer volume of education research creates a daunting obstacle for school leaders seeking to use research in decisionmaking. A veteran evaluator commented that "there is so much they [school leaders] have to wade through before they get to something that is relevant to them—either the findings are too abstract or the context doesn't fit and many journals are so eclectic that it is a struggle to find the kind of research they are looking for. Time wasted with the bad or irrelevant research, or deciphering an article that was written for another academic instead of a practitioner, reinforces the idea that they [school leaders] don't have time to spend on understanding the research." A rural principal and a rural district leader concurred and argued that efficient access to key databases was essential for improved research utilization in decisionmaking.[53]

Originally, federally funded regional education labs (RELs) were designed to conduct and disseminate applied research to school leaders. However, none of the school leaders contacted for this paper mentioned that RELs played any helpful role in their daily practice. One explanation is that regional education labs are too broad in focus. A perusal of REL websites found an astonishing array of projects, from data-driven strategies to reforms at each organizational level (elementary, middle, and high school), to early childhood, professional development, and technology. On the other hand, more localized research centers, such as the Consortium on Chicago School Research (CCSR), have generally been accorded a meaningful role in shaping policy and practice. The CCSR's mission statement is instructive: the CCSR "conducts research of high technical quality that can inform and assess policy and practice in the Chicago Public Schools. We seek to expand communication among researchers, policymakers, and practitioners as we support the search for solutions to the problems of school reform."[54] In essence, CCSR functions as the research and evaluation arm of the Chicago Public Schools, albeit with greater resources and access to multiple experts with substantial technical and research skills—beyond that found in even the largest districts' research and evaluation departments. CCSR's "focus on one place" makes it an invaluable and readily accessible resource for school leaders seeking to use research to inform decisionmaking.

Inadequate and incorrect interpretation of data by school leaders also makes it difficult to evaluate school programs effectively. A superintendent observed, "Educators are typically not good research consumers . . . They don't have good judgments about research methodology."[55] Most leadership preparation programs require a course or two in statistics or evaluation but seldom does it constitute more than a small fraction of the total time spent in coursework and in the field experience. Rick Hess and Andrew Kelly analyzed a sample of course syllabi used in administrator preparation programs and found that only 16 percent of coursework was devoted to assessment, evaluation, data management, accountability, decisionmaking, and organizational change. Only 11 percent of course time was devoted to analysis of statistics, data, or empirical research.[56] Lorna Earl and Steven Katz assert that, "For the most part, educators have not seen statistics as a useful addition to their tool kit for decisionmaking."[57]

However, hope is on the horizon. Several university-based preparation programs, along with other leadership development organizations, have begun to emphasize research and data utilization in decisionmaking. Rather than a one-day seminar, some preparation programs infuse research and data-based decisionmaking throughout the curriculum, teaching school leaders how to use and disaggregate real school data, how to make tables and graphs, and how to analyze and accurately interpret data. Texts on data-based decisionmaking have proliferated in recent years and have become standard features of programmatic reform in leadership preparation. A report from the Southern Regional Education Board titled, "Schools Can't Wait," ranked the use of data to make decisions about changes in school and classroom practices as the top priority for university-based leadership preparation.[58] Other organizations, such as New Leaders for New Schools and the Broad Superintendents Academy, similarly emphasize the development of data-based decisionmaking skills and best practices for school leaders.

Many school leaders question the relevance of research to their daily work lives and its efficacy in improving school system performance.[59] Research findings are subject to so many qualifications and limitations, while often producing findings of little practical significance, that they offer little clear guidance as to "what works." When the Department of Education launched its "What Works Clearinghouse" website, so few studies passed methodological muster that its creators worried that practitioners would not use it.[60] Thus, one barrier to the comparative lack of impact or use of research by educators is "too few rigorous and relevant studies."Scientific research in education is "extremely difficult, time-consuming, and costly—and thus very rare," although recent advances in education research hold some promise for resolving some of these issues.[61]

School leaders seldom read scholarly research journals and published research reports. Instead, they read professional association journals such as *Educational Leadership*, *Phi Delta Kappan,* and *Education Week* that may contain brief synopses of research but not original, peer-reviewed research studies.[62] *Educational Leadership*, published by the Association for Supervision and Curriculum Development (ASCD) and marketed to K–12 education leaders, contains snapshots and anecdotal articles about what works in schools, but rarely gives details about specific studies. *Educational Leadership* also contains a two-page synopsis titled Research Matters, as well as occasional two-page Special Reports summarizing recent research studies. *Principal Leadership*, a magazine published by the National Association of Secondary School Principals (NASSP), focuses on best practices and contains examples of successful programs in middle and high schools. While full of practical tips and advice for school principals, it contains no research studies beyond anecdotal reports of successful programs in individual schools. NASSP also publishes a scholarly, peer-reviewed journal, the *NASSP Bulletin*, which contains research-based articles; however, the target market and readership is vastly different— the *Bulletin* is targeted toward professors, not practitioners. In January 2006, NASSP launched the *Principal's Research Review*, a bimonthly e-journal that contains short summaries of research on a topic, but it is unclear how many members actually read and use the research synopses. The American Association of School Administrators (AASA) publishes *The School Administrator*, targeted at superintendents, but it contains no research articles and only occasionally presents synopses of research studies; however, it is full of practical advice for superintendents. Finally, Phi Delta Kappa publishes the *Phi Delta Kappan*, which is focused on research and leadership and is marketed as the professional journal for educators. Each issue presents research summaries, but many of the articles are nonresearch-based opinion pieces, essays, or thought pieces rather than research-based analyses of education interventions. Based on a review of research-based articles found in *Educational Leadership*, *Principal Leadership*, *The School Administrator*, and the *Phi Delta Kappan* from January 2005 to June 2007, only the *Phi Delta Kappan* (21 percent) contained any significant research studies; the other three leading journals included only single-digit coverage of research.[63]

Furthermore, professional educator conferences such as AASA or ASCD rarely focus on research and serve primarily as networking venues where sessions devoted to benefits and retirement planning attract the largest audiences. Researchers and school leaders seldom attend the same conferences. AASA's annual conference now includes sessions for the presentation of academic research (the "Conference Within a Conference") but few superintendents or district administrators attend these sessions. Principals are often so busy engaging in crisis management, administrivia, and the daily operations of schooling that they have little time to devote to thoughtful, reflective, research-based strategic planning and improvement. Principals and teachers seldom have time to collaborate, discuss the data and research, and strategically plan interventions.[64] An award-winning principal commented that "one of the biggest barriers to effective use of [research and] data is *time* built into the work day of educators to understand, analyze, and use data."[65] Her thoughts were echoed by nearly all of the principals and superintendents contacted for this chapter. Further, as one veteran principal observed, "Principals are still viewed as middle-level managers in spite of the label of instructional leader."[66]

Compounding this problem is the fact that some school leaders find it difficult, in the words of a rural school district official in North Carolina, "to accept generic research data that may have occurred states away as being relevant to the familiar context of one's school or district."[67] One professional evaluator refers to this as the "unit of analysis" problem. He stated, "Research in education is rarely if ever related to my teaching, my kids, in my classroom. If I am a leader of a North Carolina school, what am I to do when I learn that students are failing elsewhere?" He went on to say that often, "the best [research] data are drawn from the largest sample of anonymous students from across the nation," but that such research is seldom helpful for school leaders who want to know how or whether the intervention will work with their students in their schools.[68] Many school leaders want personalized research and data analyses—their kids, their teachers, in their schools—and are skeptical about interventions elsewhere with different populations of students and staff.

Furthermore, our cultural conceptions of schooling—that teachers are only really working when they are "in front of students" and administrators are only working when they are engaged in the daily operations of the school—limit the time and opportunities to engage in the collaborative discussions required for research-based decisionmaking. Jonathan Supovitz and Valerie Klein note that, "Systematic data analysis is about more carefully preparing for performance," and ask, "What profession, other than K–12 teaching, spends more time performing than preparing for performance?" The researchers conclude that "the structures and opportunities to engage in these inquiries are virtually absent in the American system of education."[69]

This lack of time is symptomatic of a larger barrier to using research in decisionmaking. In the words of a former superintendent, many schools lack a "culture of inquiry" and a "culture of improvement" to promote and use research to inform practice.[70] To create a culture of inquiry and improvement in schools, a superintendent stated, "adults [in schools] must learn from one another first before they can learn from experts."[71] Unfortunately, remarked a superintendent, many school leaders suffer from an ADD (attention deficit disorder) culture whereby they quickly move, in a faddish fashion, from this year's new thing to the next.[72] As Rick Hess observed in his study of urban school reform, education leaders are quick to adopt, almost unthinkingly, the latest reform program—regardless of whether research has demonstrated its effectiveness.[73] In districts lacking a culture of inquiry and a culture of improvement, adult learning is largely absent from systemic organizational processes.

In another illustrative example, one veteran principal commented that he "hasn't had a conversation about research in 30 years," and that when he asked staff at his new school where the school's professional library with research publications was located, they told him that it did not exist.[74] This suggests that perhaps the question is incorrect. A former superintendent in North Carolina stated that the question is not "why don't schools change?" but rather "why don't people change?" The research on adult learning makes one thing clear: Incentives and support must be created in schools for systemic learning to occur. All too often, school leaders assume that a culture of inquiry and improvement is a given in education systems. However, as several examples in this chapter illustrate, that is often not the case. A superintendent stated that a large part of the problem is that "schools aren't structured for systemic organizational learning."[75] Leaders tend to operate in a day-to-day crisis or survival mode, in which a good day is when nothing bad happens. This is understandable given the enormous pressure and daily demands placed on school leaders.

DATA-BASED DECISIONMAKING IN EDUCATION

Although school leaders are not frequent users of traditional academic research (few regularly read published research studies in academic journals) they do use data in decisionmaking. While this clearly is not traditional academic research, it may be viewed as action research. A growing body of evi-

dence suggests that school leaders in districts across the nation are incorporating data-driven practices into decisionmaking, often producing substantial
improvements in student learning and achievement.[76] Data-driven decisionmaking is a common characteristic of high-performing schools and requires
a paradigm shift from process- to results-focused outcomes.[77] Kati Haycock
of the Education Trust asserts that data-based decisionmaking "can basically
take us out of the dark ages of just kinda teaching and hoping, which is what
a lot of folks have done for a very long time."[78]

A number of school districts and states have adopted data-driven decisionmaking as a model for school improvement. In Connecticut, the state
mandated the creation of data teams in schools to use data to drive instruction. Principals are required to indicate in their annual school improvement
plans how data is being used to improve student achievement. Furthermore,
state officials are conducting statewide research studies on reading and math
instruction.[79] To produce long-term results, data-based decisionmaking must
be incorporated into the school improvement planning process.

In schools and districts that have institutionalized data-based decisionmaking and action research and made it part of the organizational culture,
data graphs and charts are on display (and used) on classroom walls, in hall-
ways, in school principals' and district leaders' offices, and even in school
board meeting rooms. In North Carolina and Connecticut, schools compete
for the most effective "data walls." In Florida, the superintendent of the Jack-
sonville school district created a war room in which the district's strategic
progress is continually reviewed and assessed. In Georgia, schools are creating data rooms in which officials analyze student subgroup performance and
target interventions.[80] Scott Cowart, superintendent of the Monroe County
(GA) schools, stated that, "The data doesn't lie—it's kind of in your face."[81]
A Georgia superintendent concurred, stating, "To really know where you're
at you have to have it in your face all the time. You look to see the gaps. You
identify best practices, determine how to teach."[82] Teachers and school leaders meet regularly throughout the year in various teams (horizontal and vertical teams) to disaggregate state and local performance data and assess what
is working and what is not in their particular context and with their students. In Wake County, North Carolina, schools that fail to make adequate
yearly progress are encouraged to create data teams of administrators and
teachers to analyze school performance and develop intervention plans for
school improvement. A combination of state-, district-, and classroom-level
assessments is used, avoiding reliance on single measures of student performance. Teachers make instructional adjustments and develop targeted interventions based on these collaborative meetings, which contrast sharply with

the traditional culture of isolation common to teaching.[83] Data-based decisionmaking is also useful as a tool to ensure alignment between local curricular programs and state tests.[84]

INCENTIVES TO ENCOURAGE RESEARCH UTILIZATION AND DATA-BASED DECISIONMAKING

With its extensive testing requirements and demands to eliminate the achievement gap among subgroups of students in the No Child Left Behind Act (NCLB), federal policymakers have created a strong incentive for school leaders to use action research and data and become more research-based in decisionmaking, although many districts used data-based decisionmaking long before NCLB came along.[85] One district official stated that NCLB has forced districts and schools to examine data "much more closely to understand the specific academic needs of students."[86] Data can be a powerful tool for school leaders in initiating and sustaining change. NCLB requires state education agencies to engage in immense data collection and analysis, although a report by the Education Commission of the States found that less than one-third of states have the requisite capacity to handle the task. A report by the Data Quality Campaign concluded that only one state (Florida) has all ten essential elements of a longitudinal data system, and only eight states have at least eight of these elements.

School leaders can facilitate the incorporation of research and data-based decisionmaking into school systems through sustained professional development.[87] Superintendents must take the lead and create an environment where evidence-based practices are implemented and valued.[88] This requires providing release time for school leaders—district office and principals—to meet regularly and to share and discuss data. Districts dedicated to data-based decisionmaking have created district-level teams and study groups to review evidence of the effectiveness of various programs.[89] Others have created research and evaluation departments to evaluate and disseminate best practices, although attention must be paid to the politics of in-district evaluations, particularly when evaluation findings are contrary to district-led (or superintendent-led) initiatives; as well as to the politics of bringing in external evaluators, who sometimes find that favored programs are ineffective. Research and evaluation is useful only when school leaders are willing to accept and act upon the results of that research. In Los Angeles, the school district shelved the Waterford Early Reading program after two district evaluations concluded that the program failed to improve reading performance in the early grades (in fact, by taking time away from student's primary literacy lessons, it actually produced declines in student achievement). District officials concluded that the district's nearly $50 million investment in the program was not producing the promised results.[90]

Evaluating data using building- and district-level teams is crucial. A former superintendent stated that using data teams in decisionmaking encourages innovation and engages "the creative power of practitioners."[91] To do so, however, school leaders must be well trained in principles of applied research methods, strategic planning, and evaluation; and equipped with the technological expertise to collect, organize, and analyze student performance data.[92]

While it is true that some educators need to improve their data collection and statistical analysis skills, and that some do little more than collect mandated data, many highly effective school leaders actively use data and incorporate data-driven decisionmaking models into the culture of their schools and school systems.[93] A culture of inquiry needs to be created to foster and encourage the use of evidence-based and data-based decisionmaking.[94] Doing so, however, requires that school leaders, staff, and school boards become data-literate.[95] A veteran New York superintendent commented that in his experience, it is not always easy to get school boards to buy into using research and data as the basis for decisionmaking. He stated that with limited resources, leaders must justify the expenditure of resources, including time and money, to boards faced with competing demands, such as "putting up new curtains and fixing the boilers," which are "more visible and easier to justify."[96]

Thus, for school leaders to create a culture of inquiry and make research-based, data-driven decisionmaking a reality in education, they must spend time educating not only themselves and their staffs, but the school board and the community as well.[97] A school district in Ohio created a series of data classes for district administrators, principals, and teachers to help them develop competence and confidence in the application of statistics, the creation and management of data information systems, and data-based strategic planning.[98] To be useful to educators, state and district data management systems (such as data warehouses) must provide raw data that educators can rework and format to meet their instructional needs.[99]

Other incentives that encourage research utilization and evidence-based best practices in schools include incorporating student performance into teacher and administrator evaluations.[100] Principals are still judged primarily on input measures and classroom/school management factors rather than primarily by student performance. Holding everyone directly accountable and tying evaluation to student performance would force educators to more critically and thoughtfully evaluate the effectiveness of programs and would increase the use of action research-based, data-driven decisionmaking in education.

Finally, a significant increase in federal funding for education research would facilitate the use of research and data-based decisionmaking by school leaders. A former superintendent remarked that Nintendo spends more on research and development than the federal government spends on education research.[101] Foundations such as the Wallace Foundation have played an instrumental role in helping fund programs to train school leaders in evidence-based practice and data-based decisionmaking.[102] The Institute for Education Sciences (IES) is funding the creation of data academies to facilitate the use of data in decisionmaking by school leaders.

In addition, greater collaboration between researchers, school leaders, and staff in developing research proposals based on practitioners' needs is necessary if research is to play a more prominent role in decisionmaking.[103] A superintendent remarked, "There may be less than one percent of the existing research that's really meaningful to teachers. Much is for researchers, for getting funding, for career advancement, or for advocacy."[104] As one superintendent stated, "Researchers must take the practitioners' perspectives and raise questions from the practitioners' standpoint" rather than pursuing "their own interests and their own questions."[105] A principal in North Carolina agreed, stating that researchers need to "ask school systems about their problems and needs" if they want school leaders to pay attention to and use research in decisionmaking.[106] A Texas superintendent noted that she had "a limited amount of time to sift through research" and called on researchers to, "Highlight it for me. If what I read is the first page of the articles in administrator magazines, then give me a one-page, readable highlight of the most current research and it will stick in my mind. If you want it read, then put it in the format that I consume." She pleaded, "Help us with this one. Adapt to what our needs are."[107]

By conducting collaborative action research projects using data-based decisionmaking, researchers and school leaders will be able to discover "what works," thereby making research more useful and relevant to practitioners' needs. Furthermore, state and federal governments should facilitate the creation of more city-based, narrowly focused research consortiums such as the CCSR in Chicago. Given the massive problems faced by school leaders operating urban school systems, such research and development centers could provide valuable, targeted, research-based assistance to school leaders initiating school improvement efforts.

CONCLUSION

Research-based and data-based decisionmaking allows school leaders to use research and student performance data to improve student achievement by identifying what works. Instead of constantly reinventing the wheel, or making decisions through a trial and error method (or worse still, making decisions in the dark—a not uncommon education practice), school leaders who use research and engage in data-based decisionmaking are able to promote more coherent and effective system-wide reform.

This chapter's examination of the extent of research utilization in education shows that the topic is more complex and nuanced than is commonly believed. Although several ways in which research utilization could be improved and made more relevant for school leaders have been suggested in these pages, implementation will require structural as well as cultural changes—neither of which will occur absent time, money, and sustained professional development.

What Gets Studied and Why: Examining the Incentives That Drive Education Research

Dan D. Goldhaber and Dominic J. Brewer

On May 22–23, 2006, a conference was held at the Brookings Institution. Like many such gatherings held by august Washington, D.C., think tanks, the goal was to bring together the city's "policy wonks" with esteemed academics. This particular event attracted prominent education researchers and focused on what was known about the effects of school and class size on student learning. During lunch, an informal conversation started about why we were having the conference. On the one hand, it made sense to study and review what we know about important policies that are actively being advocated and implemented around the nation. Over the last decade class size reduction policies have been implemented in numerous states at a cost of billions of dollars. Similarly, smaller school sizes had become a "hot" reform, fueled by the Bill & Melinda Gates Foundation to the tune of more than $100 million. On the other hand, several at the table noted that there are a plethora of studies on class and school size. Why did these topics continue to be researched, particularly when the findings of existing studies are paid so little attention, either by educators in schools or by the policymakers that allocated resources?[1] Further, why was critical information on the relative cost-effectiveness of different reform strategies so limited?

THE MORE THINGS CHANGE, THE MORE THEY STAY THE SAME

On the face of it, the education research enterprise in the United States has never been healthier. The American Educational Research Association (AERA) has a record number of members, and more than 14,000 budding research-ers and onlookers attended their last annual conference. There are more academic journals catering to education scholars than ever before, and in recent years, numerous education-focused online journals and forums have sprouted. "Handbooks" and encyclopedias of education research are being compiled at a fast clip.[2] The number of education doctorates produced by the nation's universities was 7,088 in 2003, an increase of 10 percent over the previous five years.[3] Many of these graduates go on to be full-fledged aca-demics or enthusiastic "action" researchers that continue to conduct research and nurture hoards of graduate students who generate more studies. Barely a week goes by without a major national media outlet reporting on the latest education research finding.

The growth in research can be traced to an interrelated combination of factors. For example, as globalization and new technologies have rapidly changed the economic and social landscape, a strong consensus has emerged that "education is more important than ever." There is keen interest in the performance of the education system, and much of the new scholarship on education has been directed toward understanding the various influences on student achievement. This line of research can be traced back at least to the 1966 Coleman Report,[4] but the passage of the No Child Left Behind Act (NCLB) in 2001 and the institution of state-level accountability systems in states like Florida, North Carolina, and Texas, have accelerated the pace of education research. Accountability demands knowledge about how effective schools and teachers are, and how to boost productivity.

New outcomes-oriented research has generated important insights into how schools function and the effects of various education reform initiatives. For example, recent studies showing the considerable heterogeneity between teachers who hold similar credentials are not only an important finding, but fly in the face of what was once conventional wisdom.[5] Research on topics such as the effects of class size or increased school choice has shown that these reforms are not the panaceas that advocates often claim them to be.

However, a cursory examination of the latest issues of education research journals or the program of the AERA annual conference suggests that the bulk of education research is neither outcomes-oriented nor utilizes methods that support strong inferences about causality. Despite a renewed emphasis on randomized research designs and on the use of sophisticated quasi-ex-perimental methods (particularly using comprehensive student-level longi-tudinal data), the proportion of the entire education research enterprise that would pass muster for scientific rigor in other fields is shockingly small.[6]

Consequently, for policymakers striving to craft effective policies, the research base in which underlying causal relationships have been uncovered with some degree of certainty remains quite thin. Many educators and researchers seem to believe that "context is king," and therefore each situation is unique; under this view, there is little utility in large-scale quantitative studies that seek to uncover causal effects. Implementation of reforms on a large scale in education has been shown to be difficult and uneven, so translating research findings into policy-actionable results can be problematic.[7] Much education research is not related to a specific policy level or decision point. Furthermore, scholars tend to focus on small-scale studies that utilize existing datasets or rely on qualitative methods; researchers focus on the same issues again and again. Ultimately, this may lead to a "chipping away" at key issues, but the process is slow, costly, and unlikely to generate clear conclusions.

Perhaps more important, the consumers of education research (as well as many of the producers) have little knowledge of what constitutes sound research design, and consequently, poor studies with results that fit a popular ideological perspective or serve stakeholder interests often dominate. In fact, funders may look to intermediary indicators of research "impact" such as citations by politicians or prominent placement in newspapers. This, combined with the fact that there are now many more avenues to distribute research (listservs, podcasts, new online journals, and so on), has led to a shift in incentives for researchers toward publicity and away from the establishment of a scholarly track record (for example, through journal publications). There is by no means an inconsistency between the two—many high-quality studies receive a good deal of publicity—but the concern is that a significant amount of less-credible research also gets considerable play in the media.

Electronic media has allowed researchers to push their product out and (depending on its content) the product's message may get amplified many times over. A good example of this is report on the efficacy of the National Board for Professional Teaching Standards (NBPTS) prepared by J. E. Stone.[8] The report uses scores from the well-known Tennessee Value Added Assessment System (TVAAS) and reaches the conclusion that "At the very least, [they suggest that] public expenditures on NBPTS certification and teacher bonuses should be suspended until it can be clearly and independently established that NBPTS certification delivers what it promises." Whether this conclusion is correct is not so relevant in terms of our focus as is the fact that its analysis was based on a sample of only 16 teachers; and that despite this, the study was so widely disseminated and debated that the Education Commission of the States commissioned a panel (of which one of us, Brewer, was a member) to analyze the report, resulting in a damning critique.[9]

It seems that the most credible studies do not result in a crystal-clear message that can easily be packaged. For example, one of us (Goldhaber) found mixed results when conducting research on NBPTS with colleague Emily Anthony.[10] National Board Certified Teachers (NBCTs) appeared to be more effective than non-NBCTs, on average, but the results were context (e.g., grade level) contingent, and we did not find that going through the NBPTS process itself improved teacher effectiveness. So what was made of these messy results by intermediaries or synthesizers of education research? (The role of synthesizers is discussed more extensively by Paul Manna and Michael J. Petrilli in chapter 4.) Well, the National Education Association (NEA) headline suggested the research largely supported NBPTS: "Kids Learn More from Teachers with National Board Certification"; and the article stated, "New research underscores the importance of NEA's support of and promotion of National Board Certification."[11] Of course, not everyone interpreted the results the same way. The Education Consumers Clearinghouse, for instance, concluded that, "Despite widespread reports to the contrary, the evidence brought forth by Goldhaber and Anthony does not strengthen the claim that NBPTS-certified teachers are substantially more effective than their colleagues in bringing about student achievement. If anything, the case for NBPTS certification may now be weaker."[12]

The above example makes it clear that research findings may be spun in quite different directions when the inherent nuances are glossed over. The consequences of this can be profound, resulting in bad policy design that hurts kids, disrupts schools, and wastes billions of dollars. Perhaps no better illustration of the decidedly imperfect use of education research is the California class-size reduction policy, which in terms of sheer size and scope is probably one of the largest education interventions in history. Despite its availability, California policymakers paid little attention to a relatively well-designed, large-scale demonstration in Tennessee that yielded specific findings on the beneficial effects of classes of 13 to 17 students for poor students in certain grades.[13] In 1996, with political pressures paramount, California implemented a statewide policy of 20 students per teacher for grades K–3 at a few months notice, with no initial evaluation planned. The policy remains in place more than a decade later, and despite a subsequent evaluation effort, few if any of its recommendations on increased flexibility, teachers' professional development, or alternative funding mechanisms have been heeded.

It is not that consumers are not listening to the recommendations of research. Rather, there is sometimes so much research and purposeful interpretation of it that consumers default to the research that tends to buttress their preconceived notions. There is a desire for a simple bottom line—"NBPTS doesn't work" or "small class sizes matter"—and little patience for "details," despite the fact that it is those very details that determine the efficacy of the policy. Unfortunately, there is no group that is respected and trusted enough that their recommendations supersede what consumers might hear about the literature or particular studies from the media or those who have a vested interest in "spinning" the results to suit their purpose.

In this chapter, we describe how these and other features of the education research enterprise play out in the context of an examination of what gets studied and why. We lay out a supply-and-demand framework that provides a roadmap to the incentives faced by individuals and organizations in the education research business. By understanding the forces that drive the production of education research, we hope to better understand the questions researchers choose to address and the methodologies they utilize, and how funding and policy shifts affect the nature, quality, and policy relevance of the scholarship that is produced. Many of our conjectures are based on our personal experiences over the past fifteen years conducting education research on a range of topics and producing both academic peer-reviewed journal articles and nontechnical reports for a broader audience; our employment in different types of organizations (a topic-specific think tank, a broad-based policy think tank, a university soft-money center and a university school of education); soliciting and receiving external funding from a variety of federal and private sources; and our service on editorial boards of various academic journals and national, state, and other panels.

We begin by laying out a supply-and-demand framework, and then discuss the rigor and policy relevance of education research and how the incentives facing the institutions and individuals conducting this research affect its production. Our analysis suggests that the market for education research may not function efficiently, in the sense that not enough of the research that is needed gets done, and too much of what is not needed is produced. Incentives are misaligned, and our conclusion offers some thoughts on steps that might be taken to increase the production of high-quality, policy-relevant education research.

THE MARKET FOR EDUCATION RESEARCH

What are the factors that influence the production of scholarly knowledge? As economists, we think a supply-and-demand framework may be usefully applied in this context. Of course, the market for education research, like many markets, is complex. Broadly speaking, consumers in the market for education research are the policymakers, educators, and parents who "demand" research evidence to make critical choices—about how to allocate resources, how to teach kids, how to choose schools, and so on. The suppliers of education research are the individuals and organizations who produce the studies, reports, and findings. Most markets are brought into equilibrium by changes in price, the critical signal that tells consumers to demand more or less, or suppliers to produce more or less. Prices to some extent reflect costs of production, as well as the value that consumers place on the product. In the case of education research, the "price" might be considered the monetary value placed on any given research study of a given quality, although it is rarely observed directly. In fact, the consumers and the funders are *not* synonymous in education research—both operate in institutional settings that are often political, and market signals are decidedly murky.

The Demand Side: Who Wants Education Research?

Anyone making an education decision, who desires to make it on the basis of empirical evidence rather than intuition, casual observation, tradition, or ideology, might be considered a consumer of research. If research is needed in order to help with decisionmaking, it is worth asking *who* is making these education decisions and in need of research evidence.[14] At the level of the individual student, classroom, or school site, it is educators themselves who are the most frequent decisionmakers, deciding what strategies to use with particular students, how students should spend their time, who teaches them, and so on. Many of these decisions are made with little advance planning. Further, in the context of a bureaucratic and hierarchical government-operated and financed K–12 system, many decisions are made at levels "above" the school through political oversight and involving all branches of government. In fact, thousands of individuals and organizational entities have some involvement in education decisionmaking, ranging from individual legislators and their staff to lobbyists, judges, and school board members, to mention only a few. Special interest groups such as private education companies (textbook publishers, supply vendors, education management companies, testing outfits), organized collectives of employees in the form of labor unions, concerned businesses/employers and their organizations, private nonprofit organizations such as philanthropic foundations, or wealthy or influential individuals, all seek to influence education decisions. Finally, ordinary citizens (whether they are individual parents on school governing boards or the PTA; city residents in a school board election; or voters in state legislative, gubernatorial, congressional, or presidential elections) exercise political oversight over these education decisionmakers. This fragmented consumer base, with numerous and diffuse players that have different missions, goals, ideologies, and needs, suggests a complex market in which the signals may be unclear as to what research is demanded.

Finally, the producers of education research are also important consumers, even though they may not use it directly to make education decisions. Research output is primarily produced in a format designed for consumption by other researchers rather than policymakers or practitioners. It is also used to get organizational rewards such as tenure at universities. This suggests that producers have the ability to affect market conditions, and perhaps reduce the influence of other consumers. One could argue that in the long run, even producers acting as consumers would seek to ensure that their output was useful, relevant, and "correct" on average (although they still might have an incentive to produce "too much" of it). However, there is no inherent reason why the incentives of various consumers would be aligned. In fact, the picture we have painted is one of multiple interests and a highly fragmented demand for education research, with few mechanisms to ensure that the message about what is being demanded is clearly conveyed to many potential providers of that research.

The education sector differs from other parts of the economy in several key ways. First, in most private sector markets, consumers who demand and use a product pay for it, directly or indirectly. Consumers buy products that they assume do what they are purported to do, and if the good or service does not perform, they switch to others. Producers, therefore, have an incentive to invest in research and development (R&D) financed through revenue raised from selling their products. Consumers of K–12 public education services usually pay for them through general taxation, and in most cases cannot exercise the power of "exit" by switching providers.[15] There are few mechanisms for individual parents or teachers to get organized to raise funds or to mount any kind of research effort; teachers, schools, or districts are not major purchasers of education research. Providers receive funds directly from government sources and their livelihood is only weakly tied to their success at delivering a high-quality product. Most service providers in the K–12 education sector have poor incentives to pay for research, and do not worry too much about losing consumers if they fail to do a good job.

Second, in the private sector, sales or profits are used to gauge whether an enterprise is investing in the right kind of research. Schools, in contrast, are producing a complex final product: student learning. There is often disagreement about what should be taught in schools, and these decisions are made not directly by markets, but through political processes. As a consequence, "education research" can encompass many different foci.

Third, education research is typically a public good. In other words, the findings of a research study are usually placed in the public domain and freely available to any decisionmaker who wants to draw on them. This norm is driven in part by incentives for the suppliers of research whose reward structure demands open publication, and peer review that (in principle) promotes the quality and objectivity of the research produced. Individual parties (notably parents, educators, schools, and school districts) rarely have enough incentive to pay for research. Even if a study design could be convincing and implemented at a cost that was reasonable relative to the decision being made, there is a strong incentive to "free ride"—to hope that someone else will pay for the study that is needed. The incentive for free riding undoubtedly helps explain why the federal government is one of the primary sources of funding for education research, even though it has the least direct influence over the sector in terms of aggregate expenditures. K–12 schooling is constitutionally a state enterprise and highly decentralized to school districts—yet neither states nor districts fund much of the research.

Fourth, markets need informed consumers to function well. This is problematic in education. For example, it may not always be known in advance whether research is worth doing, particularly because the costs and benefits of a given policy action may be quite unclear, or the context too uncertain. Not all decisions require research, and few would suggest that a major study is needed to determine whether a school system should buy pencils or pens, although manufacturers of these goods might lobby for such a study. In addition, because education research is a scientific endeavor, its methods and analyses are often mysterious to those consuming it. A decisionmaker obtaining education research may be unable to tell whether the study is good or bad, believable or usable. It is easier to consume work aimed at a broad audience that is straightforward, has "face validity," and accords with priors as to the "right answer." More complex and sophisticated methods may produce reliable and valid results but are hard to explain. Intermediaries (including the special interests noted earlier or those motivated by ideology) and the media may be relied upon to interpret and synthesize the research, and it is almost inevitable that something gets "lost in translation." The importance of context-specific factors, the statistical uncertainty of the findings, the practical insignificance of the results, and the difficulty of transferring the results to large-scale policy all tend to get lost.

The Supply Side: Who Produces Education Research?

Just as the consumer side of the market for education research is complex and diffuse, so is the producer side. Research is produced by individuals, but individuals (with the exception of a handful who are self-employed) are nested within organizations. For education research, we might distinguish between two main types of organizations: think tanks or other private firms, and universities. Within each, considerable differentiation exists that may be important in determining the type and quality of education research that gets done.

Think Tanks

The incentives to engage in education research for think tanks or for individuals operating in private sector companies are relatively straightforward, because they are dependent on "soft money" in the form of grants or contracts. These individuals face considerable pressure to raise funds from public and private agencies, as their salary trajectory and job security are directly related to the success of any fundraising endeavors. In some cases, researchers or organizations may be approached directly by funders and asked to conduct a particular research study. In other cases, researchers themselves may contact funders and inquire about their interest in conducting a particular study.[16] Government agencies, however, are usually bound by some restrictions that require a competitive bidding process for each piece of work to be conducted, or at the very least a competitive process that establishes a longer-term agreement permitting a series of many studies—for example, through a task order agreement or a Federally Funded Research and Development Center (FFRDC). Private sector researchers therefore compete with each other for contracts or grants from federal sources, foundations, private companies, and gifts from individual wealthy donors.

The upside of the research supplied by soft-money institutions is that it is likely to be policy-relevant because it is "client-driven," formulated to inform a specific issue for which there is an audience. Over the long term, the work produced is likely to match the expectations of the funders in terms of quality, timeliness, relevance, and so on; if it does not, then such suppliers would find themselves with less work and eventually go out of business. The type and quality of individuals employed in such organizations flows directly from the type of work conducted. They hire and fire staff, typically under standard "at will" professional contracts, giving the labor market some flexibility and helping to drive quality and relevant products.

Many, but not all, players in this market are nonprofits, operating under specific government guidelines that permit them to receive tax exemptions (such as 501(3)(c) status). They might be viewed as maximizing their revenues, employment, or some other bundle of characteristics, including reputation. As with many nonprofits that are not permitted to carry a surplus each year, firms that more than cover their costs make other uses of those funds. Most of these nonprofits have an explicit "public service" mission—committed to "improving policymaking" or "improving understanding"—which implies that they do more than simply maximize their workload and keep current clients happy. Nonprofits may also have charters stipulating that their work be largely in the public domain (with a few exceptions, such as national security). This creates a dilemma for many: if the work demanded by consumers does not fully reflect the institution's view of "what is needed" to fulfill its mission, or if most work barely covers operating costs, flexible funding to enable such non-client-specific research will be in short supply. Hence, most nonprofits can be seen actively raising philanthropic funds or pursuing increasing volumes of contract work that have some margin.[17]

It is worth emphasizing that research varies in quality and scope according to the source of the research; and the funders of research, to a large extent, shape these sources. In particular, the degree to which research organizations depend on clients, and how many clients they serve, will have a marked impact. This point is underscored by the presence in the market of some nonuniversity institutions, such as the Heritage Foundation, that have large-enough endowments ("hard money") so that it is not necessary for them to "sell" research services. On the one hand, individuals operating in such institutions may be far less immune to the direct pressures of the market, but such organizations typically have a definitive ideological bent, which enhances the likelihood that the research they conduct is designed to buttress a particular ideology rather than to be truly independent. This is partly because individuals working in such institutions are predisposed toward its prevailing ideology, and also because they may feel internal pressure to shape their work to conform to institutional expectations.

The reality is that the competition is actually taking place in many slightly differentiated markets. Institutions that compete for large federal grants and contracts differ. Some are large and diversified across numerous types of work and content areas (such as American Institutes for Research or Mathematica). Others are narrower and may specialize in contract work or a particular topic area. (There are a plethora of "Beltway Bandit" firms that rely almost exclusively on federal funding for their activities, often from one agency with which they establish a close relationship.) Entities may also rely on grant funding (for example, many university centers), which is no surprise given that contracts often entail a scope of work requiring significant institutional infrastructure. Some research outfits are focused on single or closely aligned issues and, rightly or wrongly, may be seen as issue advocacy organizations (such as Education Trust), while others have a broader scope and trade on their reputation for independence (for instance, RAND). As funding ebbs and flows, suppliers can come into existence, grow, decline, and go out of business. As the nature of government funding changes—for example, the use of restrictive contracts as opposed to more flexible grants—so, too, does the character of the suppliers of education research.

Universities

Although many for- and nonprofit firms and think tanks are highly influential in producing education research, the bulk of the research output is generated by academics who are based in universities. We cannot review the large research literature on all facets of universities and colleges, including their internal incentive structures and hiring policies, but these factors clearly influence the type and quality of research that is conducted.[18] Academics carry out research on education issues across departments, schools, and centers within universities. Because (most) universities are organized into departmental "silos" that operate semi-autonomously with their own norms, policies, and expectations (which affect who gets hired and promoted, the incentives to secure external funding, and so on), there is often relatively little interaction and collaboration across these boundaries. This autonomy has important implications; for example, it reinforces the production of work based on one disciplinary-based view of the world, and it minimizes the sharing of methods and new developments and institution-level scrutiny of the quality of research. This tends to limit the extent to which cumulative learning occurs and to slow the development of a strong research base in education.

Faculty at research universities are expected to produce scholarly work, so the incentives that come with these expectations merit elaboration. The main impetus for scholarly work is tenure, which guarantees lifetime employment under most conditions, and permits the tenured faculty members to write about whatever they choose—in other words, "academic freedom." Assistant professors are evaluated through what is typically a six-year process of "apprenticeship," and those found worthy are promoted to associate and full professor ranks with tenure. Universities differ greatly in their tenure requirements, but usually require publishing in peer-reviewed journals (which are mainly read by other academics). There is significant variation in the quality of journals (as judged by, say, the rejection rates) and in their foci. In most cases, a premium is placed on technical sophistication rather than policy relevance. Tenure-track professors are expected to teach and undertake service requirements, and spend typically 40 percent of their time on research activities. Salaries are paid by the institutions, and cover 100 percent of the faculty members' time with "hard money."[19]

Although there is an incentive to produce high-quality, high-volume research under the tenure process, there may not be an incentive for that research to be funded. This tends to bias work in favor of less-costly qualitative case studies that do not yield generalizeable findings, or quantitative studies that use data collected by others (for example, large federal databases collected by the National Center for Education Statistics). We, in fact, built much of our early careers around research that focused almost exclusively on studies that utilized datasets like *High School and Beyond* or the *National Longitudinal Survey of 1988.*[20] These data sources are certainly valuable, but also limited in key ways. For instance, for those wishing to study student outcomes, one is generally limited to research on math and reading achievement in grades three through eight. Surveys, like those administered by the Department of Education, are not going to be able to cover the range of interventions that school systems might be trying. Large-scale demonstration projects or complicated randomized field trials are far more expensive in terms of time and money, and therefore less likely to be done. Due to the shift by the Institute for Education Sciences toward "scientifically based research," university research under the tenure process has started to move increasingly toward experiments, but this type of work still represents only a small fraction of the studies that are undertaken.

The university system also provides no guarantee that the research will be useful or relevant for policymakers or practitioners, only that their academic peers will value it.[21] Of course, many institutions encourage the generation of external funding for research as a way to offset salaries and other costs of employment. But at all but a handful of the most highly ranked research institutions, funding is not required for promotion and tenure.[22]

INCENTIVES AFFECTING THE RELEVANCE AND RIGOR OF EDUCATION RESEARCH

Applying a supply-and-demand lens helps explain some of the incentives that affect the production of education research. In this section, we zero in on two related components of that research output, relevance and rigor. Work that is *relevant* addresses questions that decisionmakers need answers to. This does not imply studies of cause-and-effect alone, but it does imply focusing on questions whose answers can be used to change policy or practice. Education research has to employ *rigorous* research design, so that the results are credible and usable; studies must have internal and external validity to the maximum extent possible. An examination of the incentives for both producers and consumers in the education research market suggests a bias exists in favor of small, fragmented studies that focus mainly on process, rather than on large, definitive studies that emphasize outcomes. While some mechanisms exist that push the system toward rigor, strong forces are also present that keep standards low and perpetuate the *overproduction* of weak research from which few policy conclusions can be drawn, and perpetuate the *underproduction* of strongly designed and executed efforts that give decisionmakers what they need. To a large degree, the explanation for this derives from the level and patterns of funding for education research.

University Silos and Schools of Education

A key feature of the education research market that limits relevance and rigor is that much of the enterprise is supply-driven—in other words, studies are self-initiated and often unfunded, particularly in universities. Much of the university-based research on education is carried out in schools of education. But the primary goal of most universities' schools of education is training practitioners. All but a handful of these schools are dependent on tuition revenue (or state support tied in part to enrollments), so local school district administrators and teachers make up an important constituency to be served. Inevitably, then, the education research agenda may get focused on fragmented, disparate, and parochial concerns. It might examine only narrow problems that can be studied in a time frame and on a scale that can be completed quickly.

Most universities have little direct financial incentive to demand longer-term, more rigorously designed studies because they are dependent on student enrollments for their survival. And because most of the practitioners pursuing degrees are part of the traditional K–12 public monopoly, they have relatively little incentive to want to critically study issues of productivity and costs. This point is further compounded by the fact that studying schools and school districts requires access. Cordial relationships must be established, nurtured, and preserved. Although this may not mean researchers pull punches with respect to their findings, it does suggest that there is an incentive to study issues that are not likely to embarrass the key constituencies and undermine the relations that will allow for future studies.

Well-designed experiments, necessary for making definitive causal inferences, are expensive and logistically complex (and raise ethical issues when they involve children). It is, therefore, hardly surprising that academics have limited ability to carry out such studies. However, sophisticated quasi-experimental education research is increasingly possible at relatively low cost, due to the growing availability of state student-level longitudinal data that permits researchers to track the progress of individual students over time, and, in some states, link them to their individual teachers. This data structure has allowed researchers to get far more precise and credible estimates on how various school resources contribute toward student learning, the impact of policy interventions, and the extent to which research methods influence findings in a nonexperimental setting.[23] It is clear, for instance, that the nonrandom distribution of teachers across schools and classrooms, when unaccounted for by a research design, will often lead researchers to overstate the value of teacher experience and credentials.[24] These more recent data and findings show that much of what was done in the past simply is not credible.

The structure of universities, reflecting the historical differentiation of disciplines, also severely limits both the relevance and rigor of education research. To fully utilize newly available data, a solid grounding in statistical methods is needed. However, universities' education departments are dominated by qualitative researchers. University researchers outside of education schools that do have the necessary methodological training are less likely to understand classroom practices, school operations, and education policymaking. This "silo" effect is compounded by disciplinary boundaries. With emphasis on diverse methods, and disparate and separate outlets for work (tied to different traditions and internal incentive structures), even the work that is produced is fragmented. For example, it is not uncommon for researchers from one discipline studying a particular issue to totally ignore a robust literature on that issue outside of their discipline.

Funders and Funding

Notwithstanding the insularity of academia, a significant driver of relevance and rigor in education research are funders, notably the federal government and foundations. In terms of federal funding, four features are noteworthy.

First, the overall levels of funding for education research are extremely low. The entire federal investment in education research is quite small when compared to health, energy, or other important fields of public policy. (See chapter 3 in this volume by Jeffrey R. Henig for more details.) The lack of funding severely limits the efficacy of the research produced. For example, the kind of randomized trial that would continue for five to ten years and have sufficient numbers of sites to ensure some external validity would likely cost tens or hundreds of millions of dollars. Although creative researchers have tried to develop efficacious studies with lots of "in kind" resources, it is incredibly difficult to produce work that addresses policymakers' needs in a convincing way.

Second, funding for research is split across multiple agencies and among many topics. The agency with the greatest interest in the efficacy of school reform, the U.S. Department of Education, has the least funding, and furthermore splits its limited budget across multiple subdepartments and across several different contract and grant vehicles. Thus, a small amount of money is spread around—lessening the possibilities of large-scale, long-term research studies that are likely to yield convincing answers to policy-relevant questions. Some Department of Education funding is in grant form and some is "field-initiated," in that the topics to be studied are left largely to the suppliers of research. In addition, the Department of Education funds regional laboratories that conduct small-scale research designed to meet the needs of specific regions.[25] Another major vehicle through which federal research on education is carried out is through education "centers" that focus on a theme (such as data-driven reform) or student population (for example, English language learners).[26] The research priorities of centers funded under the current Bush administration are quite different than the research previously funded through this vehicle.[27] These centers have the advantage of producing a coherent stream of research that is tied together, and tend to be awarded to the nation's elite university-based academics. They do, however, have their own tendency toward many small projects, so as to reward the coalitions that form in order to win the funding.

Third, the determination of what should be funded (and, indeed, whether research is valued at all)[28] is carried out in a political context. Consider, for instance, the federal government and the role that a major event, such as a change in the presidency or control of Congress, might play in determining the topics that research is expected to address. The passage of NCLB in 2001 has had a profound impact on education research through its emphasis on measuring student achievement on standardized tests, but the shift of political power that occurred in 2000 has also had a somewhat less-visible impact on the topics that are studied. The mere fact that politics helps drive what is studied is not necessarily a negative. However, because political cycles are short and politicians fickle, it does tend to limit the extent to which large-scale, long-term studies can be carried out. It also limits research topics to those that politicians wish to see examined. For example, the transition from the Clinton to the Bush administrations coincided with greater interest in studying issues such as school choice and teacher pay reforms and less interest in studying whole-school reform models.

Fourth, because the federal government is a significant funder of education research, the methodological standards it insists upon, in addition to the topics it chooses, will be important. Almost all federal research is at some point subject to a selection process, one that most frequently involves significant involvement from research suppliers in the form of peer review. The Institute of Education Sciences (IES) has recently made major progress in increasing the rigor of peer review for much of its research portfolio, with serious attention to research design and the use of "standing panels" of highly regarded academics that deliberate in detail over the merits of research proposals.[29] However, because the supply side is replete with hard-to-change universities, and the levels of funding are so small, the impact of this trend takes time.

Over the last decade, foundations have become a much more important source of education research funds, driven in large part by the Bill & Melinda Gates Foundation. And while foundations are not subject to the same political-cycle dynamic as the federal government, they do have foci that shift over time. Education philanthropy follows several models for funding: *issue oriented*, with The Walton Family Foundation being a good example; *field initiated,* such as the Spencer Foundation, which funds proposals solicited through a call for proposals; or a *blended strategy*, as exemplified by the Carnegie Foundation, which not only funds research through a call for proposals, but also funds research on their own initiatives (for example, Teachers for a New Era).[30]

As Henig points out in a forthcoming volume, some foundations are focused on a particular education program area; they may also pay for research that examines the effectiveness of their programs.[31] Foundations that have a "dog-in-the-hunt" may be inclined to fund researchers who are thought to be sympathetic to a particular policy position; researchers who find evidence suggesting that a foundation is making a bad bet on a particular program face the difficult task of reporting findings so as not to jeopardize their ability to garner future funding.

Consumers

The fact that there are suppliers of both good and bad research would not be a problem if consumers of education research were able to distinguish between the two. Intermediaries such as mainstream newspapers, specialized publications like *Education Week*, and nontechnical practitioner-oriented journals such as *Phi Delta Kappan* are important here. Technology has made it possible to disseminate information in ways that bypass conventional gatekeepers, and this has important implications for the types of education research that gets widely disseminated. There has been an explosion of websites and blogs, and listserves and podcasts are widely used to "push" information out. This is important because most consumers of education research are unlikely to distinguish between a newsflash on a new study from a RAND-type organization that trades on its reputation for independent analysis, or a Lexington Institute–type organization that has an agenda (in this case, a limited federal government role) to promote. Research is hungrily picked up by the media and in nonacademic and often politically charged environments where a "sexy" story is much more important than solid methodology. Consequently, policymakers and practitioners are more likely to consume education research that has not undergone adequate peer review.

Perhaps more importantly, because research is complex and consumers are not well-informed, poor studies with results that fit a popular ideological perspective or serve stakeholder interests often dominate. In fact, one might hypothesize that the existence of such organized interests and their relative power affect the extent to which publicity is sought and what story dominates. Research that is mixed or cautionary and that has no powerful constituency to champion it is likely to get less attention. For example, research on teacher certification or teacher pay that finds traditional structures effective will appeal to teacher unions and schools of education, while more nuanced findings have no natural constituency. Research on school choice, both for and against, tends to attract a great deal of attention, in part because there are powerful forces on each side that seek to generate publicity about findings.

Both suppliers and funders exacerbate this problem, in that they benefit from publicity and point to newspaper headlines as evidence that their research is having an "impact." Publicity is much more likely if research is new and newsworthy, criteria that often require bold definitive statements and the short-circuiting of traditional (slow) review processes. Some academics seem quite willing to generate publicity for their own work well before it has undergone significant review—it seems part of being a "star" in the field is now tied to one's ability to generate press coverage rather than simply high-quality, peer-reviewed publications. The fact that professors at tier I institutions rush to put results from working papers into the *Wall Street Journal* or *New York Times* suggests that the self-policing incentives within academia are not functioning as well as they have in the past. Institutions and colleges do not appear to punish such behavior, suggesting that it no longer falls outside the norms of the profession. Tenure undoubtedly severely limits the ability of institutions to sanction individuals; our conjecture would be that young assistant professors are more apt to stick with guarded statements and nuanced findings in academic journals. But the phenomenon exists, in part, because research findings that generate a great deal of publicity are likely to match the interests of key stakeholders, and provide visibility and contacts, which subsequently attract future funding. A cycle such as this, in which academics can get drawn into an agenda of work, serves a particular interest. Funding makes for a more comfortable professorial life, and provides benefits to institutions. University administrators are happy to have their institution cited in a newspaper story, regardless of scientific accuracy, no doubt hoping that well-heeled alumni and others will take the publicity as a sign of institutional prowess. As a consequence, at least some of what is sold under the guise of education research is really advocacy and advertising. Although there may be some damage to individual reputations from "overselling" research findings, it seems from the frequency of this behavior that the benefit from enhanced attention and funding for research exceeds any cost.

CONCLUDING THOUGHTS: HOW MIGHT THE INCENTIVES FOR EDUCATION RESEARCH BE IMPROVED?

The supply-and-demand approach used in this chapter to help understand why, and how, some education issues are studied yields some important insights into how the education research enterprise currently works, and provides some clues as to how it might be made better. We find considerable support for the commonly held view that education research is methodologically weak. This section summarizes our major points and offers suggestions on how the market for education research could work better. Because many of our diagnoses stem from the public monopoly nature of the K–12 delivery system, and the deeply engrained traditions of academe, we are not naïve in thinking that the strong incentives governing the relevance and rigor of research can be changed overnight. We do believe, however, that federal, state, and local policymakers can take steps that will lead to improvements.

Two themes recur throughout our analyses—disconnectedness and fragmentation. The disconnect between consumers and funders of research has important implications for the incentives that each group faces. Research is demanded because it is a useful guide for decisionmakers. Funding is crucial for conducting research on a large-enough scale and with sufficiently rigorous research design to make it useful. But the school, district, and state policymakers who ideally would rely on research to make informed decisions do not typically fund it. Consequently, they have limited influence over what actually gets funded, and, thus, what gets researched. The mechanisms for aggregating the preferences of this lower level are decidedly imperfect. One view is that no individual or organization, with the exception of a handful of very large states, has the resources required to fund research. A more cynical view is that despite the billions spent on the operation of K–12 public schooling, the operating agencies do not really care to know what does and does not work, and, hence, are unwilling to devote even a small percentage of their budgets to research. There are few private sector providers willing to pay for R&D. Until the relatively recent onset of the accountability movement in the late 1980s and 1990s, culminating in NCLB, there were enormous societal consequences for producing poor outcomes, but few consequences directly influencing the districts and schools that are, at least partially, responsible for producing these outcomes. Accountability creates incentives for schools to use research-tested education strategies and to demand better research.

One possible avenue of reform, then, would be to broaden this accountability beyond schools to other private interests that play a role, albeit sometimes indirectly, in influencing student achievement. Textbook publishers, for instance, have a vested interest in selling books. We would like to see more emphasis (along the lines of the What Works Clearinghouse) placed on providing them with incentives to make sure that the books they sell are in fact aligned with student achievement goals. In general, it would be helpful for policymakers to try to ensure that those private interests that play a key role in the education process have incentives encouraging high-quality, independent analysis of the products and services they provide.

Disconnectedness also helps reinforce a tendency toward fragmentation in education research. Large-scale efficacy studies would require millions of dollars over a sustained period, but the federal government's research effort is split among many agencies, and then into even smaller pots of money within each agency, and each state acts largely on its own. While there are strong pressures to divvy up funds among many small projects and powerful constituencies, the exponentially greater power of consolidated efforts must be highlighted. States and localities could learn much more about the effectiveness of their policies if they took more of a lead in funding, maybe through consortia organized by region or common interest, encouraged by federal government incentives or facilitation.

Federal and state accountability efforts are undoubtedly increasing the demand for and attention to research. However, because much of the effort is centered around state standards and student assessments that differ widely from state to state, it is difficult for researchers to analyze cross-state policies. It also suggests that as a nation we have not agreed upon what students should be learning in schools. National tests would not only facilitate coordinated research efforts by bringing about consistency of measures of student outcomes, but such tests would also allow better research quality checks since they would eliminate one potential source of variation in findings. Finally, they would serve to send a message to funders that, yes, through the political process, we have reached a national consensus as to what students ought to know. This message might help clarify what should be funded, thereby reducing the fragmentation of outcomes that could be studied.

One or two well-designed, large-scale randomized trials or quasi-experimental studies, for example, seem much more likely to generate useful findings than the current hotchpotch of underpowered efforts. Furthermore, to the extent possible, research should be undertaken on policies or programs *before* they are enacted on a large scale.[32] In some cases, this might mean studying interventions that take place in select localities or states, but the general point is that the more well-established a program or policy, the more likely that research on it will take place in an environment with entrenched interests, and thus, the less likely that the research will have much influence.[33] A good example of where this could be useful today is studying pay-for-performance. A number of states and localities are pushing forward in this area, but we do not know much about how such plans should be structured.[34] We would learn a lot by studying, for instance, the impacts of the various types of plans enacted under Q-Comp in Minnesota.[35] This would help policymakers not only to figure out whether pay-for-performance is a good idea, but, if so, how to design plans that are most effective—which is important, as ineffectively structured or implemented programs could serve to undermine the very notion that such a policy could work.

Foundations and the federal government request some "demand-driven" research, but a striking feature of education research is the extent to which the standards and the topics valued by research suppliers have a significant impact on what gets done. This is not an issue if the suppliers are attuned to the needs of the field, and have high-quality standards. However, for all sorts of historical, organizational, and other reasons, this is not the case. Yet, promising developments are occurring on this front: Some foundations actively seek to fund research that is built upon school districts' priorities, and the Council of the Great City Schools has recently announced a IES-funded fellowship that will result in senior education researchers being embedded in a large urban school district and focused on producing research that is both rigorous in nature and relevant to the specific challenges facing such districts. At a policy level there is some prospect that the increasingly severe sanctions of NCLB and state accountability systems will generate greater demand for good data and research that can inform decisionmaking.[36]

Finally, we believe that education research needs more quality-control mechanisms to help policymakers distinguish good research from bad. Education gatekeeping can, and does, happen on both the front and back ends of research. Some foundations have quite rigorous review processes, and IES reviews of research proposals are far more focused on methodology than has historically been true at the Department of Education. However, the impact of such efforts is limited by the modest overall funding levels. Funders could be clearer about the research standards they expect of their funded research, outlining specifically the methods they deem acceptable for making causal inferences. Furthermore, all funders ought to do more to avoid funding that creates conflicts of interest.

Gatekeeping happens on the back end as well. Academic journals that publish education research vary in prestige, in part based on the rigor required of the research they accept (for more on this, see chapter 9 by Lance D. Fusarelli). Efforts such as the What Works Clearinghouse and the Campbell Collaborative, and initiatives of the National Academy of Education and (even) the American Educational Research Association, have gradually increased the awareness of the importance of research design. At the same time, it appears that the growth in research media outlets is exceeding the capacity of gatekeeping institutions to separate good research from bad. This is deeply problematic, because most consumers of the work will not have the time or capacity to judge its quality.

Many of our diagnoses stem from the complex nature of the K–12 delivery system, and the deeply engrained traditions of academe, so we do not naïvely think that the strong incentives governing the relevance and rigor of education research can be changed overnight. But we do believe that federal, state, and local policymakers can take steps that would lead to necessary improvements. Without such changes, we suspect that the education research enterprise will always be a pale imitation of that in other fields, such as health.

We thank Rick Hess, Kathleen McCartney, Mike McPherson, and Russ Whitehurst for helpful comments on an earlier draft of this paper, and Carol Wallace for editorial suggestions.

CHAPTER 10

Considering the Politics in the Research Policymaking Nexus

Kenneth K. Wong

American political and social institutions have maintained a clear division of responsibility and labor between those who investigate the nature of societal problems and those who make policy choices to address the problems. These two spheres of activities, which may be broadly characterized as the research community and the electoral-oriented policy institutions, operate under different governing principles and incentive structures. As C. P. Snow observed almost half a century ago, "there is a sharp difference in the intellectual and moral temperaments" between science and government. Snow described the "two cultures":

> To be any good, in his youth at least, a scientist has to think of one thing, deeply and obsessively, for a long time. An administrator has to think of a great many things, widely, in their interconnections, for a short time . . . I agree that scientists in their creative periods do not easily get interested in administrative problems and are not likely to be much good at them.[1]

While electoral success is often dependent on broad-based constituency support, academic institutions value specialization, independence, and originality.

Snow's depiction of two cultures is echoed by many social scientists. In accepting the John Gaus Award for his lifetime of exemplary scholarship in the joint tradition of political science and public administration in 1994, political scientist James Q. Wilson observed, "The study and the practice of public administration were once nearly identical. . . . Today, study and practice have increasingly gone their separate ways. As the academic theory of public organizations has become more abstract, the reform of public management has become detached from scholarly research."[2] To a great extent, policy researchers, particularly those who work in the academic setting, are driven by the theoretical and methodological concerns of their academic discipline or their specialized field of study. In his seminal work on agenda setting, political scientist John Kingdon specified the different mindset of the "policy community" and the "political people." He observed, "The policy community concentrates on matters like technical detail, cost-benefit analyses, gathering data, conducting studies, and honing proposals. The political people, by contrast, paint with a broad brush, are involved in many more issue areas than the policy people are, and concentrate on winning elections, promotion parties, and mobilizing support in the larger polity."[3]

Given the two cultures, to what extent and in what manner can researchers exercise influence in the policymaking process? What is the incentive for policymakers to use and not use research in their decisionmaking? How do public officials use research? What are the conditions under which researchers can exercise greater influence in the policy process? Are there ways that the two communities can collaborate for the public good? In addressing these questions, this chapter focuses on the political side of the research–policymaker nexus. Too often, researchers pay little attention to the political dynamics in the policymaking process. Electoral interests, distribution of power, and partisan-oriented agenda must be taken into consideration in understanding the use and influence of research in the policy process.

ELECTORAL INTEREST AND POLICY DIRECTION

A major goal of elected officials is to be re-elected. This electoral interest constitutes a fundamental rationale behind the behaviors of elected officials. Electoral concerns determine politicians' allocation of time, use of political capital, choice of words during media events, selection of information, affiliation with groups and organizations, alliance with other public officials, and votes in the decisionmaking process. Members of the U.S. Congress, for example, are known to effectively use their influence to leverage resources for their constituencies, thereby consolidating their electoral base for re-election. Indeed, congressional elections in recent decades are dominated by incumbents who do not face serious challengers.[4]

Elected officials, though driven by their self-interest in winning elections, are keenly aware of their role in shaping policy direction. In a populist democracy such as the United States, political representation is a process whereby the electorate entrusts the decisionmaking power to their chosen representatives for a designated period of time. In this governing arrangement, public officials are held accountable for their use of power to address the concerns of their constituencies, which includes not only those who reside in their home jurisdiction, but also the broader community that identifies with the policy disposition of the elected officials. Elected officials who hold either a liberal or a conservative perspective on the role of government are likely to receive campaign support from different coalitions across the country. Building on the legacy of the civil rights movement, black elected officials, for example, tend to support redistributive policy. Because minorities comprise a disproportionate share of the economically disadvantaged population, minority officials are particularly keen advocates for public programs that aim to alleviate the economically deprived state of their constituencies, both locally and nationally.[5]

Elected officials in the executive branch, such as the president, governors, and mayors, provide ample examples of how public officials build a policy record so that they can leave a legacy on issues they and their constituencies care about.[6] Politician-executives can be expected to behave in an electorally calculating and competitive fashion in order to stay in office. From this perspective, public officials choose to involve themselves in public policy issues because they expect that the political benefits will outweigh the political risks or costs. In prioritizing their limited political resources, they frequently revisit their strategic use of time, energy, personnel, and political influence in advancing their policy agenda.

At the same, the chief executive office, such as the U.S. presidency and the office of the mayor, constitutes an important institution that is embedded in its own tradition, reputation, status, and identity. Even though politician-executives are keenly aware of the necessity of running successful political campaigns, many also aspire to leave behind a policy legacy. From this perspective, public officials are motivated by issues pertaining to the collective good, such as revitalizing economically depressed communities, improving public schools, raising the quality of life, and making the government more efficiently serve its clients.

To be sure, the self-interest motivation and a sense of institutional mission are not mutually exclusive. While President George Bush received measurable public support for the passage of the No Child Left Behind Act, he viewed high-stakes accountability as an instrument to change the landscape of education policy.[7] When mayors become involved in schools, they tended to maintain a mix of political calculation and institutional mission and legacy.[8] In his successful re-election bids, Mayor Richard Daley of Chicago was able to cite school improvement to address the criticisms launched by his opponents. In other words, electoral popularity depends on "good government" and policy accomplishments. Clearly, elected officials are motivated to build their policy impacts while making every effort to win their next election.

Finally, the scope of policy issues pursued by elected officials is likely to vary across the three levels of our federal system. There are two broad strands of literature on the differentiated policy role. First, the literature on fiscal federalism suggests that local government faces more structural constraints.[9] Local communities cannot regulate the flow of productive resources, such as labor and capital investment, and do not have control over monetary and tariff policy. Instead, local communities have to compete with one another in luring investment, in attracting property taxpayers, and in exporting their goods and services. While the federal and state governments enjoy more elastic taxing mechanisms (such as income tax), localities have to raise their revenues largely through the more restrictive "benefits-received" principle.

These structural constraints suggest a functional division of responsibilities. At the federal level, Congress and the president can address poverty and other redistributive issues because they face fewer fiscal constraints when compared to local communities. In contrast, locally elected officials have to pay primary attention to how their policy decisions influence local property values and residential choices of productive labor. Consequently, when the federal government pursues its goals on equal education opportunities for disadvantaged students, it is not surprising to see local and state resistance.[10]

A second strand of literature on federalism focuses on states and localities as sources for policy innovation.[11] When new policy ideas are found to have worked in a small number of communities, they are likely to be instituted at the national level. This view of states as policy laboratories can be illustrated by examples across policy arenas. Social security, for example, was a successful program in Wisconsin before it was federalized and applied across the nation.

Public school reform offers many examples of policy experimentation. To a greater or lesser extent, states are engaging in several major reforms that are subject to ongoing evaluation, including charter schools, vouchers, and school district takeover. At the same time, states do not design or implement these reforms uniformly. While some states have restrictive charter laws, others allow for diverse service providers and keep raising the number of approved charters with full reimbursement schemes. Given these variations in the scope of policy initiatives, state and local officials are particularly keen on focusing on accountability and innovations that work in education. In short, facing structural realities in our federal system of public policy, elected officials at different levels of the federal system may pay attention to issues that are consistent with their strategic priorities at their particular institutional level.

WEAK INCENTIVES TO USE RESEARCH IN POLICYMAKING

While the research community encounters difficulties in gaining policy influence, electoral-oriented policy institutions may lack sufficient incentives to pay attention to research knowledge in their decisionmaking. Among the likely impediments are the nature of pluralist democracy, the policymaking cycle, federalism, and bureaucratic inertia.

Pluralist Democracy Limits Expert Influence

Pluralist democracy does not solely rely on research for setting policy priorities. In *Speaking Truth to Power*, Aaron Wildavsky reminded us:

> In an aspiring democracy, the truth we speak is partial. There is always more than one version of the truth and we can be most certain that the latest statement isn't it. This is not only democracy's truth, it is also democracy's dogma . . . Policy analysis and policy analysts in a democracy never will (and never should) be that powerful.[12]

Clearly, policymakers need to pay attention not only to expert knowledge but also preferences from organized interests and their own political ties and philosophical beliefs.[13] As Mary Jo Bane, an expert in social welfare policy, suggested, the need is "to shift our perception from seeing ourselves mostly as expert problem solvers to seeing ourselves mostly as participants in democratic deliberation."[14] The policy influence of experts in a liberal democracy, thus, is likely to face a "ceiling effect."

Further, in his study of "nonpartisan research organizations" that are under the direction of the state legislation, John Hird found that state lawmakers did not consider these actors as influential when compared with other competing interests in the legislative process. There are, however, variations within these nonpartisan research organizations. Lawmakers see greater influence among those that have strong staffing capacity to address longer-term analytic tasks that go beyond providing information-gathering services in the short term.[15]

Timing is Everything

It is not a surprise that policymakers need timely research to inform policy decisions. Electoral cycles necessitate that elected officials rapidly move their agenda forward . The timeliness of education research poses a challenge. The following exchange during a Congressional hearing between Milton Goldberg, the acting assistant secretary of the Office of Educational Research and Improvement in 1981, and Congressman Silvio Conti, is indicative of the tension between the electoral-policy cycle and the longer span of research undertakings:

> *Congressman Conti:* Dr. Goldberg, look, before you go any further, can I ask you to do something for me? . . . Don't begin your remarks by telling me that research takes a long time. Because your predecessors have done that.

> *Dr. Goldberg:* Unfortunately, Mr. Conti, it is true that research takes a long time. On the other hand, if you support enough research, over long enough periods of time, I ought to be able to tell you, at any point in time, that some stuff has borne fruit. And I ought to be able to tell you enough about that stuff so that you will permit us to continue doing that other work that may not be fruitful for another five or six years.[16]

In recent years, the growing impatience of policymakers with the lack of timely research has encouraged the Institute of Education Sciences to engage for-profit organizations to bid on research centers, regional labs, and research projects. This effort to promote public–private partnerships in research undertakings constitutes an extension of the practice in other agencies (including the National Science Foundation) and industries, as well as the National Institutes of Health and for-profit hospitals and pharmaceutical companies.

A Decentralized System of Education Creates Data Barriers

Policy researchers face enormous political difficulties in gaining access to data at the school and student level. Structurally, the general lack of data access is closely associated with the way school systems are organized in the United States. Districts are independent entities that are governed by an independently elected school board, financed with their own fiscal authority, and managed by rules and regulations that are constrained, in many states and districts, by collective bargaining agreements. Each of the 14,000 districts has its own governing culture and bureaucratic inertia. Research is often seen as a nuisance that dilutes staffing resources from the central task of regulatory compliance. Very few researchers can leverage a sufficient amount of influence to build an ongoing research relationship with districts and schools. As discussed later in the paper, this high cost of entry can only be managed efficiently when a network of researchers collaborate.

Intra-Organizational Politics

Competition for control among organizational units within the government sector tends to destabilize the research agenda and government commitment in research funding. In reviewing the history of the organization of federal education research, Kaestle (1994) described "a merry-go-round" process whereby the National Institute of Education (NIE) was replaced by the Office of Educational Research and Improvement (OERI) in 1984.[17] The latest attempt to clarify the mission and authority of the federal research agency saw the creation of the Institute for Education Sciences (IES), whose directorship is designed not to be subject to partisan shift in the White House during the 6-year appointment. Nonetheless, each round of reorganization took about six to eight months in transition, often disrupting the ongoing relationship between the agency and researchers. Agency restructuring is further complicated by partisan changes in Congress and the White House. Partisan shift tends to destabilize appropriations for research because the policy priorities are likely to change. For example, the Bush administration has prioritized its funding to support the research and implementation of the recommendations of the Reading Panel.

Inertia of the Status Quo

Research that addresses school choice and other innovative management arrangements tends to be challenged by the power of the status quo. Policymakers are constrained by existing institutional norms, procedures, and regulations in defining the scope of policy options. In summarizing recent innovative efforts, Frederick Hess observed institutional barriers against the opening of new charter schools and the involvement of external providers to deliver supplemental services under NCLB.[18] At the state and local level, policymakers face collective bargaining agreements between management and unions. In this regard, teachers unions can be understood to have both economic interests in protecting jobs and compensation, and broad-based policy interests in promoting high-quality teaching and learning in public schools. These two interest strands have been labeled "traditional" unionism versus "new" or "reform" unionism.[19] Reform unionism is generally more favorable to charter schools, stressing the need for high-quality teachers, accountability, and assessment. This sentiment can be seen in the unions' call for legal provisions that maintain high standards. On the other hand, traditional unionism aims to promote job security, high wages, and benefits[20]—economic interests that remain prevalent despite the rise of new unionism.[21] Terry Moe, skeptical of new unionism, contends that the primary goal of unions is still to protect jobs, wages, and benefits.[22] Most relevant to this discussion is the role that teachers unions play in the state-level political process.[23] Moe argues that the unions' "massive memberships and awesome resources give them unrivaled power in the politics of education, allowing them to affect which policies are imposed on the schools by government—and to block reforms they don't like."[24] Whether or not their power is unrivaled, it is widely acknowledged that unions have the potential for significant influence in the statehouse. As Hess and Martin West point out, both kinds of major teachers unions have made strategic donations to protect their economic interests.[25]

It has long been recognized that education services do not always function as markets with very few constraints. Economists have engaged in much work on the empirical realities of these markets. Recent work in this area has pointed us toward the political aspects of the education marketplace. The quasi-market for education services is substantially regulated by legislative and administrative authorities. After all, charter schools exist because of enabling state legislation. Charter schools are not simply firms supplying educational services. Jeffrey Henig and his associates provide evidence that the locational pattern of charter schools is affected by political and practical considerations.[26] In short, charter schools are linked in many ways to the politics and bureaucracy of their surroundings. Exactly how that interaction will take place will depend upon the context of local and state politics, but it could very well play a significant role in the effectiveness of teaching and learning. In this politicized context, even well-designed research can be overshadowed by political calculus.

Political interests have been recognized in other contexts as well. Bryan Hassel and Meagan Batdorff have shown that the charter re-authorization process can be influenced by politics and a lack of needed information.[27] Both of these limitations can hamper the way in which policy decisions are made on charter schools. Always operating in the background are the interest-based politics of school choice, which may break down along traditional partisan lines. Joshua Phillips, Omer Gokcekus, and Edward Tower observed that politicians with stronger links to teachers unions are more likely to vote against such proposals, while representatives of districts with larger African-American or Republican populations are more likely to vote in favor.[28] It remains to be seen whether research can play a key role in issues that are polarized.

WHEN RESEARCH GAINS POLICY ATTENTION

Notwithstanding these institutional impediments in the policymaking process, education policy research can exercise some influence under certain conditions in the policy process. Several examples can be cited in the second half of the twentieth century, when social science research gained the attention of policy actors. In 1954, Kenneth Clark's experiment on children's racial identity was included as a footnote in the Supreme Court's *Brown v. Board of Education* decision.[29] (For more on education and the courts, see chapter 8 by Joshua Dunn and Martin West.) Commissioned by the Office of Education, a 1966 report on education opportunities, under the direction of James Coleman and Ernst Campbell, played a key role in defining how federal investment in education acts as a strategy to address poverty issues.[30] Research on early childhood education by Benjamin Bloom and Edward Zeigler, among others, provided the empirical evidence that supported federal commitment to Head Start programs. During the late 1960s, the NAACP Children's Defense Fund challenged the growing misuses of Elementary and Secondary Education Act Title I funds by state and local agencies. The study led to the Congressional passage of the 1969 provision on "supplement not supplant" that exists today. In the early 1980s, the Heritage Foundation's series on the White House transition provided a framework that shaped Ronald Reagan's domestic agenda.

Networks of Researchers

In recent years, the Koret Task Force at the Hoover Institution and Harvard's Civil Rights Project have attracted ongoing federal and state government attention to their research on education accountability, equity, and choice. A Google search in early March 2007 for "Koret Task Force Testimony" yielded 277 results, while a search for "Testimony for Civil Rights Project at Harvard" yielded 1,140 results since NCLB. Members of the Koret Task Force, for example, testified several times in Congress on school finance issues. The Civil Rights Project's school dropout study alone received 233 results in the Google Search, which included media reporting.

   These examples suggest several institutional conditions that enable researchers to gain policy attention. First, membership in the research and policy networks has become increasingly permeable. Government officials are hired to direct research centers, while prominent researchers are recruited to lead policy units. Of the ten members of the Koret Task Force on K–12 Education at the Hoover Institution, three serve on the board of directors of the National Board for Education Sciences, which sets broad policy for the

Institute for Education Sciences. Two were former assistant secretaries at the Office of Educational Research and Improvement. Williamson Evers, a member of the Koret Task Force, is currently on leave to serve as the U.S. assistant secretary of education for planning, evaluation, and policy development. Similarly, the former co-director of the Harvard Civil Rights Project was an assistant secretary in the U.S. Justice Department.

Further, researchers are more effective when they team up to provide comprehensive research analysis in response to the needs of policymakers. The Koret Task Force was invited by state policymakers in Texas, Arkansas, and Louisiana to provide statewide reform recommendations. In Texas, these recommendations ranged from teacher compensation reform to charter schools and accountability. The Task Force proposal on school vouchers was endorsed by the governor, Speaker of the House, lieutenant governor, and the chair of the House Select Committee on Public School Finance in 2004.[31] There was also a legislative attempt to advance the Koret Task Force's recommendation to expand outsourcing of public school services to private management organizations.[32] However, these proposals were not approved by the Texas legislature.

When policymakers are ready to address a major policy challenge, research and expert opinions can play a role in framing policy redirection. The March 2005 release of a major study on school dropouts by the Harvard Civil Rights Project generated citywide discussion in Los Angeles, where, the study estimated, only 45 percent of high school freshmen graduated in four years. In March 2006, Los Angeles Mayor Antonio Villaraigosa declared that the dropout challenge was "the new civil rights issue of our time."[33] In response to public pressure, the district consolidated dropout and adult education programs and launched the "Diploma Project" for credit recovery and work-based learning.

Opportunities in the Context of Paradigmatic Shift

Ironically, research experts' general lack of political influence may place them in a unique role under circumstances of uncertainty. An example is the commission that issued the influential 1983 report, *A Nation at Risk*.[34] Written by an eighteen-member commission appointed by President Reagan's secretary of education, the report's conclusions reflect competing reform perspectives both within the education community and across societal sectors. The commission members included college and university presidents (including the president-elect of the University of California, who chaired the commission), scientists, school administrators, and business representatives. During the 18-month tenure of the National Commission on Excellence in Education, it commissioned dozens of research papers and held eight meetings of the full commission, six public hearings, two panel discussions, a symposium, and a series of regional meetings.

The biggest challenge facing the commission was the uncertainty regarding the appropriate federal role during the first term of the Reagan presidency. First, consistent with its notion of devolution, Reagan's New Federalism proposed a functional "swap," shifting all the education functions to the states but federal assumption of public welfare assistance.[35] Second, the president proposed to dismantle the Department of Education, create school choice for Title I parents, and finance tuition tax credits for parents of students in nonpublic schools. In an interview with the *New York Times* during his first month as the U.S. Secretary of Education, Terry Bell pledged his commitment to the President's proposal to abolish the department, and said that he was "not sure that we need department-level cabinet status."[36] It was not until June 1987 that the administration began to shift its six-year effort to reduce federal spending in education. The shift coincided with the appointment of a pragmatic former Republican Senator from Tennessee as the White House chief of staff.[37] Third, efforts were made to streamline the administration of federal grants. Reagan's New Federalism agenda tended to shift the federal focus from one that was primarily focused on equity to one that promoted efficiency.

It was in this policy context of a seemingly historic shift in the American social welfare state that the National Commission on Excellence in Education deliberated the future role of the federal government in education. The two policy paradigms, equity and efficiency, were supported by competing powerful interests in the early 1980s. While congressional and bureaucratic support for equity-oriented programs remained strong, the Reagan administration, elected at a time of growing taxpayer dissatisfaction with government performance, clearly wanted to reduce the supply of federally funded services.

Caught in the seemingly intractable tension between the politics of demand and the politics of supply, the commission offered a "third way" that tended to instill new expectations on both the clients and the providers of the education enterprise. It would be in the nation's interest, argued the commission, for higher academic standards to be attained in our public schools and institutions of higher education. It did not "rubber stamp" any of the major education initiatives proposed by the Reagan White House. Nor was the report sympathetic with the congressional recommendation for increased education spending. Instead, *Nation at Risk* left unsettled the question of the amount and types of resources the nation might need to reverse the trend of declining education performance. Perhaps most important, instead of terminating the federal role in education, the commission called upon federal leadership to lead the movement toward "creating a learning society."

Given the fact that the commission was walking on a political tightrope, it came as no surprise that *Nation at Risk* was written to address the broad societal concerns, commonly shared values, and universalistic expectations on education. These principles are designed to lay the normative foundation for the public, educators, businesses, and politicians to develop their specific reform strategies. Program details, though provided by dozens of commissioned technical papers, were not featured prominently in the report. Any discussion of program details would have placed the commission at political risk of being perceived as yielding to White House pressure or as taking a position on the debate over the future of the social welfare state. In looking back at a White House meeting when President Reagan specified the work of the commission, Harvard physics professor Gerald Holton, a commission member, summarized the situation: "He [the president] told us that our report should focus on five fundamental points that would bring excellence to education: Bring God back into the classroom. Encourage tuition tax credits for families using private schools. Support vouchers. Leave the primary responsibility for education to parents. And please abolish that abomination, the Department of Education. Or, at least, don't ask to waste more federal money on education."[38] None of these initiatives were taken up seriously in *Nation at Risk*. The report did not go into any details of specific federal policy. It clearly did not mention programs for the disadvantaged, including Title I. As Gerald Holton reflected, the report did not address "the moral equivalent of a national 'right to proper education.'"[39] Instead, *Nation at Risk* articulated broad principles on improving learning and teaching.

To be sure, the mission of the National Commission on Excellence in Education was endorsed by the White House in the first place, thereby granting its work political legitimacy. Perhaps more important in terms of the commission's policy influence was the presidential reaction to *Nation at Risk* and its recommendations. Recognizing that education is a national challenge, the commission's report signaled the need for national leadership in reforming the entire system of education. For the first time in American history, the president used his bully pulpit to define the problems in the nation's public education system. During the first 12 months following the release of the report, the media quoted President Reagan over 100 times as referring to its findings and recommendations. Further, the commission and its activities mobilized a wide range of societal interests, resources, and expertise to address education problems. Building on the work of the commission, two subsequent national education summits involved the President, the governors, businesses, and civic and education leaders.

Marketing Research

Good research has to compete with other forces to gain the attention of policymakers. Clearly, researchers by themselves are no longer able to garner the attention of the media, the policy community, and the public. All the major think tanks, such as the Brookings Institution, the American Enterprise Institute, the Heritage Foundation, Cato Institute, and the Hoover Institution have invested heavily in their public affairs and communications offices. Marketing capacity is at least as important as, if not more important than, conducting the research itself. Making research findings readily accessible is particularly important to journalists as they face deadlines for their reporting. As political scientist Doris Garber (1993) pointed out, news reporters tend to rely on a few experts for information.[40] Foundations that fund the research projects emphasize on how the deliverables are disseminated to the policy community. Not only do policymakers expect to work with programs and organizations, foundations that hold the purse strings are increasingly looking for institutional actors to invest as a way to increase the likelihood of impact and sustainability.

Government Actor as Partner

Government endorsement suggests another facilitating condition, namely, when government actors collaborate with researchers on the design and implementation of large-scale studies. The Tennessee STAR class size reduction experiment was endorsed by Governor Lamar Alexander in the 1980s. The project earned credibility with the research community by using a randomized experimental design.[41] It also had the additional benefit of a state legislator, one who appreciated social science and policy research, actively engaged in every stage of the research. When investigators collaborate with elected officials in the design phase, it creates incentives for the latter to follow the research progress and to utilize the research findings.

Demand-Side Politics

Finally, in the context of growing accountability, policymakers will be increasingly selective in viewing the importance of education research. In focusing on NCLB accountability, the Bush administration has sent a clear signal to the public that student achievement matters and that it holds schools and districts accountable for results. In other words, the Bush administration is trying to meet the demands of education "consumers," including parents, taxpayers, and employers. Clearly, NCLB places a lot of pressure on service providers, including the education profession and the teachers unions. The Bush strategy to build a consumer-based coalition is in part facilitated by public opinion on issues associated with NCLB and school reform. In a January 2006 survey sponsored by the Pew Research Center, the respondents ranked "improving the educational system" as the second most important priority for the president and Congress. It was behind defense against terrorist attacks, but ahead of such important issues as the nation's economy, employment, social security, Medicare, and crime reduction.[42]

Public attention to education comes at a time when public confidence in the institution of public education continues its thirty-year decline. In 1977, 53 percent of the public showed a high level of confidence with public education. By May 2005, the confidence level had fallen to 37 percent.[43] However, the public seemed unwilling to give up on reforming the existing system of public schools. According to the Gallup Poll conducted in the summer of 2003, 73 percent of the respondents wanted to reform the existing public school system, while only 25 percent preferred alternative approaches (such as school vouchers).[44] This pattern was found in a 2003 poll sponsored by the Pew Hispanic Center, in which 37 percent were in favor of the government offering parents vouchers but 40 percent indicated they did not know enough to offer an opinion.[45] Finally, two-thirds of the respondents in a June 2002 Gallup Poll favored using annual tests to track student progress.[46] In other words, the accountability focus on fixing low-performing schools seemed to have broad public support.

Because of the public demand for performance-based accountability, policymakers have directed their attention to research that addresses the questions of what works, under what circumstances, for whom, and with what kind of effects on school and student outcomes. This focus on what works is not unique to education policy following NCLB. During the early 1990s, for example, the Clinton administration promoted the notions of customer accountability, greater transparency, and management reform as suggested by David Osborne and Ted Gaebler in their book, *Reinventing Government*.[47] The National Performance Review, also known as the Al Gore Commission, cited the work of John Dilulio, whose research identified the management conditions for producing safer prisons, and Donald Kettl, whose research examined government deployment of market strategies to improve services.[48]

BEYOND THE TWO CULTURES: INCENTIVES FOR POLICYMAKERS TO USE RESEARCH

Public officials are motivated by both electoral concerns and institutional mission. Given this duality, will elected officials pay more or less attention to policy research findings? What are the conditions that shape the policy-maker–research community nexus? The future, in my view, poses challenges and opportunities.

Gaining Research Credibility

First, rigorous research will continue to earn credibility. To find out how the policymaking community perceives the importance of think tanks and policy experts on regulatory issues, Andrew Rich surveyed 71 congressional staff from both parties and 54 Washington, D.C., journalists. While 28 percent of journals from national news organizations saw think tanks as "very influential," fewer than 20 percent of the congressional staff agreed.[49] The somewhat limited policy influence of think tanks seems to be consistent with Carol Weiss's argument that policymakers use research findings in a purposeful manner.[50] They use research to justify their preexisting policy positions and to test the public pulse on politically risky issues. Rich's findings also suggest the need for better-designed, rigorous research, a role that university-based research centers can undertake.

Further, policymakers and media are likely to value policy research that does not come from ideologically leaning organizations. When asked to rank think tanks that are "most credible in the political process," survey respondents identified six "centrist" organizations among the top ten. These included the Brookings Institution, RAND Corporation, Council on Foreign Relations, Carnegie Endowment for International Peace, Center for Strategic and International Studies, and National Bureau of Economic Research.[51]

Promoting Research

While credibility may be valued, policymakers are more likely to pay attention to research findings that are effectively promoted. As Rich observed in his study of congressional actions on health care and telecommunications reform, "marketing-oriented think tanks generally are more successful in having their research cited, and conservative think tanks have good fortune in obtaining space in which to promote their work, at least in the pages of the editorially sympathetic *Wall Street Journal*."[52] The way expertise is organized has changed. While experts used to come from academic institutions without having to concern themselves with any marketing strategies, today's most visible experts are ready to work with lobbyists, marketing firms, and interest-based advocacy groups throughout the policy process.

Enhancing Research Rigor

From a broader perspective on research quality, it is useful to consider the standards regarding social science research as developed by Gary King, Robert Keohane and Sidney Verba, three Harvard political scientists with different methodological and substantive orientations. In *Designing Social Inquiry*, King and his colleagues identify several criteria for improving the design and conduct of social science research in policy evaluation.[53]

First, policy researchers need to frame their research questions to satisfy a dual audience, namely, the broader community and the specialized scholarly peers. Second, policy researchers need to organize evidence to improve a particular theory or policy paradigm. After assessing the balance of the evidence in testing key hypotheses, researchers may specify the conditions under which the original theory can be revised to accommodate for emerging occurrences. For example, in their study of first grade reading and the common practice of organizing students into ability groups, Barr and Dreeben were surprised to see that some first graders were able to learn more even when placed in lower tracks. This finding ultimately led the researchers to distinguish the structure of ability groups from instructional coverage in each ability group.[54]

Further, policy analysts must be transparent about the way research is conducted. It is necessary to report on the rules, procedures, and tools employed in gathering and analyzing data. Equally important is the need to refrain from discouraging those peers who may hold a different view on the issue from asking questions on data quality. Indeed, to ensure their projects meet scientific standards for data quality, many policy researchers give priority to publishing their findings in refereed journals.

Fourth, policy researchers can improve data quality. Reliability of measurement of observable implications, replicability of results when another uses the same methods, and documentation of data sources are some of the scientific practices that all researchers are expected to follow.

Clearly, an ongoing challenge is to develop a process whereby researchers can guard against data bias. Researchers also can situate their findings in the larger context to maximize the potential for causal inference. Policymakers are concerned about program evaluation that is conducted by designers of the program. Consequently, independent, third-party evaluators are recruited to conduct program assessment. Finally, policy research needs to recognize the importance of reporting uncertainties that are associated with the results.

Mediating Divisiveness

It should be noted that divisiveness among researchers on key policy issues will remain an impediment to expert influence in the policy process. As Brookings Institution economist Henry Aaron points out, "On any given subject that is important or at all controversial, the lay reader is routinely confronted with experts saying conflicting things. And therefore, the reader is at a loss. And it tends to undercut the capacity of any of the studies to have a major influence on policy. People wield their social science research studies like short swords and shields in the ideological wars."[55] Perhaps the consensus panel as established by the National Academy of Sciences offers a feasible venue to address this challenge.[56] Adopted by many research committees in NAS, consensus panel provides a forum for incorporating diverse perspectives and approaches on a common set of policy challenges.

Separating Advocacy Claims from Research Evidence

Another challenge for the education policy community is the diminishing distinction between research and advocacy. Unlike many of their peers in related social science fields, students of education policy have a strong commitment to address education problems. At issue is whether they can set aside their advocacy for certain policy positions and carry out a program of research that is grounded in the standards of systematic inquiry as discussed above. Does the philosophical underpinning allow for a balanced consideration of rival hypotheses? Will the evidence on different rivals be treated even handedly? Just as advocacy work has its legitimate place in the policy process, research–driven policy analysis can offer societal benefits.

Drawing Lessons from Other Policy Arenas

Perhaps the creation of the National Institutes of Health (NIH) offers some useful lessons in building political support for the education research infrastructure. The NIH can be traced all the way back to 1887, when the U.S. Congress provided funding to create a one-room "laboratory of hygiene" within the Marine Hospital Service to study infectious diseases in the interest of public health.[57] It was only in 1901 that Congress saw the value of having a permanent hygienic laboratory, and funding was appropriated for the construction of a building to house the laboratory and its staff. The National Institute of Health was established in the Ransdell Act of 1930, which authorized research fellowships to examine medical and biological problems. In 1937, there was unanimous support in the U.S. Senate to establish the National Cancer Institute, the first categorical-disease structure of NIH. The number of congressionally approved, categorical institutes grew, and in 1948 Congress revised the institute's name to National Institutes (plural) of Health. By the late 1990s, the NIH had 27 categorical institutes and centers.

The congressionally approved categorical institutes suggest several advantages in terms of gaining political support. First, each categorical institute or center has its own mission, role, and expected contribution to the field. Congress can hold each institute separately accountable for performance, thereby connecting government funding to the quality and utility of the institute's research. Second, categorical institutes or centers offer flexibility in response to the nation's changing priorities. As new problems emerge, existing institutes can be phased out, consolidated, or reconstituted with an appropriate mission. Third, categorical institutes need to be focused and specialized with the primary goal of solving specific problems in the field. Disagreement among researchers is expected to be resolved or managed within the categorical institute. These lessons from NIH may be applicable to education research. For example, Congress might pass legislation establishing an institute on charter school research and development, which in turn would be held accountable as a line-item on the federal budget.

Another arrangement is suggested by the establishment of the Federal Reserve System. Following a series of crises in financial institutions in the late-nineteenth and early-twentieth centuries, Congress established the 1913 Federal Reserve Act "to provide for the establishment of Federal reserve banks, to furnish an elastic currency, to afford means of rediscounting commercial paper, to establish a more effective supervision of banking in the United States, and for other purposes." While its functions have expanded over the years, the Federal Reserve System (FRS) maintains its independence from the federal executive branch even though its board and its chair are presidential appointees. The FRS decisions do not require the approval of Congress or the President. At the same time, FRS has established a complex network of subsystems at the regional level. The current Institute for Education Sciences resembles FRS in some ways, including independence and regional networks. Unlike the way financial institutions are responding to the FRS prime rate decisions, however, the Institute of Education Sciences does not have much leverage in shaping the behaviors of school districts and state systems.

CONCLUSION

This chapter draws on the political science literature to illuminate the "political" dimensions of the research–policymaker nexus. The research community often overlooks the prominence of electoral interest in driving the behaviors of elected policymakers. Electoral concerns significantly influence policymakers' strategic choices and resource allocation. In this context, I differentiate two overlapping considerations—self-interest in winning elections and a sense of institutional mission in solving societal problems, such as improving education performance. The dynamics of rebalancing self-interest and institutional mission shapes the terms and the timing of political leaders' engagement in public school reform issues.

As the education reform agenda encourages innovation and experimentation, the policy community and the public face competing views pertaining to such controversial issues as school vouchers, performance-based compensation for teachers, and defining adequacy in state funding. These emerging issues are likely to be divisive, as elected officials choose the policy positions that are consistent with their policy disposition and their electoral interests. In this context of paradigmatic shift, researchers will be given the opportunity to play a critical role in shaping the terms of the debate. In short, the policymaker–researcher nexus will continue to evolve.

CHAPTER 11

Conclusion: Education Research and Public Policy

Frederick M. Hess

Even as paeans to "scientifically based research" and "evidence-based practice" have become a staple of education policymaking in recent years, the tangled relationship of education research to policy has received little serious scrutiny. Frustrated by a sprawling research community that offers few demonstrable advances and little reliable policy guidance, funders and policymakers have sought a greater emphasis on "science" and increasingly demanded clear and actionable answers. Researchers, wooed by the attention, eager to attract funds, and interested in contributing to policy deliberations, have sometimes encouraged such expectations. Meanwhile, larger questions about what role research can and does play in education policy have been largely shunted aside.

There is a natural inclination in penning a conclusion of this kind to advise researchers, policymakers, journalists, and others about how to do their jobs better; or to preach what actions must be taken if research is to be useful. However, the reality is that these actors are typically doing what existing professional incentives encourage them to do. Rather than bemoan this state of affairs or scold researchers, policymakers, and intermediaries for acting rationally, it may be more fruitful to reflect upon the pressures and dynamics of their world and—if we are not satisfied with the status quo—how those might be altered so that these actors are rewarded for producing more satisfactory outcomes.

It is not, however, merely a question of getting the incentives right for researchers and policymakers. Research is produced and used within a larger political economy—an ecosystem comprised of researchers, public officials, education groups, advocacy organizations, and journalists—that stretches to encompass district leaders, board members, courts, state boards of education, and educators. How these various constituencies motivate, interpret, and employ research may have an enormous impact on how research matters for formal and informal policymaking.

Several of the contributors to this volume note that some of the problems endemic to the education research–policy dynamic result from a proliferation of mediocre journals, a lack of uniform norms for research quality, a failure to communicate findings in accessible prose, and a lack of investment in the research enterprise. Popular remedies for these dilemmas include calls for a scholarly education journal analogous to *The Journal of the American Medical Association*, increased funding for "relevant" scholarship, and admonitions that researchers should avoid political debates. While such suggestions typically have merit, they are limited by an emphasis on technical frustrations that can be readily "fixed" through one intervention or another, and are unlikely to fully address the challenges posed by a vibrant, complex, and adaptive network.

For instance, in chapter 7, Howell provides provocative new research illustrating the constrained role that research may play in informing public preferences, suggesting that a finding can have a substantial impact on public attitudes, but only (at least in the case of school choice) when it comports with deeply held beliefs. Howell's results offer little reason to believe that research alone will prompt the public to revisit ingrained assumptions; and may help us understand why public confidence in the value of smaller class sizes, increased school spending, or National Board teaching certification might remain largely unaffected by research findings that question their efficacy. Howell's research sounds an important caution for those who are tempted to put exaggerated faith in the ability of research to mold public preferences or set policy agendas.

In the end, the contributors show why it is necessary to revisit assumptions about how research should be disseminated, how researchers should participate in public debates, how policymakers ought to consume and apply research, and about the interplay between funding, research, and policy. Now, I do not mean to make things more complicated than is necessary here; it is indisputably true that the Institute of Education Sciences' push for randomized field trials and its investment in the rigorous methodological training of young scholars have brought a healthful rigor to bear. At the same time, we should recognize the limits and the unintended consequences of such efforts. In this concluding chapter, I will step back and broadly address five key dynamics that are evident today.

THE LIMITS OF "SCIENTIFIC" POLICY RESEARCH

As the discussion of class size in the introduction makes clear, and as authors Ingersoll, Dunn, and West discuss, advocates and policymakers are frequently incautious when discussing how even rigorous, high-quality research might inform policy. This is due in large part to a flawed understanding of how the "medical research model" works and how it applies in medicine or education. The medical model, with its reliance on randomized field trials in which drugs or therapies are administered to patients under explicit protocols, is enormously powerful but also limited in its application. There are two types of interventions in fields like medicine or education. One relates to specialized knowledge of how the mind or body works, and the other to the manner in which we manage organizations and provide services.

Medical research is prescriptive and reliable when recommending interventions for certain illnesses, but few imagine it as authoritative when instructing policymakers on the merits of universal health coverage or how best to hold hospitals accountable for patient outcomes. While the Food and Drug Administration (FDA) monitors and approves drug therapies, its approval is not required before doctors, hospitals, or health-care firms can change management practices, compensation strategies, or accountability metrics.

In education, research into pedagogical and curricular interventions that relate to the development, knowledge, and skills of individual students entails the application of discrete treatments to identifiable subjects under specified conditions. Such interventions are readily susceptible to randomized field trials, which yield results that can reasonably be extrapolated to other populations and serve as the basis for prescriptive policymaking. However, reforms relating to governance, management, compensation, deregulation, and other innovations intended to improve organizational effectiveness are rarely precise, do not take place in controlled circumstances, and are not administered to discrete subjects. While research can shed light on how such reforms work and how their impact is affected by context, it will rarely be able to answer the question of whether a particular policy is "correct." Of course, this kind of work tends to have a smaller constituency among legislators and to draw less interest among the press because it does not "answer" the "big" questions. Nonetheless, the frustrating reality is that research into topics like merit pay or decentralization will always be more useful as a proximate guide for particular program elements than as a conclusive basis for prescriptive policymaking.

In truth, policies like charter schooling and merit pay are not really "education" innovations in any meaningful sense. They are decisions about how to arrange and deliver services, similar to those made in other public agencies and private enterprises. Asking research to conclusively confirm that school districts should seek to pay good employees more than mediocre ones—and never mind the 1,001 wrinkles that might explain why a merit pay program does or does not work as intended—is to ask more than research can plausibly deliver. The failure to make this distinction has been a problem for the No Child Left Behind Act, for instance, which, as Manna and Petrilli note in chapter 4, embraced "scientifically based research" as a convenient slogan with little attention to its precise meaning or how it might be implemented.

THE DEMOCRATIZATION OF DISSEMINATION

In chapter 3, Henig points out that modern technology has changed the mores governing scholarly publication. Thirty years ago, it was unusual for academics to release their work directly to a policy audience; there was no convenient way to do this except to mail it to designated recipients. Today, of course, the Internet has fundamentally altered that calculus. Indeed, of the thirteen studies that Editorial Projects in Education identified in 2006 as the most influential of the previous decade, only three were primarily released through refereed scholarly journals (i.e. academic journals in which submissions are judged by other scholars through an anonymous review process).[1] The "conventional" approach to dissemination, in which scholars rely on academic conferences, professional associations, books, and scholarly journal articles to communicate their findings, has been challenged by the emergence of a more entrepreneurial and free-wheeling model. The proliferation of national- and state-level think tanks and advocacy groups, and their success in utilizing inexpensive dissemination strategies, means the policy world is today suffused with research, syntheses, and policy briefs.

The transformation has opened up the discourse, raised new questions about how research quality can be ensured, and has helped inundate policymakers with a wealth of competing research, syntheses, and briefs. For instance, a 2007 Google search for "pre-k research" yielded more than 1.7 million results; a similar search for "merit pay research" more than 1.9 million. Forced to sort through this bonanza of information, public officials and their staffers have sought useful shortcuts. Meanwhile, equipped with new tools and encouraged by funders eager to influence public policy, a growing number of prominent researchers have adopted the dissemination practices pioneered by think tanks and advocacy groups, such as issuing press releases and policy briefs, holding launch events, writing op-eds, and wooing interested reporters. What percentage of researchers use these techniques? How frequently do they do so and with what effect? We don't know and have not asked, but these are questions deserving scrutiny.

It has become routine for policy-relevant research to be widely disseminated and posted on the Web within days or weeks of its completion. Think tanks and reform advocates seeking to maximize the impact and readership of those releases have little or no interest in scholarly publication. University scholars frequently author reports for these organizations or release "working papers" online—through proprietary websites or more formal outlets such as the National Bureau for Economic Research. In many cases, scholarly publication in a refereed publication is now the culmination of a body of research, sometimes appearing years after a number of earlier studies have entered the public debate and potentially influenced public policy.

While a source of concern for some, this development is the natural response to a culture of academic publication that long made it difficult for researchers to speak effectively to current and evolving debates. It can be extraordinarily challenging for research to contribute to contemporary policy debates if scholars wait while their work is reviewed, revised, and then published by scholarly journals before speaking in the public square. Take, for instance, a researcher studying NCLB. If he began his research in fall 2002 (when the law was first implemented), studied its effects in 2002–03, analyzed his data in summer and fall 2003, wrote up his findings in spring 2004, and submitted them to a scholarly journal in summer 2004, it is entirely possible that his research analyzing the law's initial implementation would first appear in print in 2007, when the issues framing the NCLB reauthorization debate were vastly different from those that marked initial implementation efforts. Such a delay can lead policymakers, funders, and reformers to deride research as irrelevant and has the unintended consequence of elevating the import of those speedier analysts unconcerned with scholarly review or publication. Consequently, the incentive for scholars to bypass traditional review channels and seize on new methods of dissemination is easy to fathom.

In bypassing conventional scholarly journals and forums, researchers from institutions ranging from the RAND Corporation to Yale University to the Heritage Foundation vet their work as they see fit, which may entail submission to internal mechanisms rather than to agreed-upon external referees. This development has enabled organizations that are more careful about vetting research to tout their institutional quality controls as a competitive advantage. Thus, in pursuing access and contracts, research and evaluation think tanks trade on the fact that their work goes through a standard, formalized review process before being released.

Similarly, University researchers have professional incentives to safeguard their academic credibility. Most academic incentives encourage them to pursue project funding and professional success through technical proficiency and by becoming an authority on an identifiable niche. As a general rule, generating controversy or attracting notoriety are consequently unhelpful, although some researchers have gained visibility and funding by publishing high profile policy-relevant studies whose validity or reliability have been questioned.

In the more laissez-faire research environment that has evolved over the past decades, institutional integrity has become a valuable tool in helping universities, think tanks, and researchers gain attention and attract funding (although little is known about how scholarly credibility compares to a savvy press strategy or flashy graphics in terms of impact). It is also unclear to what degree grant-based work encourages institutions that brand themselves based on internal review processes—like RAND or the Urban Institute—to be exemplars of careful research, or to what degree it may encourage them to be so deferential to their clients and so cautious in reporting findings that their conclusions are rarely critical, definitive, or highly directive.

Unlike academic or contract-dependent research institutions, advocacy and membership groups that pursue explicit policy agendas have cause to care more about policy outcomes than research rigor. These groups may well find that the attention and controversy generated by the release of even problematic research can be useful—and have little incentive to adopt vetting processes that slow their rate of activity or hamper their ability to issue bold conclusions and expansive policy recommendations. Advocacy groups may well enjoy more success in fundraising, influence, and visibility by issuing more studies and generating more headlines than by being overly scrupulous about technical considerations. Champions of more rapid and open dissemination suggest that such activity has resulted in a more heterodox and timely body of education research, and question whether research quality has been compromised by this shift.

Confronted with enormous variation in the quality of research, consumers must rely on proxies to sort through often conflicting findings reported by diverse institutions operating in accord with divergent norms. Reporters note that they are often more comfortable highlighting work that draws upon federal data because they feel confident as to its provenance—though experience has shown that findings derived using federal data or the policy implications drawn from such research can be just as problematic as those generated using privately collected data. The very notion of impartiality— itself a valuable lodestar as a platonic ideal, even if ultimately unobtainable on more than a fleeting basis—can become a branding and positioning technique for research entities. The result is that journalists and public officials may place undue emphasis on proxies for neutrality or rigor while more substantial considerations, such as the technical merit or ingenuity of the research design, go unmentioned. Meanwhile, in seeking cues as to the possible agenda of researchers, reporters typically focus on personalities, funding, reputations, and politics rather than arid technical discussions—potentially giving readers a distorted picture of the scholarly debate and fueling doubts about the reliability of the research enterprise.

Those who cheer the new education research marketplace argue that the slow pace of conventional scholarly mechanisms and biases implicit in the profession are evidence of the need for significant change. After all, as Kim explains in chapter 5, the professional associations and publications have been anything but neutral arbiters in the world of reading research. Editors, established authorities, and dominant interests influence what gets disseminated through "official" outlets and have at times marginalized or stifled work by contrarian thinkers. Recall Kim's discussion of scholarly reviewers who unapologetically dismissed research addressing the value of phonics-based instruction. If scholars feel their research or analysis is not receiving a fair hearing in the academy, it is only sensible for them to appeal directly to the public and to policymakers—and to regard such a move as an escape from the shackles of a cloistered field in the name of intellectual inquiry. In short, proponents regard the ability to bypass gatekeepers as an enormously positive development.

While proponents praise the benefits of democratization, however, Henig argues in chapter 3 that there are substantial costs to conducting debates about the merits of research findings in public spaces. Contributors including Henig, Kim, and Ingersoll show that when research gets caught up in larger political debates and is wielded by interested parties, it can become more difficult for scholars to argue about technical considerations, such as sample size or measurement error, as researchers rather than as partisans.

To the degree that debates are methodological disputes about how best to employ statistical models, measure key variables, or construct samples, there are good reasons why it may be beneficial to hash these issues out within the research community rather than in press releases or newspaper stories. After all, the value of the FDA is in part its ability to provide the public with a clear professional consensus on the product in question; there is good reason to believe that the FDA would be markedly less useful if research regarding the efficacy of new drugs were debated in the court of public opinion, with inexpert public officials expected to sort out the merits of the competing claims.

Yet, given the norms of the 1970s and 1980s, it would be a mistake to suggest that it is obviously, on balance, a bad thing for contemporary debate over education policy research to take place in the public forum. While sorting out the merits and demerits of the new landscape, we should seek to find ways to facilitate technical debate, encourage researchers to police their work quality, and help consumers make sense of the enormous variation in the credibility of published research.

This might include devising ways to support professional organizations or associations that encourage and reward self-policing; funding federally-sponsored reviews of available research by scholars as is being attempted in the case of the What Works Clearinghouse; boosting the attention that foundations pay to these considerations; and fostering efforts by organizations such as Editorial Projects in Education (publisher of *Education Week*) to assess and gauge the rigor of high-profile scholarship and the reliability of the work produced or sponsored by various entities.

INTERMEDIARIES AND THE POLICY DEBATE

The cluttered information environment requires someone to distill, explain, promote, and convey research to public officials if it is to be understood or influential. One of the most intriguing and overlooked developments in the world of education research and policy may be the role of the intermediaries which, as noted previously, play a critical role in disseminating research. In a limited number of cases, these tasks are undertaken by researchers themselves; but most scholars are reticent to do so, because academe doesn't reward such behavior, because doing so may raise doubts about their impartiality, and because many may lack the requisite skill set. Consequently, as Manna and Petrilli suggest in chapter 4, the job typically falls to a menagerie of intermediaries. The degree to which these liaisons attend to the quality and rigor of research is critical if policymakers are to make informed decisions. Observers would hope that these intermediaries would be quality-conscious, but incentives to be so vary significantly across organizations.

While there are literally hundreds of intermediaries operating at the state and national level, they can generally be grouped into three categories. The first category is that of "expert" and nonpartisan groups, such as the Education Commission of the States, Editorial Projects in Education, or the regional education research and development laboratories. These groups trade on their credibility and perceived impartiality, but are therefore more focused on synthesizing available scholarship than on actively promoting particular findings.

A second category includes membership groups, such as the National Education Association, the Council of the Great City Schools, or the National School Boards Association. These have a natural interest in promoting research findings which align with the interests of their members and their existing policy agendas.

A third category includes mission-driven or ideological organizations, including the Education Trust, the Heritage Foundation, the Center for Education Reform, and the Center for American Progress (CAP), which seek to promote work that advances their various policy agendas.

Not surprisingly, there is a strong preference among the cognoscenti for those organizations perceived as nonpartisan and expert. However, experience has raised questions about how effective these organizations can be. Because they are nonpartisan, their arguments are not as sharply defined as those of interest-based groups or advocacy organizations and they lack a defined audience that looks to them for cues. Membership groups often enjoy influence based on the size and import of their members, with the national teachers unions, for instance, able to tout research directly to major media organs and to a network of allies in state legislatures or on Capitol Hill. Nonpartisan groups, however, lack this kind of muscle.

Mission-driven groups tend to garner the most skepticism within the research community, but entities like the Education Trust and the Thomas B. Fordham Foundation have proved immensely influential because their clarity, policy focus, and energy make them highly effective disseminators. While leaders of membership groups must take care to stay in step with their members, mission-driven groups are permitted to act and speak with more crispness and agility. Meanwhile, harried staffers at the Department of Education, on Capitol Hill, or in state departments of education have limited time to search systematically through briefings and are therefore most likely to turn to intermediaries known to share their aims and that are willing to offer clear, actionable interpretations of the research. This helps to explain the influence of organizations like the Heritage Foundation and the Center for American Progress.

Intermediaries and advocacy groups inhabit a murky space, exerting enormous influence as they operate in a variety of unexamined ways. Research regarded as helpful to the agenda of influential interests can win a researcher visibility, contacts, access, and funding, while research that serves the interest of no organized constituency is likely to attract less notice and yield fewer professional rewards. For instance, Petrilli and Manna note that in 1998 the Education Trust issued an influential policy brief on teacher quality[2] that prominently featured research William Sanders had been conducting in which he used value-added testing to document how much teachers influenced gains in student achievement. Petrilli and Manna illustrate how the Education Trust publication had a dramatic impact on national awareness of Sanders' work, boosting Sanders' influence and professional reputation.

The implications of this dynamic are not well understood. In practice, a researcher whose work is embraced by the teachers unions, advocates for early childhood education, or the charter school community has incentives to depict his work in ways that the organizations will find congenial and to remain quiescent if they stretch the findings or recommendations in the course of their efforts. Researchers perceived as "friendly" may well face informal pressures from funders and allies if later work points to different policy implications. Ingersoll's discussion in chapter 6 suggests how difficult it can be for a researcher to remain independent and prevent his work from being misrepresented, and how modest the incentives or resources are for that kind of vigilance.

Rather than bewailing the influence of intermediaries or their necessary role, the more useful tack is for scholars to examine this dynamic and for reformers to understand their role in disseminating, explaining, and promoting research findings. For interested reformers, there are at least three possible strategies worth exploring.

One response is to "stock the pond"—to alter the mix of intermediaries that exists. Two ambitious efforts to do this in the past decade include the launch of the Washington, D.C.-based groups CAP and Education Sector. Education Sector seeks to position itself as a neutral voice in education, while CAP is engaged in the full panoply of policy issues and is unapologetically aligned with the Democratic Party. Each has sought to influence the education debates by commissioning new research, promoting select findings, and reaching public officials. In doing so, they joined a raft of influential advocacy intermediaries launched in the 1990s—including the Center for Education Reform, the Thomas B. Fordham Foundation, and the Education Trust. The rise of these groups has diluted the once-unchallenged influence of the National Education Association, American Federation of Teachers, and other membership associations in the public debates. Creating an aggressive organization committed to a particular reform philosophy can generate interest among researchers and journalists and alter the terms of the public debate.

A second response to concerns about intermediaries is to foster norms that will signal quality scholarship and encourage mediators to emphasize that work. For instance, in the medical industry, lobbying groups hesitate to approach legislators using research that fails to meet FDA standards because of a consensus about what constitutes valid and rigorous research; efforts to use research deemed sub-par could undercut a mediator's credibility. In education, the lack of such clear-cut norms or standards allows groups to aggressively market work that fails to meet a reasonable degree of rigor. One consequence, of course, is that criticism of research tends to engender doubts about the larger enterprise and can leave policymakers uncertain about how to judge sophisticated technical disputes. For that reason, it is worth pondering mechanisms by which the research community might more effectively signal its judgment regarding the merits of policy-relevant research. One approach, as several authors suggest, would be fostering a research journal regarded as authoritative in the field. Another is for one or more respected groups to begin systematically assessing and publicly reporting on the credibility and rigor of the research that various intermediaries report and advocate.

A third tack in policing quality is to consider ways in which intermediaries, foundations, or the Department of Education might encourage researchers at the entire array of existing institutions—including advocacy think tanks and universities—to take care regarding the claims they make when issuing policy-relevant research, and to take responsibility for how they represent their findings. Foundations might insist that university scholars pay more serious attention to "dissemination"; today, many university-based researchers are encouraged to regard such expectations as trifling nuisances. Similarly, funders could condition support on new standards and measures that ensure that intermediaries are relying on work that has met some reasonable degree of rigor and reliability. Rather than attempt to address this behavior through statute or regulation, it would be more appropriate and useful for private entities committed to rigorous research—such as the National Academy of Science, the Spencer Foundation, Knowledge Alliance, or the Bill & Melinda Gates Foundation—to encourage and support private action via researchers and intermediaries.

THE PERILS OF OVEREMPHASIZING RELEVANCE

Ultimately, the questions and insights that research generates may matter at least as much as the answers it can produce. Helping policymakers understand why more spending may not deliver improved achievement, what teachers-in-training are or are not receiving in the course of their preparation, how educator pension and benefit systems affect the teacher labor market, or how much time school leaders spend on paperwork and trivia, are all valuable lines of inquiry that are more valuable for the questions and cautions they pose than for their ability to deliver prescriptive guidance to policymakers. For researchers to play such a role, they must be able to obtain the requisite data and financial support.

One consequence of the standards and accountability movement has been to shift research away from basic inquiry and toward applied evaluation. While this has brought a discipline and focus to education research that was previously lacking, it has imposed real costs. The 2014 target for "universal proficiency" enshrined in NCLB, and the law's push for rapid efforts to close achievement gaps, has been particularly significant here. As intended, NCLB has encouraged state and district officials to operate on a much shorter time horizon and to seek immediate remedies. Yet this short-term perspective is at odds with the scientific process. Focusing attention and resources primarily on what might be relevant in the near term has the potential to distort research agendas and weaken support for long-term efforts to collect broad descriptive data.

An exaggerated focus on findings that are useful in the short-term can blind observers to the kind of research that will ultimately be the most significant. After all, the research that has transformed medicine or physics has typically not been the field trials that promise useful products or interventions within the decade, but the searching inquiry that may take a generation to yield its fruits. Nobel Prize–winning biochemist Roger Kornberg has, for instance, bemoaned the fact that NIH funding decisions in recent years have become overly focused on short-term benefits. "If the work that you propose to do isn't virtually certain of success, then it won't be funded. And, of course, the kind of work that we would most like to see take place, which is ground-breaking and innovative, lies at the other extreme."[3] Kornberg, whose own work was seminal in understanding DNA, highlights the tension that inevitably exists between the desire for applicable "lessons" and the investigation of more fundamental questions which may not offer obvious or immediate benefits. An essential role for the federal government is the collection and maintenance of large datasets, both descriptive and longitudinal. These efforts, housed at the National Center for Education Statistics, are less likely to deliver immediate pay-offs than more narrowly pitched or evaluative work, but are essential to sustaining a vibrant environment of inquiry.

During the twentieth century, foundations played a very different role than the leading funders of K–12 schooling do today. Historian Robert Kohler has observed, "The Rockefeller Institute for Medical Research (1901) and the Carnegie Institution of Washington (1902) were created to undertake research on large, fundamental problems that university or government scientists could not and should not tackle." At the same time, Kohler has noted that the large foundations of the Progressive Era were frequently "resistant to scientists' overtures. Growing out of nineteenth-century traditions of voluntary activism . . . foundations had much larger social ambitions than furthering science per se."[4] Today, foundations have an interest in sponsoring useful knowledge, but limited interest in the kind of basic research that may yield unanticipated insights or advance the field in unexpected ways.

A valuable and instructive case of philanthropy investing in the creation of knowledge—with a decades-long time horizon in mind—is that of the National Assessment of Educational Progress (NAEP). The NAEP is touted today by the Department of Education as "the Nation's Report Card"; in 2006, a survey by Editorial Projects in Education identified NAEP as the nation's most influential education information source and its reports as the most significant line of research in the previous decade.[5] Support from the Carnegie Corporation of New York was crucial to NAEP's creation. In 1964, responding to demands for better data on the impact of education reforms, the Carnegie Corporation supported a major study into the feasibility of a regular assessment of U.S. education progress.[6] In 1969, Carnegie gave large grants to the Committee on Assessing the Progress of Education to finalize its assessment tools and to the Education Commission of the States, which assumed control of the newly created NAEP. Today, NAEP is regarded as the gold standard when it comes to gauging state performance. The NAEP makes it possible to keep an eye on state performance claims, facilitates research into the effects of different state policies, and provides a consistent metric for measuring changes in achievement over time.

In another example, the Carnegie Corporation, in the late 1930s, sought to evaluate the efforts that foundations had been making to improve education in the American South. In search of a fresh perspective, Carnegie recruited European economist Gunnar Myrdal to head up the research. After spending several years doing field research and collecting descriptive data, Myrdal penned *An American Dilemma: The Negro Problem and Modern Democracy*.[7] While Carnegie officials appeared disappointed that the volume did not provide the practical guidance or evaluation they had sought (historian Ellen Condliffe Lagemann has noted that the report "seem[ed] by and large to have been ignored" by Carnegie),[8] the book went on to be cited by the U.S. Supreme Court in its 1954 *Brown v. Board of Education* ruling and helped shape the thinking of leaders of the civil rights movement.

Given diffuse, uncertain, and long-term benefits, and the reality that even "successes" may be difficult to explain to a donor or board of directors, this kind of investment finds few enthusiasts among foundation staff in today's accountability-driven environment. While the tension between the desire for applicable "lessons" and the investigation of more fundamental questions which may not offer obvious or immediate benefits is not soluble, education research and policy would both be better served if we wrestled with the implied challenge and sought to strike a coherent balance between the two, rather than simply cartwheel from one extreme to the other.

THE POLITICAL ECONOMY OF EDUCATION RESEARCH

The "supply and demand" framework of research production that Goldhaber and Brewer proffer in chapter 10 offers a valuable way to understand the incentives which motivate scholars. From that chapter and others, there emerge at least three critical points regarding the "political economy" of education research.

First, scholars compete fiercely for the right to evaluate high-profile reform initiatives, and typically require support from interested funders and access to the schools, districts, or programs under study. Winning that access is a delicate process, one that requires careful attention to building relationships and cultivating a reputation for probity and rigor. Leading researchers have often achieved that reputation based on their previous work—meaning they are frequently asked to conduct new research by parties who embrace their previous findings. Whatever the intent, positive findings can yield a symbiotic relationship that serves both subject and researcher. Evaluators operate under incentives to avoid being too negative when examining projects they have been selected to evaluate if they intend to conduct additional work (especially because researchers are often partisans of the reforms they are asked to examine). Scholars are inevitably more likely to study states, districts, schools, or programs where they have established and cordial relationships—and where they have an incentive to protect those relationships.

Second, the incentive for good econometricians to work with existing datasets encourages them to study the questions for which good data already exist and to shy away from murky questions where it does not. In this way, research and data collection on a given topic tends to attract imitators, while more difficult to capture questions go unexplored. In recent years, the magnetic pull of available data has driven enormous attention to measuring school performance in reading and math for children in grades three to eight, or to assessing high school reform in terms of graduation rates; scant attention has focused on questions where systematic data is less readily available. At the same time, pressing policy questions—such as how school districts actually respond to choice-based interventions, how principals respond to NCLB-style accountability, how philanthropic investment affects district reform, or how districts hire and assign teachers to schools—have attracted little disciplined scrutiny. In this volume, contributors have noted the attention that available data have afforded the "out-of-field" teaching problem or charter school performance, while a lack of comparable data has led researchers to neglect equally important topics or the causal dynamics that explain the observed effects.

Federal agencies have a vital role to play in the collection of a comprehensive and appropriately heterogeneous set of data. Because academics will gravitate toward those questions for which systematic data is available, investing in collecting comprehensive, descriptive and longitudinal data on an array of topics is critical. As Goldhaber and Brewer point out, a limited body of available data fosters a culture in which academics study what is readily available. Given the existence of 1,300 schools of education nationwide, the limited methodological training provided to many education scholars, and a sizable population of professors whose expertise is in schooling rather than research, it should come as no surprise that this has led to a preponderance of research focusing on case studies of local schools, teachers, or training programs to which professors could obtain ready access.

Third, as Fusarelli makes clear, education leaders have trouble framing tractable questions or communicating clearly to researchers the kind of queries that would benefit practice—so research is frequently driven by the enthusiasm of researchers, foundations, or petitioners in ways that hinder its ability to inform decisionmaking. Practitioners and reformers are invested in their programs and naturally predisposed to regard them as effective. These educators are frequently correct—pilot programs frequently impress because of the advantages of impassioned leadership, extra resources, exceptional faculty, and a common culture forged by a shared bond. They are primarily interested in evaluative research that can document the success of their efforts and thereby open the door to additional resources and opportunities. Foundations enthusiastic about their successes are more likely to find studies of these happy cases. Consequently, educators have strong incentives to provide access and data to friendly researchers and little cause to provide access to researchers perceived as skeptical or whose work is not evaluative in nature. The result may be research documenting or evaluating best practices that are difficult to replicate or implement.

CONCLUSION

Research has a vital role to play in democratic policy debate. That role is not to dictate outcomes or to presume that public officials should be the handmaidens of researchers, but to ensure that public decisionmaking is informed by all the facts, insights, and analyses that the tools of science can provide. Researchers can raise questions about simple-minded verities, challenge casual assumptions, provide realistic estimates about what reforms may or may not accomplish, help innovative ideas gain a foothold by offering credible evidence of their plausibility, and—in some circumstances—provide insight into the relative merits of multiple interventions.

It is not simply a question of getting the research right. The soft tissue involved in marrying research to policy matters as much as the technical merits of research and the desire of policymakers to be guided by compelling findings. For instance, the federal Reading First program drew on a wealth of rigorous and sophisticated research, built upon a consensus report issued by the National Reading Panel, and made an unprecedented federal investment in reading with strong bipartisan backing. Nevertheless, the program's awkward construction and predictably problematic implementation have severely compromised its natural advantages. The political and legal travails of Reading First have undercut its political support, raised questions about the program's legitimacy, undermined support for program funding, and illustrated how perilous this course can be if it is not informed by attention to institutional design and political dynamics. In comparison, the National Institutes of Health works as well as it does precisely because researchers, findings, and funding are embedded in a set of routines and protocols that reward rigorous research, police malfeasance, and reassure policymakers about the integrity of the enterprise.

Ultimately, in a world marked by the proliferation of think tanks, advocacy groups, a massive proliferation of published research, and independent research entities, there is a need to rethink the role that education researchers can and should be expected to play. The answer that emerges from these pages suggests that the dispassionate "scientist" is an uncommon figure in education policy debates; those who play that role require a high degree of institutional, financial, and professional remove, and a determination to avoid getting entangled in policymaking. Not only is this figure rare, but it is not clear that he should be the ideal. It would be strange indeed, as Terry Moe has eloquently observed in *Schools, Vouchers, and the American Public*,[9] if scholars did not have strong, informed opinions about subjects that they have spent years or even decades studying. It would be a peculiar kind of reticence that encourages a scholar to remain mum about her own conclusions and sit on the sidelines even as others, less expert, opine freely while using (and misusing) her work. In particular, one should be wary of reforms targeted at careful researchers that would discourage them from speaking or writing clearly on public issues, as such prohibitions would only increase the prominence of those less scrupulous about heeding the limitations of research or less familiar with the complexities of the issue.

Nonetheless, if academics are to avoid compromising their ability to serve as independent sources of insight and knowledge—and to avoid being seen as engaged in the service of political projects—they must retain the ability to discuss ideas, ask hard questions, and change their minds when they believe that the preponderance of evidence justifies it. This is more challenging than it may seem. Relevance in policy debates requires alliances with the intermediaries and policymakers who make things happen; forming these alliances risks compromising the researchers' ability—should they encounter data, theory, or arguments that alter their thinking—to change their minds without worrying unduly about the impact on allies, financial support, or professional status.

This state of affairs encourages successful researchers to adopt one of two courses: either focus on narrow technical work and studiously avoid offering opinions on policy, or become enmeshed with one or another side in heated public debates. Neither course seems optimal, but the resources, professional norms, and incentives that might encourage more researchers to negotiate a middle path are in short supply—and there has been little attention paid to how they might be augmented. How the research community wrestles with this tension in the years ahead will be critical to the nature and influence of education policy research.

The contributors in these pages teach that the pressures on researchers are not immutable but are partly the product of circumstance. There are steps that researchers, policymakers, the federal government, foundations, and the profession's leadership can take or encourage that will advantage researchers who are careful about respecting the data and who avoid casual or careless claims—steps which can incline researchers to seek a healthy independence from partisan conflict. These involve helping policymakers and the public understand what research can and cannot contribute, supporting self-policing within the research community, encouraging the development of professional norms about what constitutes appropriate and constructive involvement in public debate, steering more funding toward research that is vetted by knowledgeable researchers, and investing more heavily in large public datasets. How best to accomplish these goals, and how to do so without stifling far-reaching inquiry or unduly narrowing the body of scholarship, are questions that researchers and policymakers will continue to confront in the years to come.

In the end, it is worth remembering that the immutable tension between those engaged in accumulating knowledge and those engaged in making policy is a frustrating but healthy tension in a democratic nation. Efforts to make research useful to policymakers ought not go so far that they compromise the ability of researchers to provide a check on the enthusiasms of advocates and public officials. Nor, in the end, should the pursuit of relevance obscure the reality that research cannot provide all the answers officials seek—but is frequently most valuable when it helps sheds new light on problems and favored solutions.

Notes

FOREWORD

Lorraine M. McDonnell

1. Carol H. Weiss, ed., *Using Social Research in Public Policy Making*, (Lexington, MA: Lexington Books, 1977); Laurence E. Lynn, ed., *Knowledge and Policy: The Uncertain Connection* (Washington, DC: National Academy of Science, 1978); and Keith Cohen and Charles E. Lindblom, *Usable Knowledge: Social Science and Social Problem Solving* (New Haven, CT: Yale University Press, 1979).
2. Lynn, *Knowledge and Policy*, 4.
3. Weiss, *Using Social Research*, 2.
4. For example, Linda J. Nelson and Michael W. Kirst, "What Are the Information Preferences of State Educational Policymakers?" in *Policy Research and Educational Policy-Making: Toward a Better Connection*, ed. Michael W. Kirst (Palo Alto, CA: Institute for Research on Educational Finance and Governance, Stanford University, 1981), pp. 30–113; and Susan Fuhrman and Lorraine M. McDonnell, *Mapping Instate Information Networks in Education Policy: An Exploratory Study* (Alexandria, VA: State Education Policy Consortium, 1985).
5. Alan Schick, "Informed Legislation: Policy Research Versus Ordinary Knowledge," in *Knowledge, Power, and the Congress*, ed. William H. Robinson and Clay H. Wellborn (Washington, DC: Congressional Quarterly, 1991), 99–119; David E. Price, "Comment," in *Knowledge, Power and the Congress*, ed. William H. Robinson and Clay H. Wellborn (Washington, DC: Congressional Quarterly, 1991), 126–29; and Mark A. Peterson, "How Health Policy Information Is Used in Congress," in *Intensive Care: How Congress Shapes Health Policy*, ed. Thomas E. Mann and Norman J. Ornstein (Washington, DC: American Enterprise Institute and the Brookings Institution, 1995), 79–125.
6. Carol H. Weiss, "Policy Research in the Context of Diffuse Decision Making," *The Journal of Higher Education* 53 no. 6 (1982): 619–39; and Carol H. Weiss, "Congressional Committees as Users of Analysis," *Journal of Policy Analysis and Management* 8 no. 3 (1989): 411–31.
7. Weiss, "Congressional Committees"; Peterson, "How Health Policy Information Is Used"; and James L. Sunquist, "Research Brokerage: The Weak Link," in Lynn, *Knowledge and Policy*, 126–44.

INTRODUCTION

Frederick M. Hess

1. Carl F. Kaestle, "Comment," in *Brookings Papers on Education Policy: 2000*, ed. Diane Ravitch (Washington, DC: Brookings Institution, 2000), 384.

2. Alice O'Connor, *Social Science for What? Philanthropy and the Social Question in a World Turned Rightside Up* (New York: Russell Sage Foundation, 2007), 23.

3. Carol Weiss, "The Many Meanings of Research Utilization," *Public Administration Review* 39, no. 5 (1979): 426.

4. Quoted in Fiona Graff and Miranda Christou, "In Evidence Lies Change: The Research of Whiting Professor Carol Weiss," *Harvard Graduate School of Education News*, September 10, 2001. Available at http://gseweb.harvard.edu/news/features/weiss09102001.html (accessed July 24, 2007).

5. Carol Weiss, "Congressional Committees as Users of Analysis," *Journal of Policy Analysis and Management* 8, no. 3 (1989): 411–31.

6. John Kingdon, *Agendas, Alternatives, and Public Policies* (Boston: Little, Brown & Co., 1984).

7. Readers primarily interested in these issues, see Michael Feuer, *Moderating the Debate: Rationality and the Promise of American Education* (Cambridge, MA: Harvard Education Press, 2006).

8. Doug Harris, "Class Size and School Size: Taking the Trade-Offs Seriously," in *Brookings Papers on Education Policy: 2006/2007*, ed. Tom Loveless and Frederick M. Hess (Washington, DC: Brookings Institution Press, 2007), 137–61.

9. American Educational Research Association (AERA), "Class Size: Counting Students Can Count," *Research Points* 1, no. 2 (2003): 4.

10. AERA, "Class Size," 4.

11. Eric Hanushek, "Some Findings from an Independent Investigation of the Tennessee STAR Experiment and from Other Investigations of Class Size Effects," *Educational Evaluation and Policy Analysis* 21, no. 2 (1999): 143–63.

12. Hanushek, "Some Findings from an Independent Investigation," 147.

13. Frederick Mosteller, Richard J. Light, and Jason A. Sachs, "Sustained Inquiry in Education: Lessons from Skill Grouping and Class Size," *Harvard Educational Review* 66, no. 4 (1996): 797–842.

14. Harris, "Class Size and School Size," in Loveless and Hess, *Brookings Papers*, 145.

15. Gene V. Glass and Mary Lee Smith, "Meta-analysis of Research on Class Size and Student Achievement," *Educational Evaluation and Policy Analysis* 1, no. 1 (1979): 2–15.

16. Peter Schrag, "Policy from the Hip: Class-Size Reduction in California," in Loveless and Hess, *Brookings Papers 2006*, 235.

17. Richard D. Kahlenberg, "Economic School Integration," The Century Foundation, February 2000, 2. Available at http://www.tcf.org/Publications/Education/School_Integration.pdf (accessed November 2, 2007).

18. Schrag, "Policy from the Hip," 235–236.

19. Gerald Holton, "Introduction," in "ERRORS: Consequences of Big Mistakes in the Natural and Social Sciences," ed. Gerald Holton and Arien Mack, *Social Research* 72, no. 1 (1998): viii.

20. Quoted in Holton, "Introduction," viii.

21. Grover J. (Russ) Whitehurst, "Statement before the Subcommittee on Education Reform, U.S. House of Representatives," 2002, http://ies.ed.gov/director/speeches2002/02_28/2002_02_28.asp (accessed July 13, 2007).

22. Arthur Levine, *Educating Researchers* (Washington, DC: The Education Schools Project, 2007), 53.

23. Maris Vinovskis, "Fixing Federal Research," *Education Next* 1, no. 4 (2001): 62–67.

24. Howard Gardner, "You Can't Test Lessons the Way You Do Meds," *Newsday*, December 30, 2002, A23.

25. William Ayers, "Trudge toward Freedom: Educational Research in the Public Interest," in *Education Research in the Public Interest: Social Justice, Action, and Policy*, ed. Gloria Ladson-Billings and William F. Tate (New York: Teachers College Press, 2006), 81.

CHAPTER 1
Structure and Science in Federal Education Research
Andrew Rudalevige

1. As noted below, federally sponsored education research is also carried out under the auspices of other offices, such as the National Institutes of Health and the National Science Foundation. Although this chapter will reference that work, it focuses on the role of the Department of Education in such efforts.
2. National Advisory Committee on Education, *Federal Relations to Education, Part I: Committee Findings and Recommendations* (Washington, DC: National Capital Press, 1931), 72.
3. Institute of Education Sciences, "Director of the Institute of Education Sciences," http://ies.ed.gov/director/ (accessed July 19, 2007).
4. Christopher T. Cross, *Political Education* (New York: Teachers College Press, 2004), 124.
5. James March, foreword to *Organizing an Anarchy: Belief, Bureaucracy, and Politics in the National Institute of Education* by Lee Sproull, Stephen Weiner, and David Wolf (Chicago: University of Chicago Press, 1978), x.
6. Diane Ravitch, "Enhancing the Federal Role in Research in Education," *Chronicle of Higher Education* (April 7, 1993), A48. And see yet another head of OERI, Chester E. Finn, Jr., "What Ails Education Research," in *Knowledge for Policy: Improving Education through Research*, ed. Don S. Anderson and Bruce J. Biddle (Philadelphia: Falmer Press, 1991), 39.
7. Gerald Sroufe, "Legislative Reform of Federal Education Research Programs: A Political Annotation of the Education Sciences Reform Act of 2002," *Peabody Journal of Education* 78 (2003): 224.
8. Carl F. Kaestle, "The Awful Reputation of Education Research," *Educational Researcher* 22 (January–February 1993): 23–31. It should be noted that Kaestle does not argue that reputation is justified.
9. See, for example, Gene V. Glass, "Policy for the Unpredictable (Uncertainty Research and Policy)," *Educational Researcher* 8 (September 1979): 12–14.
10. Ellen Condliffe Lagemann, "Contested Terrain: A History of Education Research in the United States, 1890–1990," *Educational Researcher* 26 (December 1997): 5.
11. Douglas D. Christensen, quoted in Debra Viadero, "Bill Would Remake OERI into 'Education Sciences' Academy," *Education Week* 21 (March 6, 2002): 31.
12. Terry M. Moe, "The Politics of Bureaucratic Structure," in *Can the Government Govern?*, ed. John Chubb and Paul Peterson (Washington, DC: Brookings Institution Press, 1989), 267–329.
13. See, for example, the comments in Carl F. Kaestle's hugely useful *"Everybody's Been to Fourth Grade": An Oral History of Federal R&D in Education* (Madison: Wisconsin Center for Education Research, 1991), 36–37; Maris Vinovskis, *Revitalizing Federal Education Research and Development: Improving the R&D Centers, Regional Educational Laboratories, and the "New" OERI* (Ann Arbor: University of Michigan Press, 2001), 102–3; and Sharon Begley, "Just Say No—To Bad Science," *Newsweek*, May 7, 2007, 57.
14. Quoted in Vinovskis, *Revitalizing*, 6.

15. Thomas Hammond and Paul A. Thomas, "The Impossibility of a Neutral Hierarchy," *Journal of Law, Economics, and Organization* 5 (1989): 155–84; and Moe, "Politics of Bureaucratic Structure," 268.

16. Sproull et al., *Anarchy,* ix; and see Cross, *Political Education,* 153–54.

17. David E. Lewis, *Presidents and the Politics of Agency Design* (Stanford, CA: Stanford University Press, 2003), 5, 30–35.

18. Lewis, *Presidents and the Politics of Agency Design,* 30–35, 46–47.

19. Carl F. Kaestle, "Comment," in *Brookings Papers on Education Policy: 2000,* ed. Diane Ravitch (Washington, DC: Brookings Institution, 2000), 383–84.

20. See Kenneth R. Mayer, "Closing Military Bases (Finally): Solving Collective Dilemmas through Delegation," *Legislative Studies Quarterly* 20 (August 1995): 393–413; Richard S. Conley, "Derailing Presidential Fast-Track Authority," *Political Research Quarterly* 52 (1999): 785–99; and, more generally, Jon Elster, *Ulysses Unbound: Studies in Rationality, Precommitment, and Constraints* (New York: Cambridge University Press, 2005).

21. Howe was speaking specifically of NIH. He is quoted in Kaestle, *Fourth Grade,* 51.

22. The text of the law (14 Stat. L., 434) may be found in Darrell Hevenor Smith, *The Bureau of Education: Its History, Activities, and Organization,* Institute for Government Research Service Monograph No. 14 (Baltimore, MD: The Johns Hopkins Press, 1923), 2–3. Banks is quoted in Charles H. Judd, *Research in the United States Office of Education,* Advisory Committee on Education Staff Study No. 19 (Washington, DC: Government Printing Office, 1939), 5.

23. Donald R. Warren, *To Enforce Education: A History of the Founding Years of the United States Office of Education* (Detroit: Wayne State University Press, 1974), 42–44.

24. Warren, *To Enforce Education,* 39, 47–54, 77–91. The quoted section of an 1865 resolution is on p. 78.

25. Warren, *To Enforce Education,* 109.

26. Smith, *Bureau of Education,* 3–4, 10–11. Note that while the official title of the organization was as an "Office," it was referred to (even in appropriations legislation) as a "Bureau."

27. David L. Clark, "Federal Policy in Educational Research and Development," *Educational Researcher* 5 (January 1976): 5.

28. Smith, *Bureau of Education,* 14.

29. Warren, *To Enforce Education,* 151, 172.

30. *Colorado School Journal,* May 1914, quoted in Smith, *Bureau of Education,* 17.

31. U.S. Department of the Interior annual report for fiscal year 1929, quoted in Judd, *Research,* 8.

32. National Advisory Committee on Education, *Federal Relations,* 76. For a broader discussion of the "panacea" of science in education, see Richard A. Dershimer, *The Federal Government and Educational R&D* (Lexington, MA: D.C. Heath, 1976), 37.

33. National Advisory Committee on Education, *Federal Relations,* 77.

34. Judd, *Research,* 49.

35. Dershimer, *Federal Government,* 41; see also Clark, "Federal Policy," 5–6; and David L. Featherman and Maris A. Vinovskis, "Growth and Use of Social and Behavioral Science in the Federal Government since World War II," in *Social Science and Policymaking,* ed. David L. Featherman and Maris A. Vinovskis (Ann Arbor: University of Michigan Press, 2001), 40–82.

36. Cooperative Research Act, Public Law 83-531, 83rd Cong., 2nd sess. (July 19, 1954).

37. The 1960 figure is from Maris A. Vinovskis, "Changing Federal Strategies for Supporting Educational Research, Development, and Statistics" (Washington, D.C.: U.S. Dept.

of Education, National Educational Research Policy and Priorities Board, September 1998), Section III, http://www.ed.gov/pubs/FedStrat/research.html (accessed November 11, 2007); 1965 from Richard C. Atkinson and Gregg B. Jackson, eds., *Research and Education Reform: Roles for the Office of Educational Research and Improvement* (Washington, D.C.,: National Academy Press, 1992), 55.

38. Dershimer, *R&D*, 47.

39. Sproull, Weiner, and Wolf, *Anarchy*, 19.

40. Vinovskis, *Revitalizing*, 9–10, 36–37.

41. Dershimer, *R&D*, 86.

42. Manuel J. Justiz and Lars G. Bjork, "Academic Science and Public Policy," in *Higher Education Research and Public Policy*, ed. Manuel J. Justiz and Lars. G. Bjork (New York: American Council on Education/Macmillan, 1988), 13; Vinovskis, *Revitalizing*; Sproull, Weiner, and Wolf, *Anarchy*, 18–19, and (for the findings of Rep. Edith Green's 1967 special subcommittee on the subject) 24–25; and Dershimer, *R&D*, 71.

43. Stephen Bailey, "The Office of Education and the Education Act of 1965," Inter-University Case Program #100 (Indianapolis: Bobbs-Merrill, 1966), quoted in Dershimer, *R&D*, 73.

44. Sproull, Weiner, and Wolf, *Anarchy*, 34; and see Dershimer, *R&D*, 8.

45. Sproull, Weiner, and Wolf, *Anarchy*, 27, figure 1.1. A subsequent reorganization briefly created a deputy assistant secretary who would directly oversee a National Center for Educational Research and Development (NCERD). See Dershimer, *R&D*, 120–26.

46. Richard Nixon, "Special Message to the Congress on Education Reform," *Public Papers of the President*, March 3, 1970. http://www.presidency.ucsb.edu/ws/?pid=2895 (accessed October 25, 2007). See also Richard Nixon, "Special Message to the Congress on the Administration's Legislative Program," *Public Papers of the Presidents*, September 11, 1970. http://www.presidency.ucsb.edu/ws/?pid=2656 (accessed October 25, 2007).

47. Emerson Elliott, interview with author, April 11, 2007. A number of interviews with past and present political actors were conducted for this paper. Where anonymity has been requested, it has been granted.

48. Education Amendments of 1972, Public Law 92-318, 92nd Cong., 1st sess. (June 23, 1972); and Sproull, Weiner, and Wolf, *Anarchy*, 61–62.

49. Quoted in Sproull, Weiner, and Wolf, *Anarchy*, 65.

50. John Brademas and Lynne P. Brown, *The Politics of Education* (Norman: University of Oklahoma Press, 1987), 18–19, 75; Sproull, Weiner, and Wolf, *Anarchy*, 67ff.

51. Chester (Checker) E. Finn, Jr., interview with author, April 13, 2007.

52. P. Michael Timpane, "Federal Progress in Educational Research," in *Higher Education Research and Public Policy*, ed. Manuel Justiz and Lars Bjork (New York: American Council on Education/Macmillan, 1988), 20.

53. Sproull, Weiner, and Wolf, *Anarchy*, 79–80.

54. James Welsh, "NIE: Lining Up the Leaders," *Educational Researcher* 1 (October 1972): 17–18; Evan Jenkins, "Institute of Education Gets a Lesson in How Not to Win More Money," *New York Times*, October 22, 1973, 64; and interviews with author.

55. March 1974 testimony before Senate Appropriations committee, quoted in Sproull, Weiner, and Wolf, *Anarchy*, 95.

56. Subcommittee Hearings, in Sproull, Weiner, and Wolf, *Anarchy*, 101.

57. Kaestle, *Fourth Grade*, 56.

58. Christopher Cross, interview with author, April 5, 2007.

59. Vinovskis, *Revitalizing*, Ch. 4; and Joe Schneider (former executive director of CEDaR), e-mail message to author, May 22, 2007.

60. Kaestle, *Fourth Grade*, 32–33, 50.

61. Vinovskis, *Revitalizing*, 102–4.

62. Vinovskis, *Revitalizing*, 102–4.

63. Vinovskis, *Revitalizing*, 102–4.

64. Finn interview.

65. Michael Kirst quoted in David G. Savage, "Education Research: Anatomy of U.S. Agency that Failed," *Los Angeles Times*, October 1, 1985, A1.

66. Finn interview; David Stephens, "President Carter, the Congress, and NEA: Creating the Department of Education," *Political Science Quarterly* 98 (Winter 1983–84): 641–63; and *The Department of Education Organization Act*, Public Law 96-88, 96th Cong., 1st sess. (October 17, 1979).

67. Vinovskis, *Revitalizing*, 109.

68. The Higher Education Amendments of 1986, Public Law 99-498, 99th Cong., 2nd sess. (October 17, 1986).

69. Sally Kilgore (Office of Research Commissioner), quoted in Kaestle, *Fourth Grade*, 57.

70. Kilgore, quoted in Kaestle, *Fourth Grade*, 34; and see Gene V. Glass, "What Works: Politics and Research," *Educational Researcher* (April 1987): 5–10, and the OERI reply in the October 1987 issue, 24–26.

71. Chester E. Finn, Jr., quoted in Vinovskis, *Revitalizing*, 111.

72. Chester E. Finn, statement before the U.S. House Subcommittee on Select Education, 99th Cong., 2nd sess., February 19, 1986, 8.

73. After Finn, three acting assistant secretaries combined to last one year, followed by a similar stretch of instability in the mid-1990s. On the 1980s, see Jaemin Kim, "As New Head of Education Research, Ravitch Brings Her Advocacy of Tough Standards to Reform Efforts," *Chronicle of Higher Education*, September 11, 1991, A31.

74. Diane Ravitch, "Enhancing the Federal Role," and "State of the Agency," *OERI Bulletin* (Winter 1992–93), http://www.ed.gov/bulletin/winter1993/winter92-3.html (accessed April 29, 2007).

75. This should be sung to the tune of "Love and Marriage." Quoted in Vinovskis, *Revitalizing*, 158.

76. House Staff Report, 1988, cited in Vinovskis, *Revitalizing*, 119; and Gerald Sroufe, interview with author, April 17, 2007.

77. Gerald Sroufe, "Legislative Reform of Federal Education Research Programs: A Political Annotation of the Education Sciences Reform Act of 2002," *Peabody Journal of Education* 78 (2003): 221–22.

78. Kent McGuire, interview with author, April 6, 2007.

79. Arthur Wise was another key actor. See Kaestle, *Fourth Grade*, 58–59.

80. "Education Research Renewal Would Reorganize Office," *CQ Weekly* 51, no. 44 (November 6, 1993), 3056; and Vinovskis, *Revitalizing*, 121–28.

81. Vinovskis, *Revitalizing*, 128.

82. Christopher T. Cross, "The Federal Role in R, D, & D: A Vision of the Future," in *Collection of Background Materials for OERI Reauthorization*, National Educational Research Policy and Priorities Board (Washington, DC: OERI, August 1999), 53–58.

83. Vinovskis, *Revitalizing*, 141–44 (the quote is from 143).

84. McGuire, interview; Vinovskis, *Revitalizing*, 141–44.

85. Quoted in Kaestle, "Comment," 384; and see Vinovskis, *Revitalizing*, 134–35; and McGuire, interview. On NIE comparison, see Maris Vinovskis, *History and Educational Policymaking* (New Haven, CT: Yale University Press, 1999), 55.

86. Vinovskis, *Revitalizing*, 175.

87. *Education Sciences Reform Act of 2002*, HR3801, 107th Cong., 2nd sess., *Congressional Record* 148, no. 51 (April 30, 2002): H 1739.

88. Quoted in Richard Morgan, "Lawmakers Criticize Research Office," *Chronicle of Higher Education*, March 15, 2002, A27; the hearing was held February 28, 2002.

89. *Scientifically Based Education Research, Statistics, Evaluation, and Information Act of 2000*, HR 4875, 106th Cong., 2nd sess., *Congressional Record* 146, no. 93 (July 18, 2000): E1271; see also Debra Viadero, "Research Bill Clears House without Fuss," *Education Week*, May 8, 2002, 1.

90. House Committee on Education and the Workforce, *Education Sciences Reform Act of 2002*, 107th Cong., 2nd sess., H. R. 107-404, 139. See also Rep. Ron Kind of Wisconsin, speaking for the Education Sciences Reform Act on April 30, 2002 on the House floor, 107th Cong., 2nd sess., *Congressional Record* 148, no. 51 (April 30, 2002): H1742.

91. Sroufe, "Legislative Reform," 227, and interview with author.

92. Debra Viadero, "Senate May Vote on Overhaul of OERI before Fall Elections," *Education Week*, July 10, 2002, 37.

93. A National Center for Special Education Research was added to the roster after the reauthorization of the Individuals with Disabilities Education Act in 2004.

94. Richard Morgan, "House Passes Legislation to Reform Educational Research Office," *Chronicle of Higher Education*, May 10, 2002, A26; and *Education Sciences Reform Act of 2002*, Public Law 107-289, 107th Cong., 2nd sess. *Congressional Record* 148, no. 51. (October 15, 2002): S10480.

95. Cross, *Political Education*, 150. After all, as Carl Kaestle observes, "everybody's been to fourth grade."

96. Viadero, "Bill Would Remake OERI," 31.

97. Bruce Hunter, quoted in Lisa Fine Goldstein, "Senate Panel Passes Federal Research Bill," *Education Week*, October 2, 2002, 27.

98. Karl Hostetler, "What Constitutes 'Good' Educational Research?" *Educational Researcher* 34 (August/September 2005): 16–21; Debra Viadero, "Push for Science-Based Research is Expanded," *Education Week*, February 2, 2005, 32; Debra Viadero, "Ed Dept Issues Practical Guide to Research-Based Practice," *Education Week*, January 7, 2004, 12; and Therese Mageau, "Determining 'What Works,'" *T.H.E. Journal* 31 (January 2004): 32–37.

99. Debra Viadero, "IES Gets Mixed Grades as It Comes of Age," *Education Week*, September 27, 2006, 1, which includes the Sroufe quote; and McGuire, interview.

100. Jim Kohlmoos, interview with author, April 6, 2007; and interviews generally

101. Viadero, "IES Gets Mixed Grades as It Comes of Age," September 27, 2006, 1.

102. Grover J. (Russ) Whitehurst, interview with author, April 30, 2007; National Board for Education Sciences, *Annual Report 2006* (Washington, D.C., U.S. Department of Education, July 2006), 10; and Debra Viadero, "Review Process for U.S. Education Research Approved," *Education Week*, February 1, 2006, 24.

103. Debra Viadero, "'One Stop' Research Shop Seen as Slow to Yield Views that Educators Can Use," *Education Week*, September 27, 2006, 8.

104. Interviews; and see Vinovskis, *Revitalizing*, 131–32.

105. Kathleen Kennedy Manzo, "Scathing Report Casts Cloud Over Reading First," *Education Week*, October 4 ,2006, 1; Debra Viadero and Kathleen Kennedy Manzo, "Out-of-Favor Reading Plan Rated Highly," *Education Week*, March 28, 2007, 1; Amit Paley, "Software's Benefits on Tests in Doubt," *Washington Post*, April 5, 2007, A1; and Debra Viadero, "What Works Reviewers Find No Learning Edge for Leading Math Texts," *Education Week*, January 24, 2007, 1.

106. Anonymous interview; Spellings quoted in Viadero, "IES Gets Mixed Grades," 9.

107. Whitehurst interview.

108. U.S. Department of Education, *Strategic Plan, 2002–2007* (Washington, DC: U.S. Department of Education, 2002); and U.S. Department of Education, *Strategic Plan, 2007–2012* (Washington, DC: U.S. Department of Education, 2007), especially the draft for public comment dated February 2007. (IES received some additional attention in the final draft published in May 2007.)

109. George W. Bush, "President's Statement on H.R. 3801: Act to Provide for Improvement of Federal Education Research," Office of the White House Press Secretary, November 5, 2002, http://www.whitehouse.gov/news/releases/2002/11/20021105-4.html (accessed July 25, 2007); and Debra Viadero, "New Research Agency's Independence in Question," *Education Week*, November 13, 2002, 26. In an interview, Whitehurst, however, argued there have been "no issues," as IES has implemented the relevant section, §186(a), as written in statute: "the signing statement is not the law." Interview with author, April 30, 2007.

110. Finn interview, April 13, 2007.

111. Debra Viadero, "Control of Regional Education Labs Shifting," *Education Week*, March 29, 2006, 32; and Kohlmoos, interview.

112. Debra Viadero, "Shift in Regional Education Labs' Role Stirs Concern," *Education Week*, March 14, 2007, 8; and Kohlmoos, interview.

113. Grover J. (Russ) Whitehurst, quoted in Debra Viadero, "New Group of Researchers Focuses on Scientific Study," *Education Week*, February 1, 2006, 16.

114. See, e.g., Panel on Improving Education Research report on OERI reauthorization, *Recommendations for the Improvement of the Federal Education Research Program* (Washington, DC: AERA, 2000).

115. Cross, *Political Education*, 124–25.

116. Whitehurst, interview. For Bush, measurement issues, and NCLB, see Andrew Rudalevige, "Forging a Congressional Compromise," in *No Child Left Behind? The Politics and Practice of School Accountability*, ed. Paul E. Peterson and Martin R. West (Washington, D.C.,: Brookings Institution Press, 2003).

117. Chester Finn, quoted in Debra Viadero, "New Research Agency's Independence in Question," *Education Week*, November 13, 2002, 29.

118. Harold Laswell, *Politics: Who Gets What, When, and How* (New York: Meridian Books, 1958).

CHAPTER 2
The Evolving Relationship between Researchers and Public Policy
Jeffrey R. Henig

1. Carl F. Kaestle, "The Awful Reputation of Education Research," *Educational Researcher* 22, no. 1 (1993): 23, 26–31. Kaestle's point was that this reputation was not fully deserved.

2. Maris A. Vinovskis, "The Presidential Address 1995: The Changing Role of the Federal Government in Educational Research and Statistics," *History of Education Quarterly* 36, no. 2 (1996): 118.

3. Frederick M. Hess and Laura LoGerfo., "Chicanas from Outer Space," *The National Review*, May 8, 2006: http://article.nationalreview.com/?q=ZDYwOGExMmUxOWYOZ DgxNGQxMGEwZjg4NTNhMzQ2M2M= (accessed October 22, 2007)

4. Ellen Condliffe Lagemann, *An Elusive Science: The Troubling History of Education Research* (Chicago: University of Chicago Press, 2000).

5. Stephen A. Stephan, "Prospects and Possibilities: The New Deal and the New Social Research," *Social Forces* 13 (1935): 515.

6. Maris A. Vinovskis, "The Changing Role of the Federal Government in Educational Research and Statistics," *History of Education Quarterly*, Vol. 36, No. 2 (Summer 1996): 117.

7. This paradox is noted in Lorraine M. McDonnell, "Can Education Research Speak to State Policy?" *Theory/into Practice* 27, no. 2 (1988): 91–97; also Michael W. Kirst, "Bridging Education Research and Education Policymaking," *Oxford Review of Education* 26, no. 3&4 (2000): 379–91.

8. The What Works Clearinghouse can be accessed at http://www.whatworks.ed.gov/ (accessed October 18, 2007).

9. Jeffrey Henig, *Spin Cycle: How Research Is Used in Policy Debates. The Case of Charter Schools* (New York: Russell Sage Foundation, 2008).

10. Peterson's paper contradicting Witte's findings was co-authored by Jay Greene and Jiangtao Du, although it is Peterson who is featured in the *Wall Street Journal* article. Jay Greene, Paul Peterson, and Jiangtao Du, "The Effectiveness of School Choice in Milwaukee: A Secondary Analysis of Data from the Program's Evaluation," Paper read at American Political Science Association Annual Meeting, August 29 to September 1, 1996, San Francisco, CA.

11. Bob Davis, "Class Warfare: Dueling Professors Have Milwaukee Dazed Over School Vouchers—Studies on Private Education Result in a Public Spat About Varied Conclusions—Candidates Debate the Point," *Wall Street Journal*, October 11, 1996, A1.

12. Michael J. Petrilli, "Review: Key Issues in Studying Charter Schools and Achievement, A Review and Suggestions for National Guidelines," *Education Gadfly*, May 2006, http://www.fordhaminstitute.org/foundation/gadfly/issue.cfm?edition=&id=246#2891 (accessed July 25, 2007).

13. Caroline Hoxby, "Do Charter Schools Help Their Students? Review of Reviewed Item," Manhattan Institute, *Civic Bulletin*, February 2005, http://www.manhattan-institute. org/html/cb_38.htm (accessed July 20, 2007); and Educational Policy Institute, "Focus on Results: An Academic Impact Analysis of the Knowledge Is Power Program (KIPP)," August 2005, http://www.educationalpolicy.org/pdf/KIPP.pdf (accessed July 25, 2007).

14. Jon E. Hilsenrath, "Making Waves: Novel Way to Assess School Competition Stirs Academic Row to Do So, Harvard Economist Counts Streams in Cities; A Princetonian Takes Issue," *Wall Street Journal*, October 24, 2005, A1.

15. Caroline M Hoxby. "Does Competition among Public Schools Benefit Students and Taxpayers?" *The American Economic Review* 90, no. 5 (2000): 1209–38.

16. Jesse Rothstein, "Does Competition among Public Schools Benefit Students and Taxpayers? A Comment on Hoxby (2000)," NBER Working Paper #11215 (March 2005). Available at SSRN: http://ssrn.com/abstract=689396 (accessed October 18, 2007).

17. National Bureau of Economic Research, "History of the NBER," http://www.nber.org/ info.html (accessed July 25, 2007).

18. Caroline M. Hoxby, "Competition among Public Schools: A Reply to Rothstein," National Bureau of Economic Research, 2004, http://www.nber.org/papers/w11216 (accessed July 18, 2007).

19. Hilsenrath, "Making Waves," A1

20. Kathleen Kennedy Manzo, "E-Mails Reveal Federal Reach over Reading Communications Show Pattern of Meddling in 'Reading First,'" *Education Week*, February 20, 2007, 1–3.

21. Debra Viadero and Kathleen Kennedy Manzo, "Out-of-Favor Reading Plan Rated Highly," *Education Week*, March 28, 2007, 29.
22. These counts were taken February 17, 2007. http://www.eduwonk.com
23. Howie Schaffer, e-mail message to author, February 21, 2007.
24. Caroline M. Hoxby, "Do Charter Schools Help Their Students? Review of Reviewed Item," in Manhattan Institute, *Civic Bulletin*, 2005, http://www.manhattan-institute. org/html/cb_38.htm (accessed July 18, 2007); and Educational Policy Institute, "Focus on Results."
25. As explained below (note 28), there was more than one version of the Hoxby paper. The first is dated September. *Education Week* and the *New York Post* received copies in time to run articles on September 8, 2005. In the first paper, Hoxby used two sets of comparison schools, one comprising what she said was the nearest conventional public school, and the second the nearest public school with a similar racial composition. This was a clever approach, and definitely worth pursuing. But whether it represents an improvement over statistical controls is not clear. There is too little that we know, at this point, about where charters draw their students from and what factors go into their choice of location to be confident in the assumption that spatial proximity effectively controls for student background.
26. http://www.edexcellence.net/foundation/gadfly/issue.cfm?id=162&edition= (accessed October 22, 2007).
27. Center for Education Reform, *Newswire*, September 14, 2004, Vol. 6, No. 36. http://www.edreform.com/index.cfm?fuseaction=document&documentID=1860 (accessed October 29, 2007).
28. Howard Nelson and Tiffany Miller, "A Closer Look at Caroline Hoxby's 'A Straightforward Comparison of Charter Schools and Regular Public Schools in the United States'" (Washington, DC: American Federation of Teachers, 2004). Unpublished report, available from hnelson@aft.org. In a later (December 2004) version of the paper, Hoxby corrected some of these elements of the initial paper. As a result, her results for the District of Columbia changed dramatically. In the September paper, she had claimed that the nearest D.C. public schools with a similar racial composition had 36.6% higher proficiency rates in reading and 41.5% in math, compared to charter schools; in the December paper, the comparable figures were 12.3 and 13.0. Despite this, based on other changes, her bottom-line estimate of the national charter school advantage was even higher than in the earlier version.
29. Researchers' willingness to bypass traditional peer review is controversial, with some arguing peer review is a critical ingredient for quality control and others arguing it is not only slow, but itself biased against new ideas that challenge the status quo. For a heated exchange on the subject, see Edward Muir, "They Blinded Me with Political Science: On the Use of Non-Peer Reviewed Research in Education Policy," *PS: Political Science and Politics* 32 (1999): 62–64; followed by articles in *PS: Political Science and Politics* 33, no. 2 (2000): Jay P. Greene and Paul E. Peterson, "Should Public Discussion of Political Science Research Be Controlled? Why Interest Group Recommendations on the Proper Procedures for Reporting Research Should Be Treated with Skepticism," 220–24; Jay P. Greene and Paul E. Peterson, "If the Peer Review Attack Fails, Attack Something Else," 229–31; and Edward Muir, "Social Science Should Be a Process, Not a Bloody Shirt," 235–37.
30. For example, the role of new technologies and media in by-passing scholarly journals and peer review, as already discussed, and the relative increase in contracting versus

grant funding and the growth of think tanks and private research organizations (both of which are discussed below).

31. Lagemann, *An Elusive Science*, 179.

32. Within the mix, I hasten to add, were some innovative, enlightening, and well-executed empirical studies. But in the massive, scattered, and heterogeneous brew of education literature, these examples were as easy to miss as the striped-shirted title character amidst the crowd scenes of the well-known *Where's Waldo?* series of children's books.

33. Alex Molnar, David Garcia, Margaret Bartlett, and Adrienne O'Neill, *Profiles of For-Profit Education Management Companies, 2005–2006* (Tempe, AZ: Arizona State University, Education Policy Studies Laboratory, 2006).

34. Homepage for the National Council of Education Providers, "Quality Schooling Options in Communities Nationwide," http://www.educationproviders.org/financial.htm (accessed July 18, 2007).

35. Jeffrey R. Henig, "The Political Economy of Supplemental Educational Services," in *No Remedy Left Behind: Lessons from a Half Decade of NCLB*, ed. Frederick M. Hess and Chester E. Finn, Jr. (Washington, D.C.: AEI Press, 2007), 66–94.

36. Thomas Toch, *Margins of Error: The Education Testing Industry in the No Child Left Behind Era* (Washington D.C.: Education Sector, 2006), 6.

37. Toch, *Margins of Error*, 6.

38. Author's calculations are based on data provided in Institute for Education Sciences, *Biennial Report: Grants, Cooperative Agreements, and Contracts over $100,000 Receiving Funding FY2002 through FY2004.* (Washington, D.C.: Department of Education, Institute of Education Sciences, 2005).

39. Edison Schools, "Edison Hails RAND Report," 2005, http://www.edisonschools.com/edison-schools/edison-news/b-edison-hails-rand-report-b (accessed July 18, 2007).

40. Educational Policy Institute, "Focus on Results: An Academic Impact Analysis of the Knowledge Is Power Program (KIPP)," August 2005, available at http://www.educationalpolicy.org/pdf/KIPP.pdf (accessed October 29, 2007). It is worth noting that the report itself takes some care not to claim that KIPP students' higher scores are attributable to the schools. It notes: "It is also impossible, considering this data set, to make comments about the comparability of the findings here to those in a random assignment design . . . Although this study design does not allow for claims of causality, we feel confident that the following findings are reflective of what is happening in KIPP schools. Future studies will need to be conducted before we can fully attribute outcomes to the schools."

41. The *Washington Post*, for example, published Jay Mathews, "Study Finds Big Gains For KIPP: Charter Schools Exceed Average," *Washington Post*, August 11, 2005, A14. Mathews mentions in the second paragraph that the data for the study were provided to the research firm by KIPP, but does not mention that the analysis was done under contract.

42. Marcia Angell, "Is Academic Medicine for Sale?" *New England Journal of Medicine* 342 (2000): 1516–18; and Troyen A. Brennan, "Health Industry Practices that Create Conflicts of Interest: A Policy Proposal for Academic Medical Centers," *Journal of the American Medical Association* 295, no. 4 (2006): 429–33.

43. See Goldhaber and Brewer, chapter 10 in this volume, for a discussion of the demand for research within the context of the incentives that researchers face.

44. National Science Foundation, "Federal Funds for Research and Development: Fiscal Years 2003–2005. Detailed Statistical Tables," http://www.nsf.gov/statistics/nsf06313/tables.htm#group15 (accessed October 29, 2007). Author's calculations.

45. Ronald L. Meeks, Project Officer, *Federal R&D Funding by Budget Function: Fiscal Years 2004–06* (Arlington, VA: National Science Foundation, Division of Science Resource Statistics, 2006), 1.

46. National Science Foundation, "Federal Funds for Research and Development: Fiscal Years 2003–2005. Detailed Statistics Tables," http://www.nsf.gov/statistics/nsf06313/tables.htm#group15 (accessed July 18, 2007).

47. Department of Education, Institute of Education Sciences, "Biennial Report: Grants, Cooperative Agreements, and Contracts over $100,000 Receiving Funding FY2002 through FY2004," March 2005, https://www.ies.ed.gov/doc/biennialrpt05.doc (accessed July 25, 2007).

48. Bryan C. Hassel and Amy Way, "Choosing to Fund Choice," in *With the Best of Intentions,* ed. Frederick M. Hess (Cambridge, MA: Harvard Education Press, 2005), 177–98.; and Ray Bacchetti and Thomas Ehrlich, "Foundations and Education: Introduction," in *Reconnecting Education and Foundations,* ed. Ray Baccheti and Thomas Ehrlich (New York: John Wiley & Sons, 2007), 3–20.

49. Original calculations based on data download from the Foundation Center website, http://fconline.fdncenter.org/.

50. Nancy Hoffman and Robert Schwartz, "Foundations and School Reform: Bridging the Cultural Divide," in *Reconnecting Education & Foundations,* ed. Ray Baccheti and Thomas Ehrlich (San Francisco, CA: Jossey-Bass, 2007), 107–38.

51. On localism generally, see Katherine McDermott, *Controlling Public Education: Localism versus Equity* (Lawrence KS: University Press of Kansas, 1999); on the myth of the end of localism in supplemental education services, see Jeffrey R. Henig, "The Political Economy of Supplemental Educational Services," in *No Remedy Left Behind:Lessons from a Half Decade of NCLB,* ed. Frederick M. Hess and Chester E. Finn, Jr. (Washington, DC: AEI Press, 2007), 66–94; and on suburban localism and resistance to vouchers, see Chad d'Entremont and Luis A. Huerta, "Irreconcilable Differences? Education Vouchers and the Suburban Response," *Education Policy* 21, no. 1 (2007): 40–72.

52. Paul Manna, *School's In: Federalism and the National Education Agenda* (Washington, DC: Georgetown University Press, 2006); and Patrick McGuinn, *No Child Left Behind and the Transformation of Federal Education Policy 1965–2005* (Lawrence, KS: University Press of Kansas, 2006).

53. Jeffrey R. Henig and Clarence N. Stone, "The Distractions of Dogma and the Potential for a New Politics of Progressive Pragmatism: Rethinking School Reform," *American Journal of Education,* forthcoming. See also Douglas S. Reed, *On Equal Terms: The Constitutional Politics of Educational Opportunity* (Princeton, NJ: Princeton University Press, 2003), who makes a similar argument about why school finance battles are easier to resolve politically than those over racial integration.

54. Paul Manna, *School's In.*

55. William L. Sanders and Sandra P. Horn, "Research Findings from the Tennessee Value Added Assessment System (TVAAS) Database: Implications for Educational Evaluation and Research," *Journal of Personnel Evaluation in Education* 12, no. 3 (1998).

56. Julian Betts, Paul Hill, and Patrick McEwan, "Key Issues in Studying Charter Schools and Achievement: A Review and Suggestions for National Guidelines," white paper, National Charter Schools Research Project, 2006. http://www.ncsrp.org/cs/csr/view/csr_pubs/5 (accessed October 18, 2007).

57. Sarah A. Binder, *Stalemate: Causes and Consequences of Legislative Gridlock* (Washington, DC: Brookings Institution Press, 2003); Jacob S. Hacker and Paul Pierson, *Off Center: The*

Republican Revolution & the Erosion of American Democracy (New Haven, CT: Yale University Press, 2005); Lawrence R. Jacobs and Robert Y. Shapiro, *Politicians Don't Slander: Political Manipulation and the Loss of Democratic Responsiveness* (Chicago: University of Chicago, 2000); and Carl Kaestle, "Federal Education Policy and the Changing Polity for Education, 1955–2005," in *To Educate a Nation: Federal and National Strategies of School Reform,* ed. Carl F. Kaestle and Alyssa E. Lodewick (Lawrence, KS: University Press of Kansas, 2007), vii–x.

58. Elizabeth DeBray-Pelot, "Dismantling Education's 'Iron Triangle': Institutional Relationships in the Formation of Federal Education Policy between 1998 and 2001," in Kaestle and Lodewick, *To Educate a Nation,* 64–89.

CHAPTER 3
Double Standard? "Scientfically Based Research" and The No Child Left Behind Act
Paul Manna and Michael J. Petrilli

1. Kevin M. Esterling, "Buying Expertise: Campaign Contributions and Attention to Policy Analysis in Congressional Committees," *American Political Science Review* 101, no. 1 (2007): 106. On the goal-oriented behavior of members of Congress, for example, see R. Douglas Arnold, *The Logic of Congressional Action* (New Haven, CT: Yale University Press, 1990); Richard F. Fenno, Jr., *Congressmen in Committees* (Boston: Little, Brown, 1973); Richard F. Fenno, Jr., *Home Style: House Members in Their Districts* (Boston: Little, Brown, 1978); and David R. Mayhew, *Congress: The Electoral Connection* (New Haven, CT: Yale University Press, 1974). A more pessimistic view about the use of research to inform policy is Walter Williams, *Honest Numbers and Democracy: Social Policy Analysis in the White House, Congress, and the Federal Agencies* (Washington, DC: Georgetown University Press, 1998).

2. House Subcommittee on Early Childhood, Youth and Families of the Committee on Education and the Workforce, *Options for the Future of the Office of Educational Research and Improvement,* 106th Cong., 2nd sess. (May 4, 2000). Available online at http://commdocs.house.gov/committees/edu/hedcew6-107.000/hedcew6-107.htm (accessed October 26, 2007).

3. Bryan D. Jones, *Politics and the Architecture of Choice: Bounded Rationality and Governance* (Chicago: University of Chicago Press, 2001); Bryan D. Jones and Frank R. Baumgartner, *The Politics of Attention: How Government Prioritizes Problems* (Chicago: University of Chicago Press, 2005); and Giandomenico Majone, *Evidence, Argument, and Persuasion in the Policy Process* (New Haven, CT: Yale University Press, 1989).

4. Lynn Olson and Debra Viadero, "Law Mandates Scientific Base for Research," *Education Week,* January 30, 2002, 1. NCLB's formal definition of scientifically based research appears in § 9101(37) of the law.

5. Olson and Viadero, "Law Mandates." 1.

6. *No Child Left Behind Act of 2001,* Public Law 107-110, 107th Cong., 1st sess. (January 8, 2001), Title II, Part A, Subpart 1, § 2112. Emphasis added. Hereafter referred to as NCLB.

7. NCLB, Title II, Part D, Subpart 1, § 2416. Emphasis added.

8. Title I, Part B contains these programs: Reading First, Early Reading First, the William F. Goodling Even Start Family Literacy Programs, and an additional subpart focusing on literacy and school libraries.

9. Many of these references are to "scientifically based reading research," which NCLB defines in § 1208(6): "The term 'scientifically based reading research' means research that—(A) applies rigorous, systematic, and objective procedures to obtain valid knowledge relevant to reading development, reading instruction, and reading difficulties; and (B) includes research that—(i) employs systematic, empirical methods that draw on observation or experiment; (ii) involves rigorous data analyses that are adequate to test the stated hypotheses and justify the general conclusions drawn; (iii) relies on measurements or observational methods that provide valid data across evaluators and observers and across multiple measurements and observations; and (iv) has been accepted by a peer-reviewed journal or approved by a panel of independent experts through a comparably rigorous, objective, and scientific review."

10. Information on the National Reading Panel is available at its homepage, http://www. nationalreadingpanel.org/ (accessed February 28, 2007).

11. During that year, the inspector general of the U.S. Department of Education (and some independent journalists and researchers) made allegations of favoritism and mismanagement in the billion-dollar Reading First program. Coverage appears in Michael Grunwald, "Billions for Inside Game on Reading," *Washington Post*, October 1, 2006; Jennifer Smith Richards, "Report Rips Federal Reading Initiative," *Columbus (Ohio) Dispatch*, October 4, 2006; and Diana Jean Schemo, "U.S. Audit Faults Grants for Reading in New York," *New York Times*, November 7, 2006.

12. Peter Simon, "New Reading Plan Faulted," *Buffalo News*, November 27, 2006, B1.

13. Frank R. Baumgartner and Bryan D. Jones, *Agendas and Instability in American Politics* (Chicago: University of Chicago Press, 1993); and Walter J. Oleszek, *Congressional Procedures and the Policy Process*, 4th ed. (Washington, DC: CQ Press, 1996).

14. We obtained NCLB's legislative history from the Congressional Information Service Index, via the Lexis-Nexis Congressional Universe library. A copy of this history is available from the authors.

15. Some witnesses in the research and program development type are affiliated with groups that also do advocacy. We omitted them from the association or advocacy group type because individuals in that type came from groups whose primary reason for being there appeared to be group representation or lobbying.

16. House Subcommittee on Education Reform of the Committee on Education and the Workforce, *From Research to Practice: Improving America's Schools in the 21st Century*, 107th Cong., 1st sess. (July 17, 2001), 30.

17. Additional sources commenting on the quality of education school research that parallel and extend Fuhrman's point are Geraldine J. Clifford and James W. Guthrie, *Ed School: A Brief for Professional Education* (Chicago: University of Chicago Press, 1988); and Arthur Levine, *Educating Researchers*, (Washington, DC: The Education Schools Project, 2006).

18. A difference of proportions test confirms that the difference between these two values is real in statistical terms. The p value associated with a test of the difference is 0.047, which means there is less than a 5 percent chance that we would observe the difference we observed if there actually were no real difference between the two numbers.

19. Christopher B. Swanson and Janelle Barlage, *Influence: A Study of the Factors Shaping Education Policy* (Bethedsa, MD: Editorial Projects in Education, Research Center, October 2006).

20. National Commission on Teaching and America's Future (NCTAF), *What Matters Most: Teaching for America's Future* (New York: NCTAF, 1996).

21. NCTAF, *What Matters Most*, 10.

22. NCTAF, *What Matters Most*, 53.

23. NCTAF, *What Matters Most*, 52.

24. NCTAF, *What Matters Most*, 56.

25. Thomas B. Fordham Foundation, "Kati Haycock: Happy Warrior," 2007, http://www.edexcellence.net/doc/2007_Prizes_Haycock.pdf (accessed March 12, 2007).

26. Kati Haycock, "Good Teaching Matters: How Well-Qualified Teachers Can Close the Gap," *The Education Trust, Thinking K–16*, Summer 1998.

27. Swanson and Barlage, *Influence*, 41.

28. William L. Sanders and June C. Rivers, *Cumulative and Residual Effects of Teachers on Future Student Academic Achievement* (Knoxville, TN: University of Tennessee Value Added Research and Assessment Center, November 1996). An alternative explanation for the jump in Google Scholar hits is simply that the number of documents available in electronic form has increased since the 1990s. Low numbers during the 1990s, as measured by the Google Scholar citation counts, might understate the initial impact of the Sanders and Rivers study. Overall, according to Google Scholar, this piece was cited by 240 others. That number is relatively large. As a basis of comparison, consider that John Chubb and Terry Moe's seminal book on school vouchers, *Politics, Markets, and America's Schools* (Washington, DC: Brookings Institution, 1990), has been cited by 879 other pieces in the Google Scholar database.

29. Haycock, "Good Teaching Matters," 3.

30. Thomas B. Fordham Foundation, "The Teachers We Need and How to Get More of Them" (Washington, DC: Thomas B. Fordham Foundation, 1999), http://www.edexcellence.net/institute/publication/publication.cfm?id=15&pubsubid=41&doc=pdf (accessed June 26, 2007). This chapter's second author worked at the Fordham Foundation at the time and helped to develop this manifesto.

31. Marci Kanstoroom and Chester E. Finn, Jr., ed., *Better Teachers, Better Schools* (Washington, DC: Thomas B. Fordham Foundation, 1999).

32. Fordham Foundation, *The Teachers We Need*, 4.

33. Fordham Foundation, *The Teachers We Need*, 9.

34. NCTAF, *What Matters Most*, dedication.

35. Jeff Archer, "Sanders 101," *Education Week*, May 5, 1999, 26.

36. Haycock, "Good Teaching Matters," 2.

37. See Thomas B. Fordham Foundation, "Mission," http://www.edexcellence.net/foundation/global/page.cfm?id=6 (accessed June 26, 2007).

38. In Paul J. Quirk and Sarah H. Binder, eds., *The Legislative Branch* (New York: Oxford University Press, 2005). See the editors' "Congress and American Democracy: Assessing Institutional Performance," 525–50; and Binder's, "Elections, Parties, and Governance," 148–70.

39. *The Student Results Act of 1999*, HR 2, 106th Cong., 1st sess. *Congressional Record* (October 20, 1999): H 10423—H 10514. Section 1610(2) defines this term.

40. House Committee on Education and the Workforce, Subcommittee on Early Childhood, Youth, and Families, *Teacher Preparation Initiatives*, 105th Cong., 2nd sess. (February 24, 1998), 49.

41. House Committee, *Teacher Preparation Initiatives*, 55.

42. House Committee, *Teacher Preparation Initiatives*, 10.

43. U.S. Department of Education, Office of Postsecondary Education, Office of Policy Planning and Innovation. *Meeting the Highly Qualified Teachers Challenge: The Secretary's Annual Report on Teacher Quality* (Washington, DC: Government Printing Office, 2002).

44. Department of Education, *Meeting the Highly Qualified Teachers Challenge*, 15.

45. Department of Education, *Meeting the Highly Qualified Teachers Challenge*, 19.
46. Studies cited include: Dan D. Goldhaber and Dominic J. Brewer, "Teacher Licensing and Student Achievement," in *Better Teachers, Better Schools*, ed. Chester E. Finn, Jr., and Marci Kanstoroom (Washington, DC: Thomas B. Fordham Foundation, 1999); http://www.edexcellence.net/institute/publication/publication.cfm?id=15 (accessed on October 26, 2007). Michael Podgursky and Dale Ballou, *Personnel Policy in Charter Schools* (Washington, DC: Thomas B. Fordham Foundation, 2001); C. Emily Feistritzer and David T. Chester, *Alternative Teacher Certification: A State By State Analysis 2002* (Washington, DC: National Center for Education Information, 2002); Kati Haycock, *Good Teaching Matters . . . A Lot* (Washington, DC: The Education Trust, 1998); Kate Walsh, *Teacher Certification Reconsidered: Stumbling for Quality* (Baltimore, MD: The Abell Foundation, 2001); Frederick Hess, *Tear Down This Wall: The Case for a Radical Overhaul of Teacher Certification* (Washington, DC: Progressive Policy Institute, 2001); and Margaret Raymond and Stephen Fletcher, "Teach for America," *Education Next* 2, no. 1 (Spring 2002): 62–8.

CHAPTER 4
Research and the Reading Wars

James S. Kim

1. Art Levine, "The Great Debate Revisited," *Atlantic Monthly* 274, no. 6 (December 1994): 38.
2. James McKeen Catteell, "The Time It Takes to See and Name Objectives," *Mind* 11 (1886): 63–65.
3. National of Child Health and Human Development, *Report of the National Reading Panel: Teaching Children to Read: An Evidence-based Assessment of the Scientific Literature on Reading and its Implications for Reading Instruction*. NIH Publication No. 00-4754 (Washington, D.C.,: Government Printing Office, 2000). Hereafter cited as *NRP*.
4. William S. Gray, *On Their Own Reading* (Chicago: Scott, Foresman, 1948), 19.
5. Rudolph Flesch, *Why Johnny Can't Read and What You Can Do About It* (New York: Harper & Brothers, 1955). Flesch's book was on the bestseller list for over 30 weeks and received widespread coverage in the popular press.
6. John Edwin Cowen, *A Balanced Approach to Beginning Instruction, A Syntheses of Six Major U.S. Research Studies* (Newark, DE: International Reading Association, 2003), 11.
7. Jeanne Chall, *Learning to Reading: The Great Debate* (New York: McGraw-Hill, 1967), 75.
8. Chall, *Learning to Reading*, 137.
9. Kenneth S. Goodman, "Reading: A Psycholinguistic Guessing Game," *Journal of the Reading Specialist* 6 (1967): 126.
10. Goodman, "Reading," 127.
11. Kenneth S. Goodman, "Analysis of Oral Miscues: Applied Psycholinguistics," *Reading Research Quarterly* 5, no. 1 (1969): 15.
12. Goodman, "Analysis of Oral Miscues," 29.
13. Frank Smith, *Understanding Reading: A Psycholinguistic Analysis of Reading and Learning to Read* (New York: Holt, Rinehart & Winston, 1971).
14. Smith, *Understanding Reading*, 209.
15. Smith, *Understanding Reading*, 230.
16. Frank Smith, *Psycholinguistics and Reading* (New York: Holt, Rinehart, and Winston, 1973), 196.

17. Frank Smith, *Reading Without Nonsense* (New York: Teachers College Record, 1979), 166.

18. Keith E. Stanovich, *Progress in Understanding Reading* (New York: Guilford Press, 2000), chapter 1.

19. Richard F. West and Keith E. Stanovich, "Automatic Contextual Facilitation in Readers of Three Ages," *Child Development* 49 (1978): 717–27.

20. Linnea Ehri, "Research on Learning to Read and Spell: A Personal-Historical Perspective," *Scientific Studies of Reading* 2, no. 2 (1998): 97–114; Linnea Ehri and Kathleen T. Roberts, "Do Beginners Learn Printed Words Better in Contexts or in Isolation?" *Child Development* 50, no. 3 (September 1979): 675–85; and Linnea Ehri and Lee Wilce, "Do Beginners Learn to Read Function Words Better in Sentences or in Lists?" *Reading Research Quarterly* 15, no. 4 (1980): 451–76.

21. Keith Rayner, "Eye Movements in Reading and Information Processing," *Psychological Bulletin* 85 (1979): 618–60.

22. Isabelle Y. Liberman, Donald Shankweiler, F. William Fischer, and Bonnie Carter, "Explicit Syllable and Phoneme Segmentation in the Young Child," *Journal of Experimental Child Psychology* 18, no. 2 (October 1974): 201–12.

23. David Laberge and S. J. Samuels, "Toward a Theory of Automatic Information Processing in Reading," *Cognitive Psychology* 6 (1974): 293–323; and Tom Nicholson, "Do Children Read Words Better in Context or in Lists? A Classic Study Revisited," *Journal of Educational Psychology* 83, no. 4 (1991): 444–50.

24. Richard L. Venezky, "Research on Reading Processes, A Historical Perspective," *American Psychologist* 32, (May 1977): 344.

25. National Institute of Education (NIE), National Academy of Education Commission on Reading, *Becoming a Nation of Readers,* (Washington, DC: NIE,1985), viii.

26. NIE, *Becoming a Nation of Readers*, vi.

27. Carl F. Kaestle, "The Awful Reputation of Education Research," *Educational Researcher* 22, no. 1 (January–February, 1993): 26.

28. Marilyn Jager Adams, *Beginning to Read: Thinking and Learning about Print* (Boston: MIT Press, 1990).

29. Michael Pressley, *Reading Instruction That Works* (New York: The Guilford Press, 2002), 171.

30. Steven A. Stahl and Patricia D. Miller, "Whole Language and Language Experience Approaches to Beginning Reading: A Quantitative Research Synthesis," *Review of Educational Research* 59, no. 1 (1989): 87–116; and Keith E. Stanovich and Paula J. Stanovich, "Fostering the Scientific Study of Reading Instruction by Example," in *Reading Research at Work*, ed. Katherine A. Dougherty Stahl and Michael C. McKenna (New York: The Guilford Press, 2006), 36–44.

31. P. David Pearson, "Reading the Whole Language Movement," *Elementary School Journal* 90, no. 2 (1990): 231.

32. Jerome C. Harste, "The Future of Whole Language," *Elementary School Journal* 90, no. 2 (1990): 248.

33. Kenneth S. Goodman, "Whole-Language Research: Foundations and Development," *Elementary School Journal* 90, no. 2 (1990): 208.

34. Goodman, "Whole-Language Research," 215.

35. Goodman, "Whole-Language Research," 219.

36. Timothy Shanahan, "The Shift from Polarization in Reading: Relying on Research Rather than Compromise," in *Reading Research at Work*, ed. Katherine A. Dougherty Stahl and Michael C. McKenna (New York: Guilford Press, 2006), 78.

37. Tom Loveless, "The Use and Misuse of Research in Educational Reform," in *Brookings Papers on Education Policy 1998*, ed. Diane Ravitch (Washington, DC: Brookings Institution, 1998), 289; and Jeanne S. Chall, *The Academic Achievement Challenge* (New York: The Guilford Press, 2000), 34.

38. California State Department of Education, *English-Language Arts Framework for California Public Schools: Kindergarten through Grade Twelve* (Sacramento, CA, 1987), 2.

39. Ina V. S. Mullis, Jay R. Campbell, and Alan E. Farstrup, *NAEP 1992 Reading Report Card for the Nation and the States: Data from the National and Trial State Assessments* (U.S. Department of Education, National Center for Education Statistics, 1993).

40. Scholars have also disagreed about the links between California's NAEP scores and whole-language practice. On one hand, Marilyn J. Adams infers a link between teacher practice and student outcomes by concluding that demographic changes alone could not explain the precipitous decline in California's NAEP scores. She notes that while one hypothesis "was that California's outcomes were a consequence of demographics . . . an equally immediate hypothesis was that whole language was at least partly to blame." Marilyn J. Adams, "Comments," in *Brookings Papers on Education Policy 2005*, ed. Diane Ravitch (Washington DC: Brookings Institution Press, 2005), 232. On the other hand, Jeff McQuillan argues that there were also differences in teacher practice within California that seemed to contradict the cross-state comparisons. Fourth grade teachers were asked to indicate their approach to reading and given three options: whole language, literature based, phonics. Children in whole-language classrooms (40% of teachers) had an average score of 220, children in literature-based classrooms (49% of teachers) had an average score of 221, and children in phonics classrooms (11% of teachers) had an average score of 208. Jeff McQuillan, *The Literacy Crisis, False Claims, Real Solutions* (Portsmouth, NH: Heinemann, 1998), 14.

41. Loveless, "Use and Misuse of Research," 289–90.

42. Frances R. A. Paterson, "The Politics of Phonics," *Journal of Curriculum and Supervision* 15, no. 3 (Spring 2000): 179–211.

43. In the late 1990s, Washington state lawmakers allocated $9 million to K–2 classrooms to prevent reading failure, which seemed widespread on the 1998 WASL test revealing that 43% of children were below proficiency. The bill viewed phonics as an essential component of effective reading instruction and as a potential remedy for the fourth-grade reading crisis. Writing in a *Seattle Times* editorial, the chair of the Senate Education Committee declared, "Reading is phonics! Writing is phonics!" Some local districts responded by urging schools to replace sustained silent reading with more teacher-directed instruction. Subsequent analyses of children falling below proficiency on WASL indicated that many children had good word recognition skills and did not need phonics instruction. See Marsha Riddle Buly and Sheila W. Valencia, "Below the Bar: Profiles of Students Who Fail State Reading Assessments," *Educational Evaluation and Policy Analysis* 24, no. 3 (Fall 2002): 219–39.

44. Keith E. Stanovich, "Romance and Reality," *The Reading Teacher* 47, no.4 (1994): 285–86.

45. Honig is quoted in Loveless, "Use and Misuse of Research," 289.

46. John W. Kingdon, *Agendas, Alternatives, and Public Policies*, 2nd ed. (New York: Harper Collins, 1995), 196–97. Also see Mengli Song, Jane G. Coggshall, and Cecil G. Miskel, "Where Does Policy Usually Come From and Why Should We Care?" in *The Voice of Evidence*, ed. Peggy McCardle and Vinita Chabra (Baltimore, MD: Paul H. Brookes, 2004), 445–62.

47. McCardle and Chabra, *The Voice of Evidence*; and G. Reid Lyon, Sally E. Shaywitz, Bennett A. Shaywitz, and Vinita Chabra, "Evidence-Based Reading Policy in the United States: How Scientific Research Informs Instructional Practices," in Ravitch, *Brookings Papers on Education Policy 2005*, 209–50.

48. Duane Alexander, David B. Gray, and G. Reid Lyon, "Conclusions and Future Directions," in *Better Understanding Learning Disabilities*, ed. G. Reid Lyon, David B. Gray, James F. Kavanaugh, and Norman A. Krasnegor (Baltimore: Paul H. Brookes, 1993), 349.

49. Although focused initially on basic research about the etiology of reading difficulties, especially among students with disabilities, the NICHD began to fund more experimental studies on reading instruction during Reid Lyon's tenure in the 1990s, and Lyon played an influential role in shaping the Reading First legislation. See, for example, Cecil Miskel and Mengli Song, "Passing Reading First: Prominence and Processes in an Elite Policy Network," *Educational Evaluation and Policy Analysis* 26, no. 2 (Summer 2004): 89–110.

50. Catherine E. Snow, M. Susan Burns, and Peg Griffin, ed., *Preventing Reading Difficulties in Young Children* (Washington, DC: National Academy of Sciences, 1998), vi.

51. Snow, Burns, and Griffin, *Preventing Reading Difficulties*, vii.

52. Snow, Burns, and Griffin, *Preventing Reading Difficulties*, 343.

53. *Departments of Labor, Health and Human Services, and Education and Related Agencies Appropriation Bill 1998*, 105th Cong., 1st sess. (July 24, 1997): S Rep 105–58.

54. National Institute of Child Health and Human Development, *Report of the National Reading Panel: Teaching Children to Read: An Evidence-Based Assessment of the Scientific Literature on Reading and Its Implications for Reading Instruction* (Washington, DC: U.S. Government Printing Office, 2000).

55. The chairs of the subgroups reviewing alphabetics, comprehension, fluency, and methodology were national leaders in the field of literacy research, members of the Reading Hall of Fame, and former editors of academic journals. Linnea Ehri, chair of the alphabetic subgroup, had received the Oscar Casey award for her work on early literacy, the stages of sight-word reading, and phonics. Michael Kamil, chair of the comprehension subgroup, was coeditor of volume II and III of the *Handbook of Reading Research* (Mahwah, New Jersey: Lawrence Erlbaum Associates, 1991, 2000) which contains authoritative and comprehensive reviews of reading theory, processes, and practice. S. Jay Samuels, cochair of the reading fluency subgroup, had been editor of *Reading Research Quarterly*, a leading reading research journal. And the cochair of the methods chapter, Timothy Shanahan, an education professor at the University of Chicago–Illinois and Sally Shaywitz, a pediatrics professor and reading scholar at Yale, were both experts in research methods, and published widely using meta-analysis, experimental design, and longitudinal data analysis.

56. See Minority View, in *NRP*, 1.

57. Thus, the NRP's decision to review studies with high internal validity was essentially the same standard "normally used in research studies of the efficacy of interventions and psychological and medical research." *NRP*, Section 1, page 5.

58. Timothy Shanahan, "The National Reading Panel: Using Research to Create More Literate Students," 1999, http://www.readingonline.org/critical/shanahan/panel.html (accessed on June 20, 2007).

59. *NRP*, Section 2, page 136.

60. *NRP*, section 3, page 20.

61. Commenting on this finding, the NRP concluded that "the demonstrated effectiveness of guided oral reading compared to the lack of demonstrated effectiveness of strategies encouraging independent silent reading suggest the importance of explicit compared to more implicit instructional approaches for improving reading fluency." *NRP*, section 3, page 4.

62. Jeanne Chall, *The Academic Achievement Challenge* (New York: Guildford Press, 2000).

63. See, for example, Gregory Camilli, Paula M. Wolfe, and Mary Lee Smith, "Meta-Analysis and Reading Policy: Perspectives on Teaching Children to Read," *Elementary School Journal* 107, no. 1 (September 2006): 27–36; Elfrieda Hiebert, "A Review of the National Reading Panel's Studies on Fluency: The Role of Text," *Elementary School Journal* 105, no. 5 (May 2005): 443–61.

64. In the Reading First applications of the five largest U.S. states (California, New York, Texas, Florida, Illinois), which received over 40% of Title I dollars in 2004–05, the five areas of reading instruction are mentioned over 150 times.

65. International Reading Association, *Evidence-Based Reading Instruction: Putting the National Reading Panel Report into Practice* (Newark, DE: International Reading Association, 2002), 2.

66. Louisa C. Moats, *Teaching Reading Is Rocket Science* (Washington, DC: American Federation of Teachers, 1999), 31.

67. For criticisms of the recommendations flowing from the NRP's meta-analysis on phonics instruction, see Elain M. Garan, "Beyond the Smoke and Mirrors: A Critique of the National Reading Panel Report on Phonics," in *Big Brother and the National Reading Curriculum: How Ideology Trumped Evidence*, ed. Richard Allington (Portsmouth, NJ: Heinemann, 2002), 90–111.

68. Timothy Shanahan, "Response to Elaine Garan," *Language Arts* 79 (2001): 70–71.

69. Richard L. Allington, "Accelerating in the Wrong Direction: Why Thirty Years of Federal Testing and Accountability Hasn't Worked Yet and What We Might Do Instead," *Big Brother*, 235–63.

70. Paul Starr, *The Social Transformation of American Medicine, The Rise of a Sovereign Profession and the Making of a Vast Industry* (New York: Basic Books, 1982), 4.

71. Thomas S. Kuhn, *The Structure of Scientific Revolutions*, 3rd ed. (Chicago, University of Chicago Press, 1996), 10.

72. Chall, *Learning to Read*, 314.

73. Stanovich, *Progress in Understanding Reading*, 406.

74. Kuhn, *Structure of Scientific Revolutions*, 158.

75. National Academy of Education, Committee on Reading. *Toward a Literate Society* (New York: McGraw-Hill, 1975), 15.

76. Kuhn, *Structure of Scientific Revolutions*, 405–6.

77. Louisa C. Moats, *Speech to Print, Language Essentials for Teachers* (Baltimore, MD: Paul H. Brookes, 2000), 6.

78. Barbara Mellers, Ralpha Hertwig, and Daniel Kahneman, "Do Frequency Representations Eliminate Conjunction Effects? An Exercise in Adversarial Collaboration," *Psychological Science* 2001, no. 4 (July 2001): 269–75. It should be noted that the paper was received on July 26, 2000, and accepted on August 25, 2000, an unusually fast review process for a peer-reviewed journal.

79. See, for example, chapter 6 by Richard Ingersoll and chapter 8 by Josh Dunn and Martin West.

80. Kuhn, *Structure of Scientific Revolutions*, 168.

81. Gary W. Ritter and Robert F. Boruch, "The Political and Institutional Origins of a Randomized Controlled Trial on Elementary School Class Size: Tennessee's Project STAR," *Educational Evaluation and Policy Analysis* 21, no. 2 (Summer 1999): 111–26.

82. According to Frederick Mosteller, the Project STAR study is "one of the most important educational investigations ever carried out and illustrates the kind and magnitude of research needed in the field of education to strengthen schools." See Frederick Mosteller, "The Tennessee Study of Class Size in the Early Grades," *Future of Children, Critical Issues for Children and Youths* 5, no. 2 (Summer/Fall 1995): 113.

83. Daniel P. Moynihan, *Maximum Feasible Understanding, Community Action in the War on Poverty* (New York: Free Press, 1969), 193.

84. *NRP* "The Minority View," 2.

85. When faced with the challenge of improving reading achievement in underperforming schools, leaders in the Labour Party formed a Literacy Task Force to review the research on teaching reading. One half of the members of the United Kingdom's Literacy Task Force were teachers and none of the task force members had a national reputation for their academic expertise in teaching reading, or for their scholarship. For more on the Literacy Task Force and the policies it recommended, see Dominic Wyse and Russell Jones, *Teaching English, Language and Literacy* (London: Routledge & Falmer, 2001); and Literacy Task Force, "A Reading Revolution: How We Can Teach Every Child to Read Well," February 1997, http://www.leeds.ac.uk/educol/documents/000000153.htm (accessed July 26, 2007).

86. International Reading Association, "IRA, NICHD Collaboration Continues," *Reading Today* (April/May 2007), 17.

87. Starr, *Social Transformation of American Medicine*, 15.

CHAPTER 5

Researcher Meets the Policy Realm: A Personal Account

Richard M. Ingersoll

1. See, for example, Eric Hirsch, Julie Koppich, and Michael Knapp, *Revisiting What States Are Doing to Improve the Quality of Teaching: An Update on Patterns and Trends* (Seattle, WA: University of Washington, Center for the Study of Teaching and Policy, 2001); Wendy Kopp, "Reforming Schools of Education Will Not Be Enough, *Yale Law and Policy Review* 10 (1992): 58–68; and Emily Feistritzer, *Alternative Teacher Certification: A State-by-State Analysis 1997* (Washington, DC: National Center for Education Information, 1997).

2. James Conant, *The Education of American Teachers* (New York: McGraw-Hill, 1963).

3. Albert Shanker, "Education's 'Dirty Little Secret'" *New York Times*, October 27, 1985.

4. See, for example, Sharon Bobbitt and Marilyn McMillen, *Qualifications of the Public School Teacher Workforce* (Washington, DC: National Center for Education Statistics, 1995); Victor Bandeira de Mello and Steve Broughman, *SASS by State* (Washington, DC: National Center for Education Statistics, 1996); Becky Smerdon, *Teacher Quality: A Report on the Preparation and Qualifications of Public School Teachers* (Washington, DC: National Center for Education Statistics, 1999; and Marilyn McMillen, Kerry Gruber, Robin Henke and Dan McGrath, *Qualifications of the Public School Teacher Workforce: 1987–88 to 1999–2000* (Washington, DC: National Center for Education Statistics, 2002).

5. Richard Ingersoll, *Teacher Supply, Teacher Qualifications and Teacher Turnover* (Washington, DC: National Center for Education Statistics, 1995); and *Out-of-Field Teaching and Educational Equality* (Washington, DC: National Center for Education Statistics, 1996).

6. See, for example, these publications by Richard Ingersoll (all available at www.gse.upenn. edu/faculty/ingersoll.html): "Commentary. Putting Qualified Teachers in Every Classroom," *Education Week* 16, no. 37 (1997): 60; "The Problem of Underqualified Teachers in American Secondary Schools," *Educational Researcher* 28, no. 2 (1999): 26–37; "Misunderstanding the Problem of Out-of-Field Teaching," *Educational Researcher* 30, no. 1 (2001): 21–22; *Out-of-Field Teaching and the Limits of Teacher Policy* (Philadelphia: University of Pennsylvania, Consortium for Policy Research in Education, 2003), http://depts.washington.edu/ctpmail/PDFs/LimitsPolicy-RI-09-2003.pdf (accessed November 14, 2007); and "Why Some Schools Have More Underqualified Teachers Than Others" in *Brookings Papers on Education Policy 2004*, ed. Diane Ravitch (Washington, DC: Brookings Institution, 2004), 45–71, available at http://www.gse.upenn.edu/faculty_research/docs/BPEP-RMI-2004.pdf (accessed November 14, 2007)

7. National Commission on Teaching and America's Future (NCTAF), *What Matters Most: Teaching for America's Future* (New York: NCTAF, 1996); and NCTAF, *Doing What Matters Most: Investing in Quality Teaching* (New York: NCTAF, 1997).

8. Education Trust, *Education Watch* (Washington, DC: Education Trust, 1996); Kati Haycock, "Good Teaching Matters . . . a Lot," *Thinking K–16: A Publication of the Education Trust* 3, no. 2 (1998): 3–14; K. Haycock, "No More Settling for Less," *Thinking K–16: A Publication of the Education Trust* 4, no. 1 (2000): 3–12; and Craig Jerald and Richard Ingersoll, *All Talk, No Action: Putting an End to Out-of-Field Teaching* (Washington, DC: Education Trust, 2002). Available at http://www2.edtrust.org/NR/rdonlyres/8DE64524-592E-4C83-A13A-6B1DF1CF8D3E/0/AllTalk.pdf.

9. See, for example, these issues of *Education Week*'s annual supplement, "Quality Counts: A Report on Education in the 50 States," *Education Week* 17, no. 17 (1998): 56–61; and vol. 22, no. 17 (2003): 57–61.

10. House Committee on Education and the Workforce, *Teacher Preparation Initiatives: Statement of Dr. Richard M. Ingersoll*, 105th Cong., 2nd sess., February 1998, 13–40, 163–94. Available at http://www.gse.upenn.edu/faculty_research/docs/HSE-RMI-1998.pdf.

11. NCLB allows several ways of establishing competency in a particular field: hold a major, pass a subject test, obtain advanced certification, or some other approved method.

12. Michael Cohen, James March, and Johan Olsen. "A Garbage Can Theory of Organizational Decision Making," *Administrative Science Quarterly* 17 (1972): 1–25.

13. For a detailed discussion of measures of out-of-field teaching, see Ingersoll, "Misunderstanding the Problem," 21–22. Also see Richard Ingersoll, "Measuring Out-of-Field Teaching," (2002), unpublished manuscript, available from the author; and Ingersoll, *Out-of-Field Teaching and the Limits of Teacher Policy*.

14. See, for example, Stephen Friedman, "How Much of a Problem: A Reply to Ingersoll's 'The Problem of Underqualified Teachers in American Secondary Schools,'" *Educational Researcher* 29, no. 5 (2000): 18–20.

15. For a summary of my empirical findings, see Ingersoll, "The Problem of Underqualified Teachers."

16. Richard Ingersoll, *A Comparative Study of Teacher Preparation and Qualifications in Six Nations* (Philadelphia: University of Pennsylvania, The Consortium for Policy Research in Education, 2007). Available at http://www.cpre.org/images/stories/cpre_pdfs/RB47.pdf.

17. Ingersoll, Comparative Study.

18. See, for example, Arthur Levine, Educating School Teachers (New York: Education Schools Project, 2006). For an excellent review of the many critiques of teacher educa-

tion, see David Labaree, The Trouble with Ed Schools (New Haven, CT: Yale University Press, 2004).

19. NCTAF, *What Matters Most*; and NCTAF, *Doing What Matters Most*.

20. Eric Hanushek and Steve Rivkin, "How to Improve the Supply of High Quality Teachers." in Diane Ravitch, *Brookings Papers*, 7–44; and Chester Finn, Marci Kanstoroom, and Michael Petrilli, *The Quest for Better Teachers: Grading the States* (Washington, DC.: Thomas B. Fordham Foundation, 1999).

21. See, for example, Amitai Etzioni, ed., *The Semi-Professions and Their Organizations: Teachers, Nurses and Social Workers*. (New York: Free Press, 1969); and Dan Lortie, *School Teacher* (Chicago: University of Chicago Press, 1975).

22. Michael Kane, "Validating Interpretive Arguments for Licensure and Certification Examinations," *Evaluation & The Health Professions* 17, no. 2 (1994): 133–59; and American Educational Research Association/American Psychological Association/National Council on Measurement in Education, *Standards for Educational and Psychological Testing* (Washington, DC: American Psychological Association, 1999).

23. For reviews, see, for example, Richard Murnane and Senta Raizen, "Indicators of Teaching Quality," in *Improving Iindicators of the Quality of Science and Mathematics Education in Grades K–12*, eds. Richard Murnane and Senta Raizen (Washington, DC: National Academy Press, 1988), 90–118; and Robert Greenwald, Larry Hedges, and Richard Laine, "The Effect of School Resources on Student Achievement," *Review of Educational Research* 66 (1996): 361–96.

24. See, for example, Stephen Raudenbush, Randall Fotiu, and Yuk Cheong, "Synthesizing Results from the Trial State Assessment," *Journal of Educational and Behavioral Statistics* 24, no. 4 (1999): 413–38; and Elizabeth Greenberg, Ye Rhodes, Xioalan, and Fran Stancavage, "Prepared to Teach: Teacher Preparation and Student Achievement in 8th Grade Mathematics," paper presented at the annual meeting of the American Educational Research Association, San Diego, CA, April 2004.

25. For a recent review, see Michael Allen, *Eight Questions on Teacher Preparation: What Does the Research Say?* (Denver, CO: Education Commission of the States, 2003); also available at http://www.ecs.org/tpreport (accessed November 14, 2007).

26. Ernest Pascarella and Patrick Terenzini, *How College Affects Students: Findings and Insights from Twenty Years of Research* (San Francisco: Jossey-Bass, 1991).

27. Myra Sadker and David Sadker, "Sexism in the Classroom: From Grade School to Graduate School," *Phi Delta Kappan* Vol. 67, no. 7 (March 1986): 512–15.

28. NCTAF, *What Matters Most*; and NCTAF, *Doing What Matters Most*.

29. See, for example, the syndicated columns of David Broder, Thomas Sowell, or Maggie Gallagher during the week of September 14 to 20, 1996; and Committee for Economic Development, *American Workers and Economic Change* (New York: Committee for Economic Development, 1996).

30. Sowell's column appeared in numerous newspapers, including: "Education Insiders Protect their Turf," *The St. Louis Post-Dispatch,*. September 23, 1996.

31. National Commission on Excellence in Education, *A Nation at Risk: The Imperative for Educational Reform* (Washington, DC: U.S. Government Printing Office, 1983).

32. National Association of State Directors of Teacher Education and Certification, *The 2004 NASDTEC Manual on the Preparation and Certification of Educational Personnel*. 9th edition. (Sacramento, CA: School Services of California, Inc., 2004).

33. Thomas Toch, "Why Teachers Don't Teach: How Teacher Unions are Wrecking our Schools," *U.S. News and World Report*, February 26, 1996, 62–71.

34. NCTAF, *What Matters Most*; and NCTAF, *Doing What Matters Most*.

35. For a more detailed examination of the data on the teacher shortage, see Richard Ingersoll, "Teacher Turnover and Teacher Shortages: An Organizational Analysis, *American Educational Research Journal* 38, no.3 (2001): 499–534; and Richard Ingersoll, *Is There Really a Teacher Shortage?* (Philadelphia, PA: University of Pennsylvania, Consortium for Policy Research in Education, 2003), http://www.gse.upenn.edu/faculty_research/docs/Shortage-RMI-09-2003.pdf (accessed November 14, 2007).

36. Richard Ingersoll, *Who Controls Teachers' Work?: Power and Accountability in America's Schools* (Cambridge, MA: Harvard University Press, 2003).

37. Brian Delany, "Allocation, Choice and Stratification within High Schools: How the Sorting Machine Copes," *American Journal of Education* 99, no. 2 (1991): 181–207.

38. Virginia Robinson, *Making Do in the Classroom: A Report on the Misassignment of Teachers* (Washington, DC: Council for Basic Education and American Federation of Teachers, 1985).

39. Randy Hodson and Teresa Sullivan, "Professions and Professionals," Chapter 11 in *The Social Organization of Work* (Belmont, CA: Wadsworth, 1995), 287–314.

40. D.P. Moynihan, *Miles to Go: A Personal History of Social Policy.* (Cambridge, MA: Harvard University Press, 1996), 49.

41. Raymond Callahan, *Education and Cult of Efficiency.* (Chicago: University of Chicago Press, 1962).

42. Ingersoll, "Why Some Schools."

43. For a summary of recommendations for policymakers, see Richard M. Ingersoll and Bridget K. Curran, *Out-of-Field Teaching: The Great Obstacle to Meeting the "Highly Qualified" Teacher Challenge* (Washington, DC: National Governor's Association, 2004), available at http://www.nga.org/Files/pdf/0408HQTEACHER.pdf (accessed November 14, 2007).

CHAPTER 6
Education Policy, Academic Research, and Public Opinion
William G. Howell

1. Phillip Converse, "The Nature of Belief Systems in Mass Publics," in *Ideology and Discontent*, ed. David. Apter (New York: Free Press, 1964).

2. For further discussion of the public's general lack of knowledge of education issues, see Stanley Elam and Lowell Rose, "The 27th Annual Phi Delta Kappa/Gallup Poll: Of the Public Attitudes toward the Public Schools," 1995, http://www.pdkintl.org/kappan/kpollpdf.htm (accessed November 1, 2007); Terry Moe, *Schools, Vouchers, and the American Public* (Washington, DC: Brookings Institution Press, 2001); and Steve Farkas, Jean Johnson, and Tony Felono, "On Thin Ice: How Advocates and Opponents Could Misread the Public's Views on Vouchers and Charter Schools," *Public Agenda* (1999), select findings available at http://www.publicagenda.org/specials/vouchers/voucherhome.htm (accessed November 1, 2007)

3. Donald Green, Bradley Palmquist, and Eric Schickler, *Partisan Hearts and Minds* (New Haven, CT: Yale University Press, 2003).

4. Morris Fiorina, *Retrospective Voting in American National Elections* (New Haven, CT: Yale University Press, 1981).

5. Tali Mendelberg, *The Race Card: Campaign Strategy, Implicit Messages, and the Norm of Equality* (Princeton, NJ: Princeton University Press, 2001).

6. See, for example: Samuel Popkin, *The Reasoning Voter* (Chicago, IL: University of Chicago Press, 1992); and Paul Sniderman, Richard Brody, and Phillip Tetlock, *Reasoning and Choice: Exploration in Political Psychology* (Cambridge, UK: Cambridge University Press, 1991).

7. According to a Pew Research Center report, the percentage of people who regularly read a newspaper declined from 58 percent in 1994 to just 40 percent in 2006; the percentage of people of watch the nightly network news dropped between 1993 and 2006 from 60 to 28 percent; viewers of local television news declined during the same period from 77 to 54 percent; and between 2004 and 2006, the percentage of cable television news views hovered at just 34 percent. The report is available online at: http://people-press. org/reports/print.php3?PageID=1064.

8. James Druckman, "Political Preference Formation: Competition, Deliberation, and the (Ir)Relevance of Framing Effects," *American Political Science Review* 98 (2004): 671–86.

9. Going back to Crawford and Sobel's seminal work on signaling under conditions of asymmetric information, a massive game-theoretic literature explores precisely this point. Vincent Crawford and Joel Sobel, "Strategic Information Transmission," *Econometrica* 50 (1982): 1431–51. More recently, these insights have been applied to elite-mass communications. See, for example, James Druckman, "The Implications of Framing Effects for Citizen Competence," *Political Behavior* 23 (2001): 225–56.

10. The experiment was included in the context of a larger survey conducted in the spring of 2007 by the Program on Education Policy and Governance and *Education Next*. The results from this survey are presented in: William Howell, Martin West, and Paul Peterson. "What Americans Think about their School," *Education Next*, 2007. 7 (4): 12–26.

11. This analysis isolates those respondents who took a clear position on the voucher item. Respondents who claimed to "neither support nor oppose" vouchers, as well as respondents who refused to answer the question, are not included.

12. Nonparents, meanwhile, register baseline levels of support for the conventional wisdom that are roughly halfway between those of public and private school students; and the differences they register across the four treatment conditions are similar to those of public school students.

CHAPTER 7
Calculated Justice: Education Research and the Courts
Joshua Dunn and Martin West

1. We are grateful to Martha Derthick, John Dinan, James Guthrie, Al Lindseth, Shep Melnick, Paul Peterson, Michael Podgursky, James Smith, and Matthew Springer for helpful discussions of this subject. Chris Bennett and Arthur Kim at Brown University provided valuable research assistance.

2. Edward S. Corwin, "The Supreme Court as National School Board," *Law and Contemporary Problems* 14, no. 4 (1949): 22.

3. For a survey of court decisions on education policy issues, see Mark G. Yudof, David L. Kirp, Betsy Levin, and Rachel F. Moran, *Educational Policy and the Law*, 4th ed. (Belmont, CA: West Thompson Learning, 2002).

4. Martin R. West and Paul E. Peterson, eds., *School Money Trials: The Legal Pursuit of Educational Adequacy* (Washington, DC: Brookings Institution Press, 2007).

5. *Brown v. Board of Education of Topeka*, 347 U.S. 483 (1954). For subsequent debate over the quality of the evidence cited in footnote 11, see, for example, Kenneth B. Clark,

"The Desegregation Cases: Criticism of the Social Scientists' Role," *Villanova Law Review* 5 (1959–1960): 224–40; and Harold B. Gerard, "School Desegregation: The Social Science Role," *American Psychologist* 38 (1983): 869–78.

6. Michael Heise, "Adequacy Litigation in an Era of Accountability," in *School Money Trials: The Legal Pursuit of Educational Adequacy*, ed. Martin R. West and Paul E. Peterson (Washington, DC: Brookings Institution Press, 2007), 262–63.

7. *San Antonio School District v. Rodriguez*, 411 U.S. 1 (1973).

8. Robert Boruch, "The Virtues of Randomness," *Education Next* 2, no. 3 (Fall 2002): 37–41 and Debra Viadero, "Report Urges Use of Medical-Style Research in Education," *Education Week*, November 27, 2002, 10.

9. James Traub, "No Child Left Behind: Does It Work?" *New York Times*, November 10, 2002, Section 4A, 24 (Education Life Supplement).

10. See, for example, Donald Horowitz, *The Courts and Social Policy* (Washington, DC: Brookings Institution Press, 1977); Shep Melnick, *Between the Lines: Interpreting Welfare Rights* (Washington, DC: Brookings Institution Press, 1994); and Ross Sandler and David Schoenbrod, *Democracy by Decree: What Happens When Courts Run Government* (New Haven, CT: Yale University Press, 2003).

11. Abram Chayes, "The Role of the Judge in Public Law Litigation," *Harvard Law Review* 89 (1976): 1281–1316.

12. Horowitz, *The Courts and Social Policy*, 22–67.

13. Horowitz, *The Courts and Social Policy*, 51. Michael Rebell and Arthur Block argue that, for all its apparent flaws, the courts' use of social science evidence compares favorably to that of legislative bodies. See Michael A. Rebell and Arthur R. Block, *Educational Policy Making and the Courts: A Study in Judicial Activism* (Chicago, IL: University of Chicago Press, 1982). Rebell and Block's study has been criticized for focusing exclusively on committee hearings and floor debates when examining legislative activity, when much legislative fact-finding, analysis, and persuasion occurs in other venues. See Gerald N. Rosenberg, *The Hollow Hope: Can Courts Bring about Social Change?* (Chicago, IL: University of Chicago Press, 1991), 29n19.

14. *Daubert v. Merrell Dow Pharmaceuticals*, 509 U.S. 579 (1993). The other two cases comprising the *Daubert* trilogy are *General Electric Co. v. Joiner*, 522 U.S. 136 (1997), and *Kumho Tire Co. v. Carmichael* 526 U.S. 137 (1999).

15. Previously, under the precedent established in *Frye v. United States*, 293 F. 1013 (1923), scientific evidence had to satisfy only the "general acceptance" prong.

16. See David E. Bernstein and Jeffrey D. Jackson, "The Daubert Trilogy in the States," *Jurimetrics* 44 (2004): 351–66; Bernstein, David E., "Expert Witnesses, Adversarial Bias, and the (Partial) Failure of the Daubert Revolution," George Mason Law & Economics Research Paper no. 07-11, February 2007, SSRN: http://ssrn.com/abstract=963461 (accessed October 24,2007).

17. See Sheldon Goldman, Elliot Slotnick, Gerard Gryski, and Sara Schiavoni, "W. Bush's Judiciary: The First Term Record," *Judicature* 88 (2005): 244–75.

18. For information on selection methods in the states, see American Judicature Society, "AJS Judicial Selection Materials," http://www.ajs.org/js/materials.htm (accessed March 27, 2007).

19. See Melinda Gann Hall, "State Supreme Courts in American Democracy: Probing the Myths of Judicial Reform," *American Political Science Review* 95 (2001): 317–19.

20. Kyle Cheek and Anthony Champagne, "Money in Texas Supreme Court Elections: 1980–1998," *Judicature* 84 (2000): 20–25.

21. Deborah Goldberg, Sarah Samis, Edwin Bender, and Rachel Weiss, *The New Politics of Judicial Elections 2004: Report on State Supreme Court Elections* (Justice At Stake Campaign: 2004), 13–15.
22. Sandra K. McKinley, "The Journey to Adequacy: The *DeRolph* Saga," *Journal of Education Finance* 30, no. 3 (Winter 2005): 321–81.
23. *Craig v. Boren*, 429 U.S. 190 (1976).
24. *McCleskey v. Kemp*, 481 U.S. 279 (1987).
25. *United States v. Virginia*, 518 U.S. 515 (1996).
26. *Grutter v. Bollinger*, 124 S. Ct. 2325 (2003).
27. David L. Faigman, *Laboratory of Justice* (New York: Henry Holt, 2004), 293.
28. *Brown v. Board of Education of Topeka*, 347 U.S. 483 (1954).
29. *Brown v. Board of Educationn of Topeka*, 494.
30. In Richard Kluger, *Simple Justice* (New York: Vintage Books, 1975), 255.
31. See, for example, Frank I. Goodman, "De Facto School Desegregation: A Constitutional and Empirical Analysis," *California Law Review* 60 (1972): 275–437; and Mark G. Yudof, "School Desegregation: Legal Realism, Reasoned Elaboration, and Social Science Research in the Supreme Court," *Law and Contemporary Problems* 42 (1978): 57–109.
32. See Paul L. Rosen, *The Supreme Court and Social Science* (Urbana: University of Illinois Press, 1972).
33. *Plessy v. Ferguson*, 163 U.S. 537 (1896).
34. Kenneth B. and Mamie Clark, "Racial Identification and Preference in Negro Children," in *Readings in Social Psychology*, ed. Theodore M. Newcomb, and Eugene L. Hartley (New York: Henry Holt, 1947), 169–78.
35. Morroe Berger, "Desegregation, Law, and Social Science," *Commentary* 23 (1957): 476.
36. *Green v. County School Board of New Kent County*, 391 U.S. 430 (1968).
37. *Swann v. Charlotte-Mecklenburg Board of Education*, 402 U.S. 1 (1971).
38. *Keyes v. Denver School District No. 1*, 413 U.S. 189 (1973).
39. Quoted in J. Harvie Wilkinson, *From Brown to Bakke* (Oxford, UK: Oxford University Press, 1979), 200.
40. *Milliken v. Bradley I*, 418 U.S. 717 (1974).
41. *Milliken v. Bradley II*, 433 U.S. 267 (1977).
42. For an overview of that transformation, see Eleanor Wolf, *Trial and Error* (Detroit, MI: Wayne State University Press, 1981), chap. 19.
43. For evidence that public opposition to busing influenced the Court's decision in *Milliken I*, see James E. Ryan and Michael Heise, "The Political Economy of School Choice," *Yale Law Journal* 111 (2002): 2043, 2052–56.
44. See Christine Rossell, *The Carrot or the Stick for School Desegregation Policy* (Philadelphia, PA: Temple University Press, 1990).
45. *Missouri v. Jenkins*, 495 U.S. 33 (1990).
46. *Jenkins v. Missouri*, 77-0420-CD-W-4, Western District of Missouri, May 10, 1985, transcript of record at 24,453.
47. For an overview of the effective schools literature, see Susan J. Rosenholtz, "Effective Schools: Interpreting the Evidence," *American Journal of Education* 93 (1985): 352–88; and Stewart C. Purkey and Marshall S. Smith, "Effective Schools: A Review," *The Elementary School Journal* 83 (1983): 426–52.
48. Arthur Benson, interview with Joshua Dunn, Kansas City, Missouri, January 17, 2001. The interview was conducted for Joshua Dunn, "Complex Justice: Educational Policy,

Desegregation Law, and Judicial Power in *Missouri* v. *Jenkins*," dissertation, University of Virginia, 2002.

49. Christine Rossell has pointed out that "the civil rights leadership's almost single-minded pursuit of mandatory reassignment plans in school desegregation litigation from the late 1960s through the early 1990s has either ignored or disregarded the attitudes of ordinary parents." Christine Rossell, "The Convergence of Black and White Attitudes on School Desegregation Issues," in *Redefining Equality*, ed. Neal Devin and Davison M. Douglas (New York: Oxford University Press, 1998), 120.

50. *Board of Education of Oklahoma City v. Dowell*, 498 U.S. 237 (1991); *Freeman v. Pitts*, 503 U.S. 467 (1992); and *Missouri v. Jenkins III*, 515 U.S. 70 (1995).

51. *Parents Involved in Community Schools v. Seattle School District No. 1*, and *Crystal Meredith v. Jefferson County Board of Education*, 127 S. Ct. 2738 (2007).

52. James E. Ryan, "The Limited Influence of Social Science Evidence in Modern Desegregation Cases," *North Carolina Law Review* 81 (2003): 1674.

53. *Parents Involved in Community Schools v. Seattle School District No. 1*, 2755.

54. *Parents Involved in Community Schools v. Seattle School District No. 1*, 2792.

55. James S. Coleman, E.Q. Campbell, C.J. Hobson, J. McPartand, A.M. Mead, F.D. Welnfeld, and R.L. York, *Equality of Educational Opportunity* (Washington, DC: U.S. Government Printing Office, 1966).

56. See, for example, Eric A. Hanushek, "The Economics of Schooling: Production and Efficiency in Public Schools," *Journal of Economic Literature* 24 (1986):1141–77; Eric A. Hanushek, "School Resources and Student Performance," in *Does Money Matter? The Effect of School Resources on Student Achievement and Adult Success*, ed. Gary Burtless (Washington, DC: Brookings Institution Press, 1996), 43–73.

57. See, for example, L. V. Hedges, R. D. Laine, and R. Greenwald, "Does Money Matter? A Meta-Analysis of Studies of the Effects of Differential School Inputs on Student Outcomes," *Educational Researcher* 23, no. 3 (1994): 5–14. R. F. Ferguson, "Paying for Public Education: New Evidence on How and Why Money Matters," *Harvard Journal on Legislation* 28, no. 465 (1991): 465–97 and Alan B. Krueger, "Economic Considerations and Class Size," *Economic Journal* 113 (February 2003): F34–F63.

58. John E. Coons, William H. Clune, and Stephen D. Sugarman, *Private Wealth and Public Education* (Cambridge, MA: Harvard University Press, 1970); and Arthur E. Wise, *Rich Schools, Poor Schools: The Promise of Equal Educational Opportunity* (Chicago, IL: University of Chicago Press, 1969).

59. *McInnis v. Shapiro*, 293 F. Supp. 327 (N.D. Il. 1968).

60. *Burrus v. Wilkerson*, 310 F. Supp. 572 (W.D. Va. 1969, *aff'd per curium*, 397 U.S. 44 (1970)

61. John E. Coons, William D. Clune, and Stephen D. Sugarman, *Private Wealth and Public Education* (Cambridge, MA.: Harvard University Press, 1970):25.

62. As school finance experts Robert Berne and Leanna Stiefel explain, "Works of the 1960s and 1970s that questioned the link between resources and effects in education may have had a very particular influence on the development of school finance equity concepts by convincing those working with school finance equity to stick more closely to inputs and processes, waiting for more definitive, less controversial findings on the link to outputs before using output concepts." Robert Berne and Leanna Stiefel, "Concepts of School Finance Equity: 1970 to the Present," in *Equity and Adequacy in Education Finance* (Washington, DC: National Research Council, 1999), 7–33, 15.

63. *Serrano v. Priest*, 5 Cal.3d 584, 487 P2d 1241 (1971).

64. Mark G. Yudof, David L. Kirp, Betsy Levin, and Rachel F. Moran, *Educational Policy and the Law,* 4th ed. (Belmont, CA: West Thompson Learning, 2002), 780.

65. *Rodriguez v. San Antonio Independent School District,* 337 F.Supp. 280 (W.D. Tex. 1971).

66. *San Antonio Independent School District v. Rodriguez,* 411 U.S. 1 (1973).

67. *San Antonio Independent School District v. Rodriguez,* 42–43.

68. *San Antonio Independent School District v. Rodriguez,* , 43.

69. *Serrano v. Priest,* 18 Cal.3d 728 (1976).

70. Molly McUsic, "The Use of Education Clauses in School Reform Litigation," *Harvard Journal of Legislation* 28 (1991): 307–41.

71. William A. Fischel, "Did Serrano Cause Proposition 13?" *National Tax Journal* 42, no. 4 (December 1989): 465–74; and William A. Fischel, "How Serrano Caused Proposition 13," *Journal of Law and Politics* 12, no. 4 (Fall 1996): 607–36.

72. Martin R. West and Paul E. Peterson, "The Adequacy Lawsuit: A Critical Appraisal," in *School Money Trials: The Legal Pursuit of Educational Adequacy,* ed. Martin R. West and Paul E. Peterson (Washington, DC: Brookings Institution Press, 2007), 1–22.

73. *Brigham v. State,* 166 Vt. 246, 692 A.2d 284 (Vt. 1997).

74. *Brigham v. State,* 14.

75. *Rose v. Council for Better Education, Inc.* 790 S.W.2d 186 (Ky. 1989).

76. West and Peterson, "The Adequacy Lawsuit."

77. Richard Briffault, "Adding Adequacy to Equity," in West and Peterson, *School Money Trials,* 27.

78. National Access Network, "Casting Out," http://www.schoolfunding.info/policy/CastingOut/factsheetlist.php3 (accessed October 24, 2007).

79. Michael A. Rebell, "Professional Rigor, Public Engagement and Judicial Review: A Proposal for Enhancing the Validity of Education Adequacy Studies," *Teachers College Record* 109, no. 6 (2007): 1303–73.

80. *Campbell County School District v. State* (Campbell I), 907 P.2d 1238.

81. Matthew G. Springer and James W. Guthrie, "The Politicization of the School Finance Legal Process," in West and Peterson, *School Money Trials,* 102–30.

82. Springer and Guthrie, "The Politicization of the School Finance Legal Process," 114.

83. Rebell, "Professional Rigor."

84. Eric A. Hanushek, "The Alchemy of 'Costing-Out' an Adequate Education," in West and Peterson, *School Money Trials,* 77–101.

85. Rebell, "Professional Rigor."

86. Quoted in Hanushek, "The Alchemy of 'Casting-Out' an Adequate Education," 96.

87. Frederick M. Hess, "Adequacy Judgments and School Reform," in West and Peterson, *School Money Trials,* 159–94.

88. See quotations in Andrew Rudalevige, "Adequacy, Accountability, and the Impact of the No Child Left Behind Act," in West and Peterson, *School Money Trials,* 246.

89. See Peter Schrag, *Final Test: The Battle for Adequacy in America's Schools* (New York: New Press, 2003), 120.

90. Nathan Glazer, "Should Judges Administer Social Services?" *The Public Interest* 50 (1978): 78.

91. See R. Shep Melnick, *Regulation and the Courts: The Case of the Clean Air Act* (Washington, DC: Brookings Institution Press, 1983); and Melnick, *Between the Lines.*

92. Springer and Guthrie, "The Politicization of the School Finance Legal Process," 117–20.

CHAPTER 8
Flying (Partially) Blind: School Leaders' Use of Research in Decisionmaking
Lance D. Fusarelli

1. Biddle and Saha note that such criticism is not limited to the United States—education leaders in England, Australia, and other English-speaking countries are also criticized for not using education research to improve practice. Bruce J. Biddle and Lawrence J. Saha, "How Principals Use Research," *Educational Leadership* 63, no. 6 (March 2006): 72–77.

2. Tom Corcoran, "The Use of Research Evidence in Instructional Improvement," in *CPRE Policy Briefs* (Philadelphia: Consortium for Policy Research in Education, November 2003): 1.

3. A total of eighteen knowledgeable school personnel from four states provided feedback for this article: five current or former superintendents, four district office officials, five principals, and four individuals with extensive experience conducting program evaluations in school districts. The names of respondents are withheld by mutual agreement.

4. The U.S. Postal Service is another example of effective organizational learning and improvement. Michael E. Milakovich, *Improving Service Quality: Achieving High Performance in the Public and Private Sectors* (Delray Beach, FL: St. Lucie Press, 1995).

5. Denis P. Doyle, "Knowledge-Based Decision Making," *The School Administrator* 59, no. 11 (December 2002): 32.

6. Carol H. Weiss, "Ideology, Interests, and Information: The Basis of Policy Decisions," in *Ethics, the Social Sciences and Policy Analysis*, ed. Daniel Callahan and Bruce Jennings (New York: Plenum Press, 1983), 219; and Bruce J. Biddle and Lawrence J. Saha, *The Untested Accusation: Principals, Research Knowledge, and Policy Making in Schools* (Westport, CT: Ablex Publishing, 2002).

7. Kennedy believes that policymakers may have a faulty expectation of what research utilization should look like in education, and asserts that research has had a significant influence on policymakers' thinking and on the climate of opinion about education reform. See Mary Kennedy, "Infusing Educational Decision Making with Research," in *Handbook of Educational Policy*, ed. Gregory J. Cizek (San Diego, CA: Academic Press, 1999), 53–79.

8. Tom Corcoran, "Use of Research Evidence"; Diane Massell, "The Theory and Practice of Using Data to Build Capacity: State and Local Strategies and their Effects," in *From the Capitol to the Classroom: Standards-Based Reform in the States*, ed. Susan H. Fuhrman (Chicago: National Society for the Study of Education, 2001), 148–69.

9. Biddle and Saha, *The Untested Accusation.*

10. Gary Huang, Mindy Reiser, Albert Parker, Judith Muniec, and Sameena Salvucci, *Institute of Education Sciences Findings from Interviews with Education Policymakers* (Arlington, VA: Synectics, 2003), 13, 16.

11. Victoria L. Bernhardt, *Using Data to Improve Student Learning in School Districts* (Larchmont, NY: Eye on Education, 2006).

12. Gordon Cawelti, "Lessons From Research That Changed Education," *Educational Leadership* 60, no. 5 (February 2003): 18–21.

13. Susan H. Fuhrman, "The Politics of Coherence," in *Designing Coherent Education Policy*, ed. Susan H. Fuhrman (San Francisco: Jossey-Bass, 1993): 1–34; National Governors Association, "Maintaining Progress through Systemic Education Reform," 2002, http://www.nga.org/cda/files/000125EDREFORM.pdf (accessed July 27, 2007); and James J.

Scheurich, Linda Skrla, and Joseph J. Johnson, "State Accountability Policy Systems and Educational Equity," paper presented at the annual meeting of the American Educational Research Association, Seattle, WA, April, 2001.

14. Michael J. Petrilli, "The Key to Research Influence," *Education Next* 7, no. 2 (Spring 2007): 77.

15. Daniel Callahan and Bruce Jennings, "Introduction," in *Ethics, the Social Sciences and Policy Analysis*, ed. Daniel Callahan and Bruce Jennings (New York: Plenum Press, 1983), xiii.

16. David K. Cohen and Janet A. Weiss, "Social Science and Social Policy: Schools and Race," in *Using Social Research in Policy Making*, ed. Carol H. Weiss (Lexington, MA: Lexington Books, 1977), 67–83.

17. Harris Cooper, "Speaking Power to Truth: Reflections of an Educational Researcher After 4 Years of School Board Service," *Educational Researcher* 25, no. 1 (January–February 1996): 29–34.

18. Ellen Condliffe Lagemann, *An Elusive Science: The Troubling History of Education Research* (Chicago: University of Chicago Press, 2000).

19. Huang et al., *Institute Findings*, 17–18.

20. Carl F. Kaestle, "The Awful Reputation of Education Research," *Educational Researcher* 22, no. 1 (January–February 1993): 29.

21. Huang et al., *Institute Finding*.

22. This is not to suggest that practitioners in these other areas where research is used in decisionmaking do not also act in ways contrary to what research suggests. For example, some critics of arthroscopic surgery to treat osteoarthritis of the knee assert that too little research on its effectiveness has been conducted; that the quality of research on the procedure is poor, with many studies based on anecdotal evidence and few randomized controlled trials; and that credible information, even when available, is not quickly incorporated into clinical practice. See Alan S. Gerber and Eric M. Patashnik, "Sham Surgery: The Problem of Inadequate Medical Evidence," in *Promoting the General Welfare: New Perspectives on Government Performance*, ed. Alan S. Gerber and Eric M. Patashnik (Washington, DC: Brookings Institution Press, 2006), 43–73. In the same edited volume, Clifford Winston asserts that urban transportation policy is shaped by political forces that have led to excessive labor costs, poor service, bloated bureaucracies, and construction-cost overruns. Clifford Winston, "Urban Transportation," 74–99.

23. Paul A. Sabatier, "Toward Better Theories of the Policy Process," in *PS: Political Science & Politics* 24, no. 2 (1991): 148.

24. Carol H. Weiss, "Introduction," in *Using Social Research in Public Policymaking*, ed. Carol H. Weiss (Lexington, MA: D.C. Heath, 1977), 14.

25. Frank W. Lutz, "Policy-Oriented Research," in *Policy Paradox and Political Reason*, ed. Deborah A. Stone (Glenview, IL: Scott, Foresman, 1988).

26. Todd Oppenheimer, "Selling Software," *Education Next* 7, no. 2 (Spring 2007): 25.

27. Lorna Earl and Steven Katz, "Painting a Data-Rich Picture," *Principal Leadership* 5, no. 5 (January 2005): 19.

28. Steve Fleischman, "Moving to Evidence-Based Professional Practice," *Educational Leadership* 63, no. 6 (March 2006): 87–90.

29. Personal correspondence, superintendent, April 16, 2007.

30. Personal correspondence, evaluator, April 19, 2007.

31. Mary E. Hawkesworth, *Theoretical Issues in Policy Analysis* (Albany: State University of New York Press, 1988).

32. Jerry L. Patterson, Stewart C. Purkey, and Jackson V. Parker, *Productive School Systems for a Nonrational World* (Alexandria, VA: Association for Supervision and Curriculum Development, 1986).

33. Frans L. Leeuw and Richard C. Sonnichsen, "Introduction: Evaluation and Organizational Learning: International Perspectives," in *Can Governments Learn? Comparative Perspectives on Evaluation & Organizational Learning*, ed. Frans L. Leeuw, Ray C. Rist, and Richard C. Sonnichsen (New Brunswick, NJ: Transaction Publishers, 1994), 1–2; and Harris Cooper, "Speaking Power to Truth."

34. Robert T. Stout, Marilyn Tallerico, and Kent P. Scribner, "Values: The 'What?' of the Politics of Education," in *The Study of Educational Politics*, ed. Jay D. Scribner and Donald H. Layton (London: Falmer Press, 1995), 5–20.

35. Hawkesworth, *Theoretical Issues*, 4.

36. Personal correspondence, superintendent, April 19,2007.

37. Paul A. Sabatier and Hank C. Jenkins-Smith, eds., *Policy Change and Learning: An Advocacy Coalition Approach* (Boulder, CO: Westview Press, 1993).

38. P. David Pearson, "The Reading Wars," *Educational Policy* 18, no. 1 (2004): 216–52; Alan H. Schoenfeld, "The Math Wars," *Educational Policy* 18, no. 1 (2004): 253–86.

39. As former Seattle superintendent John Stanford, a retired U.S. Army General, was quick to discover. John Stanford, *Victory in Our Schools,* (New York,: Bantam Press, 1999).

40. Bruce S. Cooper and E. Vance Randall, eds. *Accuracy or Advocacy: The Politics of Research in Education* (Thousand Oaks, CA: Corwin Press, 1999); Debra Ingram, Karen R. Seashore Louis, and Roger Schroeder, "Accountability Policies and Teacher Decision Making: Barriers to the Use of Data to Improve Practice." *Teachers College Record* 106, no. 6 (2004): 1258–87.

41. Corcoran, "Use of Research Evidence," 2.

42. Personal correspondence, principal, April 6, 2007.

43. Corcoran, "Use of Research Evidence," 2.

44. Oppenheimer, "Selling Software," 28.

45. Personal correspondence, principal, April 17, 2007; Personal correspondence, principal, April 6, 2007.

46. Stephen H. Davis, "Bridging the Gap between Research and Practice: What's Good, What's Bad, and How Can One be Sure?" *Phi Delta Kappan* 88, no. 8 (April 2007): 569–78.

47. AERA alone has 12 divisions and nearly 170 special-interest groups, so one can imagine the conceptual and methodological diversity of scholarship produced by members of the organization. It is doubtful that the education equivalent of *NEJM* or *JAMA* will emerge from within AERA.

48. *Cabell's Directory of Publishing Opportunities in Educational Psychology and Administration,* 8th ed. (Beaumont, TX: Cabell Publishing Co., 2007/2008). Ed. D.W.E. Cabell and D.L. English. One could argue that medical researchers face an even more daunting challenge, since an Internet search of medical libraries found more than 5,164 journals devoted to medical and public health research—although the vast majority of these journals are highly specialized to a degree not found in education journals.

49. Edward J. Miech, Bill Nave, and Frederick Mosteller, "The 20,000 Article Problem: How a Structured Abstract Can Help Practitioners Sort Out Educational Research," *Phi Delta Kappan* 88, no. 5 (January 2005): 396–400.

50. Biddle and Saha, "How Principals Use Research"; Kerry Englert, Dawn Fries, Mya Martin-Glenn, and Sheri Michael, "How Are Educators Using Data? A Comparative Analysis of Superintendent, Principal, and Teachers' Perceptions of Accountability Systems,"

Mid-Continent Research for Education and Learning, November 2005, http://www. mcrel.org/topics/products/226/ (accessed July 27, 2007); and Patricia L. Reeves and Walter L. Burt, "Challenges in Data-Based Decision Making: Voices from Principals," *Educational Horizons* 85, no. 1 (Fall 2006): 65–71.

51. Lynda E. Irvin and Donald White, "Keys to Effective Leadership," *Principal Leadership* 4, no. 6 (February 2004): 20–24.

52. Bernhardt, *Using Data*; Reeves and Burt, "Challenges in Data-Based Decision Making."

53. Personal correspondence, principal, April 3, 2007; Personal correspondence, district official, April 15, 2007.

54. Consortium on Chicago School Research, "About CCSR," 2007, http://ccsr.uchicago. edu/content/page.php?cat=1 (accessed November 9, 2007).

55. Huang et al., *InstituteFindings*, 18.

56. Frederick M. Hess and Andrew P. Kelly, "The Accidental Principal," *Education Next* 5 (Summer 2005): 1–7.

57. Earl and Katz, "Painting a Data-Rich Picture," 19.B.

58. Southern Regional Education Board, "Schools Can't Wait: Accelerating the Redesign of University Principal Preparation Programs," May 2006 http://www.wallacefoundation. org/knowledgecenter/knowledgetopics/EducationLeadership/SchoolsCantWait.htm (accessed November 9, 2007).

59. Huang et al., *InstituteFindings*.

60. Debra Viadero, "'What Works' Rates Programs' Effectiveness," *Education Week* 25, no. 37 (May 17, 2006): 22, 26.

61. Fleischman, "Moving to Evidence-Based Professional Practice," 87; and Oppenheimer, "Selling Software," 25.

62. Biddle and Saha classify these as secondary sources. In their survey of 81 principals in Missouri, the most commonly read journals were *Educational Leadership* (46 percent), *Phi Delta Kappan* (32 percent), and *Education Week* (17 percent). Biddle and Saha, "How Principals Use Research."

63. *Educational Leadership* contained 6 percent research articles; *School Administrator* only 3 percent; and *Principal Leadership* only 1 percent (data calculated by the author). This finding is significantly lower than Kenneth Henson's biennial survey of journal editors, who reported the following percentages of research articles found in these journals: *Educational Leadership* = 15 percent; *School Administrator* = 10 percent; *Principal Leadership* = 10 percent; and *Phi Delta Kappan* = 50 percent. See Kenneth T. Henson, "Writing for Publication: Steps to Excellence," *Phi Delta Kappan* 88, no. 10 (June 2007): 782.

64. Englert et al., "How Are Educators Using Data?"; Reeves and Burt, "Challenges in Data-Based Decision Making."

65. Personal correspondence, principal, April 10, 2007.

66. Personal correspondence, principal, April 4, 2007.

67. Personal correspondence, district official, April 5, 2007.

68. Personal correspondence, evaluator, April 12, 2007.

69. Jonathan A. Supovitz and Valerie Klein, *Mapping a Course for Improved Student Learning: How Innovative Schools Systematically Use Student Performance Data to Guide Improvement* (Philadelphia: Consortium for Policy Research in Education, 2003), 43.

70. Personal correspondence, former superintendent, April 28, 2007.

71. Personal correspondence, superintendent, April 26, 2007.

72. Personal correspondence, superintendent, April 162007.

73. Frederick M. Hess, *Spinning Wheels: The Politics of Urban School Reform* (Washington, DC: Brookings Institution Press, 1999).

74. Personal correspondence, principal, April 4, 2007.

75. Personal correspondence, superintendent, April 26,2007.

76. Kerri Kerr, Julie A. Marsh, Gina S. Ikemoto, Hilary Darilek, and Heather Barney, "Strategies to Promote Data Use for Instructional Improvement: Actions, Outcomes, and Lessons from Three Urban Districts," *American Journal of Education* 112, no. 4 (August 2006): 496–520; Scott McLeod, "Data-Driven Teachers," unpublished white paper, School Technology Leadership Initiative, University of Minnesota, May 2005, download.microsoft.com/download/2/5/9/259f7395-bd6a-45d0-bbe2-cb7cbc3e16a7/ThoughtLeaders_DDDM_May05.doc (accessed July 27, 2007); and Mike Schmoker, *The Results Fieldbook: Practical Strategies from Dramatically Improved Schools* (Alexandria, VA: Association for Supervision and Curriculum Development, 2001).

77. Jewell E. Cooper, Gerald Ponder, Sherri Merritt, and Catherine Matthews, "High-Performing High Schools: Patterns of Success," *NASSP Bulletin* 89, no. 645 (December 2005): 2–23; and McLeod, "Data-Drive Teachers."

78. Kati Haycock, Education Trust, quoted in Eleanor Chute, "Back to School: Performance Data Driving Education," *Pittsburgh Post-Gazette* (August 29, 2006), 1.

79. Loretta Waldman, "Teaching Strategy Yields Results," *Hartford Courant,* October 9, 2006, 1–2.

80. Julie Hubbard, "Data Rooms' Latest Tool for School Improvements in Georgia," *Macon Telegraph,* November 1, 2004, 1–3.

81. Julie Hubbard, "Data Rooms' Latest Tool for School Improvements in Georgia," 1–3.

82. Julie Hubbard, "Data Rooms' Latest Tool for School Improvements in Georgia," 2, available at http://www.macon.com/mld/macon/news/local/10066798.htm (accessed November 3, 2004)

83. Kerr et al., "Strategies to Promote"; Loretta Waldman, "Teaching Strategy Yields Results," *Hartford Courant,* October 9, 2006, 2.

84. Kerr, et al., "Strategies to Promote."

85. McLeod, "Data-Drive Teachers." This is particularly true in states with strong accountability systems, since many states have testing requirements that far exceed the mandates contained in NCLB. Bonnie Fusarelli and Lance Fusarelli argue that with its heavy emphasis on scientifically based research and implementing research-based best practices, the No Child Left Behind Act requires that superintendents assume the role of applied social scientist and that they be well grounded in research methodology and familiar with the research on best practices in effective schools. Bonnie C. Fusarelli and Lance D. Fusarelli, "Reconceptualizing the Superintendency: Superintendents as Applied Social Scientists and Social Activists," in *The Contemporary Superintendent: Preparation, Practice, and Development*, ed. Lars G. Bjork and Theodore J. Kowalski (Thousand Oaks, CA: Corwin Press, 2005: 187–206).

86. Personal correspondence, district official, April 22, 2007.

87. Bernhardt, *Using Data.*

88. Fusarelli and Fusarelli, "Reconceptualizing the Superintendency."

89. Corcoran, "Use of Research Evidence"; and Massell, "Theory and Practice."

90. Todd Oppenheimer, "Selling Software," *Education Next,* Spring 2007, Vol. 7, no. 2, 23–29.

91. Personal correspondence, former superintendent, April 28, 2007.

92. Fusarelli and Fusarelli, "Reconceptualizing the Superintendency"; and Supovitz and Klein, *Mapping a Course.*

93. Irvin and White, "Keys to Effective Leadership," 21.

94. Massell, "Theory and Practice."

95. Earl and Katz, "Painting a Data-Rich Picture."

96. Personal correspondence, superintendent, April 15, 2007.

97. This also explains, in part, why districts are reluctant to commission external evaluations of school programs, as even small budgetary expenditures appear large and appear to take funds away from teachers and students in classrooms.

98. Leigh Burgess, "Data 101: Going Back to School," *Principal Leadership* 7, no. 2 (October 2006): 22–25.

99. McLeod, "Data-Drive Teachers."

100. John Stanford, former superintendent of schools in Seattle, was shocked by how little teachers or school principals evaluate the effectiveness of their professional practice. See also Massell, "Theory and Practice."

101. Personal correspondence, former superintendent, April 28, 2007.

102. The Wallace Foundation has awarded State Action for Education Leadership Project (SAELP) grants to state departments of education to train school leaders in data-based decisionmaking. See Van E. Cooley, Jiaping Shen, Deborah S. Miller, Peter N. Winograd, John Mark Rainey, Wenhui Yuan, and Lisa Ryan, "Data-Based Decision Making: Three State-Level Educational Leadership Initiatives," *Educational Horizons* 85, no. 1 (Fall 2006): 57–64.

103. Corcoran, "Use of Research Evidence."

104. Huang et al., *InstituteFindings*, 16.

105. Personal correspondence, superintendent, April 12, 2007. The disconnect between researchers and practitioners leads to mutual feelings of disrespect and distrust. See Huang et al., *Institute Findings*, 16.

106. Personal correspondence, principal, April 16, 2007.

107. Personal correspondence, superintendent, April 12, 2007. One solution is the use of structured abstracts in education journals. Miech, Nave, and Mosteller, "The 20,000 Article Problem."

CHAPTER 9

What Gets Studied and Why: Examining the Incentives That Drive Education Research

Dan D. Goldhaber and Dominic J. Brewer

1. Indeed, one former California policymaker indicated, under questioning, that the research wouldn't really have influenced his support for smaller classes, no matter what it showed—and this from an official who believed research was worth doing.

2. We alone have contributed within the last year to the AEFA *Handbook on Education Finance and Policy*, the AERA *Handbook on Education Policy Research*, *The Handbook of Research on School Choice*, and the *International Encyclopedia of Education*.

3. Includes PhD, EdD, and comparable degrees at the doctoral level.

4. James S. Coleman, E. Q. Campbell, C. J. Hobson, J. McPartland, A.M. Mood, F.D. Weinfeld, and R.L. York, *Equality of Educational Opportunity* (Washington, DC: U.S. Government Printing Office, 1966). Other reports have also been influential. For example, National Commission on Excellence in Education, *A Nation at Risk: The Imperative for Educational Reform* (Washington, DC: U.S. Government Printing Office, 1983); Carnegie Forum on Education and the Economy, Task Force on Teaching as a Profession, *A Nation Prepared: Teachers for the 21st Century*, Eric Digest no. 268 120 (May 1986); and

National Commission on Teaching and America's Future (NCTAF), *What Matters Most: Teaching for America's Future* (New York: NCTAF, 1996).

5. See, for example, Donald J. Boyd, Pam Grossman, Hamilton Lankford, Susanna Loeb, and Jim Wyckoff, "How Changes in Entry Requirements Alter the Teacher Workforce and Affect Student Achievement," *Education Finance and Policy* 1, no. 2 (2006): 176–216; Dan D. Goldhaber, "Everyone's Doing It, But What Does Teacher Testing Tell Us about Teacher Effectiveness?" *Journal of Human Resources* (forthcoming); Thomas J. Kane, Jonah E. Rockoff, and Douglas O. Staiger, "What Does Teacher Certification Tell Us about Teacher Effectiveness? Evidence from New York City," National Bureau of Economic Research Working Paper N12155, 2006, http://www.ksg.harvard.edu/pepg/PDF/events/colloquia/KaneOnCertification.pdf (accessed July 27, 2007); Steven G. Rivkin, Eric A. Hanushek, and John F. Kain, "Teachers, Schools, and Academic Achievement," *Econometrica* 73, no. 2 (2005): 417–58; and Jonah E. Rockoff, "The Impact of Individual Teachers on Students' Achievement: Evidence from Panel Data," *American Economic Review* 94, no. 2 (2004): 247–52.

6. What Works Clearinghouse (WWC) is a federally funded effort aimed at categorizing research studies and making findings available to practitioners. From 2002 to 2006, WWC managed to identify only 76 major reform interventions with convincing evidence to support claims of positive effects on student outcomes. This is not due to a lack of research on a given topic—they reviewed 237 studies over this period—but because most studies do not meet the WWC standards of evidence. These standards can be found at http://ies.ed.gov/ncee/wwc/overview/review.asp?og=pi (accessed October 31, 2007).

7. See, for example, Amy Bacevich, Kerstin Carlson Le Floch, James Stapleton, and Beth Burris, *High Implementation in Low-Achieving Schools: Lessons from an Innovative Pilot Program* (Washington, DC: American Institutes for Research, 2005); Robert Cooper, *Socio-Cultural and Within-School Factors That Affect the Quality of Implementation of School-Wide Programs*, report no. 28 (Baltimore, MD: Center for Research on the Education of Students Placed at Risk, 1998); Amanda Datnow and Sam Stringfield, "Working Together for Reliable School Reform," *Journal of Education for Students Placed at Risk* 5, (2000): 183–204; Anja Kurki, Daniel Aladjem, and Kevin R. Carter, *Implementation: Measuring and Explaining the Fidelity of CSR Implementation* (Washington, DC: American Institutes for Research, 2005); Joseph F. Murphy and Amanda Datnow, eds., *Leadership Lessons from Comprehensive School Reform* (Thousand Oaks, CA: Corwin Press, 2003); Brian Rowan, Delena M. Harrison, and Andrew Hayes, "Using Instructional Logs to Study Mathematics Curriculum and Teaching in the Early Grades," *Elementary School Journal* 105, no. 1 (2004): 103–27; and Jonathan A. Supovitz and Henry May, "A Study of the Links between Implementation and Effectiveness of the America's Choice Comprehensive School Reform Design," *Journal of Education for Students Placed at Risk* 9, no. 4 (2004): 389–419.

8. J. E. Stone, "The Value-Added Achievement Gains of NBPTS Certified Teachers in Tennessee: A Brief Report, "May 1, 2002, http://www.education-consumers.com/oldsite/briefs/stoneNBPTS.shtm (accessed October 30, 2007).

9. The panel consisted of Dominic Brewer, Susan Fuhrman, Robert Linn, and Ana Maria Villegas. Synthesis of Reviews of "The Value-Added Achievement Gains of NBPTS Certified Teachers in Tennessee: A Brief Report," http://www.ecs.org/html/special/nbpts/PanelReport.htm. (accessed October 31, 2007).

10. This study was based on a considerably larger sample of tens of thousands of teachers and students in North Carolina. For further details, see Dan Goldhaber and Emily

Anthony, "Can Teacher Quality Be Effectively Assessed? National Board Certification as a Signal of Effective Teaching," *Review of Economics and Statistics* 89, no. 1 (2007): 134–50.

11. "Kids Learn More from Teachers with National Board Certification." This NEA statement can be found online at http://www.nea.org/nationalboard/goldhaber.html (accessed October 30, 2007).

12. See "Getting Involved in Your Child's Education from a Consumer's Perspective." http://www.education-consumers.com/briefs/june2004.shtm (accessed October 30, 2007).

13. See, for example, Peter Schrag's "Policy from the Hip: Class Size Reduction in California," http://www.brook.edu/GS/brown/bpepconference/Schrag_Paper.pdf (accessed June 8, 2007). A broader discussion of the evidence on class size from Tennessee, California, and elsewhere may be found in Ronald G. Ehrenberg, Dominic J. Brewer, Adam Gamoran, and Doug Williams, "Class Size and Student Achievement," *Psychology in the Public Interest*, Vol. 2, no. 1(May 2001): 1–30. The California effort is reviewed in a series of reports completed by a consortium led by RAND and the American Institute for Research; the studies may be found at CSR Research Consortium, http://www.classize.org (accessed October 30, 2007).

14. Needless to say, there is a huge literature on education governance and the intricate processes though which education decisions are made. See, for example, Michael Kirst and F. Wirt, *The Political Dynamics of American Education*, 3rd ed. (Berkeley, CA: McCutchan, 2005), 29–62. For this paper, we do not delve deeply into these formal and informal mechanisms.

15. With the advent of within-district choice, magnet schools, charter schools, and other hybrid options, this statement is becoming less true. However, for the vast majority of parents across the country, the local, public, government-operated school remains the only viable option.

16. Projects that can be funded in this way tend to be small and, therefore, limited in scope. Officers at many philanthropic foundations may be able to fund small projects (say, $50,000) without the need for board approval or external review; larger efforts typically require a more extensive process of proposal development, review, and board approval. Government agencies rarely can fund projects at the discretion of lower-level staff or simply because they like an idea brought to them. They do, however, have a number of funding vehicles available that may permit funding at some point (for example, issuing a sole-sourced task order, or generating an RFP/RFA/RFQ on the topic and inviting bids).

17. Most U.S. government federal contracts permit "fees" over and above actual costs, typically in the 7 percent to 12 percent range. Grants usually do not allow for added margins above costs. However, each firm doing business with the government has a negotiated indirect cost rate that permits the recovery of expenditures above direct labor, facilities, equipment, and other costs. If companies make a profit, they may return the surplus to shareholders or to their employee owners or private investors.

18. For example, see William F. Massy and Robert Zemsky, "Faculty Discretionary Time: Departments and the 'Academic Ratchet,'" *Journal of Higher Education* 65, no. 1 (1994): 1–12; and William Zumeta, "Meeting the Demand for Higher Education without Breaking the Bank: A Framework for the Design of State Higher Education Policies for an Era of Increasing Demand," *Journal of Higher Education* 67, no. 4 (1996): 367–425.

19. In many cases, professors are on nine-month contracts, able to supplement their base salaries with two or three months' additional salary if they perform other administrative or teaching duties, or to raise research funds from other sources.

20. High School and Beyond; National Longitudinal Study of 1988. Details on these data may be found at NCES Surveys and Programs http://nces.ed.gov/surveys/surveygroups. asp?group=1 (accessed October 31, 2007).

21. Other disciplines (for example, health) manage to produce a great deal of useful and rigorous research of critical importance to policymakers and practitioners, while still operating in a largely university-based, tenured-faculty environment. This suggests that while these features of the suppliers of education research are important, they may not be paramount.

22. For instance, many universities have missions other than research. Public universities have a mission to "serve interests of [the] state" from which they receive the bulk of their funding. This includes aiding in state economic development, including relevant research as well as teacher training and so on. State funds are often targeted toward specific state-operated institutions for specific research projects. Most research funding at the federal level ends up at one of the major research universities, notably Penn, Stanford, Princeton, Harvard, and Vanderbilt—all private institutions with considerable endowments, none of which are dependent on external funding for their "survival."

23. For research on school resources, see Daniel Aaronson, Lisa Barrow, and William Sander, "Teachers and Student Achievement in the Chicago Public High Schools," *Journal of Labor Economics* 25 (2007): 95–135; Steven G. Rivkin, Eric A. Hanushek, and John F. Kain, "Teachers, Schools, and Academic Achievement," *Econometrica* 73, no. 2 (March, 2005): 417–58; and Jonah E. Rockoff, "The Impact of Individual Teachers on Students' Achievement: Evidence from Panel Data," *American Economic Review* 94, no. 2 (2004): 247–52. For research on the impact of policy interventions, see Dan Goldhaber and Emily Anthony, "Can Teacher Quality Be Effectively Assessed? National Board Certification as a Signal of Effective Teaching," *Review of Economics and Statistics* 89, no. 1 (2007): 134–50.

24. For example, see Charles T. Clotfelter, Helen F. Ladd, and Jacob L. Vigdor, "How and Why Do Teacher Credentials Matter for Student Achievement?" CALDER working paper no. 2 2007, http://www.caldercenter.org/research/publications.cfm (accessed October 31, 2007).

25. The effectiveness of these "labs" has long been debated, and several administrations have attempted (unsuccessfully) to eliminate them. On the one hand, these labs are in a position to be directly responsive to the demanders of research, but on the other hand, they may be parochial and low-quality.

26. For more specific information about current centers, see National Research and Development Centers http://ies.ed.gov/ncer/projects/randdcenters/index.asp (accessed October 30, 2007).

27. Deborah Viadero, "Whole-School Projects Show Mixed Results," *Education Week*, July 11, 2001, 19.

28. There is clear "endogeneity" here. With the quality of education research generally poor, and small-scale studies producing unexciting results, funders are less likely to commit to enhanced funding. This feeds a cycle of low-relevance, low-rigor research.

29. Both authors serve as standing members of the Systems and Reform panel.

30. See respective foundation websites for details.

31. Jeffrey R. Henig, forthcoming.

32. A good example of such research is work by Kane and Staiger on the implications of various definitions of "adequate yearly progress" for the number of schools that would be judged to be failing to meet standards. For more details, see Thomas Kane and Doug-

las Staiger, "The Promise and Pitfalls of Using Imprecise School Accountability Measures," *The Journal of Economic Perspectives* 16, no. 4 (2002): 91–114.

33. We would, for example, know far more about the value of small schools had the Bill & Melinda Gates Foundation invested a fraction of the money that was spent on implementation of a small schools policy on studying the impacts of small schools. Now there is an infrastructure built up around small schools, and the Foundation itself may be reluctant to see studies undertaken that would have the potential to show that a very large investment was not terribly productive (we are not suggesting this is the case, just that this could be true).

34. See Dan Goldhaber, *Teacher Pay Reforms: The Political Implications of Recent Research* (Washington, DC: Center for American Progress, December 2006), available at http://www.americanprogress.org/issues/2006/12/pdf/teacher_pay_report.pdf (accessed October 30, 2007)

35. Minnesota Department of Education. http://education.state.mn.us/MPE/Teacher_support/Qcomp/index.html (accessed October 31, 2007).

36. While accountability systems help to drive data collection, it is clear that divergent state standards, and the absence of national high-stakes testing, undermine efforts to assess many cross-state policies.

CHAPTER 10
Considering the Politics in the Research Policymaking Nexus
Kenneth K. Wong

1. Charles Percy Snow, *The Two Cultures and the Scientific Revolution* (New York: Cambridge University Press, 1959), 72.

2. James Q. Wilson, "Reinventing Public Administration," *PS: Political Science and Politics* 27, no. 4 (December 1994): 667.

3. John Kingdon, *Agendas, Alternatives, and Public Policies*, 2nd ed. (New York: Harper Collins College Publishers, 1995), 228.

4. Morris Fiorina, *Congress: Keystone of the Washington Establishment* (New Haven, CT: Yale University Press, 1977).

5. J. David Greenstone and Paul E. Peterson, *Race and Authority in Urban Politics: Community Participation and the War on Poverty* (Chicago: University of Chicago Press, 1973); and Rufus P. Browning, Dale R. Marshall, and David H. Tabb, *Protest Is Not Enough: The Struggle of Blacks and Hispanics for Equality in Urban Politics* (Berkeley: University of California Press, 1984).

6. Paul Light, *The President's Agenda: Domestic Policy Choice from Kennedy to Carter* (Baltimore: Johns Hopkins University Press, 1982).

7. Kenneth K. Wong and Gail Sunderman, "The Bush Presidency and Education Accountability," *Publius: The Journal of Federalism*, 37, no. 3 (2007), 333–50.

8. Kenneth K. Wong, "The Political Dynamics of Mayoral Engagement in Public Education," *Harvard Educational Review* 76, no. 2 (2006): 164–77.

9. Charles M. Tiebout, "A Pure Theory of Local Expenditures," *The Journal of Political Economy* 64, no. 5 (October 1956): 416–24; and Paul E. Peterson, *City Limits* (Chicago: University of Chicago Press, 1981).

10. Paul E. Peterson, Barry Rabe, and Kenneth K. Wong, *When Federalism Works* (Washington, DC: Brookings Institution, 1986); and Kenneth K. Wong, *Funding Public Schools* (Lawrence: University Press of Kansas, 1999).

11. Morton Grodzins, *The American System: A New View of Government in the United States* (Chicago: Rand McNally, 1966); and Virginia Gray, "Innovation in the States: A Diffusion Study," *American Political Science Review* 67 (December 1973): 1174–85.

12. Aaron Wildavsky, *Speaking Truth to Power* (Boston: Little, Brown, 1979), 404–405.

13. Carol Weiss, "Ideology, Interests, and Information: The Basis of Policy Positions," in *Social Service and Policy Analysis*, ed. Carol Weiss and others (New York: Plenum, 1983), 213–45.

14. Mary Jo Bane, "Presidential Address—Expertise, Advocacy, and Deliberation: Lessons from Welfare Reform," *Journal of Policy Analysis and Management* 20, no. 2 (2001): 195.

15. John A. Hird, *Power, Knowledge, and Politics.* (Washington, D.C.,: Georgetown University Press, 2005).

16. From Carl F. Kaestle, *Everybody's Been to Fourth Grade: An Oral History of Federal R & D in Education* (Madison: Wisconsin Center for Education Research, April 1992), 23.

17. Carl F. Kaestle, "The Awful Reputation of Education Research," *Educational Researcher* 22, no. 1 (January–February, 1993): 23–31.

18. Frederick M. Hess, *Educational Entrepreneurship: Realities, Challenges, Possibilities* (Cambridge, MA: Harvard Education Press, 2006).

19. Adam Urbanski, "Reform or Be Reformed," *Education Next* 1, no. 3 (Fall 2001): 51–54; Lawrence Hardy, "Public Interest vs. Self-Interest: Debating Reform Unionism," *American School Board Journal* 192, no. 7 (July 2005): 6–8; and Bess Keller, "Unions Turn Cold Shoulder On Charters," *Education Week* 21, no. 28 (March 2002): 1–3.

20. See, for example, Randall W. Eberts and Joe A. Stone, *Unions and Public Schools: The Effects of Collective Bargaining on American Education* (Lexington, MA: Lexington Books, 1984); William H. Baugh and Joe A. Stone, "Teachers, Unions, and Wages in the 1970s: Unionism Now Pays," *Industrial and Labor Relations Review* 35, no. 3 (April 1982): 368–76; Randall W. Eberts and Joe A. Stone, "Teacher Unions and the Cost of Public Education," *Economic Inquiry* 24, no. 4 (October 1986): 631–43; and Gregory M. Saltzman, "Public Sector Bargaining Laws Really Matter: Evidence from Ohio and Illinois," in *When Public Sector Workers Unionize*, ed. Richard B. Freeman and Casey Ichniowski (Chicago: University of Chicago, 1988), 41–80.

21. A Hess and West study shows that collective bargaining arrangements, a hallmark of traditional union activity, remain central to the unions' agenda. See Frederick M. Hess and Martin R. West, *A Better Bargain: Overhauling Teacher Collective Bargaining for the 21st Century* (Cambridge, MA: Harvard University, Program on Education Policy & Governance, 2006).

22. John E. Chubb and Terry M. Moe, *Politics, Markets, and America's Schools* (Washington, D.C.: The Brookings Institution, 1990); and Terry M. Moe, "A Union by Any Other Name," *Education Next* 1, no. 3 (Fall 2001): 40–45.

23. Teachers unions have also been shown to have significant influence at the local level, primarily through school board elections. See, for example, Terry M. Moe, "Teachers Unions and School Board Elections," in *Besieged: School Boards and the Future of Education Politic*, ed. William G. Howell (Washington, D.C.,: Brookings Institution Press, 2005), 254–87.

24. Terry M. Moe, "Taking on the Unions," *Hoover Digest.* Available at http://www.hoover.org/publications/digest/4509501.html (accessed October 31, 2007).

25. Hess and West, *A Better Bargain*, 36.

26. Jeffrey Henig, Thomas Holyoke, Natalie Lacireno-Paquet, and Michael Moser. "Privatization, Politics and Urban Services," *Journal of Urban Affairs* 25, no. 1 (2003): 31–54.

27. Bryan C. Hassel and Meagan Batdorff, "High-Stakes: Findings From a National Study of Life-or-Death Decisions by Charter School Authorizers," *Public Impact*, February 2004, http://www.brookings.org/gs/brown/hassel0204.pdf (accessed July 27, 2007).

28. Joshua J. Phillips, Omer Gokcekus, and Edward Tower, "School Choice: Money, Race and Congressional Voting Behavior," working paper no. 02-27 (Duke University, Department of Economics, 2002).

29. James S. Coleman, et al. *Equality of Educational Opportunity.* (Washington, D.C.,: U.S. Government Printing Office, 1966).

30. Coleman, *Equality of Educational Opportunity.*

31. April Castro, "Committee Considers School Finance Recommendations," Associated Press state and local wire service, February 18, 2004; Aman Batheja, "House Soundly Rejects Vouchers," *Fort-Worth Star-Telegram*, March 31, 2007, B1.

32. Garnet Coleman, "When Public Schools Go to Profiteers, All of Texas Loses; Misguided House Bill Would Set Up Campuses for Failure," *The Houston Chronicle*, March 25, 2005, B11.

33. Mitchell Landsberg, "L.A. Mayor Sees Dropout Rate as 'Civil Rights Issue,'" *Los Angeles Times*, March 2, 2006, B1.

34. National Commission on Excellence in Education, *A Nation at Risk: The Imperative for Educational Reform* (Washington, DC: U.S. Government Printing Office, 1983).

35. Claude E. Barfield, *Rethinking Federalism: Block Grants and Federal, State, and Local Responsibilities* (Washington, D.C.: American Enterprise Institute for Public Policy Research, 1981).

36. "Education: Secretary Bell's View of a Department in Transition," *New York Times*, February 3, 1981, 11, 13.

37. Edward Fiske, "Bennett, In Shift, Urging an End to Drive for Big Education Cuts," *New York Times*, June 11, 1987, A14.

38. Gerald Holton, "An Insider's View of 'A Nation at Risk' and Why it Still Matters," *The Chronicle of Higher Education*, April 25, 2003, B13.

39. Holton, "An Insider's View," B15.

40. Doris Garber. *Mass Media and American Politics.* (Washington, D.C.,: Congressional Quarterly Press, 1993).

41. Educational Resources Information Center, "The Class-Size Reduction Program Boosting Student Achievement in Schools Across the Nation: A First-Year Report." (Washington, D.C.,: U.S. Department of Education, Office of Education Research and Improvement, Educational Resources Information Center, 2000).

42. Public Agenda, http://www.publicagenda.org/issues (accessed November 1, 2006).

43. Public Agenda. http://www.publicagenda.org/issues

44. 2003 Gallup Poll

45. Public Agenda http://www.publicagenda.org/issues

46. Public Agenda. http://www.publicagenda.org/issues

47. David Osborne and Ted Gaebler, *Reinventing Government: How the Entrepreneurial Spirit Is Transforming the Public Sector* (Reading, MA: Addison-Wesley, 1992)

48. Albert Gore, "From Red Tape to Results: Creating a Government That Works Better and Costs Less," Report of the National Performance Review, September 7, 1993, http://govinfo.library.unt.edu/npr/library/nprrpt/annrpt/redtpe93/23ba.html (accessed July 27, 2007).

49. Andrew Rich, *Think Tank, Public Policy, and the Politics of Expertise* (Cambridge: Cambridge University Press, 2004), 77.

50. Carol Weiss and Eleanor Singer, *Reporting of Social Science in the National Media* (New York: Russell Sage Foundation, 1988).

51. Rich, *Think Tank*, 84.

52. Rich, *Think Tank*, 102–03.

53. Gary King, Robert O. Keohane, and Sidney Verba, *Designing Social Inquiry: Scientific Inference in Qualitative Research.* (Princeton, NJ: Princeton University Press, 1994).

54. Robert Dreeben and Rebecca Barr, "The Formation and Instruction of Ability Groups," *American Journal of Education* 97, no. 1; 34–64.

55. Quoted in Rich, *Think Tank*, 215.

56. National Academy of Sciences panel.

57. Victoria A. Harden, "History of National Institute of Health," http://history.nih.gov/exhibits/history/index.html (accessed July 27, 2007).

CHAPTER 11
Conclusion: Education Research and Public Policy
Frederick M. Hess

1. Editorial Projects in Education, "Influential Research Studies," December 13, 2006, http://www.edweek.org/ew/section/tb/2006/12/13/1141.html?qs=Influential+Studies (accessed August 7, 2007).

2. Kati Haycock, "Good Teaching Matters: How Well-Qualified Teachers Can Close the Gap," The Education Trust, *Thinking K–16*, Summer 1998.

3. Christopher Lee, "Drop in NIH Funding Could Take Toll on Research," *Washington Post*, May 28, 2007, A6.

4. From Robert E. Kohler "Science, Foundations, and American Universities in the 1920s," *Osiris* 3, no. 2 (1987): 136.

5. Editorial Projects in Education, "Influential Information Sources," December 13, 2006, http://www.edweek.org/ew/section/tb/2006/12/13/1140.html?qs=most+influential+information+sources (accessed August 7, 2007).

6. For more information on the Carnegie role, see Steve Schindler, "Case 30: Measuring American Education Reform: National Assessment of Educational Progress," 1964, Carnegie Corporation of New York, http://www.pubpol.duke.edu/dfrp/cases/descriptive/national_assessment_of_educational_progress.pdf (accessed August 7, 2007).

7. Gunnar Myrdal, *An American Dilemma: The Negro Problem and Modern Democracy* (New York, NY: Harper & Brothers, 1944).

8. Ellen Condliffe Lagemann, *The Politics of Knowledge: The Carnegie Corporation, Philanthropy and Public Policy* (Chicago: University of Chicago Press, 1989), 123–46. Quote is from p. 146.

9. Terry M. Moe, *Schools, Vouchers, and the American Public* (Washington, D.C.,: The Brookings Institution Press, 2001).

About the Contributors

Dominic J. Brewer is the Clifford H. and Betty C. Allen professor in urban leadership and professor of education, economics, and policy at the University of Southern California (USC). Brewer is a labor economist specializing in the economics of education and education policy. Prior to joining the USC faculty in 2005, Brewer was a vice president at RAND Corp., where he directed its education policy research program for more than five years. He has overseen major projects focusing on educational productivity and teacher issues in both K–12 and higher education. He has published more than fifty academic economics and education journal articles, book chapters, and monographs. His work on class size includes a review of the research published in *Scientific American* and a report for the U.S. Congress on the costs of class-size reduction under different policy designs. Brewer is currently a coeditor of the economics section of the *International Encyclopedia of Education*.

Joshua Dunn is an assistant professor of political science at the University of Colorado–Colorado Springs, where he teaches courses on constitutional law. He has also taught at the College of William & Mary and was a fellow in contemporary history, public policy, and American politics at the Miller Center of Public Affairs in Charlottesville, Virginia. His research has focused on judicial policymaking, desegregation, and the role of Supreme Court doctrine in shaping remedial decrees. He is the coauthor of a forthcoming book, *Complex Justice* (UNC Press, 2008) on *Missouri v. Jenkins*, and he coauthors a quarterly column on law and education for *Education Next* with Martha Derthick.

Lance D. Fusarelli is an associate professor in the Department of Educational Leadership and Policy Studies at North Carolina State University. He has coauthored or edited six books and written more than forty journal articles and book chapters. He coauthored *Effective Communication for School Administrators* (Rowman & Littlefield, 2007) and *Better Policies, Better Schools: Theories and Applications* (Allyn & Bacon, 2004), and coedited *The Politics of Leadership: Superintendents and School Boards in Changing Times* (Information Age Publishing, 2005). His primary areas of interest focus on superintendents, systemic reform, and the politics of education. His current research centers on implementation of the No Child Left Behind Act and on how school leaders use—and do not use—data to inform decisionmaking.

Dan D. Goldhaber is a professor of public affairs at the University of Washington, an affiliated scholar of the Urban Institute, and a senior nonresident fellow at Education Sector. Goldhaber also served as an elected member of the Alexandria City School Board from 1997 to 2002. Goldhaber's work focuses on issues of educational productivity and reform at the K–12 level and the relationship between teacher labor markets and teacher quality. His current research addresses teacher labor markets and the role that teacher pay structure plays in teacher recruitment and retention; the relationship between teacher licensure test performance and student achievement; the stability of teacher effectiveness measures over time; the influence of human resource practices on teacher turnover and quality; and the role of community colleges in higher education.

Jeffrey R. Henig is a professor of political science and education at Teachers College and a professor of political science at Columbia University. He is the author or coauthor of eight books, including *Rethinking School Choice: Limits of the Market Metaphor* (Princeton, 1994); *The Color of School Reform: Race, Politics and the Challenge of Urban Education* (Princeton, 1999) and *Building Civic Capacity: The Politics of Reforming Urban Schools* (Kansas, 2001), both of which were named—in 1999 and 2001, respectively—the best book written on urban politics by the Urban Politics Section of the American Political Science Association; and *Mayors in the Middle: Race, Politics and Urban School Reform* (Princeton, 2004). His most recent book, *Spin Cycle: How Research Gets Used in Policy Debates. The Case of Charter Schools* (Russell Sage, 2008), focuses on the controversy surrounding the charter school study by the American Federation of Teachers and its implications for understanding politics, politicization, and the use of research to inform public discourse.

Frederick M. Hess is a resident scholar and director of education policy studies at AEI. His many books include *No Remedy Left Behind* (AEI Press, 2007), *No Child Left Behind: A Primer* (Peter Lang, 2006), *Educational Entrepreneurship* (Harvard Education Press, 2006), *Common Sense School Reform* (Palgrave Macmillan, 2004), *Revolution at the Margins* (Brookings Institution, 2002), and *Spinning Wheels* (Brookings Institution, 1999). His work has appeared in outlets including the *Harvard Educational Review, Urban Affairs Review, Social Science Quarterly, American Politics Quarterly, Teachers College Record, Education Week, Phi Delta Kappan, Education Next, Educational Leadership, Washington Post, Boston Globe,* and *National Review.* Hess currently serves on the review board for the Broad Prize in Urban Education, as executive editor of *Education Next,* and as a member of the research advisory board for the National Center on Educational Accountability. He is a former high school social studies teacher and former professor of education and government at the University of Virginia. He holds his MEd in teaching and curriculum and his MA and PhD in government from Harvard University.

William G. Howell is an associate professor at the Harris School of Public Policy at the University of Chicago. In addition to his research on American political institutions, he has written on a wide variety of education policy initiatives, including school vouchers, charter schools, and the No Child Left Behind Act. He is the principal coauthor, with Paul Peterson, of *The Education Gap: Vouchers and Urban Schools* (Brookings Institution Press, 2002), and editor of *Besieged: School Boards and the Future of Education Politics* (Brookings Institution Press, 2005). He is the deputy director of the Program on Education Policy and Governance at Harvard University; a member of the board of technical advisors for the federal government's evaluation of the D.C. voucher program; and a coprincipal investigator of a multiyear Institute of Education Sciences grant for the Center on School Choice, Accountability, and Achievement.

Richard M. Ingersoll, a former high school teacher, is currently a professor of education and sociology at the University of Pennsylvania. Ingersoll's research focuses on the management and organization of elementary and secondary schools and the character and problems of the teaching occupation. Over the past decade, he has done extensive research on the problems of teacher shortages and underqualified teachers. His research on these issues has been widely reported in the media and featured in numerous major education reports. Ingersoll has been invited to present his research to numerous federal, state, and local legislators and policymakers. In 2004 he received the Outstanding Writing Award from the American Association of Colleges for Teacher Education for his book, *Who Controls Teachers' Work? Power and Accountability in America's Schools* (Harvard University Press, 2003).

James S. Kim is an assistant professor of education at the Harvard Graduate School of Education. Prior to joining the faculty at Harvard, he was an assistant professor at the University of California, Irvine. He is a former history teacher in an ethnically diverse middle school, where he served as chair of the history and civics department. His research interests include the use of quantitative methods to assess the effectiveness of compensatory education policies for disadvantaged students, and the impact of reading programs on adolescent learning. He is currently conducting experimental studies of voluntary summer reading, middle school literacy, and teacher professional development in Title I schools.

Paul Manna is an assistant professor in the Department of Government and a faculty affiliate with the Thomas Jefferson Program in Public Policy at the College of William and Mary. His research and teaching focus on American public policy, elementary and secondary education, federalism, and applied research methods. In education, he has written and published on No Child Left Behind, school vouchers, charter schools, teachers unions, and education governance. His book, *School's In: Federalism and the National Education Agenda* (Georgetown University Press, 2006), analyzes the development of the federal role and federal-state relationships in K–12 education since the 1960s. Manna holds an MA and PhD in political science from the University of Wisconsin and a BA from Northwestern University.

Lorraine M. McDonnell is a professor of political science at the University of California, Santa Barbara (UCSB) and president-elect of the American Educational Research Association. Prior to joining the UCSB faculty, McDonnell was a senior political scientist at RAND for sixteen years, where her research focused on the design and implementation of education policies and their effects on school practice. In her most recent book, *Persuasion, Politics, and Educational Testing* (Harvard University Press, 2004), she examined the politics of student testing, particularly the curricular and political values underlying state assessment policies. She is a member of the divisional committee for the behavioral, social sciences, and education of the National Research Council (NRC), and was a member of the NRC's Board on Testing and Assessment for seven years. She has also served on the executive committee of the American Educational Research Association and has chaired its government relations committee.

Michael J. Petrilli is vice president for national programs and policy at the Thomas B. Fordham Foundation, a Washington, D.C.–based school reform organization. He served as a George W. Bush administration appointee in the Department of Education, where he helped coordinate No Child Left Behind's public school choice and supplemental services provisions and oversaw discretionary grant programs for charter schools, alternative teacher certification, and high school reform. His work has appeared in the *New York Times*, the *Wall Street Journal*, *Education Next*, *Education Week*, *The Public Interest*, and other publications.

Andrew Rudalevige is an associate professor of political science at Dickinson College and currently directs its global education program in London and Norwich, England. In 2004–05 he was a visiting research scholar at Princeton University's Center for the Study of Democratic Politics. His research addresses national political institutions, inter-branch relations, and public policy processes and implementation. He previously worked in the Massachusetts State Senate and served a term as an elected city councilor in his hometown of Watertown, Massachusetts. His first book, Managing the President's Program (Princeton, 2002), won the American Political Science Association's Richard E. Neustadt Award. Most recently, he coedited *The George W. Bush Legacy* (CQ Press, 2008).

Martin West is an assistant professor of education and political science at Brown University. He also serves as the research editor of *Education Next,* a journal of opinion and research on education policy and is a research associate of the Program on Education Policy and Governance at Harvard University. West is a coeditor of *School Money Trials: The Legal Pursuit of Educational Adequacy* (Brookings, 2006) and of *No Child Left Behind? The Politics and Practice of School Accountability* (Brookings, 2003), and the author of numerous articles and papers on education policy and politics. He received a PhD in government and social policy from Harvard in 2006 and an MPhil in economic and social history from Oxford University in 2000.

Kenneth K. Wong is the Walter and Leonore Annenberg Chair for Education Policy and the director of Urban Education Policy Program at Brown University, where he is also a professor of education, political science, and public policy. He was the founding director of the federally funded National Center on School Choice, Competition, and Student Achievement. He is nationally known for his research in the politics of education, policy innovation, outcome-based accountability, and governance redesign. His research has received support from the National Science Foundation, the Department of Education, the Social Science Research Council, the Spencer Foundation, the Joyce Foundation, the Broad Foundation, the British Council, Japan Society for the Promotion of Science, and the Rockefeller Foundation. He has advised the U.S. Congress, state legislature, and governors' and mayoral offices, and has provided leadership in several large urban school systems on how to redesign their accountability frameworks. His most recent book is *The Education Mayor: Improving America's Schools* (Georgetown University Press, 2007).

Index